Tony Gray is an experienced journalist, author and script-writer who started his career as a junior leader-writer at the *Irish Times* in 1940. Since then he has worked on various newspapers, including a spell as Features Editor of the *Daily Mirror*, and has enjoyed a successful career in television scriptwriting and production.

He is the author of over a dozen books including *Fleet Street Remembered*, a history of the Street incorporating the personal reminiscences of such famous old hands as Keith Waterhouse, Nigel Dempster, Jeffrey Bernard and Lord Rothermere.

He is married, with two grown up children, and divides his time between Surrey and France.

Also by Tony Gray

FICTION
Starting from Tomorrow
The Real Professionals
Gone the Time
Interlude
The Last Laugh

NON-FICTION
The Irish Answer
The Record-Breakers
Psalms and Slaughter
The Orange Order
Buller (with Henry Ward)
Champions of Peace
The White Lions of Timbavati (with Chris McBride)
Some of My Best Friends are Animals (with Terry Murphy)
Operation White Lion (with Chris McBride)
The Road to Success: Alfred McAlpine, 1935–85
Fleet Street Remembered
Mr Smyllie, Sir
Europeople
Saint Patrick's People
The Lost Years: The Emergency in Ireland 1939–45

IRELAND
THIS
CENTURY

Tony Gray

WARNER BOOKS

A *Warner* Book

First published in Great Britain by Little, Brown and Company 1995
This edition published by Warner 1996
Reprinted 1997

A CIP catalogue record for this book
is available from the British Library.

ISBN 0 7515 1391 1

Printed and bound in Great Britain by Clays Ltd, St Ives plc

Warner Books
A Division of
Little, Brown and Company (UK)
Brettenham House
Lancaster Place
London WC2E 7EN

For Pat

Remembering all those endless hours
(and days and weeks)
in sunny Colindale

Acknowledgements

A glance at the dedication will be a sufficient indication – to anybody who knows the British Newspaper Library at Colindale – of the amount of work the preparation of this book has involved for my wife Pat, who went through the century's Irish newspapers with me, page by page, day by day, week by week, month after month, year after year. She is in every sense co-author with me of this book, and I am extremely grateful to her for all her help, and to the staff at Colindale for theirs. I would also like to thank the staff at Richmond Reference Library for all the trouble they have taken in helping me to solve a number of problems.

I must acknowledge, too, all the help and assistance given to me during the course of this project by James Hale, my agent, by Alan Samson and Andrew Wille of Little, Brown (UK), and, above all, by my brother Ken, who for a greater part of this century than either of us would care to acknowledge, worked for the *Irish Times* in a number of capacities, including Deputy Editor and a member of the Board of Directors, and who has gone through the book at various stages and made numerous invaluable contributions.

Contents

Contents

About The Use Of Irish

All languages change in the course of a century, but I think Irish
has changed more than most. For example, I can think offhand
of three ways in which the Roman form of Irish for the county
formerly known as King's County has recently been spelled –
Leix, Laoighis and Laois – and I notice that it has now become
fashionable to spell the house of the President Aras (an
Uachtaran) although at the time of Dev's 1937 Constitution and
for a long time afterwards, it was spelled Arus (an Uachtaran),
and I note from my copy of Father Dinneen's Irish dictionary
that 'arus' is the way he spells the Irish for 'house'.

So, in general I have used the form of spelling which was in
favour at the time about which I was writing, and was then being
most widely used in the newspapers.

Accents were a bit of a problem, too, so I decided to simplify
it, both for myself and for my editor, by leaving out all Irish
accents. Those who speak the language will insert them automatically; others will not miss them.

Also, I apologise to Irish language experts for my inept
attempts to give a rough phonetic indication of how an Englishman – sorry, person – might go about trying to reproduce an
approximation of some of the Gaelic words, but what can you
do? You have to give the reader some vague idea of what they
sound like.

A Note About Sources

Obviously, the principal source of all the day-to-day material in this book is the Irish newspapers, daily, and Sunday and weekly. In general, we tended to refer first to the files of the *Irish Times* because both Pat and myself can find our way around the *Irish Times* far more easily than the other newspapers, though we also consulted the *Freeman's Journal*, the *Irish Independent* and the *Irish Press* files as well as those of their Sunday and evening versions and of other Irish newspapers and magazines like *Dublin Opinion*, and, for more recent years the *Phoenix*, Ireland's *Private Eye*.

For general background material, I referred to dozens of the hundreds of books on Irish history and literature and politics that are crowding us out of house and home in Kew, invading even the toilet, but to be a bit more specific, I found F. S. Lyons's *Ireland Since the Famine* (London, Weidenfeld and Nicolson, 1971) and Robert Kee's *The Green Flag: A History of Irish Nationalism* (London, Weidenfeld and Nicolson, 1972) invaluable; other books I constantly referred to included Tim Pat Coogan's *Ireland Since the Rising* (London, Pall Mall Press, 1966), his *The IRA* (London, Pall Mall Press, 1970) and his brilliant biography of Eamon de Valera, *Long Fellow, Long Shadow* (London, Hutchinson, 1993).

For more recent events, I have used Terence Browne's *Ireland: A Social and Cultural History, 1922–79* (London, Fontana, 1981); Garret FitzGerald's *Towards a New Ireland* (Charles Knight, 1972) and his autobiography, *All in a Life* (Dublin, Gill & Macmillan, 1991); *Northern Ireland, A Chronology of the Troubles 1968–1993* by Paul Bew and Gordon Gillespie (Dublin, Gill & Macmillan, 1993); and, for details on the Haughey years, *The Haughey File* by Stephen Collins (Dublin, The O'Brien Press, 1992) and *Operation Brogue* by John M. Feehan (Dublin and Cork, The Mercier Press).

For matters relating to the arts, Christopher Fitz-Simon's *The Arts in Ireland: A Chronology* is indispensable; I also used *Irish Art from 1600* by Anne Crookshank, published by the Irish Department of Foreign Affairs in 1979, and while I am on to the subject of Government publications, I got a lot of background information from some of the many excellent handouts on all aspects of Irish life which are available from the Irish Tourist Board and the Department of Foreign Affairs. The most generally useful is *Facts About Ireland*, which, so far as I remember, used to be published annually, but now seems to appear only intermittently.

For matters specifically referring to the Abbey Theatre, Sean McCann's *The Story of the Abbey Theatre* (London, New English Library, 1967) is useful, and for details of the newspaper scene, there is Hugh Oram's *The Newspaper Book* (Dublin, MO Books, 1983).

Finally, D. J. Hickey and J. E. Doherty's *A Dictionary of Irish History Since 1800* (Dublin, Gill & Macmillan, 1980) is an extremely user-friendly encyclopaedia of Irish history and politics.

Introduction

❧

New Century's Eve

December 31, 1899, was not only New Year's Eve, it was also the eve of the twentieth century, so you might have expected great scenes of jubilation, as there normally are on New Year's Eve in the Dublin streets as the bells of Christ Church cathedral clang out twelve o'clock midnight.

But in 1899, New Year's Eve fell on a Sunday, which meant that if there had been any balls or house parties to celebrate the occasion, they would have been held on the Saturday night, which isn't quite the same thing. This particular New Year's Eve, there had been no state ball, and very few private celebrations. For the Boer War was at its height, and every day the Irish newspapers carried long lists of names of Irishmen – officers from the big houses, troops and NCOs from the cottages in the country and from the towns and cities – killed or missing in South Africa.

By midnight on December 31, 1899, the pubs had been closed for two hours and the last of the horse trams had left the city centre for the suburbs. It is unlikely that the few scattered revellers still left in the streets paused to consider what the dying century had meant to Ireland. It hadn't been a good century for Ireland, but then, what century had?

By now most of the Irish people had forgotten, if they ever knew, that a century earlier, Ireland had had its own parliament, with 300 members sitting in College Green in the splendid building that is now the headquarters of the Bank of Ireland. It was a parliament without a great deal of power, but a parliament, nevertheless, always known as Grattan's Parliament though Grattan was a member of the opposition. Dublin had enjoyed the status of a proud capital city with a very lively season. In fact, until 1800, the city had been widely regarded as one of the European capitals with which to be reckoned by any fond mother anxious to run her daughter in the Matrimonial Stakes.

After Britain's decision to abolish the Irish Parliament and run the country from Westminster – where Ireland was represented by only 100, and later 105 members, plus four peers – from September 1800,* Dublin had changed almost overnight into a shabby provincial city in an alien kingdom of which London was the capital. The proud Georgian houses of Gardiner Street, Mountjoy Square and Rutland Square were almost all deserted as the Irish MPs obliged to sit at Westminster bought or rented accommodation in London. Their former homes and those of their camp-followers and friends degenerated into slums. Many of the rich Anglo-Irish who had previously been happy enough to sow their wild oats during the Dublin season, and indeed throughout the year and throughout their entire lives at house parties in the big houses all over the country, now took houses in London and did all their socialising there instead.

For a century now, the whole territory of the British Isles had been the United Kingdom of Great Britain and Ireland, with the cross of St Patrick (diagonal red on a white background), added to the cross of St George (red on a white background) and St Andrew (diagonal white on a blue background) to make the flag which is correctly called the Union Jack only when it is flown from the jackstaff of a naval vessel. Wales is not represented in the union flag because it was, and still remains, a Principality

---

*For events before 1800 I have appended a brief historical sketch in Appendix 1, pages 345–52.

technically ruled by the eldest son of the monarch, the Prince of Wales.

For much of the century, the Irish MPs at Westminster had been doing their best to secure the repeal of the Act of Union, latterly under the far more effective slogan of Home Rule, and towards the end of the century two Home Rule bills had been introduced, and had been vetoed by the House of Lords. But the matter was of no great interest to the bulk of the Irish people. In the country, they were far more interested in getting a better deal from their landlords, mostly English and mostly absentee, and in the cities and towns they were far more interested in trying to get to England, or better still, to America, where there was more chance of earning a decent living wage.

Among the intellectuals and those of the smart set who had stayed on in Ireland, Irish language and literature had become very fashionable, and organisations like the Gaelic League were extremely popular; but the ordinary Irish people were not interested in the distant past of their country. They knew all about the recent past, the famine years, when the failure of the potato crop, combined with the crass maladministration of the Irish authorities, had led to a situation in which 1,500,000 Irish men, women and children died trying to keep body and soul together on grass and seaweed, and another 1,000,000 travelled, battened down in the holds of cargo ships, to the States, where, as soon as they had set foot ashore, they began to organise themselves into societies dedicated to getting the British out of Ireland once and for all.

The Irish authorities were, in the main, a collection of British and Irish civil servants working for Dublin Castle. For although legislation had passed to Westminster, executive authority was vested in the Lord Lieutenant or Viceroy (one and the same person), also known as the Governor-General. He represented the Crown in Ireland and signed all proclamations, legislation and other paperwork on the monarch's behalf, and Dublin Castle was the administrative centre. But the real power lay in the hands of the Chief Secretary for Ireland, who was always a Westminster MP and usually a member of the Cabinet, and the law was enforced by the Royal Irish Constabulary, an armed militia force, 11,000-strong in 1899, as well as by the unarmed Dublin Metropolitan Police.

There was also a very considerable British Army presence in Ireland, North and South, but at this period it was never contemplated that the army would ever be used, or even needed, to quell a rebellion. Although there hadn't been a serious attempt at a rising for over a century, there were plenty of nationalists in Ireland still, both in the Nationalist Parliamentary Party, and in the country at large, but none of them at this stage contemplated anything more revolutionary than some form of Home Rule under the safe and stable regimen of the British Crown.

1900–1910

&

Nationalist Party Re-united

At the end of January 1900, all sections of the Irish Nationalist Parliamentary Party met in London to pledge themselves to the restoration of unity within their ranks, adopting a new title – the United Irish League – to underline their determination to forgive and forget past differences.

These differences included the disastrous split over whether Parnell should have resigned following a divorce case brought against him by one of his followers, Captain William O'Shea, with whose wife he had been openly having an affair. Parnell did not defend the suit and, after her divorce, married Kitty O'Shea, a pretty flagrant piece of improbity in Victorian Ireland.

Charles Stewart Parnell was a wealthy land-owner who had succeeded Dan O'Connell, the Co Kerry Catholic lawyer who defied the ban on Catholics at Westminster, won an election with a huge majority and, as leader of the Irish Nationalist Parliamentary Party in the Commons, was largely responsible for Catholic Emancipation in 1829.

Parnell had succeeded in getting the Liberal Party to adopt Home Rule officially, and Gladstone, the Liberal leader, had made the first of many attempts to pacify Ireland by disestablishing the Anglican Protestant Church of Ireland. This had

5

removed one of the Irish Catholic farmers' deepest grievances, the necessity to pay 10 per cent of their farms' gross income to an alien church.

Parnell's chief accomplishment, however, was the destruction of the power of the landlords in Ireland. By continuously obstructing the business of the Parliament at Westminster, he had succeeded in drawing public attention to the Irish Question, and he had also strongly supported the Land League, a sort of trades union of Irish tenants, founded in 1879 by Michael Davitt. Members of the Land League would offer a reduced rent to a landlord, and if the landlord refused to accept it, all League members would immediately withhold payment of all rents. Naturally, the landlords reacted with their standard penalty, eviction, whereupon the members of the Land League would then turn to their favourite weapon, the boycott.

So-called after the first man against whom it was used, a Captain Boycott who was agent for an absentee landlord in the west, it was a powerful device. If a man was boycotted, the entire neighbourhood would refuse to have anything to do with him, his agents, his family or his servants. Any man who took land from a landlord who had been boycotted was himself instantly included in the boycott. Nobody would work for him, or sell him anything, or feed his animals, or talk to him or his children, or even bury his dead.

It was crude, but it worked. A series of Land Acts was hurriedly passed through Parliament which transferred the power to fix rents from the landlords to the courts and which gave tenants complete security of tenure so long as they paid the rents fixed by the courts. Rents in Ireland went down by an average of four shillings in the pound, about one fifth. But the Land War was far from over, and it was not until well into the twentieth century that it was finally settled.

Parnell's other major achievement was to inculcate, into the Irish peasant mind, some feeling of nationalism alongside the overweening desire for some sort of security of tenure.

For a time, after Parnell's marriage to Kitty O'Shea, the Irish Nationalist Parliamentary Party stood by their leader, but when Gladstone threatened to withdraw his support for Home Rule unless Parnell resigned, the party split down the middle, and it seemed as if the Irish Nationalist Parliamentary Party, having lost its leader, had also lost all heart.

The split was healed under the party's new leader, John Redmond, MP for Co Wicklow, whose first action in 1900 was to table an amendment to the Queen's speech to Parliament at Westminster, disapproving of the Boer War and demanding recognition of the Transvaal and the Orange Free State.

There was, needless to say, a brigade of Irish Volunteers out in South Africa, fighting on the side of the Boers, as well as thousands of Irishmen fighting in the British regiments. The latter fought so bravely that Edward VII later rewarded them by creating a new regiment, the Irish Guards. Most Irish people were still basically loyal to the British Crown and on March 1, 1900, there were mildly enthusiastic celebrations to mark the surrender of Cronje, the Boer leader, and the relief of Ladysmith.

In September 1900 two Nationalist journalists, Arthur Griffith and William Rooney, founded a new political party called Cumann na NGhaedheal (Tribe of the Gaels) but more widely known as Sinn Fein. The words simply mean 'ourselves', but with a slightly aggressive overtone, like *nous-mêmes* in French, and they were chosen by Griffith to describe a policy of total non-cooperation with Britain; it was based on Hungary's persistent, passive resistance to the Austro-Hungarian Empire, and was publicised in Griffith's newspaper, *The United Irishman*.

In April 1902, nine counties of Ireland were proclaimed under the Criminal Law and Procedure (Ireland) Act, 1887, popularly known as the Coercion Act; in fact, 105 Coercion Acts, giving Dublin Castle special emergency powers during what were considered to be times of unrest, were passed between 1800 and 1921. These proclamations enabled persons charged with crimes in any of the proclaimed counties to be tried by special juries far from their place of domicile, a device designed to eliminate or reduce the risk of 'packed' or intimidated juries. What particularly inflamed the Irish nationalists about the proclamation of these counties – followed in September by the final insult of the proclamation of the City of Dublin – was the fact that the country had rarely been more peaceful in living memory.

In an effort to find a final solution to the Land War, a conference of landlords, tenants and Unionists, convened in December 1902 by the Under-Secretary of State for Ireland, Sir Antony MacDonnell, made its recommendations early in 1903. It suggested a massive non-compulsory scheme for the purchase of rented land in Ireland by the British Government at subsidised prices designed to tempt the British landlords to sell. By 1908, 7,000,000 acres had been sold to the tenants at what was then a very fair price of £12 an acre. The money to buy the land was raised in Britain by a public stock issue.

The members of the Land Conference were so pleased with the results of their work that they suggested the same conference system should be used to sort out the problems presented by Home Rule, and in 1904, Lord Dunraven outlined a scheme which would have transferred some of Dublin Castle's legislative and financial functions to an Irish Assembly. The scheme was turned down by the Chief Secretary on the grounds that it would lead to a confusing multiplicity of legislative bodies within the United Kingdom.

But support for Home Rule and resentment against England continued to grow. When the Westminster Parliament re-assembled after the summer recess, a noisy effort on the part of the Nationalist MPs to protest against the proclamation of Dublin was countered by the suspension of one of them and the Commons were informed that ten Irish MPs had been arrested since the adjournment.

The third Sinn Fein convention in 1908 officially adopted a resolution refuting the right of the Westminster Parliament to legislate for Ireland. If elected, its members would refuse to sit at Westminster but would set up a separate independent assembly in Dublin. Griffith saw this parliament as operating under the mantle of the British monarchy, as Grattan's Parliament had operated before the Act of Union. The notion of demanding a republic wouldn't have occurred to Griffith at this stage; republicanism was regarded as a highly unstable, continental conception.

The Sinn Fein movement soon began to attract a great following. Huge crowds attended their meetings and several

Nationalist MPs, including the party whip, resigned their seats and joined the new movement. Soon, Griffith was telling meetings of the London Irish that Sinn Fein's aim was now 'to clear the British out of Ireland, bag and baggage'.

Despite the Land Act, agrarian violence, including cattle-driving, was again on the increase in Ireland. Driving cattle off the big ranching estates and then ploughing up the pasture-land while the police were busy trying to restore the rustled cattle to their rightful owners was one of the chief means by which the still landless members of the peasantry hoped to achieve the Irish Dream – a little farm of their own, a few acres where they could grow their own crops and raise a couple of pigs and a few hens. When they eventually got it, most of the farms proved to be too small to be viable and the new landed gentry were obliged to work on the roads for part of the year.

The late spring and early summer of 1909 were dominated in Britain and Ireland by Lloyd George's 'People's' Budget, so-called because it provided for increased old-age pensions, introduced tax-free allowances for people with young children, set up a network of labour exchanges and financed road improvements to cope with the ever-increasing motor traffic. Lloyd George, Chancellor of the Exchequer, needed to raise £15,000,000 to pay for these things as well as to build eight dreadnoughts for Admiral Jellicoe's Grand Fleet. One of the ways he proposed to do this was by increasing the tax on tobacco by £1,900,000 and the excise duty on spirits by £1,200,000.

The Irish Nationalist Parliamentary Party – financially dependent on contributions from distillers and publicans, as well as on votes from electors, most of whom were heavy smokers and drinkers – was bitterly opposed to such measures and voted against the budget on the second reading and abstained on the third.

The budget was eventually passed in November 1909 but was rejected by the Lords. For years it had been accepted constitutional practice that the Lords would never reject any money bills passed by the Commons, and this lapse was to cost them their veto.

Although they didn't realise it at the time, this row between the Lords and the Commons and its conclusion were vital to the Irish Nationalist Parliamentary Party because the end of the Lords' veto meant that if a third Home Rule Bill could be successfully manoeuvred through the Commons, the Lords could no longer block it as they had previously done, but could merely delay it.

1900

BRITISH LABOUR PARTY FOUNDED: KING UMBERTO OF ITALY ASSASSINATED: COMMONWEALTH OF AUSTRALIA PROCLAIMED: TRANSVAAL ANNEXED BY BRITAIN: ASHANTI RISING IN BRITISH WEST AFRICA SUPPRESSED: FIRST ZEPPELIN FLIGHT: DAILY EXPRESS FOUNDED IN LONDON

Parnell had died in 1891, and a committee had been formed to collect subscriptions and decide on a suitable memorial for him. On January 2, its members met in the Mansion House in Dublin to report the successful collection of £6,000 in the United States. They had initially resolved to provide £3,000 for the purchase of Avondale, his old home in Co Wicklow, but they didn't succeed in acquiring it. (It is now the property of the Irish Department of Agriculture and provides a handsome college for students of forestry and a museum.) At this meeting they resolved to raise a total of between £8,000 and £10,000 for a fitting monument to their lost leader. This eventually took the form of the column with at its foot a statue of Parnell, inexplicably wearing two overcoats, which now stands at the Parnell Square end of Upper O'Connell Street.

A civic committee set up to inquire into the excessively high mortality rate in Dublin announced on February 13, to nobody's great surprise, that the contributory causes included overcrowded tenement slums, defective sewage, poverty and intemperance.

It is possible to glean from the headlines in the *Freeman's*

Journal (motto: Ireland a Nation) some idea of how the nationalists felt about the Boer War. The newspaper openly rejoiced at every British reverse in South Africa and talked about the Irish Brigade 'covering itself in glory' after it had captured another unit composed of Dublin Fusiliers, fighting on the British side. Even as early as this, it carried a column in Gaelic and openly referred to the British administration in Dublin as the 'Castle hacks'.

If the Irish Volunteers did not exactly cover themselves in glory in South Africa, they did at least enjoy the dubious distinction of assisting in the capture of Winston Churchill, then working as a war correspondent. On December 30, 1899, the *Irish Times* carried a despatch from Churchill referring to his capture by the Boers, though not mentioning the part played in the affair by the Irish Brigade.

I happen to have heard what must have been one of the last first-hand accounts of that famous incident from a very old man called O'Reilly, who owned a pub in Sandymount in the late Forties; he had been in the Irish Brigade during the Boer War. 'We had Winston Churchill firmly under lock and key,' he told me, 'only the way it was, it was at Christmas time, and we'd all of us had a sup taken and we weren't watching and didn't we let the bugger excape on us?'

On April 4, to the salute of many guns, and amid the greatest concentration of naval vessels ever seen in Kingstown (now Dun Laoghaire) harbour, Queen Victoria arrived for a three-week visit. On the surface, her reception was rapturous, with flowers and flags and bunting everywhere, but again the *Freeman's Journal* had a different story to tell: 'Civil but strange, curious and unenthusiastic, were the masses who went out to see the Queen enter Dublin on Wednesday . . . Even at the official reception, the cheering was polite but feeble. The attempt to sing *God Save the Queen* broke down in feeble piping and the effort to raise a rouse for the Inniskilling Fusiliers absolutely failed.'

Although it was not prominently displayed in any of the newspapers, the Irish Transvaal Committee did try to organise a protest against the visit; both Arthur Griffith, who with Maud

Gonne and Major John MacBride, had founded the committee in 1899, and James Connolly, an Irish Labour leader, were injured in a police baton charge as Maud Gonne was addressing a crowd of 20,000 people. Maud Gonne, the daughter of a British officer who had served abroad and was now stationed in Ireland, was an ardent Irish nationalist. MacBride had worked in South Africa and all his sympathies were with the Boers.

During Victoria's visit the Royal Dublin Society met to consider a proposal that a statue of the queen be erected on Leinster Lawn, in front of their premises in Kildare Street, Dublin. It is perhaps ironical that the town house of the Dukes of Leinster, which had become the headquarters of the RDS – a basically well-intentioned West British society devoted to horse-breeding, agriculture and indeed culture of all kinds – should later be chosen as the most suitable building in which to house the parliament of the Free State which became today's Irish Republic. Because from the moment those ex-freedom fighters moved in to Leinster House, they began to agitate for the removal of the statue which had been erected there to mark this State Visit.

In all conscience, it was a singularly unattractive portrait in bronze of the lady, sculpted at a period of life during which none of us looks particularly appetising. I was present to report the removal of the statue on July 22, 1948 to make way for the limousines of the new rich TDs (the words Teachtaire Dala are roughly equivalent to Member of Parliament; Dail is Gaelic for assembly) and I also chanced to see the bronze effigy of the lady – always known in Dublin as 'th'ould black bitch' – in what I assumed to have been its last resting place, the grounds of the old Royal Hospital in Kilmainham. I have since learned that it was either sold or given as a gift to Australia or Canada and has been re-erected there.

If Queen Victoria's visit to Ireland did not include the usual round of soirées and levées and late-night balls in the Viceregal Lodge in Phoenix Park, where she was staying, it must be remembered that this was a lady of eighty-three nearing the end of her life. Most of her engagements were in the afternoons and one of them was a procession of Protestant children from the Masonic and similar schools about three-quarters of a mile long and several rows deep which shuffled past her dais in the Phoenix Park on Saturday afternoon.

This 'submission', as the *Freeman's Journal* called it, of the Protestant children, was followed by a four-mile procession on July 7 when the children of the Catholic poor who had 'refused to let their little ones be insulted by royal buns and lemonade' held their own protest march against the Royal visit, organised by, among others, Maud Gonne. It was hardly a very effective protest, since it didn't take place until months after the Queen had returned to England.

To be fair to Victoria and her advisers, she had made an effort during her stay to placate the Catholics by visiting a number of Catholic institutions like the convent school at Mount Anville, and she had resolutely turned down invitations to visit Protestant Belfast. But when she left the Viceregal Lodge to travel by a Royal train to Kingstown from Kingsbridge, she probably impressed only those who would have been loyal to the Crown anyway. The visit did nothing to increase her popularity among those who felt no loyalty, either to the British throne or to its occupant. Copies of the *United Irishman* were seized because they contained an article by the irrepressible Maud Gonne headlined 'The Famine Queen'.

Just to show that they were still keeping an eye on events in South Africa, the journalists of the *Freeman's Journal* were leading their pages with headlines like: ENGLISH FORCES ALMOST ANNIHILATED; MORE BRITISH REGIMENTS CUT UP; and FEARFUL GLOOM IN LONDON. And this at a time when the British were quite clearly winning the Boer War, a fairly typical example of the Irish penchant for interpreting events in the light of their own preferences.

That July, the Kingstown Decoration Committee approved plans for an ornamental fountain on the promenade overlooking the harbour, to commemorate Victoria's visit to the port. The design was so felicitous and so right for the resort, that although it was vandalised several times over the years, presumably by young nationalists determined to wipe out every last relic of the British 'occupation', the local Corporation always voted overwhelmingly for its restoration. I have to report that a more recent bomb destroyed its intricate iron-work beyond repair, and now only the pedestal remains. For years this monument added a measure of dignified distinction to a resort which, however much some of its residents might have wished, can never shrug off its unmistakably Victorian flavour.

The City of Dublin Steampacket Company introduced a new and very rapid Royal Mail service between Kingstown and Holyhead in the late summer: two services each way daily on four Royal Mail steamers, the *Ulster*, *Munster*, *Leinster* and *Connaught*, which contrived to do the journey in two hours and 45 minutes, a good deal faster than the standard service today.

On September 25, the Dublin City and County Orange Lodge resolved to oppose a scheme by the Chief Secretary, Gerald W. Balfour, to establish a Catholic University in Ireland. The Orange Order, a semi-secret, fanatically Protestant movement run roughly along the lines of the Masonic Order, and dedicated to upholding Protestant supremacy in Northern Ireland, was founded in James Sloan's pub at Loughgall, Co Antrim, in 1795, after a battle between Protestant and Catholic agrarian gangs. It has since proved one of the most enduring and divisive elements in the fabric of Northern Ireland.

Oscar Wilde died in Paris on November 30, declaring that he was dying as he had always lived, beyond his means, an aphorism probably far more memorable than it was truthful, because the small Hotel d'Alsace on the Left Bank of the Seine could not have been regarded as any evidence of wild (or even Wilde) extravagance.

The Limerick Corporation decided on December 14 to offer the freedom of their city to ex-President Kruger of the Transvaal and to the indomitable Miss Maud Gonne.

1901

KAISER WILHELM VISITS ENGLAND: PEACE OF PEKING
ENDS BOXER RISING IN CHINA: PRESIDENT MCKINLEY
SHOT: NOBEL PRIZES INSTITUTED: FREUD POPULARISES
PSYCHOLOGY: J.P. MORGAN FOUNDS US STEEL CORPORA-
TION: TAFT BECOMES GOVERNOR-GENERAL OF PHILIPPINES

Trouble over Accession Oath

The year 1901 opened in deep gloom with reports on the
queen's illness. The *Freeman's Journal* attributed the 'sad state of
her health' to the fact that the court officials had decided to
reveal to her at last the grave news from the Boer War and commented: 'The breakdown in Her Majesty's health . . . is due to
the excessive tension produced by the untoward course of
events in South Africa.' In point of fact, at this stage, things
were going very well for the British in South Africa; Kruger had
fled to Germany, and Britain had annexed the Orange Free
State and the Transvaal.

According to the *Irish Times*, 'Dublin was tense with anxiety',
and while this is undoubtedly a gross exaggeration, when Queen
Victoria died on January 22, there were dead peals from St
Patrick's cathedral, flags flew at half-mast all over the city, many
blinds were drawn and many shops shuttered. On January 23 a
vote of condolence at Dublin Corporation was rejected by 42
votes to 35, and even when resubmitted after expressions of
horror at the implied disrespect, it passed by only 30 votes to 22,
with a great many abstentions. The Irish in general had very little respect for the Crown and no love at all for Victoria; and
there were no great signs of marked enthusiasm when Edward
VII was proclaimed king at Dublin Castle on January 24.

The new Chief Secretary George Wyndham told a deputation
of Catholics on January 30 that they were not entitled to any
benefits under the Erasmus Smith Scholarship Scheme. In a
country like Britain, where there were many scholarship
schemes, this would not have mattered greatly; but the Erasmus

Smith scheme, an endowment intended to help needy Protestant children with sufficient ability to achieve a good, free education was one of the very few foundations of its kind in the country. The Catholics argued that Smith's principal pre-occupation must have been educational rather than religious, and that therefore the scholarships should be made equally available to Catholic students, thereby showing a rather naïve faith in Protestant impartiality. It was to be many years before the situation was finally resolved, if not exactly according to E. Smith's intentions, at any rate to meet the demands of a by then overwhelmingly Catholic state.

The first motorcycles to be seen in Ireland went on sale in Dublin in 1901, priced around £70. The Local Government Board sanctioned a loan of £245,000 to the Dublin Corporation to provide electric lighting and power for the city, which until then had been lit by gas. Although the street lighting in Dublin mostly changed over to electricity, many houses in Dublin and other Irish towns were gaslit until the late Twenties, and most houses in the country were lit by paraffin until much later than that. I was still a small child when our house in Sandymount was converted to electricity in 1932 or 1933 and I still clearly remember the fragile beauty of the gas mantle with its blue-green-orange-yellow, flickering perimeter and the slight, not unpleasant fug that gas lighting generated.

When the new session of Parliament at Westminster was opened by Edward VII, three of the Irish MPs signed their names to the roll in Gaelic. Maud Gonne went on a tour of America with Major John MacBride to drum up support for the Irish Nationalist cause, and the Dublin County Council protested against the form of the Coronation Oath and called on the Government to remove those portions of it which were offensive to the Irish Nationalists. The reference was to a declaration in the Oath of Accession in which the monarch was obliged to deny the doctrine of transubstantiation and affirm that the invocation and adoration of the Virgin Mary were superstitious and idolatrous practices. The Oath was quietly modified about ten years later.

The Orangemen marched to celebrate the 'Glorious Twelfth'

(July 12), the anniversary of the Battle of the Boyne, in which the Protestant King 'Billy' (William III of Orange) had defeated the Catholic King James II, thus ensuring forever the Protestant succession. The battle actually took place on July 1, 1690, but is celebrated on July 12 because of a subsequent correction to the calendar. The term 'Orange' comes – though the Ulster Unionist supporters of King Billy wouldn't be too pleased to know this – from the ancient Roman town of Orange or *Arausio*, near the uppermost limit of the first Roman province in trans-Alpine Gaul, the *Provincia* from which Provençe derives its name. Orange became a separate principality in Carolingian times, as a result of the feudal disintegration of the Kingdom of Arles, and the titles of those early Princes of Orange went eventually to the House of Nassau, which held scattered possessions in the Netherlands and Germany as well as in France, and were ratified by the Holy Roman Emperor himself.

This year one of the ways in which the Orangemen celebrated the Glorious Twelfth was to meet in Dublin to protest against any modification of the Coronation Oath and any attempt to set up a University in Ireland for Roman Catholics. This latter protest exposed one of the true aims of the Orangemen; they wanted the Irish Catholics to remain uneducated, second-class citizens for as long as that seemed even remotely possible, and certainly forever in their own tight little corner of the island.

The Commons discussed a Shannon Water and Electricity Bill to examine the possibility of developing hydro-electric power from the river, an indication that the British were at last trying to think constructively about solving some of Ireland's problems.

There was rioting in the shipyards on Queen's Island, Belfast, where Catholic workers had to be protected from their Protestant fellow workers by the police and the army.

In Roscommon, on September 9, Maud Gonne told a meeting that Ireland's freedom could easily be achieved if only Irishmen would take advantage of the next difficulty in which Britain happened to find herself.

General Baden-Powell, founder of the Boy Scout movement,

visited Dublin Castle to study the Royal Irish Constabulary's heavy-handed methods of dealing with the rebellious natives with a view to adopting some of their techniques in the South African police force which he was in the process of setting up.

George Moore, the author, spent part of the year in the west of Ireland learning Gaelic, and one of the plays of the year was *Casadh an tSugan* (*The Twisting of the Rope*) written in Gaelic by Douglas Hyde, later to become Ireland's first president.

Although Marconi transmitted the first trans-Atlantic message by wireless from Cornwall to Newfoundland in 1901, radio as a form of entertainment was still far away in the future, and the newspapers were full of advertisements for DIY home entertainment in the form of pianos, harmonicas, American organs and Campbell's melodeons to provide 'charming music for summer evenings!' as one advertisement put it.

1902

RUSSO–CHINESE AGREEMENT ON EVACUATION OF MANCHURIA: COAL STRIKE IN US: NATIONAL BANKRUPTCY IN PORTUGAL: BOER WAR ENDS: ASWAN DAM OPENED: GERMANS IMPOSE TARIFFS: KIPLING'S JUST-SO STORIES PUBLISHED: TIMES LITERARY SUPPLEMENT IS LAUNCHED

Irish Boycott Coronation

The growing nationalism which had been evident in Southern Ireland in 1900 and 1901 seemed to increase steadily throughout 1902, when Nationalist MPs for the first time condemned enlistment in the British Army and John O'Donnell, a Nationalist MP, was sentenced to two months' imprisonment for inciting tenants not to pay their rents at French Park, Co Roscommon. The General Synod of the Church of Ireland passed a resolution opposing the setting up of a university for Catholics in Ireland, thereby demonstrating that religious bigotry among the

Protestants of Ireland was by no means confined to members of the Orange Order.

When the Boers finally appeared to have surrendered on May 31, the weekly *Freeman's Journal* led with the headline: THE BRITISH DEFEATS – THE TALE OF DOCTORED DESPATCHES. And when it became clear that the surrender papers had at last been signed, it came back with headlines like: BRITAIN'S RELEASE! – RELIEF IN ENGLAND AT PEACE WITH IGNOMINY.

The coronation, originally fixed for June 26, had to be postponed because of the king's sudden illness, and the *Freeman's Journal* could hardly conceal its morbid delight: KING REPORTED SINKING FAST, it reported, quoting its London correspondent: 'There is no hope of surviving the operation which was delayed too long.'

Nevertheless, the king was soon fit enough to go through the arduous and boring coronation ceremony in the absence of the Lord Mayor of Dublin and all the Irish Nationalist MPs who met in Dublin instead and passed a resolution declaring that: 'Ireland separates herself from the rejoicing of her Imperial oppressors'.

One of the social occasions of the year was the Winter Exhibition of the Royal Hibernian Academy at its premises in Abbey Street; so popular was the event that the Academy started to rent out its premises to Dublin hostesses who sought more impressive surroundings than their own homes in which to entertain Dublin society. The Academy insisted, however, that every guest should pay the standard one shilling admission fee. The idea of charging the guests was Hugh Lane's; as a gallery official, he argued that if the guests were not specifically charged admission to the gallery, they wouldn't bother to look at the pictures. A nephew of Lady Gregory's who had gone into the art dealership business, it was said of Lane that if he was ever in need of money, he could always buy a picture from some art dealer in Bond Street, London, and sell it five doors down to another dealer for twice the price.

It was in 1902 that William Butler Yeats wrote the one-act play, *Cathleen Ni Houlihan*, probably the most inflammatory piece of rebellious propaganda so far, though clothed in mythology and imagery to such an extent that the Dublin Castle authorities didn't realise that the old lady in the play represented Ireland. By depicting her as entreating the young men of Ireland to help her regain her four green fields (the provinces of Ulster, Munster, Leinster and Connaught) from the foreigner, Yeats was openly advocating rebellion, yet he was never accused of sedition.

It almost goes without saying that when the play was produced the old lady who turned into 'a young girl with the walk of a queen' was played by Maud Gonne, Ireland's Joan of Arc, as she was described by an enthusiastic journalist during her visit to the States.

1903

CASEMENT BEGINS AGITATION OVER ATROCITIES IN BELGIAN CONGO: MURDER OF KING ALEXANDER I AND QUEEN DRAGA OF SERBIA: KRUPPS ARMAMENT WORKS FOUNDED AT ESSEN: US-PANAMA TREATY ON CANAL ZONE: FIRST HEAVIER THAN AIR FLIGHT: SUFFRAGETTES FOUNDED

Maud Gonne Marries in Paris

In February in Paris, Maud Gonne was received into the Catholic Church and was married to Major John MacBride. A bill was introduced to make St Patrick's Day a public holiday in Ireland and another to enable the Gordon Bennett road race to be held there. The Treasury agreed to provide £1,000 towards the cost of employing 2,700 men to assist in policing the 370-mile route through Carlow and Kildare. This event took place on July 2 and was won by Mikhael Jenatzy in a Mercedes. Known as the Red Devil because of the colour of his beard, he held a world record as the first man to reach the staggering speed of a mile a minute, achieved in 1898 in the North of France.

A Dublin Corporation meeting on July 3 to consider an address to King Edward VII on the occasion of his forthcoming visit, was broken up by an uproar in the gallery led by Mrs Maud Gonne MacBride.

Dublin was ablaze with illuminations for the State Visit of Edward VII and Queen Alexandra which took place from July 21 to August 2. Even Maynooth College, that dour stronghold of Catholic orthodoxy, and its principal seminary (it's now a coeducational university) was transformed with decorations in the king's racing colours and pictures of his winning horses.

In a grand gesture Lord Iveagh, the principal proprietor of the family firm of Arthur Guinness, Son & Co, manufacturers of Ireland's national drink, presented £50,000 to the king for distribution among Dublin's hospitals.

From the newspaper reports, it seems clear that Edward VII received a much warmer welcome than his mother. One reason for this may have been that everybody knew Edward VII was a bit of a lad, and the Irish have always had a soft spot for playboys.

The new Land Act received the Royal Assent on August 14 and a couple of weeks later Lord Talbot de Malahide posted up the first notice of sale, summoning his tenants to a meeting to purchase the lands they had been renting from him. In September, the Duke of Leinster sold off most of his land to his tenants, retaining only the sporting rights, and in October, John Redmond sold his estates to his tenants in Co Wicklow. In the same month the new Irish National Theatre Company announced a season of plays in the Molesworth Hall, Dublin, to be presented by the brothers W. G. and F. J. Fay with a cast which included Sara Allgood and many actors and actresses who later became stars of the Abbey Theatre.

At the end of that month, the Imperial South African Association in London announced a scheme to encourage Irish settlers to take up farms in South Africa and the Dublin Fusiliers (2nd Battalion) returned to Dublin after nearly 20 years of foreign service in India and South Africa.

Irish artist Sarah Purser founded An Tuir Glaoine (Tower of

Glass), a stained glass studio in Dublin, and one of the best-sellers of the year was a spy thriller, *The Riddle of the Sands*, written by Erskine Childers, who later was to play a major part in the Irish struggle for independence.

1904

RUSSO-JAPANESE WAR STARTS: GILLETTE INVENTS SAFETY RAZOR: JAPAN OCCUPIES SEOUL: TEDDY ROOSEVELT US PRESIDENT: ROLLS ROYCE FOUNDED: NEW YORK SUBWAY OPENS: US ACQUIRES PANAMA CANAL COMPANY: PUCCINI'S OPERA MADAME BUTTERFLY STAGED

Abbey Theatre Founded

On New Year's Day, 1904, a new Act regulating the use of motor cars came into force. Cars had to be registered for the first time, for a fee of one pound, and would be obliged to carry number plates, so that they could be easily identified and their owners traced. A driving licence – fee five shillings (25p) – was also required by law, and licences would be issued only to people over 17 years of age. Speed limits were fixed at 20 miles per hour for motor cars, and 14 mph for motorcycles.

By 1904, the main tramway services had been electrified but a number of the shorter routes were still operated by horse trams. Although almost 3,000 miles of railway line now connected all the principal towns, most families still went visiting by pony and trap or horse-drawn carriage and there was still a coach and four with outside seats on the Dublin–Bray route, via Ballybrack, which set out every day from the Shelbourne Hotel, St Stephen's Green.

As a result of Gaelic League pressure, all public houses were closed by law on St Patrick's Day. The same organisation held an 'Irish Week' beginning on March 23 which was inaugurated by a great procession of floats through Dublin, mainly attended, the

Irish Times reported with some surprise, 'by young well-dressed people of both sexes'.

In June the White Star Line announced a reduction in its third-class fares on certain trans-Atlantic liners to £2 15s (£2.75). Children under twelve travelled at half rates, and under one year for ten shillings (50p). It was the start of the Atlantic price war. A few days later the America Line reduced third-class fares to £2 5s (£2.25) and many Irish emigrants who had made good in the States were able to travel back to the ould sod to visit the friends and relatives they had left behind. In June, too, at Trinity College, Dublin, degrees were conferred on women graduates for the first time.

A rich Manchester heiress, Miss Anna Frederika Horniman, applied for a patent to turn part of the Mechanics' Institute in Lower Abbey Street, Dublin, into an Irish National Theatre. The building had had a chequered history. It had been built in 1820 as a theatre, but was burnt down within a few years. The ruins were bought by the Mechanics' Institute and turned into a lending library, a chemical laboratory and concert rooms which became a vaudeville music hall for Dublin's poorer classes, as they were always referred to in those far-off days.

The belief that the theatre was haunted – very strong among Abbey patrons in the days before the second disastrous fire in 1951 – probably sprang from the fact that the Mechanics' Hall had been used for the lying-in-state of Terence Bellew McManus, one of the heroes of the Young Ireland 1848 Insurrection at Ballingarry, when permission for his body to lie in state in the Catholic Pro-Cathedral had been refused by the Catholic Archbishop of Dublin.

The building next door to the Mechanics' Theatre had been at one time a bank, and later a morgue (another possible explanation of the widespread belief that the place was haunted), and this building was also bought by Miss Horniman as a site for the Peacock Theatre, a tiny auditorium used initially by the Abbey School of Acting, and subsequently by the Micheal MacLiammoir–Hilton Edwards Gate Theatre. She next negotiated a merger between the Fay brothers' National Dramatic Company and the Irish Literary Theatre Society, and put up the money for the conversion of the two buildings into the Abbey and Peacock Theatres.

The Abbey was an extremely oddly-shaped theatre with a proscenium opening 21 feet wide, with only 16 feet 4 inches between the tabs and the back wall. All the scenery had to be stored under the stage, and any players who were required to exit from one side of the stage and re-enter from the other, had to go out of the theatre into the streets and thread their way along a narrow side alley behind the theatre.

The auditorium was extremely Spartan and very uncomfortable, and right from the beginning one of its distinctive features was an immense gong, three strokes of which reverberated around the house as a warning that the performance was about to begin.

Pay in the Abbey was abysmal; W. G. Fay, as principal producer and frequent leading actor, was considered by other members of the company to be grossly overpaid at £4 a week. A receipt dated January 11, 1905 and signed by Sara Allgood was found at the time of the 1951 fire; it was a receipt for £1, one week's salary for the theatre's biggest star, who went on to a highly lucrative career in Hollywood.

In November, Guinness's new brewery in St James's Street, Dublin was completed and there was an exhibition at the Royal Hibernian Academy of pictures from the collection of Hugh Lane (by now Sir Hugh) which were intended to form the nucleus of a gallery of modern art for Dublin.

The Abbey Theatre opened on December 27 with a performance of Lady Gregory's one-act play *Spreading the News* and *On Baile's Strand* by W. B. Yeats, a verse play based on an old Celtic myth.

```
                            1905

TROOPS FIRE ON WORKERS IN ST PETERSBURG: GREEKS IN
CRETE REBEL AGAINST TURKISH RULE: JAPANESE ANNI-
HILATE RUSSIAN FLEET: TSAR NICHOLAS FORMS DUMA:
REVOLUTION IN PERSIA: MOSLEM RISING IN GERMAN WEST
AFRICA: FIRST FEATURE FILM SHOWN IN PITTSBURGH
```

Evictions Continue

The first issue of the *Irish Independent* appeared on January 2, 1905. It had been formed by a merger between the Parnellite *Irish Daily Independent*, founded in December 1899, and William Martin Murphy's *Daily Nation*. It was rather patronisingly welcomed by the *Irish Times*, founded in 1859, as 'a readable little paper fully worth the halfpenny that is charged for it'. It also later incorporated the *Freeman's Journal*.

On January 16, philanthropist Sir John Nutting offered £5,000 to endow entrance examinations at Trinity College, Dublin, and another £5,000 towards the erection of a Catholic chapel in the University. The following day, Cardinal Logue warned the Catholic Archbishops to be on their guard against bribes to their flocks designed to entice them into attending Trinity College.

February 4 saw the first production of J. M. Synge's play *The Well of the Saints* at the Abbey Theatre. It was poorly received by the critics but on February 13, George Moore, the novelist, wrote to the *Irish Times* urging the public not to miss it.

And still the evictions went on. In May, the MP and journalist T. P. O'Connor called the attention of the Commons to the fact that an armed force, financed by the tax-payer, had been landed by sea on Dursey island off the Irish coast, in order to assist the bailiffs in evicting a tenant with 70 acres valued at £12 and four cows .

The SS *Cambria* arrived in Ballinaskelligs Bay in Co Kerry to lay a new Atlantic telegraph cable between Waterville and Nova Scotia; three clipper barques arrived in Queenstown (now Cobh) in Co Cork, after a 99-day, 20,000-mile passage from Melbourne;

and on July 17, Mrs Pat Campbell and Madame Sarah Bernhardt appeared together in Maeterlinck's *Pelleas et Mélisande* at the Gaiety Theatre, Dublin. Major John MacBride and Maud Gonne MacBride were divorced in Paris in August, with custody of their child, Sean, given to the mother.

At Sterling, Scotland, in November, the Liberal leader Sir Henry Campbell-Bannerman announced a new step-by-step policy towards Home Rule, and two days later another Liberal, Lord Rosebery, announced that he would not serve under any Home Rule banner. Later, the Liberal Party denied rumours of a split in their ranks and announced that the re-introduction of the Home Rule Bill would not feature in their election manifesto, an indication that politicians then were every bit as unreliable and inconsistent as they are now.

It was the year of the first feature film, *The Great Train Robbery*, and the plays of the year included two by George Bernard Shaw, *John Bull's Other Island* and *Man and Superman*. In *John Bull's Other Island*, George Bernard Shaw said so much about the Irish character and the Irish condition that he inhibited a whole generation of playwrights from attempting to say anything that wasn't cloaked in heavily disguised mythology, until the arrival on the scene of realists like Sean O'Casey. As Shaw put it himself in the play: 'If you want to interest him [the Irishman] in Ireland you've got to call the unfortunate island Kathleen Ni Houlihan and pretend she's a little old woman. It saves thinking. It saves working. It saves everything except imagination, imagination, imagination; and imagination's such a torment that you can't bear it without whiskey.'

1906

VON MOLTKE BECOMES CHIEF-OF-STAFF OF GERMAN ARMY:
SIMPLON TUNNEL THROUGH ALPS OPENED: GERMANY STEPS
UP WARSHIP PRODUCTION: DREYFUS REHABILITATED: SAN
FRANCISCO EARTHQUAKE: AGA KHAN FORMS ALL-INDIA
MOSLEM LEAGUE: LIBERAL LANDSLIDE IN UK ELECTIONS

Mixed Bathing Threat

The year 1906 began, as so many years around that period had begun (and ended) with demonstrations by the Unionists in Belfast protesting against Home Rule.

A Department of Agriculture report on migratory labour in March revealed that in 1905, 25,000 Irish workers went to Scotland and England for the potato harvest, sending home to their relatives (remitting was the official word for the practice) an average of £11 a head. The San Francisco earthquake had immediate repercussions in Ireland because so many Irish families had relatives who had emigrated there, and a number of funds were opened in aid of Irish victims of the disaster.

For generations accustomed to the innocent pleasures of top-less – and indeed, bottomless – bathing and sunbathing, it is hard to credit that less than a century ago, it was believed that mixed sea-bathing, even in the grotesquely discreet costumes of those days, could lead to improper thoughts. But on May 1, 1906, Sir Edward Fitzgerald, Chairman of Cork's Public Health Committee, told Cork Corporation that while the opposition to admitting lady spectators to swimming galas came initially from the clergy, he had his own view that swimming baths 'were no place for men and women to be together'.

In June a Royal Commission was appointed to examine the affairs of Trinity College, Dublin, with a view to the establishment of a new Catholic university. In July, Trinity College came up with its own solution to the problem of university education for Catholics: it was prepared, it announced, to set up a

27

committee to safeguard the faith and morals of Catholics who chose to be educated there, as well as a Catholic chapel and a Faculty of Theology. In October the Catholic bishops responded to this offer with a resolution forbidding Catholics to reside with non-Catholics even in the non-denominational colleges then being established by the Department of Agriculture, except under special dispensation. Some Catholics believed that the solution to the problem might lie in the nationalisation of Trinity College but the Hierarchy would never have agreed to that either, unless Protestants could be totally excluded from Trinity, both as students and as professors.

The British administration and the Irish local bodies proved time and time again that they were equally small-minded; while the Anglo-Irish were still in the process of erecting a statue to Queen Victoria in front of Leinster House, the Dublin Corporation voted on June 9 to have the statue of George III removed from the round room of the Rotunda. At the other end of the scale, a ton of coal was seized from a coalman, Patrick O'Carroll, who had refused to pay a fine of 10s for not having his name 'legibly' printed on his cart; it was in fact printed in Irish and perfectly legible to anyone who could read that language.

There was a disproportionate degree of insanity in Ireland at the beginning of the century; some might claim that there still is. The Inspectors of Lunacy – splendid title, that – reported 369 new cases during 1905 as against 202 for the previous year, and a total increase of 10,383 between 1880 and 1905.

There was a disproportionate degree of poverty too. On October 11, during the course of a Government Commission of Inquiry into the Congested Districts, Monsignor Walker blamed the high rate of illiteracy in the West of Ireland on the fact that the children in that area were hired out for work from the age of four and were thus unable to attend school.

The year ended with the registration of a new Irish trademark: the words Deanta in Eireann (made in Ireland) overprinted on a vaguely Celtic symbol adapted from the *Book of Kells* would in future be stamped on all goods manufactured in Ireland. John McCormack, the Irish tenor, made his first public appearance on the Dublin stage after his triumphal return from a season at La Scala in Milan, and a verse play by W. B. Yeats, *Deirdre*, was staged at the Abbey Theatre.

1907

EARTHQUAKE IN JAMAICA KILLS 1,000: WOMEN GET VOTE IN NORWAY: EMPEROR OF KOREA ABDICATES: ELECTIONS FOR FIRST ASSEMBLY IN PHILIPPINES: FRENCH FLEET BOMBARDS CASABLANCA: OKLAHOMA ADMITTED AS US STATE: LENIN LEAVES RUSSIA: LUSITANIA LAUNCHED

Cattle Driving Rash

The new year 1907 opened with a grand motor show at Ballsbridge. Motoring was becoming increasingly popular. America had manufactured a total of 23,000 cars in 1906, and an automobile club had been opened in Dublin. Family saloons were selling for between £300 and £500 at the show, a pretty prohibitive price which represented the entire salary of a railwayman for ten years.

A Viceregal Commission was appointed to look into the workings of the Irish railways and on January 21 a Royal Commission on Trinity College recommended that a separate University be set up for Catholics as it would be impossible to alter the constitution of Dublin University (TCD) in such a way as to make it acceptable to Catholics.

There was rioting in the Abbey Theatre at the first night of J. M. Synge's *The Playboy of the Western World*. The RIC were called in and the players were inaudible over the din. The *Freeman's Journal* called the play 'an unmitigated, protracted libel upon Irish peasant men and, worse still, upon Irish peasant girlhood . . . the hideous caricature would be slanderous of a Kaffir kraal.' The disturbances continued all week despite appeals from the stage from W. B. Yeats, Lady Gregory, W. G. Fay and even the author himself. Some notion of the atmosphere in which the controversy took place can be gained from the letters to the newspapers; one writer complained that Synge had obliged a young actress to utter in public a word which 'she would probably never utter, in ordinary circumstances, even to herself': the word was shift. Curiously, only the *Daily Express* spotted what might have been a genuine objection to the play: the fact that the Playboy's principal appeal to the Widow Quinn, to Pegeen Mike and to all the other young girls in the area appeared to be that he boasted openly of having just killed his aged father.

There was a state opening on May 4 by the Lord Lieutenant of the Irish International Exhibition in Herbert Park, Ballsbridge, Dublin, which ran until November 9 and contained such Imperial exhibits as an entire African village complete with native families and their livestock. Given the comparatively clement climate of Africa, the 'kaffirs' appeared to be at least as well housed as most of the peasants in the West of Ireland. The exhibition was a huge success.

Edward VII and Queen Alexandra arrived in Kingstown on July 10 for another State Visit to Ireland.

In Belfast there was grave unrest and rioting and the troops were out on the streets in August. The trouble had started in July with serious disaffection among the ranks of the Royal Irish Constabulary over pay and working conditions; and troops were sent from Dublin to reinforce the police. Seven constables were suspended from duty in Belfast and 130 Belfast constables were transferred to other areas, their places being taken by reinforcements from Wexford, Wicklow and Kildare.

The Belfast mob expressed their support for the Belfast policemen and their resentment at the presence of police and troops from Southern Ireland in traditional fashion by tearing up the pavements, stoning the police and knocking out the street lights, causing the horses of the mounted troops to stumble on the wet streets. The military charged the crowds with fixed bayonets; there were two deaths and so many casualties that Cullingtree Barracks had to be turned into an emergency hospital. The military were eventually withdrawn from the streets of

Belfast on August 13 after the intervention of James Larkin, the Irish Labour leader and the Under-Secretary, Sir Antony MacDonnell.

Police strength had to be increased in Clare, Galway, Leitrim and King's County (now Laois) to cope with a sudden outbreak of cattle-driving and agrarian violence against cattle-ranching. Cattle-driving, though in many ways similar to the American cowboy practice of rustling, had one big difference. Unlike the cowboys, the Irish cattle drivers did not want the cattle themselves; they wouldn't have known what to do with them. What they were doing was protesting against cattle-ranching on land which they regarded as theirs.

The Cunard liner *Lusitania* called in at Queenstown on her maiden voyage to New York at the beginning of September, and in October the hierarchy warned young girls about the dangers of taking jobs in England: 'We are assured that unprotected young girls are exposed to the greatest danger in many of these places and not infrequently have been ruined.'

A young Irish writer called James Joyce published his first book, a collection of poems called *Chamber Music*, and George Bernard Shaw's *Major Barbara* had its first production.

On October 16 the Marconi wireless telegraph office at Clifden was opened for press telegrams. The Cunard liner *Mauritania* arrived in Queenstown on November 16 on her maiden voyage; Stephen Gwynn and W. B. Yeats were among the speakers at the inaugural meeting of the TCD Gaelic Society and on November 30 MP Laurence Ginnell openly advocated cattle-driving until all grazing lands had been divided up among the tenants.

1908

CARLOS I AND CROWN PRINCE OF PORTUGAL MURDERED:
TURKS STAGE REVOLT IN MACEDONIA: PAN-SLAV CONFER-
ENCE IN PRAGUE: AUSTRIA ANNEXES BOSNIA-HERZEGOVINA:
OTTOMAN PARLIAMENT HAS TURK MAJORITY: EARTHQUAKE
IN SICILY: LEOPOLD II GIVES CONGO TO BELGIUM

Sinn Fein in Local Government

In 1908, Sinn Fein made its first real mark on the political scene when on January 17 the party won 15 seats in the Dublin municipal elections. A co-operative bacon factory was opened in Roscrea, Co Tipperary and two Irish-made motor cars were on sale in Dublin, both produced in Belfast. The Viceregal Commission appointed a year earlier to inquire into the working of the Irish railways reported that the Government should purchase the railway system and hand it over as a gift to the Irish authorities.

A Municipal Gallery of Modern Art in Harcourt Street, Dublin, was opened on January 29 at 4 pm. Invitations were printed in Irish and English, and Sir Hugh Lane, who had paid for the renovations of the premises, remained outside during the ceremony, fearful that the sheer weight of le tout Dublin would bring down the ancient floors. The Chief Secretary told the Commons on March 3 that there were now 60 Resident Magistrates in Ireland, and that their number included 25 barristers and 14 RIC officers; the others were local land-owners.

On March 31, a University Bill to establish two new Catholic universities in Dublin and Belfast, with constituent colleges in Cork and Galway, was introduced by the Chief Secretary.

The Queen's Colleges established by Sir Robert Peel in Belfast, Cork and Galway to meet the Catholic demands for higher educational facilities, and Trinity College, Dublin, were none of them acceptable to the Irish Hierarchy, while the Catholic University, established under Papal authority by Cardinal Newman in 1854, had suffered from a lack of state support and its inherent inability to grant acceptable degrees.

Students from these and other educational institutions were allowed to sit for examinations set by the Royal University of Ireland which had a faculty but no students or lecturers.

A proposal was made – as early as this – to erect a station at Robertstown in the King's County (now Laois), to generate electricity from milled peat, although it wasn't until the 1950s that such a scheme became practicable.

To show that they were still keeping a close eye on things, 30,000 Orangemen turned out for the opening of a new Orange Lodge at Scarva, Co Down, site of an annual mock battle between Protestant citizens, representing the Catholic forces of King James, and the loyal Protestant troops of King Billy.

'Boss' Croker, the Irish-American Tammany Hall godfather, received the Freedom of Dublin in August, and the first pasteurised milk depot in Ireland was inaugurated by the American philanthropist Nathan Strauss at Arbour Hill, Dublin.

A bill making it compulsory to notify the disease of tuberculosis in Ireland was introduced on October 21 at Westminster. On October 22, Mr Justice Johnson, sentencing a prisoner who had been found guilty of shooting a policeman, deplored the fact that while it was illegal to carry arms in England or Scotland without a licence, there was no such restriction in Ireland.

Lord Lansdowne claimed on November 11 that the lawlessness in Ireland was an incitement to the disaffected natives in India.

On December 7, the Gaelic League demanded that the Irish language, oral and written, should be an essential subject for matriculation in the new universities.

1909

ANGLO-PERSIAN OIL COMPANY FOUNDED: GRAND VIZIER OF
TURKEY FORCED TO RESIGN BY NATIONALISTS: GENERAL
STRIKE IN BARCELONA: MURDER OF PRINCE ITO OF JAPAN
BY KOREAN FANATIC: TAFT INAUGURATED AS PRESIDENT:
PEARY REACHES NORTH POLE: BLERIOT FLIES CHANNEL

Tax on Bachelors Over 35?

On January 1, 1909, the first old age pensions in the UK were
paid out to people aged 70 years and upwards; the amounts varied from 2s to 5s (10p to 25p) a week and the pension for a
married couple, both over 70, was about 7s (35p) a week. The
Dublin streets were tarred for the first time to keep down the
dust stirred up by the ever-increasing number of motor cars.
The Labour leader James Larkin informed the Irish Transport
Workers' Union that a permanent arbitration court was to be set
up to deal with all trade and labour disputes.

On January 22, a constable was killed and two 'emergency
men', employed to assist the police in emergencies, were
wounded during an eviction on Lord Clanrickarde's estate at
Athenry, Co Galway; and cattle-driving was renewed in Co
Westmeath.

Evidence that the Irish were not really ready for self-government was always supplied most readily by the Irish themselves;
on February 3, seven cattle ready to go to the market had their
tails hacked off and were tarred and feathered as a protest
against the practice of cattle-ranching.

A Home Office report on drunkenness in Ireland was published in March. It claimed that during a 24-day period, 27,999
children had been counted as they were taken by their parents
or other relatives into 22 specified public houses which were
under police observation.

A Grand Jury at Galway Assizes was told by the judge that
trial by jury was now itself on trial in Ireland since jurors would
not convict, even on the clearest evidence.

In April Constantia Maxwell, the first woman member of the teaching staff at Trinity College, Dublin, was appointed Professor of Modern History and the Clones Board of Guardians recommended that bachelors over 35 should be heavily taxed. 'They have no right to live in single blissfulness,' the resolution stated, 'while the whole country is teeming with bright, lonely, marriageable girls.'

On September 30, University College, Dublin – one of the constituent colleges of the new National University founded under the Universities (Ireland) Act – took over the old Royal University's premises in Earlsfort Terrace, as well as Cardinal Newman's old Catholic University in St Stephen's Green and the Catholic School of Medicine in Cecilia Street.

The Engineering and Scientific Association of Ireland confidently announced on October 25 that flying through the air was not yet an accomplished fact, though it would soon become so, and added that flying would never be of any practical use. They did not appear to be aware that Blériot had flown from Calais to Dover four months earlier, and indeed five days after their meeting an Irish aviator, Moore Brabazon, won the *Daily Mail* £1,000 prize for a one-mile circular flight in a British-made plane over the Isle of Sheppey in the Thames. By the end of the following month an Irish Aero Club had been formed and was organising a flying week for Ireland.

George Bernard Shaw's *The Shewing Up of Blanco Posnet* was refused a licence by the Lord Chamberlain in London on May 23, and in a reversal of all that was to happen later, was accepted by the Abbey Theatre and staged in August, without any cuts.

Among the other plays of the year in the Abbey Theatre was one by Gerald MacNamara, unbelievably entitled *The Mist that does be on the Bog*. Margaret Burke Sheridan, gold medallist soprano at the 1908 Feis Ceoil (literally festival of music), an annual musical competition held in Dublin, gave a farewell concert in the Theatre Royal before leaving to study in Paris for her long career in Grand Opera.

But by far the most important event for Ireland in the entire decade, as mentioned in the introduction, was the rejection, in

November, by the House of Lords of Lloyd George's People's Budget, which was to lead to the loss of their power to veto any bill – including a third Home Rule Bill – likely to emerge now that the Liberals were back in power, though still dependent on the support of the Irish Nationalist Parliamentary Party.

1910–1920

❦

The Start of the Troubles

Shortly after King Edward's sudden death in May, 1910, King George V suggested that the Liberals and the Conservatives should call a truce on Asquith's Parliament Bill (immediately introduced after the Lords had thrown out Lloyd George's People's Budget and designed to curb the power of the Lords) and try to settle the affair at a round-table conference. But when they failed to reach agreement, Asquith decided to appeal to the electorate, and in a general election in December, the Liberals and the Conservatives won exactly the same number of seats each, with the Irish Nationalist Parliamentary Party once again holding the balance of power.

When it looked as if the Lords were going to throw out Asquith's Parliament Bill, it was leaked that if the Lords were going to be awkward, King George V was prepared to create enough new Liberal peers to ensure that the bill would be passed in the Lords in precisely the form in which it had left the Commons. The Lords were left with no alternative but to pass the bill, leaving the way open for a third Home Rule Bill which would this time become law after two years, even if they again tried to veto it.

The significance of this development was not lost on the

Ulster Unionists. They resolved in January 1911 to repudiate the authority of an Irish Parliament, if one should ever be constituted, and form a Provisional Government to run Ulster and resist Home Rule.

When, in April, 1911, a third Home Rule Bill was introduced at Westminster to provide for an Irish Parliament – which was to consist of the king and two houses, a Senate and a House of Commons with the power to make laws for Ireland, as well as a continuing Irish presence at Westminster – the Ulster Unionists stormed through the streets of Belfast, smashing windows and wrecking Catholic shops, houses and schools. Nearly half a million Ulster men and women signed a Solemn League and Covenant pledging themselves to oppose Home Rule by all possible means, and the Unionist leader, Sir Edward Carson, formed a volunteer army – drilled and trained by British officers – to resist Home Rule by force if necessary and began to run guns into Ulster from the continent.

Although Winston Churchill, then First Lord of the Admiralty, ordered part of the fleet to anchor off Northern Ireland and threatened that if Ulster attempted to resist Home Rule in arms, he would have the city of Belfast in ruins within 24 hours, the Army had already warned Westminster that they would take no part in suppressing a loyalist revolt in Ulster. In the British military camp at the Curragh in Co Kildare over 50 officers threatened to resign rather than be involved in any operations to force Ulster to accept Home Rule.

A similar volunteer force was soon formed in the South of Ireland to support Home Rule – one of its first recruits was a 31-year-old mathematics master called Eamon de Valera, born in New York to a Limerick emigrant and a Spanish father. By 1914, the Volunteers were 150,000 strong, training in local parish halls and carrying out manoeuvres in the mountains.

When England went to war with Germany in August, 1914, the Home Rule Bill was rushed through parliament with the proviso that it wouldn't come into effect until after the war, and Irishmen, Protestant and Catholic alike – over a quarter of a million of them – joined the British Army. There was a split in the ranks of the Irish Volunteers; those who supported the Irish

Nationalist Parliamentary Party joined up to fight for Britain, but a hard core of around 10,000 Sinn Fein followers in the Volunteers stayed on in Ireland, determined to fight for freedom at the first opportunity that presented itself.

That opportunity came at Easter 1916 when a small force of Volunteers, armed with antiquated Mauser rifles smuggled in from Germany, took over the General Post Office and several other strategic buildings in Dublin and held out against the police and the British Army – including reinforcements from England – for nearly a week.

The fifteen executions and mass deportations to British jails and internment camps which followed the rising swung world opinion over to the Irish cause, and led in Ireland to massive support for the Sinn Fein movement, which now started to put up candidates for all Westminster by-elections for Irish seats and to win them all.

In 1918, the Sinn Fein Party used the British electoral machinery to fight the post-war general election; they put up 80 candidates for the 105 Irish seats at Westminster – there was no point in putting up candidates in most of the constituencies in Unionist Ulster – and they made it perfectly clear that the candidates, if elected, would not take their seats at Westminster but would instead set up an independent parliament in Dublin which would attempt to govern the country without reference to Britain.

They won 72 of the seats they contested, and on January 21, 1919, 27 of the elected candidates – the remainder were all in jail or in exile – met as Dail Eireann (Assembly of Ireland) and formally declared Ireland an independent republic.

On the same day a party of Volunteers – who had become the Irish Republican Army from the moment they marched on the GPO on Easter Monday, 1916 – captured a supply of gelignite from a quarry in Co Tipperary, killing two policemen in the process. This raid set the pattern for hundreds of similar IRA attacks on the Royal Irish Constabulary all over the country; it marked the beginning of a long and bitter guerrilla war, now known in Ireland as the War of Independence.

The British authorities immediately imposed a curfew and all civilians were confined to their homes from ten o'clock in the evening, or in some places even earlier, while the police and military patrolled the country, raiding houses for arms, looting and ravaging, carrying away prisoners and murdering suspects in front of their families.

It was the start of the troubled times.

1910

UNION OF SOUTH AFRICA BECOMES DOMINION: JAPAN ANNEXES KOREA: MONTENEGRO GAINS INDEPENDENCE: FIRST LABOUR EXCHANGES OPENED IN BRITAIN: CRIPPEN HANGED FOR WIFE'S MURDER: MARIE CURIE PUBLISHES TREATISE ON RADIOGRAPHY: MANHATTAN BRIDGE OPENS

Home Rule in Sight?

In January 1910, an anti-Home Rule demonstration in Liverpool was attended by a crowd of 50,000 and Sir Edward Carson, a Dublin barrister with no Ulster connections whatever, accepted the leadership of the Ulster Unionist Party.

As soon as Asquith introduced his Parliament Bill to curb the power of the Lords, Lloyd George's 'People's' Budget was re-introduced, and this time, of course, the Irish Nationalist Parliamentary Party voted for it, fully aware now that by supporting the Liberals in this way they were advancing the prospects of getting a Home Rule Bill through parliament. The Lords passed the budget without a division on April 30.

When King Edward VII died suddenly on May 6, seven Sinn Fein members of Dublin Corporation voted against sending any message of condolence to King George V. Nevertheless, the Lord Mayor of Dublin attended the funeral in London in the company of eight reigning monarchs.

The conference called by King George V to enable the Conservative and Unionist Party and the Liberals to reach agreement on limiting the power of the Lords fell apart when the Conservatives refused to agree to abolishing the Lords' veto on 'constitutional issues', one of which was, of course, Home Rule. A new fortnightly publication *Irish Freedom* appeared; it was run by the Irish Republican Brotherhood, a secret society, formed in Ireland in 1858, and stronger by 1910 in the United States (where its members were known as the Fenians) than it was in Ireland. It operated through and inside other organisations such as the Gaelic League in Ireland and Clan na Gael in America; and its newspaper advocated republican government for the whole of Ireland.

Halley's Comet was visible in the skies over Dublin for half an hour on the evening of May 25 and the Senate of the new National University decided on June 23 to make Irish a compulsory subject for matriculation from 1913.

Lord MacDonnell, former Under-Secretary for Ireland, outlined his policy for devolution at a meeting of the Trinity College Historical Society on November 2.

1911

MEXICAN CIVIL WAR: REICHSTAG PASSES ARMY BILL: FIRST BRITISH OFFICIAL SECRETS ACT: NATIONAL HEALTH INSURANCE INTRODUCED: AMUNDSEN REACHES SOUTH POLE: CHINESE REPUBLIC PROCLAIMED: KING GEORGE V ATTENDS DELHI DURBAR: SUFFRAGETTES RIOT

Another Royal Visit

The year 1911 began with the largest Protestant demonstration ever held against the papal decree on mixed marriages known as Ne Temere; a resolution, passed at the Assembly Hall in Belfast at a meeting attended by 6,000, stated that the application of this decree in Ireland would cause bitterness and sectarian hatred.

The Ne Temere decree did no more than stipulate that in the case of mixed marriages, the children must in all circumstances be brought up in the Catholic faith; this had been interpreted in Ireland as giving authority to Catholic parents and relatives in mixed marriages to abduct the children if necessary and have them brought up outside the family home as Catholics. There had been a protest meeting in Dublin against the Ne Temere decree on January 30, calling on the Government to secure freedom from interference by any religious denomination for all those married in accordance with the laws of the land. And during a debate in the Commons on the king's speech on February 15, Redmond asserted that no Catholic Irishman would ever accept a settlement of the Home Rule question which would involve any oppression of Protestants. The very fact that he acknowledged the mere possibility of any oppression of Protestants struck chill in many an Orange heart.

Premier Asquith indicated on January 7 that he intended to include provision for salaries for members of the House of Commons in his next budget. Assuming this would be a nominal honorarium, the Irish members at Westminster passed a resolution approving the payment of MPs as a just democratic measure. But they requested that the money allocated to them should be devoted to some useful public purpose in Ireland. They changed their minds pretty smartly however when on May 16 it was revealed that the salary was to be £400 a year – quite a considerable sum in those days – and on August 9 it was announced that the Irish MPs had decided after all to accept a salary.

As early as March 24, a Sinn Fein meeting attended by Arthur Griffith (the architect of Sinn Fein), Countess Markievicz (Constance Goore-Booth, a member of a Sligo Anglo-Irish family married to a Polish artist, who had become an enthusiastic Sinn Fein follower) and The O'Rahilly – the head of the old Celtic O'Rahilly clan – expressed the view that no loyal address should be presented to George V during his visit.

The O'Rahilly was Michael Joseph O'Rahilly, a journalist prominent in the Gaelic League and active in the Sinn Fein movement. It is an old Gaelic tradition that the head of an Irish clan was always known as The, followed by the surname. I used to go sailing with a man I always knew as Mac O'Rahilly, but his correct title was The O'Rahilly, and he was the son and successor of the Michael Joseph O'Rahilly who so strongly opposed the notion of any loyal address to King George V in 1911, and who was killed leading a charge on a barricade during the Easter 1916 Rising.

The coronation of King George V and Queen Mary was celebrated as a public holiday in Ireland, but Major John MacBride, Countess Markievicz and Arthur Griffith celebrated the occasion by burning British flags.

Countess Markievicz burned another Union Jack on July 4 at a United National Societies open-air meeting to protest against the Lord Mayor's proposed address to welcome King George and Queen Mary to Ireland. There were disorderly scenes at a Corporation meeting the next day, when 23 warships of the Home Fleet arrived in Kingstown harbour for the Royal Visit.

On the following day the Royal Yacht arrived, preceded by that of the Duke of Connaught. The fleet was illuminated and a day later the king and queen made their state entry into Dublin. The king reviewed 17,000 troops in the Phoenix Park and despite all the previous protests there were no disturbances at all during the Royal Visit, which ended on July 12.

On August 30, the Chamber of Commerce called for a uniform time with the remainder of the British Isles; at this period Irish clocks were 25 minutes behind Greenwich Mean Time. Greenwich Mean Time was not adopted for the whole of the United Kingdom until about a year later.

A piece of sculpture by Oliver Sheppard, *The Death of Cuchulain*, was exhibited for the first time; it was later chosen as a memorial to the 1916 Rising and is now in the Dublin GPO.

1912

COMMONS REJECT VOTES FOR WOMEN BILL: TURKEY CLOSES
DARDANELLES: IMMIGRATION BILL MAKES LITERACY A
CONDITION OF ENTRY TO US: RIOTS IN LONDON DOCKS:
BULGARIANS, SERBS MOBILISE AGAINST TURKEY:
ARIZONA BECOMES AMERICAN STATE: TITANIC SINKS

No Surrender to Home Rule

The year 1912 began with the nationalisation of the telephone systems of the United Kingdom; the GPO took over the control and management of the telephone network from the National Telephone Company.

But as early as January 2, the burning topic of the year was pinpointed by the *Irish Times* which devoted two full columns to a book openly advocating an independent Irish state, *The Framework of Home Rule*. It had been written by Erskine Childers, author of *The Riddle of the Sands*, who had been born in England but brought up by relations in Ireland.

At this time, Winston Churchill was a Liberal and a firm supporter of Home Rule. His announced intention to come to Belfast to address, along with John Redmond, the leader of the Irish Nationalist Parliamentary Party, a rally in support of Home Rule caused consternation in the city. A meeting on January 19 of property-owners with premises in the vicinity of the Ulster Hall, which the Ulster Liberals had rented for the occasion, decided to petition the Belfast Corporation to cancel the booking because of the strong possibility of damage to adjoining properties in the highly likely event of a riot. Predictably the Belfast Unionists had rented the hall for February 7, the eve of the Churchill booking, making it perfectly clear that they intended to stay on in the hall and do a squat, thus preventing the Churchill meeting from ever taking place.

In the circumstances, Churchill, always a pragmatist, decided to find somewhere else to hold his meeting. As a precaution, both Liberals and Unionists had also applied for the use of the Exhibition Hall in the Botanical Gardens for the night in question, but not surprisingly in view of the temper of the times, both had been refused. Churchill in the end had to settle for the Celtic Park football field. In response to a request from the Mayor of Belfast, 5,000 troops, including cavalry, were despatched from Southern Ireland to assist in policing this potentially explosive rally.

Churchill received a very hostile reception in Belfast and was jostled on his way to the meeting, which turned out to be a bit of a damp squib. As soon as it was over, he took a train to Larne and there caught the first available cross-channel steamer back to Stranraer, while the Ulster Unionists paraded jubilantly through the streets of Belfast to the Ulster Club.

As mentioned above, starting on 'Ulster Day', September 28, 1912, 220,000 Ulster men and 230,000 Ulster women signed Carson's Solemn League and Covenant – some in their own blood – pledging themselves to resist Home Rule by every possible means. In point of fact, women were not allowed to sign the Covenant as such, but 228,991 of them signed a separate declaration to the same effect.

During the year a book was published which enjoyed a limited critical success and was, for a time, a cult book in intellectual circles: James Stephens's *The Crock of Gold*. It has now been almost forgotten, which is curious, because it was the first book to exploit a curious vein of pseudo-scientific, irreverent philosophy, later developed into an art form by Flann O'Brien. Its effect must have been sensational in 1912.

An example: 'The first person who washed was probably a person seeking a cheap notoriety, [said the Philosopher]. Any fool can wash himself, but every wise man knows that it is an unnecessary labour, for nature will quickly reduce him to a natural and healthy dirtiness again. We should seek, therefore, not how to make ourselves clean, but how to attain a more unique and splendid dirtiness, and perhaps the accumulated layers of matter might, by ordinary geologic compulsion, become incorporated with the human cuticle and so render clothing unnecessary . . . In its proper place I admit the necessity of water. As a thing to sail a ship on it can hardly be surpassed (not, you will understand, that I entirely approve of ships, they tend to create and perpetuate international curiosity and the smaller vermin of different latitudes. As an element wherewith to put out a fire, or brew tea, or make a slide in winter, it is useful, but in a tin basin it has a repulsive and meagre aspect . . .).'

The ballerina Anna Pavlova danced in the Gaiety Theatre, Dublin; in the Round Room at the Rotunda, 'new, living pictures' of the Delhi Durbar were shown to the delight of thousands of Dubliners. In Philadelphia, the Irish players were arrested after a production of Synge's *The Playboy of the Western World* 'for giving a performance calculated to injure the morals of the citizens'. The charges were later dropped and the players released.

1913

FEDERAL INCOME TAX INTRODUCED IN US: FIRST PARLIAMENT OF CHINESE REPUBLIC SITS: EMILY DAWSON FIRST WOMAN MAGISTRATE IN ENGLAND: REICHSTAG BILL INCREASES ARMY STRENGTH: BALKAN STATES SIGN ARMISTICE IN BUCHAREST:PANAMA CANAL OPENS

IRB Plans Easter Rising

On the first day of 1913, Sir Edward Carson's amendment to exclude Ulster from the provisions of a third Home Rule Bill, now going through its early stages at Westminster, was defeated by a majority of 97. The bill was passed by the Commons on January 16 and on the same day a copy of it was publicly burned at a meeting of Orangemen in front of the City Hall, Belfast; on January 30, it was rejected by the Lords.

This was a year of great labour unrest in Dublin. There had been a widespread lock-out by Dublin managements, in reaction to the growing strength of the trades unions, followed by weeks of meetings and speeches, agitations and disturbances during which the police made repeated baton charges, killing two Dublin workers and injuring many hundreds, some seriously.

On Sunday, August 30, the first of Ireland's many Bloody Sundays, the police ran amok in Sackville (O'Connell) Street after James Larkin, the Labour leader, appeared on the balcony of the Imperial Hotel and tried to make a speech at a proscribed rally. Most of the 600 people treated in hospital for injuries caused by police batons and sabres were innocent of any serious attempt to cause a riot – they were merely citizens out having a look at what was going on.

The Irish Citizen Army, commanded by the Belfast Labour organiser, James Connolly – who had come to Dublin to assist Larkin in the struggle against the lock-out — was formed to prevent a recurrence of just this sort of thing. It was ahead of its time in that women were accepted on an equal basis with men – one of its first commandants was Madame Markievicz. Later in the year, the Irish Republican Brotherhood set up a second amateur army under Professor Eoin MacNeill, a university lecturer and Vice-President of the Gaelic League.

The Volunteer movement spread like wildfire. Before long there were 150,000 of them, practising the arts of war in the fields and in the woods, among the mountains and on the seashore, using out-of-date British War Office manuals. Their big problem now was how to get arms.

Because of the rapid expansion of motor traffic, the price of petrol was increased on February 25 by 2d to 1s 9d per gallon. Horse-drawn vehicles were still far more plentiful in Dublin than motor cars and an analysis of street accidents published on March 24 found one fatal accident due to a horse-drawn omnibus, 58 due to other horse-drawn vehicles and only 41 due to mechanically propelled vehicles, seven of them tramcars. I say only since it's quite difficult to be knocked down by a horse-drawn vehicle; because of the great size of horses' feet and the careless way they stamp them about, most people tended, and still do, to stand well back at the approach of a horse-drawn vehicle, but the early motor cars looked pathetic rather than intimidating.

A meeting on April 2, of the Irishwomen's Franchise League, was informed that a cinema in Dublin employed a young girl who acted as book-keeper, office hand, cashier and pianist and stayed on at night to lock the place up, all for 3s a week; and on the same day an Irish nurse, Marjorie Hasler, died in London following injuries received during a Suffragette demonstration at Westminster.

At the annual meeting of the Association for the Housing of the Very Poor (a fine, resounding Victorian title), it was revealed that over 21,000 Dublin families were living – and, unfortunately, loving – in insanitary rooms in Dublin tenements.

The Earl of Meath protested against the apathy of the authorities in allowing an increased number of guns to be sold in Ireland: some of these guns would probably be used, he said, not only for taking pot shots at the police and other law-abiding citizens, but also even for shooting game.

Dublin Castle issued a circular addressed to the Ulster Constabulary on April 30, requesting information on drilling in the province, and on May 25, the Chief Secretary refused an invitation to the Empire Day celebrations in Belfast which were scheduled to include displays of marching and drilling by 'civilians'.

Throughout the year there had been a running controversy over a site for a new gallery to house Sir Hugh Lane's collection of modern paintings, which he had promised to bequeath to Ireland. The Municipal Art Gallery Fund had recommended Grattan Bridge as a suitable site as early as January 20, and the Corporation had provided £22,000 towards the cost of the new gallery in the same month. Sir Hugh Lane himself favoured the rather absurd notion of a gallery built on top of the Metal Bridge, for which Sir Edwin Lutyens, the famed architect of New Delhi, had designed a fanciful concept, vaguely echoing the Ponte Vecchio in Florence. Looking back on it now, it seems that both Hugh Lane and Edwin Lutyens must have been off their rockers even to contemplate such a notion: how could you possibly build a gallery on a narrow bridge over the River Liffey, without any basement for storage, toilet or restaurant facilities and without any space in any direction for development? In September, exasperated by all the arguments, of which many of his own were the most fatuous, Lane sent his French pictures to Paris and the remainder to Belfast on loan.

Sir Edward Carson was appointed Chairman of the Central Authority of the Unionist Council of Ulster; and the scheme for a Provisional Government of Ulster in the event of Home Rule was ratified. Even at this late stage, John Redmond refused to take the Ulster attitude towards Home Rule seriously, referring to it on September 28 as a 'gigantic and preposterous absurdity'.

On December 4, the whole of Ireland was proclaimed by King George V, the importation of arms was forbidden and guns were seized by the Customs at Kingstown. On the same day, Ulster motor car owners met in Belfast and agreed to put all their vehicles at the disposal of the Northern Ireland Provisional Government.

1914

WILSON SENDS US FLEET TO TAMPICO, MEXICO: LORDS REJECT VOTES FOR WOMEN: ARCHDUKE FRANZ FERDINAND OF AUSTRIA ASSASSINATED BY BOSNIAN REVOLUTIONARY AT SARAJEVO: AUSTRO-HUNGARIAN ULTIMATUM TO SERBIA: GERMANY DECLARES WAR ON FRANCE AND INVADES BELGIUM

Partition as Solution?

The labour troubles which had dominated 1913 began to peter out early in 1914, as the Employers' Federation began to get the upper hand over the unions. On January 4 the seamen and dockers who had been on strike for five months were told that there would be no more strike pay. Furthermore, over 700 'free' labourers were imported into Dublin to handle boats strike-bound in

Dublin Port. Although one of these free labourers was beaten to death on Eden Quay, the seamen gradually got the message and started to drift back to work. The Inchicore works of the Dublin United Tramway Company opened on January 19, after a closure of nearly five months, and the carters and builders' labourers, who had also been on strike, went back to work.

King George V, opening parliament once more, again expressed his desire to see a lasting settlement of the Home Rule question and on the following day, February 11, for the first time, both Houses at Westminster discussed the exclusion of Ulster, or a part of Ulster, as a distinct possibility.

When a summary of the report of the Viceregal Commission into the previous year's riots was published on February 14, it vindicated the police, despite references to 'a forest of batons' and despite the evidence of a doctor from Jervis Street Hospital that 225 citizens and 20 policemen had received treatment for their injuries; however, the report did admit that unnecessary force had been used by the police 'in isolated instances'.

A report of an Inquiry into Housing in Dublin published on February 14 revealed that about 28,000 Dubliners were living in houses 'unfit for human habitation', and named three members of the Dublin Corporation who themselves owned slum property, and were deriving rents from overcrowded, insanitary tenements.

By now it appeared less likely that Britain would attempt to impose Home Rule on the people of Northern Ireland by force. When the Home Rule Bill came up again on March 3, Prime Minister Herbert Asquith put forward the first firm proposal for partitioning Ireland, a plan which would have given each county in Ulster and the two cities of Belfast and Londonderry the right to poll themselves out of the Home Rule scheme for six years. Bonar Law, the leader of the Conservative and Unionist Party, proposed an all-Ireland referendum on the issue.

On March 20, the newspapers reported that between 60 and 70 (the actual number was 57) officers of the 3rd Cavalry Brigade stationed at the Curragh, Co Kildare, had declined to serve in Ulster and had sent in their papers to the War Office. This was the Curragh Mutiny. The Secretary of State for War resigned over the affair and a mass meeting in Hyde Park, London, protested against any attempt to use British Forces to shoot Ulster Loyalists.

There was a highly successful surprise test mobilisation of the Ulster Volunteers on April 23; the entire force was ready for action within five hours. Three days later, 35,000 rifles and 3,500,000 rounds of ammunition were landed at Larne, Bangor and Donaghadee, and were swiftly distributed among the Volunteers by a fleet of 800 motor cars.

On April 29 Carson welcomed Churchill's proposal to exclude Ulster or the North-Eastern part of Ulster until a general scheme of federation had been approved. Churchill had done what is now called a U-turn on Ulster.

By now the Irish Volunteers numbered 132,000 and the Ulster Volunteers 85,000. It was widely believed in Ireland that if the Ulster Volunteers were allowed to carry arms openly in Belfast, the Irish Volunteers ought to be able to do the same in Dublin.

Carson took over as head of the Provisional Government of Ulster on July 10, as more rifles and ammunition were landed at Belfast Quays and were carried away openly by the Ulster Volunteers. There were parades all over the province and July 12 was celebrated by the biggest ever demonstrations by members of the Orange Order.

The gun-running at Howth, for all the fuss that it caused, was a very mild affair. On July 26, a party of about 1,000 members of the Dublin Battalion of the Irish Volunteers, believing themselves to be on a normal Sunday route march, found themselves at Howth Harbour taking delivery of a consignment of arms and ammunition from a yacht, the *Asgard*, owned by Erskine Childers.

On their return, the Volunteers were intercepted at Clontarf by about 300 RIC policemen and British soldiers, and after a bit of a scuffle, about 19 guns were confiscated before the remainder of the Volunteers broke ranks and scattered away over the fields with the rest of the weapons.

As the British troops marched back through the city, they were jeered and stoned by the crowds in the street, who by this time had heard all about the gun-running. At Bachelor's Walk, the troops halted and fired on the crowd, killing two men and a woman and injuring 32.

On August 3, war was declared and hundreds of thousands of Irishmen volunteered for service with the British forces. The Home Rule Bill was rushed through its remaining stages and put on the Statute Book with the proviso that it would not become law until after the war.

1915

GERMAN SUBMARINE ATTACK OFF LE HAVRE: GERMANS USE POISON GAS ON WESTERN FRONT: ANZAC FORCES LAND AT GALLIPOLI: ITALY DECLARES WAR ON AUSTRO-HUNGARIAN EMPIRE: ZEPPELIN ATTACK ON LONDON: RASPUTIN UNOFFICIAL RULER OF RUSSIA: FRANCE BANS ABSINTHE

Lusitania Torpedoed

Although so many Irishmen had joined the British Forces and had gone off to the front, the war did not initially have a great deal of impact on Ireland. The Kingstown mailboat SS *Leinster* was chased by German submarines in the Irish Sea early in January, and during the early months of the year several hospital ships arrived in Irish ports carrying Irish casualties. After a zeppelin raid on Norfolk on January 19, there were widespread fears of a German invasion of Ireland.

A Galway postman was fined £1 on February 8 for spreading false reports that the Germans had sunk six British warships. This was the first case in Ireland brought under DORA – a series of Defence of the Realm Acts introduced by Britain on the outbreak of war.

The Rosslare–Fishguard steamer was chased by German submarines on March 13. The Pembroke Council agreed to continue to pay all members of their staff who enlisted half of their normal salaries and to keep their jobs open for them after the war.

The *Lusitania* was torpedoed by a German submarine and sunk off Southern Ireland on a passage from New York on May 7; 1,502 of the 2,150 people on board were lost, including Sir Hugh Lane. The survivors were landed at Kinsale and Queenstown.

The Chief Secretary for Ireland told the Commons that on July 6 The O'Rahilly had been prohibited from entering Cork, Kerry or Limerick, under the Defence of the Realm Acts, because he had been acting in a manner prejudicial to the safety of the state. Police notices were also served on Ernest Blythe (later to become an Irish government minister and director of the Abbey Theatre) and Liam Mellowes, a prominent republican, requesting them both to leave Ireland by July 17 under the DORA provisions. On July 30 Mellowes was sentenced to three months in prison for refusing to go. If it seems strange that the authorities could deport Irishmen from their own homes and force them to live in Manchester or Birmingham, that indeed was the practice of the period; it was the police view that 'disaffected persons' were more easily kept under control in loyal areas of Britain than in their own native districts of Ireland.

Sir Hugh Lane's will and the controversial codicil were published on October 3. In his formal will, made on October 11, 1913, Lane had bequeathed his collection of Impressionist paintings to the National Gallery in London, but before he sailed on the *Lusitania*, he had added an unwitnessed codicil dated February 2, 1915, stating that if a suitable building to house the collection should be provided in Dublin within five years of his death, the pictures would go instead to the city of Dublin.

At Liverpool, on November 6, the Cunard Steamship Company issued a notice stating that they would not accept any further bookings from British subjects who were fit and eligible for military service and over 400 would-be emigrants from the West of Ireland to the United States were turned away.

1916

FIRST ZEPPELIN RAID ON PARIS: BATTLE OF VERDUN:
ANZACS ARRIVE IN FRANCE: BATTLE OF JUTLAND:
BRITISH USE FIRST TANKS ON WESTERN FRONT: HEAVY
BRITISH LOSSES IN BATTLE OF SOMME: WOODROW WILSON
PEACE NOTE: BRITAIN ADOPTS DAYLIGHT SAVING

The Easter Rising

On January 1, 1916, the Irish Unionist Alliance, speaking on behalf of the Unionists in Southern Ireland, called for the inclusion of all Ireland in any scheme for compulsory military service. The shipping lines reported a big increase in passengers from England, notably young men arriving in Belfast from English ports, presumably attempting to dodge the draft, which was now clearly coming.

A Compulsory Service Bill requiring all British subjects between the ages of 18 and 42, unmarried or without dependent children, to enlist in the armed forces, was announced on January 5, but it excluded Ireland; on the same day the first depot for 4,000 wounded Irish soldiers was established in Tipperary.

Brigadier General Hubert Gough, leader of the Curragh Mutiny, was knighted on February 5, and on the same day the Irish Volunteers (now more widely known as the Sinn Fein Volunteers) were out in the Dublin streets in full uniforms and with fixed bayonets, carrying out street-fighting exercises.

As soon as war broke out, the IRB, both in Ireland and the United States, had reaffirmed the view expressed by Maud Gonne – that England's difficulty was Ireland's opportunity — and had begun to make plans for an armed insurrection at the first available moment. At the same time, Labour leader Connolly was also talking about a rising and was training his Citizen Army in house-to-house fighting.

Sir Roger Casement, an Irishman knighted for his work for

the British Foreign Office and an ardent nationalist, went to Germany via the US; there he hoped to form an Irish Brigade – composed of Irishmen who had joined the British Army and were now prisoners of war in Germany – which could be transported back to Ireland to fight for Irish freedom.

As early as February 1916, the German general staff had heard from the IRB in New York that they had planned a rising for Easter Sunday; the Germans had been requested to send a consignment of arms to the coast of Limerick to assist in this enterprise. As usual, the IRB hadn't bothered to tell Casement anything about this (they regarded him as a well-meaning dilettante doomed to failure) though they did tell Monteith, an IRB man they had sent along with Casement to keep an eye on him.

The arms were despatched from Germany in the 1,200-ton vessel *Aud*, flying a Norwegian flag. When Casement finally heard about the planned rising, he became convinced that without full German support (including artillery and military advisers), the rebellion could not possibly hope to succeed, and that it was now his duty to return to Ireland as quickly as possible, to persuade the leaders to call the whole thing off.

He left Germany on the night of April 11, on board a German submarine, with Monteith, the IRB man and Bailey, one of his Irish Brigade recruits. The *Aud* had arrived off Tralee on Holy Thursday. Irish Volunteers sent down to provide signals for the *Aud* had taken a wrong turning, had driven off the end of Fenit Pier and were drowned a day earlier. Finding no one there to take delivery of the 20,000 rifles and ammunition, and the seas around the coast stiff with British shipping, the skipper of the *Aud* put to sea again and scuttled his ship, arms and all.

At dawn on Good Friday, 1916, Casement and his companions came ashore in a collapsible dinghy at Banna Strand near Tralee. Monteith and Bailey went on into Tralee to try to establish contact with the Volunteers, leaving the seasick Casement hiding in a ruined fort, where he was caught and arrested during the morning, with a Berlin railway sleeper ticket still in his pocket. He was executed for treason at Pentonville Jail on August 3.

It was a spectacular cock-up, a failure so epic in its proportions that any reasonable person would have assumed that any attempt at a rising which might now take place, must prove a total failure. But, paradoxically, they would have quite been wrong.

The Rising had been planned for Easter Sunday but when the promised German arms failed to materialise, had been called off at the last minute by Eoin MacNeill, Commander in Chief of the Volunteers, who put advertisements in the papers cancelling what had been known as 'the Easter exercises'. But Patrick Pearse, the Dublin poet and school-master who commanded the Dublin Volunteers, and James Connolly, who commanded the Citizen Army, decided to go ahead with the Rising anyway.

On the morning of Easter Monday, while most of the British officers and their wives, as well as half Dublin, were on their way out to Fairyhouse Races, six members of the Irish Citizen Army walked up to the gates of Dublin Castle, shot a policeman dead and established themselves in the guard room shortly before noon. If there had been a few more of them in the party, they might well have captured the castle.

At about the same time, the main body of Irish Volunteers and members of the Citizen Army, with Pearse and Connolly at their head, took over the General Post Office in Sackville Street; they consisted of about 150 men, armed with rifles and shotguns of various sorts, sledge-hammers, pick-axes, pikes, home-made bombs, sand-bags and enough sandwiches to keep them going for a few days. From the steps of the GPO, Pearse proclaimed the Republic; the document he read had seven signatories.

Among the Post Office garrison was Michael Collins, then 26, who had returned in 1915 from England, where he had been working as a postal clerk, to join the IRB and the Volunteers. He fought in the GPO as aide-de-camp to Plunkett, one of the signatories, and after the Rising, was interned at Frongoch. On his release, he became Adjutant-General and Chief Intelligence Officer of the Irish Republican Army.

As to how many men there were in the GPO, estimates vary greatly. I once heard James Dillon tell the Dail that if even half the people who were claiming IRA pensions on the grounds that they had been in the GPO during Easter week in 1916 had actually been there, then the British troops would have found themselves hopelessly outnumbered. And I remember asking Cathal O'Shannon, James Connolly's representative in Belfast, where he had been during Easter bank holiday, 1916.

'As soon as I heard about the rising,' he told me, 'I set out for Dublin. There was no transport south of the border, but I hitched lifts and managed to get there by the Tuesday. I went straight to the GPO and knocked on the door and told them who I was. They said they were sorry, but they were full up, and fast running out of sandwiches. I asked them what I should do and they told me to go off and find myself some lodgings somewhere, until it was all over, which I did.'

All over the city of Dublin the same scene repeated itself, as various units of the Irish Volunteers and the Citizen Army took over buildings at strategic points, fortified them as best they could, ran up various Republican and Labour flags, gripped their antiquated German Mausers, smuggled to them by Erskine Childers at Howth, and waited to see how the armed forces of the greatest empire in the world would respond to their defiant gesture.

At the time, nobody in Dublin had any clear idea of what was happening. The newspapers appeared on Tuesday morning as usual carrying vague headlines like: PUBLIC BUILDINGS SEIZED: ATTEMPT TO CAPTURE DUBLIN CASTLE: LANCERS ATTACKED IN SACKVILLE STREET: REBELS DIG IN IN ST STEPHEN'S GREEN: SINN FEIN FLAG FLIES FROM GPO.

No further papers were published for the remainder of the week and all the theatres closed down from Easter Monday. The Abbey Theatre offering that week had been T.H. Nally's *The Spancel of Death* which, unluckily for the author, was never subsequently staged as another production had been billed for the following week.

It is perhaps worth making the point here that despite the desperate determination of Pearse and Connolly and many of the other leaders to shed their own blood (and, indeed, that of their comrades in arms) for Ireland's sake, at this stage nobody in Ireland took it in any way seriously. Two of my wife's uncles, in Birr on leave from service with the British Army, went up to

Dublin 'to see the gas', as they quaintly phrased it, and my uncle, Hugh Law McKee, hearing about the rebellion after a day at the seaside with his family, decided to cycle into Dublin to see for himself whether it was true that there had indeed been an 'outbreak'.

'When I got to the GPO,' he told me, 'I left my bicycle by the kerb and walked over to one of the windows. The glass had been knocked out, and there were sand-bags under it. I looked in. It was quite dark inside, but I could see groups of these fellows, sitting around with rifles across their knees. Some of them were eating sandwiches. Nobody said anything to me, so I went back to my bike and cycled back to the barricade. They let me out without a word.'

I asked him what happened then. 'Nothing,' he replied. 'I simply cycled back out to Stillorgan and told the family that yes, it was true, there was a rebellion on in Dublin, all right.'

When it was all over John Redmond, who had a great gift for saying the wrong thing at the wrong time which never deserted him until the day of his death, condemned the outbreak as 'a wicked and insane movement'.

Martial Law was proclaimed by the Lord Lieutenant on April 25, and no further newspapers were published until it was all over. The rebels held out against the British forces for six days. On the Saturday, to avoid further bloodshed, Pearse offered to surrender, and from behind the barricades and out of the battered buildings the Volunteers emerged, dazed and weary, to lay down their arms at the foot of the Parnell monument. They were mocked and jeered by women whose husbands and sons were away fighting in Flanders or the Balkans, and who had no time at all for the Shinners, as they were known in Dublin.

Sir John Maxwell, the military commander, who had been given unlimited powers to quell the revolt, soon changed all that by court-martialling all the signatories of the proclamation of the republic and all the commanding officers of the Volunteers and the Citizen Army, and executing fifteen of them, in twos and threes, over a period of about a week. Among those executed was Major John MacBride, former husband of Maud

Gonne; de Valera was sentenced to death but was reprieved because he was carrying an American passport.

Most of the Volunteers who surrendered were taken by cattle-boat to Britain and interned without trial under the Defence of the Realm Acts. Over 1,600 of them were imprisoned in one camp at Frongoch in Wales, where they spent the time discussing what went wrong and how much better they would organise things the next time. It is difficult to get hard and fast figures but the general consensus seems to be that the losses were of this order: 60 Volunteers, 30 British military and police and about 260 civilians killed and about 3,000 people wounded.

Agitations soon began for the release of the prisoners and the British, anxious to placate Irish-American opinion, had set most of them free by Christmas 1916. To their own considerable surprise, they were welcomed home with bonfires and bands and torchlight processions, and were cheered resoundingly by the very people who had jeered and spat at them nine months earlier.

Some form of Home Rule for Southern Ireland was now urgent and imperative. But Ulster, or at least the predominantly Protestant part of Ulster, would have to be excluded; on July 1, Haig had launched his Somme offensive – it continued until November – in which the British losses totalled 420,000. His forces had included the Ulster Volunteer Force, enrolled as the 36th Ulster Division; they were so decimated that hardly a Protestant family in Ulster did not lose a husband, a father, a sweetheart or a friend in the weeks and months that followed the Dublin Easter Rebellion. It was small wonder that they felt bitter about the rebels who had attacked soldiers of the army in which their loved ones had died.

In an effort to appease the Irish nationalists, the British Government set up a Convention to consider various forms of Home Rule which might solve the problem of the Northern Unionists, but as it was boycotted by Sinn Fein, by now the party representing Irish majority opinion, it could achieve nothing.

In the middle of all this turmoil, it is perhaps not surprising that not much press attention focused on a new Irish writer who had appeared on the literary scene. In 1914, when war broke out, James Joyce was in Zurich with his wife and family. He was obliged to remain in Switzerland in great poverty throughout the war, and in fact never returned to live in Dublin. In 1914, his classic collection of short stories, *Dubliners*, was published and in 1916 he published *A Portrait of the Artist as a Young Man*, which in its style and technique – and above all its effect on the English novel – was probably about the literary equivalent of Picasso's *Les Demoiselles d'Avignon*.

1917

GERMANY ANNOUNCES UNRESTRICTED NAVAL WARFARE: WOODROW WILSON ORDERS ARMING OF US MERCHANT SHIPS: FEBRUARY REVOLUTION IN MOSCOW: TSAR NICHOLAS ABDICATES: US DECLARES WAR ON GERMANY: BRITISH ROYALS RENOUNCE GERMAN TITLES, BECOME THE WINDSORS

Sinn Fein Enters Political Arena

The year 1917 began very quietly in Ireland. The Executive Committee which had been appointed to control the railways on behalf of the state met on January 2. A few days later it was announced that racing was to be curtailed, and no further 'race specials' were to be provided by the railways. On January 10, a compulsory tillage scheme was announced under which one-tenth of all holdings over ten acres had to be tilled.

By far the most significant event of the year – though it was not widely recognised as such at the time – was the by-election in February in which Count George Noble Plunkett – father of the executed Joseph Mary Plunkett, one of the seven signatories of the 1916 proclamation – went forward as a Sinn Fein candidate for the Roscommon seat in Parliament at Westminster. He was elected with a two-to-one majority over the Nationalist Parliamentary Party's candidate.

On April 6 the Government issued a proclamation forbidding meetings or processions between Sunday April 8 and Sunday April 15 (Easter Sunday); but on Easter Monday, 20,000 people gathered in front of the ruins of the GPO and cheered as the new Irish tricolour – a band of green for Ireland, a band of orange for the Ulster Unionists with a band of white between them, signifying peace – was hoisted while members of Cumann na mBan (the women's auxiliary of the Irish Volunteers) distributed copies of Pearse's 1916 proclamation overprinted with the words: 'The Republic still lives'. Masses were said all over the country for the 15 men executed after the Rising.

In a by-election on May 10, J.P. McGuinness, a Sinn Fein prisoner still in jail in Britain, won the South Longford seat from the Nationalist Parliamentary Party. The Sinn Fein election poster depicted McGuinness dressed in his convict clothes, with the slogan: 'Put him in to get him out!' Another by-election was pending in East Clare and Eamon de Valera, who had just been released from Lewes prison, was picked by Sinn Fein to contest the seat, which he won from the Nationalist Parliamentary candidate on July 11 with a majority of more than two to one.

Countess Markievicz, released from jail in June, received the freedom of the city of Sligo on July 23. Sinn Fein Volunteers in uniform, but armed only with hurley sticks, provided a guard of honour. A special Order under the Defence of the Realm Acts published on July 29 had declared the wearing of uniforms by persons other than members of the armed forces illegal and prohibited weapons of any kind from being carried in public. Despite this order, Irish Volunteers in uniform paraded to McKenna's Fort, now renamed Casement's Fort, on Carahane Strand, Tralee, on the first anniversary of Casement's execution.

Yet another Sinn Fein candidate, William T. Cosgrave, won yet another by-election in Kilkenny; it was now becoming clear that the whole country was swinging towards Sinn Fein and its ideas and aims.

There were arms seizures all over the country in August. In September, Sinn Fein raided Cork Grammar School, for arms used by the Officers' Training Corps. Thomas Ashe, a schoolmaster, was sentenced by a court martial to a year's imprisonment for making seditious speeches and Joseph MacDonagh, brother of the executed Thomas MacDonagh, was sentenced to six months with hard labour for breaches of the Defence of the Realm Acts.

Then, on September 25, the school-teacher Thomas Ashe died in the Mater Hospital in Dublin from the combined effects of a hunger strike and attempts to feed him forcibly in Mountjoy Jail. When his remains were removed to the Pro-Cathedral on September 27, a Sinn Fein demonstration held up all traffic in Dublin for two hours. De Valera acted as Commandant of the Volunteers for the occasion, and Countess Markievicz led the Citizen Army contingent. At the funeral procession to Glasnevin Cemetery on September 30, after a lying-in-state in the City Hall, there were so many mourners that the first of them had already arrived back in Dublin before the end of the procession had reached the graveside.

By the end of the year, the Volunteers were again drilling and parading all over the country, wearing uniforms and carrying arms.

1918

WOODROW WILSON'S 14-POINT PEACE PLAN: GERMAN OFFENSIVE ON RUSSIAN FRONT: RAF TO REPLACE RFC: TSAR NICHOLAS AND FAMILY EXECUTED: GERMANS RETREAT ON WESTERN FRONT: ARMISTICE SIGNED: REVOLUTION IN BERLIN: YUGOSLAV REPUBLIC IS ESTABLISHED: VOTES FOR WOMEN

Another German Plot?

By the beginning of 1918 the Ulster Unionists had realised that the Sinn Fein Party meant business and that de Valera was a force with which they would have to reckon; early in January de Valera was introduced as President of the Irish Republic at a

Sinn Fein meeting and did nothing to set the record straight despite the fact that at this particular period he hadn't been elected president of anything.

At the end of the month a meeting in Dublin demanded the return by the National Gallery in London of the collection of paintings bequeathed to Dublin in the codicil to Sir Hugh Lane's will; an Irish film, *Ireland a Nation*, was held by the Censor to be prejudicial to recruiting and was banned after two days' performances.

Sinn Fein were now taking an ever-increasing part in the day-to-day activities of the country. In January they advised Dubliners to buy their food direct from Irish farmers and asked farmers to give preference to this trade with their fellow country-men rather than exporting their produce; in February they commandeered and slaughtered 34 pigs in the Dublin streets to prevent their export to Britain. Over 100 policemen arrived on the scene but took no action as the carcasses were delivered to Donnelly's bacon factory. There were raids for arms all over the country, renewed cattle-drives, shootings of policemen, unlawful assemblies and ever more provocative displays of drilling and marching by the Volunteers.

John Dillon succeeded Redmond, who had died in March, as leader of the Nationalist Parliamentary Party. The Chief Secretary for Ireland replied to the Lord Mayor of Dublin's protest about the treatment of political hunger strikers by pointing out that during the past two months men claiming to be on 'political' hunger strike had included burglars, cattle-drivers and even men convicted for failing to pay their National Health contributions.

But the bombshell of the year was dropped on April 9 when Lloyd George introduced the Manpower Bill and announced that conscription would apply after all to Ireland.

The Nationalist MPs at Westminster called the Bill 'a declaration of war on Ireland', and warned the Government that they would not answer for the consequences of any attempt to make Irishmen fight for Britain, after all that had happened. In the end, they adopted Sinn Fein tactics and abstained altogether from Westminster.

At a conference in the Mansion House in Dublin on April 19, Sinn Fein, the Nationalist Parliamentary Party, Labour and the Independents all pledged themselves to resist conscription. The Catholic bishops, sitting at Maynooth, issued a pronouncement against conscription. The Trades Union Congress called the first general strike ever held in Western Europe in protest. A national fund to finance the defeat of conscription was set up and hundreds of thousands of ordinary people signed an anti-conscription pledge outside the churches after mass on Sunday. Things had never looked gloomier for the British administration in Ireland. Even the *Irish Times*, always a staunch supporter of English interests, had to admit on April 18: 'The whole of Ireland is now in revolt.' And still the British couldn't read the writing on the wall.

On April 22, the general strike against conscription took place. There were no trains, no trams, no restaurants nor shops nor pubs open, no deliveries, no newspapers, no theatres or places of entertainment; almost the total workforce had gone on strike. Three days later, 17 KCs at the Irish Bar approved and adopted the Hierarchy's declaration against conscription.

Then once again the British swooped. Over 80 people prominent in the revolutionary movement – among them de Valera, Arthur Griffith, Countess Markievicz, and William T. Cosgrave – were re-arrested on May 17 and carried back to British jails. This followed the arrival at Galway Bay of a single member of Casement's Irish Brigade, a man called Dowling who was transported from Germany by submarine and was arrested almost immediately after he stepped ashore. This incident was represented by the British as evidence of another German plot to attack England from the rear, and, in the climate of the times, was all that was needed.

On October 10 the mail steamer *Leinster* was sunk by a torpedo from a German submarine en route to Holyhead from Kingstown and over 500 were lost, including the captain.

The threat of conscription disappeared with the Armistice on November 11, but it was replaced by what, in many Irish eyes, seemed a far worse threat: the possibility of permanent Partition of the country which would put 500,000 Catholic Nationalists on the far side of the border from their fellow-countrymen. For Lloyd George now made yet another attempt to solve the Irish Question: he again offered the Irish a measure of Home Rule from which six of the predominantly Protestant counties of Ulster would be excluded. It was known as the 'Better Government of Ireland Bill' and it was some time before he could get it through parliament.

In the meantime, the first post-war general election was due in December. It couldn't have come at a worse time for Michael Collins, now – with de Valera and Griffith both in jail – effectively the leader of Sinn Fein. His Sinn Fein Party was constantly being proscribed as illegal; Cumann na mBan, the Gaelic League and the Irish Volunteers had all been proscribed as dangerous organisations; 47 of the Sinn Fein candidates were in English jails, others were 'on the run' from the police or military, had been deported, or had gone into exile. Sinn Fein election addresses were confiscated and even their election manifesto was heavily censored. As a final stroke of ill-fortune, their director of elections was arrested three weeks before polling day.

It was the first election in which women had a vote and it was also the first parliament in which women could sit; Countess Markievicz (Sinn Fein) was the first woman to be elected, although, as she chose not to take her seat, the first woman to sit in the House of Commons was Lady Astor.

The election results were not announced until December 28 and the year ended with considerable speculation as to what the 73 elected Sinn Fein members of the Westminster Parliament were going to do in the New Year.

1919

NATIONAL SOCIALIST PARTY FORMED IN GERMANY: PROHI-
BITION IN USA: VERSAILLES PEACE CONFERENCE:
MUSSOLINI FORMS FASCIST PARTY: GERMAN FLEET SCUTTLED
AT SCAPA FLOW: GERMANY'S AFRICAN COLONIES CON-
FISCATED: INTERNATIONAL LABOUR ORGANISATION FORMED

First Dail Eireann

The Anglo-Irish and the Castle hacks, as the *Freeman's Journal* called them, celebrated New Year's Eve at a Victory Ball in Dublin Castle.

On New Year's Day, 1919, Sinn Fein held meetings throughout Ireland to demand the release of the men still interned and imprisoned in England, including the elected MPs.

Restrictions on private motoring were relaxed, and four new Royal Mail steamers – to be called *Anglia*, *Scotia*, *Hibernia* and *Cambria* – were ordered by the London and North-Western Railway for the Kingstown–Holyhead route, to replace ships requisitioned during the war. They were narrow, dirty and uncomfortable, but extremely fast (they are also inextricably linked in my mind with the first summer holidays I remember, always spent with my uncle and aunt and cousins in sunny Rhyl, North Wales).

The police raided the Sinn Fein headquarters in Harcourt Street, Dublin, on January 11 and took away a number of documents including a draft constitution which had been prepared for Dail Eireann. Four days later, Sinn Fein issued a statement: it had been decided to summon Dail Eireann at an early date, to be announced on January 17. A special committee had been appointed to secure the release of the prisoners and the names of Eamon de Valera, Arthur Griffith and Count Plunkett were being submitted as Ireland's delegates to the post-war Peace Conference at Versailles.

Several interned men had to be 'placed in restraint' in Belfast Jail following demonstrations to celebrate the opening of Dail

Eireann in the Mansion House, Dublin on January 21; the proceedings had been opened by Cathal Brugha – deputising for Michael Collins, who was over in England arranging for de Valera's escape from jail – with the fighting words: 'We are now done with England; let the world know it.'

On January 23, the South Riding of Tipperary was proclaimed by the Government; later a reward of £1,000 was offered for information leading to the arrest of the men who had murdered the two constables at Soloheadbeg Quarry during an IRA raid for gelignite.

Sinn Fein next ordered all hunting to be stopped as a protest against the continuing detention of their fellow-countrymen in English jails without trial. They also encouraged cattle-driving to drive the herds off Irish land and redistribute it for cultivation by Irish farmers.

Twelve men were jailed on February 1 for drilling on the Clonliffe Road in Dublin, and on February 3 Eamon de Valera escaped from Lincoln Jail; two other Sinn Fein prisoners were also found to be missing from their cells.

A conference of the Irish Labour Party and the Trades Union Conference to demand a 44-hour working week with a minimum wage of 50s a week for adult workers was held on February 9. On the same day Martial Law was proclaimed in Tipperary, but the notices proclaiming it were torn down as quickly as they were posted up, and Sinn Fein announced an extension of its ban on hunting to all angling 'by alien and resident gentlemen holding anti-Irish ideas'. When King George V opened Parliament at Westminster, only the Ulster Unionists and six members of the Nationalist Parliamentary Party turned up to represent Ireland.

Sean T. O'Kelly, carrying credentials as 'envoy of the Provisional Government of Ireland', and also representing Dublin Corporation, went to Paris with the object of presenting the freedom of the City of Dublin and Ireland's case for independence to the American President, Woodrow Wilson.

There was an arms raid on Collinstown Military Airport on March 20; upwards of 50 masked men, some of them armed, seized 75 rifles and 4,000 rounds of ammunition. The raid was immediately followed by instructions to all military guards to fire on any unauthorised person who approached their posts and failed to halt when challenged.

As the year wore on, it became obvious both to ordinary readers of the newspapers, as well as to the authorities, that the attacks on the British administration were no longer random and isolated.

On June 14, two British aviators, J.W. Alcock and A.W. Brown, crash-landed in a field in Co Galway after the first air crossing of the Atlantic; they had left Newfoundland 16 hours and 27 minutes earlier.

By July, de Valera had insisted on leaving Ireland (and his wife and young family) to go on a fund-raising tour in the States, in the course of which he managed to achieve a very considerable split in the Irish-American movement.

A proclamation in the Dublin Castle *Gazette* prohibited Sinn Fein and kindred organisations in Co Tipperary. Sinn Fein replied by proclaiming the South Riding of Tipperary, warning police and persons in the pay of England (magistrates, lawyers, jurors, etc.) that they would be deemed to have forfeited their lives.

On July 12, Sir Edward Carson announced at Holywood, Co Down that if any attempt was made to revive the Home Rule Bill, he would summon the Provisional Government of Ulster, move the repeal of the bill and call out the Ulster Volunteers.

On September 22, small hand-grenades were issued to the RIC for the use of patrols if attacked, and for the protection of their barracks. On the same day Cathal Brugha announced that in future the Sinn Fein courts would settle all strikes in Ireland.

In the United States on December 2, de Valera – always presenting himself as President of the Irish Republic though his only official title at this period was Priomh-aire (first minister) of Dail Eireann – began a campaign to float a £2,000,000 bond certificate loan, the money to be repaid when the Republic had received international recognition and when the British forces had been withdrawn from Ireland.

The headquarters of Sinn Fein and Dail Eireann in Harcourt Street, Dublin, were closed by the police on December 9 and on

December 15 the struggling *Freeman's Journal* was suppressed and its machinery disconnected under DORA. It was subsequently acquired by the *Irish Independent* which added 'incorporating the Freeman's Journal' to its title.

There was an attempted assassination of Viscount French, the Lord Lieutenant, at Ashtown Gate, Phoenix Park, on December 19, in the course of which one of the would-be assassins was shot dead. Armed masked men broke into the offices of the *Irish Independent* on December 21, holding up the staff at gun-point and smashing thousands of pounds' worth of machinery.

Then, on December 22, Lloyd George came up with his 'Better Government of Ireland Bill' which became the Government of Ireland Act, under which parliaments for the 26 counties of 'Southern Ireland' and for the Six Counties of Northern Ireland were to be elected.

1920–1930

The War of Independence

The guerrilla war which Michael Collins, Chief of Intelligence of the IRA, now began to wage against the British authorities in Ireland resulted in a state of total anarchy which lasted well into the summer of 1921. Although there was a price of £10,000 on his head, Collins had so thoroughly infiltrated the forces of law and order that he was able to cycle around Dublin freely with a revolver in his pocket. There were constant IRA raids on RIC barracks and on British military installations and administrative centres, as well as bombings, burnings, murders and atrocities of all kinds on both sides.

Initially reluctant to accept that a state of war could possibly exist between the mighty British Empire and a handful of Irish rebels, Westminster left it to the RIC – aided by a couple of auxiliary forces specially recruited for the task – to contain what was now clearly a serious revolt. But by 1921 the British Army, too, had become involved in a struggle which they couldn't win – they were eventually up against an entire population of people who were either bitterly opposed to them, or were too terrified of the IRA to pretend that they were not.

And during the Irish War of Independence, the British authorities behaved as badly as they have behaved on countless occasions since, in India, in Palestine, in Cyprus, in Aden, in Africa and elsewhere, creating in Ireland a whole new communion of Irish martyrs like Terence MacSwiney, Lord Mayor of Cork, whose death in an English jail after 74 days on hunger strike made headlines around the world; and Kevin Barry, a Dublin student who was hanged for shooting a soldier despite the fact that his revolver had jammed and had clearly never been fired. By such actions the British managed to alienate even those members of the Irish public who cared nothing about politics and wanted only to be allowed to live in peace.

The courts couldn't operate, because jurors refused to serve, and the Resident Magistrates were resigning in droves. Continual raids on post offices and trains carrying mail for the British administration brought the postal services to a standstill. The Sinn Fein Dail, proscribed as an illegal organisation, couldn't really run the country, but its existence made it almost impossible for the British to run it either; at the beginning of the decade the Dublin County Council, for example, refused to furnish any returns to the Inland Revenue, claiming that such information would be available only to Dail Eireann, as the duly elected government of the country. By the middle of 1920, Sinn Fein had its own courts operating in 27 of the 32 Irish counties.

In May 1921, Lloyd George's [Better] Government of Ireland Act came into force. It provided for two Irish parliaments, one for the Six Counties of Antrim, Armagh, Derry, Down, Fermanagh and Tyrone in the North and another for the remaining 26 counties of Southern Ireland which paradoxically included Donegal, the most northerly county of them all.

This Act required elections for both parliaments, and once again Sinn Fein used the British electoral machinery to make another appeal to the country. Its candidates were returned unopposed in every single constituency in the 26 counties apart from the four Trinity College seats, and sat in Dublin as the second Dail Eireann.

This overwhelming expression of the will of the people could not easily be ignored by the democratic British. Even more importantly, perhaps, also in May, 1921, the IRA had attacked the Custom House in Dublin and had set it on fire, destroying many of the British revenue records and crippling the civil service.

Bowing to the inevitable, and encouraged by an appeal from King George V to Irishmen to work together for a solution of the problem, a truce was arranged, and Lloyd George invited de Valera to London to discuss the situation. It is perhaps worth noting, in view of the current situation, that various unofficial 'channels' had already been opened, to prepare the way for such an approach.

Lloyd George offered de Valera a measure of self-government for the 26 counties which corresponded roughly with that of Canada, though without the right of secession. He promised a border commission to consider the question of Partition in the light of the views of the inhabitants of the partitioned area at some later date. He insisted on the retention of the four British naval ports and on the same Oath of Allegiance to the king of England as British MPs were obliged to swear. This offer was put to the second Dail on August 16 and was rejected without a single dissentient vote. The possibility of permanent Partition of the country was the issue which rankled, though there was also a strong feeling that dominion status was one thing for Canada, with the broad Atlantic between it and the Mother Country, and quite a different matter for Ireland, right on Britain's doorstep.

A Dail delegation, which included Arthur Griffith and Michael Collins, but not de Valera – who claimed that his continued presence in Ireland was needed to prevent the diehards from rejecting a less generous offer from the British than they believed that they had won in combat – went to London a couple of times to try to get better terms but Lloyd George finally bulldozed them all into signing the Treaty almost exactly as it stood.

De Valera immediately declared that he could not recommend the Treaty to either the Dail or the country, and when the cabinet and subsequently the Dail – realising that this was the best offer they were likely to get for the moment and that the IRA was in no position to resume the war – voted to accept it, he announced that he intended to resign and later walked out of the chamber with his followers.

With the Sinn Fein Party and the IRA both now split on the Treaty issue, a civil war became inevitable. It dragged on until the spring of 1923. Griffith, who had succeeded de Valera as President of the Executive Council (cabinet) of Dail Eireann, died on August 13, and Michael Collins, who had taken over as Commander-in-Chief of the Free State Army, was killed in an ambush on August 22. All the dirty tricks that had been learned in the War of Independence were now employed by Irishmen against their former comrades in arms and in some cases against their own brothers and cousins. During the winter and spring of 1922–3, 77 anti-Treaty Republican Irregulars were shot, including Childers (for being in possession of a pistol which had been a present from Michael Collins).

A cease-fire on April 30, 1923, brought that particular phase of Ireland's troubles to an end. But de Valera and his followers continued to abstain from the Dail – on the grounds that the Oath of Allegiance to the British king was totally unacceptable – although they contested a general election in August 1923 and won 44 seats.

In 1924 the promised Boundary Commission collapsed in the face of stubborn Ulster recalcitrance – the Unionists refused even to put forward a delegate – and William Cosgrave, who had succeeded Griffith as President of the Executive Council, lost a certain amount of popular support for not making more effort to gain some concessions for the 500,000 Catholic Nationalists in the Six Counties.

By 1926, de Valera was beginning to grow tired of the political wilderness in which he had landed himself. He formed a new political party which he called Fianna Fail (Soldiers of Destiny, with the slight overtone provided by using one of the ancient names for Ireland, Inis Fail, the Island of Destiny). He next set about trying to get into the Dail without taking the Oath. In a general election in 1927, while Cosgrave was still suffering from the setback over the collapse of the Boundary Commission, the new Fianna Fail Party won 44 seats as against Cosgrave's 47, and de Valera led his fellow-members of the party into Leinster

House hoping that Cosgrave would let them take their seats without taking the Oath.

Not only did Cosgrave refuse to let them into the Dail chamber without first taking the Oath of Allegiance, he also introduced legislation making acceptance of the Oath obligatory before candidates could even stand for election. And when de Valera tried to organise a petition for a referendum on this issue, Cosgrave changed the Constitution to rule out any possibility of such a referendum.

De Valera now had no alternative but to take the Oath, which he did on August 12, 1927. His arrival in Dail Eireann with his Fianna Fail supporters was greeted by the Labour Party with a vote of no confidence in the Cosgrave Government . This resulted in a tie, and with the speaker's casting vote, in a victory for Cosgrave. De Valera's Fianna Fail Party remained in opposition for their first four years in the Dail.

In the meantime, the Cosgrave Government got down to the very considerable business of running the new Irish Free State, starting more or less from scratch, if not from away behind the starting line. If they didn't appear initially to make a great success of it, that's not surprising. They were an assorted collection of Gaelic language enthusiasts, lawyers, farmers, civil servants, blacksmiths and post office workers, without any experience of running anything, anywhere. They had nothing more in common than their willingness to die for Irish freedom, but started to put a country which had been in a state of total anarchy for four years back on the path to peace and prosperity. This was remarkable enough in itself, especially since a good deal of the initial Government expenditure was money which had to be spent on repairing roads and railway lines and replacing bridges and public buildings which they had themselves destroyed. That they had the gumption to come up with ideas like approaching the German firm of Siemens Shuckert with an invitation to develop a hydro-electric scheme for the Shannon River, investigating the possibility of producing sugar from Irish beet and inaugurating a sweepstake to raise badly-needed finance for the Dublin hospitals was quite extraordinary in the circumstances.

1920

LEAGUE OF NATIONS ESTABLISHED: HOLLAND REFUSES TO
SURRENDER WILHELM II: HORTHY ELECTED REGENT OF
HUNGARY: MESOPOTAMIA AND PALESTINE MANDATED TO
BRITAIN, SYRIA AND LEBANON TO FRANCE: DANZIG
DECLARED FREE CITY: FIRST BROADCAST IN BRITAIN

PR is Tried Out

In the municipal elections held on January 15 the system of
proportional representation devised by the British Government
to give the minority in Ireland some say in the government of
the country was tried out for the first time. Sinn Fein failed to
make the clean sweep the party had achieved in the 1918 general election under the straight first-past-the-post system, but it
dominated most areas.

In Derry, the Nationalists secured a majority and the first
Catholic Lord Mayor for over 300 years was elected.

Michael Collins was now not only Chief of Intelligence of
the IRA and the IRB's key man in Ireland; he was also Minister
for Finance. In this latter capacity his prime concern was a loan
which had been floated to finance the activities of Dail Eireann.
He had managed to raise £371,000 – some of it at gun-point,
from reluctant Unionists – and had deposited £25,000 of it in
cash in four boxes and a child's coffin buried under the floor-
boards of a Dublin house.

In the early months of the year 60 police barracks were
attacked; 22 income tax offices were burgled; warships arrived in
Kingstown; and the random killing of policemen continued.

Then on April 17 came a bombshell; the jury at the inquest
on Thomas MacCurtain, the Lord Mayor of Cork, who had been
awakened from his sleep and murdered in front of his family by
the police, returned a verdict of wilful murder, organised and
carried out by the RIC and directed by the British Government,
indicting Lloyd George among others by name.

On May 3 Dublin Corporation passed a resolution acknowledging the authority of Dail Eireann as the only effective government in the country. On the same day the members of the Irish Parliamentary Party announced that they would take part in no further debates on Home Rule.

By May, the country was so disturbed that Dublin Castle began to publish daily lists of what it described as 'outrages' and on July 12 it was announced that over 80 of the 90 appeals listed for hearing at Mayo Assizes had been withdrawn, as the majority of them had already been dealt with by the Sinn Fein courts. In May the Holyhead cargo sailings had been disrupted because of a strike by dockers who refused to handle munitions for the Crown Forces in Ireland and on June 4, dockers in Cork refused to unload a cargo of barbed wire for military use.

A company of the Connaught Rangers stationed at Simla in India laid down their arms and refused all duties when news of events in Ireland reached them on July 3. Two days later, Sinn Fein warned all jurors that their attendance at the British Assizes in Ireland would be regarded as an act of treason against the Irish Republic.

The Chief Secretary announced on July 22 that owing to the failure of trial by jury in Ireland, legislation had been introduced to set up special courts. On the same day Joseph O'Doherty, the Sinn Fein MP, appeared before a Special Crimes Court on charges of soliciting subscriptions for Dail Eireann; it was revealed in the course of the case that three previous courthouses in which he was to have been tried had all been burned down by Sinn Fein.

A young woman had her hair shorn off in Newport, Co Tipperary, 'for keeping company with a policeman', and the creamery in which she worked and two adjoining houses were burnt down. Two other young women in Co Longford received the same treatment for speaking to British soldiers.

The text of the Restoration of Order (Ireland) Bill, published on August 3, extended the Defence of the Realm regulations to allow for the setting up of military courts to try civil and criminal cases, with the proviso that at least one person with some legal qualifications must be included in any military tribunal trying a case which involved the death penalty.

On August 7, the Chief Secretary told the Commons that since the beginning of May, 315 magistrates and 566 members of the RIC had resigned. It was becoming clear that the Sinn Fein threat to make British administration impossible in Ireland was beginning to work, though of course nobody was prepared to admit this yet. He also added that 816 new recruits had joined the RIC, though he didn't mention the fact that they had been recruited in England.

Jurors in Cork who had failed to attend court refused to pay a total of £7,000 in fines on August 11 and on August 12, the new Lord Mayor of Cork, Alderman Terence MacSwiney, was arrested by the British Army at a Sinn Fein court in Cork City Hall. The following day, he went on hunger strike in Cork Jail in protest against his trial by a court martial.

On September 7, Dail Eireann came out into the open for the first time when a public Sinn Fein conference in Ballinrobe, Co Galway was informed that the Co Mayo courts had been set up under the authority of the Dail's Minister for Home Affairs, Kevin O'Higgins, and the laws in operation were exactly the same as those in force at the time of the Easter Rising, with the exception, obviously, of certain laws relating to treason, sedition, etc.

The Irish tenor John McCormack cancelled what would have been a highly lucrative Australian tour because an audience in Adelaide insisted on singing the British national anthem at the close of one of his concerts on September 9.

The *Irish Times* was the first newspaper to break the news that the English recruits to the RIC were the Black and Tans. Recruited in such a hurry that they had to wear makeshift uniforms – part British Army khaki, part the near black bottle-green of the RIC, hence their nickname, after a popular hunting pack – they were tough ex-soldiers, unable to find work in post-war Britain.

The other reinforcements for the police forces were the Auxiliary Cadets, all ex-officers. Both the Auxiliaries and the Black and Tans were equipped with armoured cars in which they tore around the country, drunk a good deal of the time, plundering, looting and terrorising.

Events reached a new pitch of horror in November when Kevin Barry was hanged and Terence MacSwiney died in Brixton Jail after 74 days on hunger strike. On November 1, another Irish Bloody Sunday, Collins, in an all-out effort to liquidate the British Secret Service in Dublin, sent members of his execution squad around to their lodgings and hotels at 9.30 am: fourteen men were murdered in their beds, in front of their wives, or wherever they happened to be that Sunday morning. That afternoon police and British forces retaliated by firing into the crowd at the Dublin-Tipperary Gaelic football final in Croke Park, Dublin, killing 14 and wounding 60.

1921

FIRST INDIAN PARLIAMENT MEETS: PARIS CONFERENCE FIXES GERMANY'S REPARATION PAYMENTS: HARDING INAUGURATED US PRESIDENT: FRENCH TROOPS MOBILISED FOR OCCUPATION OF RUHR: FASCISTS RETURNED IN ITALIAN ELECTIONS: EMERGENCY AFTER COLLAPSE OF D-MARK

Ireland Offered Dominion Status

With the British Army in Ireland now on active service, all pretence that the RIC and its auxiliary forces could contain the activities of the rebel gunmen was dropped. On January 1, following an ambush at Middleton, Co Cork, in which three policemen were killed, seven houses occupied by people 'presumed to have knowledge of the attack' were destroyed by soldiers acting on orders from the Military Governor of Cork.

By January 4, Martial Law had been extended to include the whole of Munster, and it was announced that after January 11 any unauthorised person found in possession of arms, ammunition or explosives was liable to be executed.

Armed men visited the homes of rates collectors in Dublin and forced them to write out personal cheques for the amount of the rates they had collected; these cheques, to the value of £100,000, were cashed and paid into Dail Eireann's funds.

On his return from America, de Valera – from what is now known as a 'safe house' in Dublin – took over the direction of Sinn Fein on January 6. He issued a statement saying that he was prepared to meet English peace negotiators on an equal footing, but that England must first recognise Ireland as a separate nation, and he ignored several unofficial peace feelers from the British.

The postal service was curtailed because of repeated armed attacks on mail trains and vans, and on January 7 Dublin Castle published a list of outrages between January 1 and December 31, 1920: 69 court-houses destroyed; 533 RIC barracks destroyed and 173 damaged; 998 raids involving confiscation of mail addressed to the military, the police and the administration; 182 policemen killed and 263 wounded; 54 members of the military forces killed and 122 wounded; and countless Anglo-Irish 'big houses' burnt to the ground. A curfew was imposed in Cork from 9 pm on January 13, and in counties where Martial Law had been proclaimed, motor cars and bicycles were prohibited between 8 pm and 6 am.

Sir Edward Carson turned down the leadership of the Unionist Party in the new parliament to be set up in Belfast, but agreed to retain chairmanship of the Ulster Unionist MPs at Westminster. A few days later, on January 20, Sir James Craig was chosen as Ulster Unionist leader for the new parliament.

On July 10, another of Ireland's Bloody Sundays, concerted attacks by the Orange Order and by special constables, resulted in 15 Catholic deaths, 68 serious injuries and the destruction of 161 Catholic homes.

At dawn on March 10 six men were executed in Mountjoy Jail, including members of the Bloody Sunday execution squads; 20,000 people kept vigil outside the jail all night.

The new Parliament of Southern Ireland – which came into being simultaneously with the new Parliament of Northern Ireland – was formally opened in Dublin on June 28. Only 15 senators and the four Commons members for Dublin University attended, and the event aroused very little interest.

After the Truce on July 11, while de Valera was in London at Lloyd George's invitation, all restrictions on motoring were removed and Michael Collins turned down an offer from a London publisher for £10,000 for his memoirs, a very considerable sum in those days.

In Dublin the Black and Tans mixed with their former enemies in the streets and throughout the country the flying columns came down from the hills. The casualties of the War of Independence were totted up. On the Irish side, about 700 had been killed, half of them members of the IRA and half of them civilians. On the British side, 366 police and 162 soldiers had been killed and 600 police and 566 soldiers wounded.

In London, de Valera and Lloyd George were at cross-purposes from the outset. Lloyd George genuinely believed that he was making de Valera a very generous offer; a measure of self-government for the 26 counties which roughly amounted to dominion status. De Valera, however, saw Ireland as an island entity with a rigid frontier (the sea), inhabited by a people utterly different in character, race, religion, and even, he liked to think, language, from her next-door neighbour. He was not disposed to accept anything less than complete independence, which included freedom from any Oath of Allegiance to the Crown. And for the whole island; he wanted nothing to do with Partition.

On the other hand, the choice of the Six Counties rather than the whole of Ulster was a cynical piece of gerrymandering which the Ulster Unionists had pressured Lloyd George into accepting. They didn't want the whole of Ulster because they couldn't have been certain of a Unionist majority in a state that included Donegal, Cavan and Monaghan. Fermanagh and Tyrone are also predominantly Catholic, and by this reasoning should also have been excluded, but the Ulster Unionists realised that this would mean that the area of partitioned Northern Ireland would have been too small to be viable. In any event, the border was not an issue. The machinery was there for its removal, if both parliaments agreed, and in the meantime, Lloyd George's offer was on the basis of a 26-county 'southern' state.

The Sinn Fein Dail Eireann met openly in the Mansion House in Dublin on July 27 and the Northern Ireland Parliament acquired the Assembly College, Belfast, as their temporary meeting place.

On August 7, the British released all Dail Eireann members who were in custody. The Sinn Fein/Dail Eireann envoys were recalled from Paris, Rome and Washington on August 11 and on August 12 the first excursion to Ireland for seven years left Euston Station in London.

The five-man delegation which de Valera had sent to London to seek a better agreement than he had been able to achieve very quickly got bogged down and appealed to him to join them there, but he refused; in the end, exasperated by de Valera's muddled instructions and deliberate indecisiveness, Griffith and Collins lost all patience, and faced with a threat of a renewal of the war within three days, caved in and signed the Treaty as it stood at 2.20 am on December 6. Collins remarked that in signing it he was almost certainly signing his own death-warrant.

On December 16, Westminster ratified the Treaty with a majority of 343 in the Commons and 119 in the Lords, while the Dail was considering de Valera's famous Document No 2 containing counter-proposals involving 'external association' with the Commonwealth.

By December 20, they were still talking without having reached any conclusion and the departure of the British Army from Queenstown was cancelled, pending ratification of the Treaty.

The Dail adjourned on December 22 until January 3, 1922, without taking a vote on the Treaty, and on December 28 Lloyd George announced that the Peace Treaty was England's final word and that there could be no re-opening of the Irish Question.

All over the country public bodies were now demanding the ratification of the Treaty. The big battalions, big business, the Church, the Government were now all in favour of acceptance, but they were all underestimating the intransigence of de Valera and a relatively small splinter-group of Sinn Fein republicans; an intransigence that was beginning to look every bit as solid as that of the Ulster Unionists.

This was the period of the great silent films and among them was *The Four Horsemen of the Apocalypse*, one of the greatest; it was about the Great War, it starred Rudolf Valentino and it was directed by an Irishman, Rex Ingram, son of the rector of Birr in Queen's County (now Co Offaly).

1922

COURT OF INTERNATIONAL JUSTICE SET UP IN THE HAGUE: GANDHI SENTENCED TO SIX YEARS FOR CIVIL DISOBEDIENCE: MUSSOLINI ELECTED ITALIAN PREMIER: TOMB OF TUTANKHAMUN FOUND: BABY AUSTIN POPULARISES MOTORING IN BRITAIN: MARIE STOPES ADVOCATES BIRTH CONTROL

IRA Split Leads to Civil War

In a division in the Dail on the Treaty on January 7, the voting was 64 in favour of the Treaty and 57 against it, a margin so narrow that it clearly called for an immediate general election. It was at this stage that de Valera resigned and left the chamber with his followers. He was succeeded as President of the Executive Council by Arthur Griffith.

It was now incumbent on the Southern Parliament to ratify the Treaty and appoint a Provisional Government to run the country until such time as all the legislature required to set up the Irish Free State had been finalised on both sides of the Irish Sea. The Irish Dail was not acceptable to the British as a negotiating body.

Accordingly, on January 15, a second meeting of this parliament was held in the Mansion House, Dublin. It was attended only by the 64 pro-Treaty members of the Dail plus the four members for Dublin University who, with the 15 elected Senators, had already attended its first session.

This parliament duly appointed a Provisional Government in which all the various departments of state were controlled by those ministers who were responsible for the same departments in Dail Eireann. As Arthur Griffith was now President of the Executive Council of Dail Eireann, Michael Collins became Chairman of the Provisional Government, though he also retained his former post as Minister for Finance in the Dail, and continued to work in close co-operation with Griffith. In one sense, the Provisional Government was simply a front, acceptable to the British in a way that the Sinn Fein Dail Eireann had never been, but in another sense it was a legal requirement, under the terms of the Treaty, which had to be ratified by the Provisional Government, as it had been ratified at Westminster, before it became law.

On January 15, Michael Collins and the members of the Executive Committee of the Provisional Government were received by the Lord Lieutenant and officially took over Dublin Castle. The Bank of Ireland was appointed Financial Agent for the new Free State on January 19 and on the same day the first 1,000 British troops left the North Wall, Dublin, for England.

A new Metropole ballroom and cinema complex was opened on February 5, on the site of the old Metropole Hotel in Sackville (O'Connell) Street, Dublin, right beside the GPO, destroyed during the fighting in 1916.

In February, too, James Joyce's *Ulysses* was published in a limited edition by Sylvia Beach's Shakespeare Press in Paris; it is perhaps not surprising, in view of what was happening in Ireland, that it did not receive much attention in the Irish press.

On February 12, de Valera denounced the Treaty, stating that the only authority he would acknowledge was the free will of the people. On the same day Collins accused him of attempting to plan a coup d'état and the withdrawal of British troops from Ireland was suspended.

At a special Sinn Fein Ard Fheis (conference) to discuss the Treaty, de Valera succeeded in getting an agreement to postpone the elections for three months. Griffith had to go to London to explain this postponement to the British Government, which didn't like it one bit. De Valera next claimed that the electoral register was invalid and asked for a further postponement of the general election to bring it up to date, which Griffith refused.

On April 1, the Irish Free State (Agreement) Bill passed its final stages in the Westminster Parliament. While the pro-Treaty members of the Dail were busy drafting a constitution for the new Free State, de Valera left for a tour of the South during which he made a number of speeches which were later claimed by pro-Treaty deputies to be tantamount to a declaration of civil war, should the Treaty be accepted. He had realised that he had lost control of the rabidly republican element in the IRA; they had already broken away from him and had set up an independent military council which refused to recognise the authority of Sinn Fein, the Provisional Government, Dail Eireann or even that of de Valera himself, and which had already started on a series of raids to get hold of arms and money to further their cause.

Eventually an election was fixed for June 16. Despite a last desperate attempt by de Valera to confuse the issue by an appeal to the old Sinn Fein Party to put up unopposed 'panel candidates', roughly representing the proportion of members for and against the Treaty before the split, when they went to the polls most people realised very clearly that they were voting for or against the Treaty.

De Valera's anti-Treaty supporters received only 36 seats out of a total of 128 and if that meant anything, it meant that an overwhelming majority of the people were now in favour of the Treaty.

The British authorities began to withdraw their troops from the barracks and towns throughout the country, though they were none too happy that many of their old barracks were being occupied, not by the army of the new Irish Free State, but by Republican IRA 'Irregulars', as they were called, pledged to carry on the fight until full freedom was achieved.

Collins, as head of the Provisional Government, was faced with a very dangerous situation in which some of the key positions in the country were held by units which would no longer take any orders from him; at least, not unless they happened to accord with their own views. One of these was entrenched in the

Four Courts complex of legal buildings, right in the heart of Dublin City.

It was at this stage that two IRA men assassinated Field-Marshall Sir Henry Wilson outside his London home. As Military Advisor to the Northern Ireland Government, Wilson was the man largely responsible for the way things were going in Ulster, where Catholics were being persecuted and turned out of their homes in thousands – but he was one of Britain's most distinguished generals, and his murder caused a sensation. Ironically, the order for his execution had almost certainly been issued by Collins who had been far too busy ever since to rescind it.

Collins was summararily ordered by the British Government to get the Republican Irregulars out of the Four Courts immediately, and on June 27, the Provisional Government used borrowed British field guns – the Irish still had not been able to get their hands on any artillery – to bombard the Four Courts. The Irish fight for freedom, begun with such lofty ideals and high hopes, now degenerated, as so many revolutions before and since have done, into a bloody and bitter civil war.

Within 48 hours, the Republican Irregular garrison had blown up the Four Courts and surrendered. The Republican positions were soon isolated and at the end of five days, when only two main strongholds remained – two fortified hotels in Sackville (O'Connell) Street – the garrisons decided to surrender to avoid further bloodshed. De Valera, who had reported back to his old battalion as a Volunteer, no more than that, went into hiding.

The surviving Republican Irregulars left the city, joined their comrades in the country and took to the hills, forming themselves into flying columns once again and resuming the guerrilla warfare, now against their own former comrades in arms.

That the hardline republican opposition to the Treaty received a certain amount of support from the public is due to a number of factors. Some elements in Irish society, particularly in the South and West – cattle-drivers and criminals, for example – had found that the signing of the Treaty and the return to law and order had made their lot far more difficult.

The people of Dublin were, however, more interested in a new type of shop – a huge, multi-floor emporium selling an enormous variety of goods of all sorts from clothes and clocks to furniture and hardware; this was Clery's, in Sackville (O'Connell) Street, almost opposite the ruins of the GPO, which re-opened on August 9 as a big department store, like Selfridge's in London.

Arthur Griffith had died on August 13, worn out and disillusioned with the way things had gone, and Michael Collins was killed in an ambush in Co Cork on August 22.

What was left of the old second Dail met on September 9 – for the first time in the RDS lecture hall at Leinster House, Kildare Street – and elected William T. Cosgrave President of the Executive Committee in succession to Griffith; he was also elected Chairman of the Provisional Government in succession to Michael Collins. The RIC had been disbanded on August 17 and a new force, known in Irish as the Garda Siochana (The Guard of the Peace) but normally referred to as the Civic Guard was formed; and on September 29 the Dail decided that this new force would not carry any arms.

In a Pastoral Letter on October 10, the Catholic Hierarchy threatened to excommunicate all those in revolt against the Provisional Government, and two days later the Government announced that they were going to set up Military Courts with the power to pronounce the death sentence and have it carried out without any further reference to the legislature.

Eleven District Justices were appointed on October 26 to replace the old Resident Magistrates. T.M. (Tim) Healy, a Nationalist MP and journalist, was appointed Governor-General on December 3, and on the following day the Irish Free State Bill received the Royal Assent, although it was not until December 6, 1922, the anniversary of the signing of the Treaty, that the Irish Free State was officially proclaimed.

On October 27 Sir James Craig, head of the Northern Ireland Government, hurried to London with an address to the king to ensure the continued exclusion of Northern Ireland from the new Free State. On the same day, a member of the Provisional Government was assassinated in Dublin and the deputy speaker of the Dail was wounded by gunshot in what was obviously another assassination attempt.

The men of the Free State Government whose hearts had turned to stone at the outbreak of the Civil War retaliated instantly by taking four of the Republican Irregulars who had been in jail since the capture of the Four Courts out of their cells in Mountjoy Jail and executing them by firing squad without warning or trial.

The Viceregal Lodge and the Chief Secretary's Lodge in Phoenix Park were handed over to the Free State troops on December 15 and on December 18, the last British troops in Ireland – apart from those manning the three ports retained by Britain under the terms of the Treaty – left for England.

1923

USSR ESTABLISHED: FRENCH AND BELGIAN TROOPS OCCUPY RUHR: PALESTINE CONSTITUTION SUSPENDED: MARTIAL LAW IN GERMANY: DISSOLUTION OF NON-FASCIST PARTIES IN ITALY: KEMAL ATATÜRK PRESIDENT OF TURKEY: ARMY DEPOSES GREEK KING: EARTHQUAKE IN JAPAN

Building a New State

The feature which dominated the year 1923 had already revealed itself right at the end of 1922; it was the new Republican Irregular policy of shooting members of Dail Eireann, and the consequent reprisal executions.

The year began with President Cosgrave's first message to the people of Saorstat Eireann, as the Irish Free State was called in Irish; it was not a markedly confident one, and in all conscience he couldn't possibly have felt too confident about the future of the new state at this particular period. On that very day, January 1, a party of Free State soldiers was ambushed in Co Kerry and two of them were killed.

There were five executions in Carlow and Tipperary on

January 16 for possession of arms, and on the following day, introducing measures to reinforce the army's powers, President Cosgrave warned the Dail: 'We cannot economise on the death penalty.'

Yet throughout all these disturbances, life went on more or less as normal. The newspapers were very interested in comparing prices in the new Free State with those in that corner of the island which had remained a part of the UK, and frequently published tables contrasting the prevailing prices of everyday commodities. In general, there was not a great deal of difference, though most items of food were marginally cheaper in Northern Ireland.

A document dated March 16 was released by the Government which made it clear that the shooting of members of the Free State Parliament, as the document called them, was only a tiny part of the new IRA Irregular policy. Fourteen categories of people were listed who could now be shot on sight, including members of the Free State Parliament who had supported the policy of executions, officers in the Free State army, judges, solicitors, members of the CID and directors of the hostile press in Ireland as well as editors, sub-editors and leader-writers. The document also listed categories of people whose houses should be burned down; they included those of all senators and 'Imperialists'.

Yet despite the continuing disturbances, the new Government were doing their best to sort things out. New Irish stamps were on sale from March; this was the period when the red pillar boxes and the small post-boxes set into walls – all still carrying the emblem of the Crown and the initials VR, ER or GR – were being overpainted in green and on April 8 the Postmaster General approved a new uniform for postmen with green piping to replace the red piping formerly worn. It was years before this tendency wore itself out; it didn't happen until the early Sixties when Dr Tod Andrews, the man who revolutionised the Turf Board and at that time was in charge of CIE, Ireland's transport monopoly, suddenly announced that Ireland had enjoyed its independence for long enough to have got over the burning need to paint everything green, and in a decision which astonished everybody, elected that the trains and buses would be painted, of all colours of the rainbow, black and tan.

On April 12, *The Shadow of a Gunman*, the first play in Sean O'Casey's powerful trilogy about the Troubles, had its premiere in the Abbey Theatre; it deals with the Black and Tan period at the height of the War of Independence and the full houses it drew saved the Abbey Theatre from bankruptcy.

But the resistance to the new state seemed to be dying and on April 18 de Valera, who had again taken over from the IRA military commanders, ordered a 'suspension of aggression' from April 30, and stated that he was prepared to consider peace proposals. In fact the word he used, typically, was to 'offer' peace proposals, though he was in no position to offer anything.

Clery's restaurant in the new department store in O'Connell Street opened on May 30; lunch cost 3s 6d and dinner was 5s 6d. The Irish Free State was admitted to the League of Nations on September 10, and on October 1, the Imperial Conference in London – to decide the future shape of the British Empire – was attended by President W.T. Cosgrave and two of his ministers.

In August there was another general election which de Valera and his followers contested. William Cosgrave revived the old Cumann na nGhaedheal title – which Griffith had initially used for the movement which became Sinn Fein – for his pro-Treaty supporters.

De Valera contested his old constituency of East Clare, and it is a tribute to the extraordinary power of his personality that the people of Clare elected him to a parliament which he refused to recognise and which he stated openly that he had no intention of attending, with almost twice as many votes as his pro-Treaty opponent. Even more surprising, perhaps, since all the newspapers in the country were violently anti-Republican, as indeed was the Catholic Church at this stage, was the fact that de Valera's party won 44 seats as against Cosgrave's 63. Needless to say, de Valera was arrested the moment he set foot on an election platform and was jailed until June the following year.

The long-drawn-out dock strike ended on November 8, and W.B. Yeats was awarded the Nobel Prize for Literature on November 14. Years later the *Irish Times* editor of that period,

R.M. Smyllie, who was also Dublin correspondent for *The Times* of London, told me that when he telephoned the great man to tell him about his good fortune and to record his lofty comments for posterity, Yeats had immediately asked: 'And tell me, Bertie, how much is it worth?' Smyllie made up a much more attic response, more worthy of a lyric poet, but as he told me, it didn't matter; *The Times* didn't use it anyway.

James Montgomery, a well-known Dublin wit, was appointed first film censor for the Irish Free State on November 9, a position which he described as one 'delicately poised between the Devil and the Holy See'. He referred to his task as trying to keep the prevailing 'Californication' out of sight of smiling Irish eyes, and later referred to Dublin's two main theatrical companies, the Gate (which was the epicentre of the not inconsiderable gay movement) and the Abbey (which specialised in healthy, earthy peasant plays) as Sodom and Begorrah.

The country saw on November 29 the first execution (for murder) under civil law since the state had been founded and a hangman had to be brought over from England; by this time, 77 IRA Irregulars had been executed by firing squad and about 12,000 of them were still in jail.

Finally, on December 5, James Weldon, a Co Westmeath school-teacher, claimed damages from his local parish priest and three parishioners for injury in his profession. His school had been boycotted because it was claimed that his son's book, *The Valley of the Squinting Windows*, had lampooned the village and its inhabitants. It was one of the first realistic modern Irish novels which ruthlessly removed the veneer of respectability covering the residents of an Irish village. The book was publicly burned, the jury disagreed, and Oliver Weldon went on to write other books and plays about the narrow meanness of Irish peasant communities under the pen-name of Brinsley McNamara.

The poet Seamus O'Sullivan founded the *Dublin Magazine* and the painter John Lavery designed the first Irish bank-notes which had, on the back, a painting of his wife Hazel, as Kathleen Ni Houlihan, with the mountains of Ireland behind her, arguably one of the most beautiful pieces of currency ever produced anywhere in the world.

1924

RAMSAY MACDONALD FORMS FIRST BRITISH LABOUR GOVERN-
MENT: LENIN DIES: BRITAIN RECOGNISES USSR: GREECE
BECOMES REPUBLIC: COOLIDGE SIGNS BILL LIMITING
IMMIGRATION AND EXCLUDING JAPANESE: NAVAL CONTROL
OF GERMANY ABOLISHED: HERTZOG SOUTH AFRICAN PM

Free State Army Crisis

The year 1924 was the first full year of peace, and it began with a proposal by the Dublin Corporation to use the unemployed to clear away the ruins in O'Connell Street which had been left there, more or less untouched, since the 1916 Rising. A great deal of the debris was dumped in Croke Park, the Gaelic sports stadium, where it formed a hill, known as Hill 16, a prime vantage point prized by followers of both hurling and Gaelic football.

On the first day of the year the balance sheet for the first nine months of the State's first financial year was published; revenue had increased by £3,801,653 and total expenditure by £8,561,510 on the corresponding period of the previous year. The latter figure reflected an abnormally high incidence of disturbances and outrages, and represented the cost of replacing all the roads and railways and bridges which had been blown up during the Troubles. The balance in the Exchequer was £7,299,915 as against a little over £1,000,000 the previous December, due to the very successful 5 per cent National Loan.

Dublin Corporation applied for an £80,000 loan to complete a new reservoir at Roundwood, Co Wicklow, to serve the Dublin area, and the new Irish Tourist Association, outlining its plans to attract tourists to Ireland and acutely aware of the proclivities of the Irish hoteliers and boarding-house proprietors, announced that these plans included 'protection against the fleecing of clients'.

The Bishops' Lenten Pastorals, issued on March 2,

condemned ballroom dancing, described by Cardinal Logue as 'the outcrop of the corruption of the age', and on May 3, the Abbey Theatre presented the first production of Sean O'Casey's *Juno and the Paycock*, set in the period of the Civil War. It was another huge success; Dublin audiences recognised themselves and their neighbours and delighted in the way O'Casey had managed to capture the Dublin dialect.

Details of the planned reorganisation of the Free State army were issued – it provided for a force of 18,000 with 1,300 officers – and the Dail tabled correspondence between the Government and Siemens-Shuckert of Berlin, outlining a scheme for a hydro-electric generating station on the River Shannon.

The first the public learned of what could have been a very dangerous situation was the announcement on March 9 that two officers of the Free State army were wanted for mutiny. They had apparently absconded from Gormanston Camp in Co Meath in a Crossley tender, taking with them arms, ammunition and other military equipment. After the disappearance of other officers and men with arms and ammunition, and the resignation of a Government Minister, it dawned on the Government that something irregular, if the pun is not too obvious, was going on in the army. A full inquiry was ordered.

In the middle of all the confusion, on March 21, in Queenstown, Co Cork, four men, dressed in Irish Free State uniforms, fired over 100 rounds from a Lewis gun into a party of British troops on leave from Spike Island; one soldier was killed and 29 people were injured, including two women. A £10,000 reward was immediately offered for information leading to the conviction of those responsible for the attack.

It was not until June 17, when the findings of the inquiry into the army crisis were published, that the general public learned what had been happening. The report revealed that two secret organisations had been responsible for the mutiny; they were the IRA Irregulars – many of whose members had joined the new Free State army alongside their pro-Treaty brother Volunteers in 1922 with the intention of continuing to work towards a republic – and the Irish Republican Brotherhood, which had infiltrated the ranks of the senior officers in an effort at a coup d'état which had been narrowly averted.

In the meantime, too, on April 24 , the Boundary Commission set up under the terms of the Treaty collapsed, and the functions reserved for a Council of Ireland under Lloyd George's 'Better Government of Ireland Act' reverted to the Government of the Six Counties which could be relied upon to do nothing whatever to further relations between the two severed parts of Ireland. The British caved in, as mentioned above, in the face of Ulster recalcitrance. Cosgrave accepted this without a word of protest in return for certain financial concessions including the writing off of Ireland's share in the British National Debt, which amounted to about £16,000,000.

Around the middle of April the Dublin cinemas began to threaten that they might have to close down because of a Government import duty of £14 on each five-reel (full feature-length) film imported, not to mention the additional impost of four guineas (£4 4s) for the essential imprimatur of the Government film censor.

On April 25, Minister for Finance Ernest Blythe introduced a series of protective tariffs in an effort to assist the Free State's ailing industries; he imposed duties on boots, bottles, soap, sugar, sweets and motor car bodies. He also reduced surtax from 6s to 4s 6d in the £ but made no change in the standard 5s in the £ income tax, although he admitted a few days later that he was puzzled that income tax in the Free State only yielded £6 15s per head of the population while the British income tax, although set at a much lower rate, yielded nearly £16 per head of the population. Anybody could have told him the answer; over 40 per cent of Ireland's working population worked on the land and paid no taxes whatever, as against about 4 per cent in Britain.

The author George Moore sought £16,289 13s 6d compensation for the destruction of his family home, Moore Hall, near Castlebar in 1923, after it had been burnt down by the Irregulars because his brother Colonel Maurice was a member of the Free State Senate. He got approximately £7,000 from the government.

Towards the end of the year the Free State flag flew for the first time legally in Britain, at the British Empire Exhibition at Wembley Stadium.

1925

TROTSKY SACKED BY RUSSIAN REVOLUTIONARY MILITARY COUN-
CIL: HINDENBERG PRESIDENT OF GERMANY: CYPRUS BECOMES
BRITISH CROWN COLONY: FIRST PARLIAMENT OF IRAQ MEETS:
UNEMPLOYMENT INSURANCE IN BRITAIN: REZA KHAN USURPS
PERSIAN THRONE: HITLER'S MEIN KAMPF PUBLISHED

Divorce Ruled Out

By January 1, 1925, the amalgamation of the Irish Free State railways was complete. The Government decided on January 9 to distribute 6,000 tons of coal and to provide meals for 15,000 children a day as part of a plan to relieve the distress caused by massive unemployment.

The troubles that had dogged the Free State army the previous year now seemed to be completely under control. On January 23 it was announced that the strength of the force now stood at 15,703 officers and men; a reduction of nearly 40,000 had been achieved partly by the demobilisation of the old IRA and partly by reorganisation. This reduction entailed, of course, the creation almost overnight of 40,000 more unemployed men.

A bill to amalgamate the old Dublin Metropolitan Police and the new Civic Guard passed its Committee stage in the Dail on February 3; on February 11, Dail Eireann passed a resolution, introduced by President Cosgrave, which would make it impossible for anyone in the Free State to obtain a divorce with the right to remarry.

Before the Treaty, Irish people who desired to petition for divorce could always do so by means of a Private Bill in the Imperial Parliament at Westminster. After the Treaty, the sovereign power in this, as in so many other legislative matters, passed to the Irish Free State Parliament, the Dail. By February 1924, three such Private Bills had been lodged but the Government had not got around to making any provisions for dealing with such matters.

When President Cosgrave's resolution reached the Senate on March 5, Chairman Lord Glenavy ruled that no parallel motion could be made in the Upper House, since the termination of an existing legal right could only be achieved by Statute, and not by a resolution.

In an effort to break the deadlock, Senator Douglas suggested a compromise: a motion requiring the full approval of both houses of the Oireachtas (Irish Parliament) before a Bill of Divorce could even start upon its legal career. This would never have happened in practice, of course, with a huge Catholic majority opposed to divorce on any grounds whatsoever in the Dail.

It was this suggestion which led to Senator W.B. Yeats's famous outburst in defence of the Protestant minority on June 25: 'We against whom you have done this thing are not a petty people. We are the people of Burke; we are the people of Swift, the people of Emmet, the people of Parnell.'

Belfast Corporation voted against the playing of any music in public parks on Sundays; and it was but a short step thence until their decision that swings and see-saws in children's playgrounds should be chained up so that they could not be used for any pleasurable purpose on the Lord's day.

The official trade returns issued on March 6 showed an adverse trade balance of over £17,000,000 for 1924; in plain language the Free State had spent £17,000,000 more than it had earned, a situation which was taken far more seriously in those days than it is today. The Free State's continuing and perilous dependence on Britain had been underlined as early as January 29, when it was reported that in 1924 the Free State had sold £40,000,000 worth of food to Britain – and almost none elsewhere – and had bought more than 70 per cent of the new state's industrial requirements from Britain.

The Intermediate Certificate examination results showed a

shattering lack of interest in foreign languages; only six pupils in the entire country took German as a subject and of these one candidate achieved only five marks out of a possible 300.

But slowly and steadily the new Government was pursuing its plans to make the Free State, if not entirely self-reliant, at any rate a great deal more self-reliant than it had been during the days of British domination. One step in that direction was the announcement on September 7 that a factory was to be set up in Carlow by a German firm to manufacture sugar from Irish beet.

An attempt to eradicate the recurring slur on 'dear, dirty Dublin' was made on September 27 when a contract for cleaning the city streets was awarded to a Paris firm, in the mistaken belief, perhaps, that it was French expertise and not the gallons of water gushing every morning from the Paris sewers that accounted for the impeccably immaculate cobblestones of the City of Light. Immediately James Larkin, the Labour leader, called a public meeting to protest against the employment of foreigners. Before long, the City Commissioners were appealing for volunteers to carry out public services in Dublin City because of a municipal workers' strike against the employment of a French firm to clean the Dublin streets.

A special committee which included John Reith, Director-General of the BBC, and Sir Hamilton Harty, the Irish conductor and composer, was appointed early in October to consider the whole question of setting up a wireless broadcasting station in Ireland, and on October 28, the Royal Dublin Society, bowing to the inevitable, moved its entire operations out to the show grounds in Ballsbridge, abandoning its Leinster House headquarters to the Dail and Senate. By December there were 800 men working on the Shannon scheme, 300 of them German.

There was a 2RN (Radio Eireann's call-sign) test broadcast of Handel's *Messiah*, originally performed in Dublin in 1759, from the Centenary Church on St Stephen's Green on December 22 and on December 27 the Abbey Theatre celebrated its 21st anniversary.

1926

BRAZIL AND SPAIN BAR GERMANY'S ADMISSION TO LEAGUE OF NATIONS: BERLIN TREATY BETWEEN GERMANY AND USSR: GENERAL STRIKE IN BRITAIN: LEBANON PROCLAIMED REPUBLIC BY FRANCE: IBN SAUD KING OF SAUDI ARABIA: STALIN VICTORY OVER LEON TROTSKY IN RUSSIA

De Valera Back in Politics

On the first day of the New Year, 2RN, Dublin's wireless broadcasting station, was officially opened, with an accompanying announcement that there would be a licence fee of £1 per year (later reduced to 10s) for crystal receiving sets; and a further announcement on January 28 that BBC programmes would be relayed from the Dublin station to supplement the pathetically few locally-produced programmes.

Despite threats from Corporation and Municipal workers to strike, the French firm of Baudeville et Cie started work on the massive task of cleaning up Dublin's streets. The first sod was turned in preparation for the new sugar beet factory at Carlow on January 5, the day on which Joseph Devlin, one of the Northern Nationalists elected to the new Northern Parliament in Belfast, appealed to other Nationalist members not to abstain but to take their seats in the Northern Ireland Parliament as a formal opposition.

When the Dail assembled after the Christmas recess on January 19, Minister for Finance Ernest Blythe proposed a bill to issue new Free State coinage. These coins would carry, on the one side, the harp of old Erin and on the other, various symbols indicating Ireland's agricultural wealth: the salmon, the hen, the cow, the horse, the hare. The original idea of having an Irish saint on the reverse of each coin was abandoned because it was feared that it might prove an insult to the saints concerned if their likenesses happened to become involved in a toss-up to decide the result of a game of bowls, or to settle an argument over a cattle-sale.

John A. Costello, later to become Premier of Ireland's first inter-party Coalition Government, was appointed Attorney-General, and because of the difficulty in collecting rates from the Aran Islands, the Galway County Council seriously suggested sending a gunboat to lay siege to the islands. Where they expected the Government to find a gunboat is not clear; it is doubtful whether at this period the Free State's armed forces' nautical equipment included even one rowing boat.

The Free State film censor rejected the first version of *The Merry Widow*, a film about as sexually explicit as *Mary Poppins*. In February, at the first production on the Abbey Theatre stage of the third play in Sean O'Casey's trilogy, *The Plough and the Stars*, which dealt with the Easter 1916 Rising, there were wild protests, mostly from women who resented the portrayal of a Dublin girl as a prostitute, though Dublin, as a seaport, had as high a percentage of prostitutes as any other seaport town. The play was also attacked by Labour supporters who thought it a libel on James Connolly and the Irish Citizen Army.

When the General Strike started in the United Kingdom on May 3, the Government announced that the situation should not be used as an excuse for any increase in the price of essential commodities. Coal was immediately rationed in Northern Ireland, and steamship services between Great Britain and the Free State were greatly curtailed with the result that before long 400 labourers were laid off in Dublin Port; within a few days that number had grown to 1,000. A state of emergency was declared in Northern Ireland, and the mails for Belfast were carried by destroyers.

The new licensing laws had been signally unsuccessful in stamping out the manufacture of illicit poteen (pronounced potcheen, a rough spirit distilled from potatoes), a fact that was poignantly illustrated on June 9 when it was revealed that a party of Civic Guards had been forced to swim across a lake in Connemara in an unsuccessful pursuit of some moonshiners.

De Valera was elected President of the new Republican Party, Fianna Fail, at that party's first convention at the Rotunda in Dublin on November 24. President Cosgrave received honorary degrees from Cambridge University and Trinity College,

Dublin, and on December 6, the Department of Posts and Telegraphs announced that there were now 24,239 telephones in the Free State.

In November, *The Importance of Being Ernest* became the first Oscar Wilde play to be produced at the Abbey Theatre. The year ended with the announcement that the Minister for Justice had received the report of a committee set up in February 1926 to examine the menace of what was known as 'Evil Literature'; no details of the report or its possible repercussions were announced at this stage.

However, the Evil Literature Committee advised the setting up of a Censorship Board, which came into being three years later, in 1929. Initially it was to consist of a representative of the Catholic Church, a doctor, a lawyer and one representative each from Trinity College and the National University. Since in practice its members were unpaid, its membership was frequently less thoroughly representative of informed opinion. From 1930 to 1946, when the Act was amended, the Censorship Board banned an average of about 30 books a month as being 'in general tendency indecent and obscene' or because they advocated or even referred to such matters as birth control. Books banned included many standard classics from Apuleius to Ernest Hemingway, as well as works by most well-known Irish writers.

Sean O'Casey received the Hawthornden Prize (then worth £100) for *Juno and the Paycock*, a pirated edition of James Joyce's *Ulysses* was published in the United States and the Radio Eireann Symphony Orchestra was established.

1927

ALLIED MILITARY CONTROL OF GERMANY ENDS: CHINESE
COMMUNISTS SEIZE NANKING: COLLAPSE OF GERMANY'S
ECONOMIC SYSTEM: BRITAIN RECOGNISES SAUDI ARABIA:
SLAVERY ABOLISHED IN SIERRA LEONE: TROTSKY EXPELLED
FROM COMMUNIST PARTY: PERSIA CLAIMS BAHRAIN

De Valera Swallows Oath

The new United States immigration quotas were announced on
January 7; the Irish Free State was to be allowed only 13,866
emigrants instead of the existing quota of 28,567.

The Royal Hospital at Kilmainham closed on January 23, after
250 years; the pensioners, all British ex-servicemen, were moved
to the Infirmary and a final service was held in the hospital
chapel, which had been consecrated in 1686.

The full text of the new Intoxicating Liquor Bill was published on February 11. One of the recommendations of a
Commission appointed to advise the Government on the matter
was that all pubs should be closed between 3 pm and 5 pm; this
was watered down, however, to the famous 'Holy Hour' break
between 2.30 and 3.30 pm, and in the cities only, to allow the
staff to clean out the premises, empty the ash-trays and get a
bite to eat.

Harry Clarke, the stained glass artist, was commissioned by
the Government to produce a stained glass window for presen-
tation to the International Labour Office in Geneva. It was
completed but was never presented to the ILO because Clarke
had chosen to depict scenes from Celtic mythology, presenting
some of the female members of his cast in full frontal nudity,
pubic hair and all, which the Government of the period felt
would give a misleading impression of Ireland, heaven only
knows why, since Irish women do not differ substantially from
women of other races in this respect. So the window, a brilliant
example of a very gifted artist's work, was locked away for years

in his Dublin studios, where it could be viewed only by special arrangement. It is now on view to one and all in Dublin's Sir Hugh Lane Municipal Gallery of Modern Art.

Charles Lindbergh's plane, The Spirit of St Louis, was spotted over Dingle Bay at 5.30 pm on May 22 en route for Paris after his solo 3,600-mile Atlantic crossing; when he arrived in Paris, he told reporters: 'I saw the green hills of Ireland and knew that I had hit Europe on the nose . . . Ireland is one of the four corners of the world.'

Kevin O'Higgins, Vice-President and Minister for Justice, was assassinated in Booterstown, Co Dublin, as he walked from his home to Mass on July 10; he was 35 years of age. The assassins were never found, nor indeed is there anything surprising about that; as the iron man of the Cosgrave Government and the man responsible, as Home Secretary, for the execution of 77 Irregulars, Kevin O'Higgins's life had been on the line from the moment that the first shots were fired by an execution squad of Free State soldiers.

Another link with the old Sinn Fein Party was broken with the death in Sir Patrick Dunn's hospital of Countess Markievicz on July 15; she was 59 years old.

On August 12, despite everything that he had said, and all the trouble he had caused by holding out against the Oath of Allegiance, de Valera took the Oath.

When I interviewed him at length in 1965 – he was quite an old man by then and I reckoned that ten minutes would be as much as I would get and kept the taxi waiting, for over two hours as it turned out – I tried to press him on this matter, and he told me that he had assured the officer charged with the task of administering the Oath that he was not prepared to take the Oath but that he was prepared to put his name down in a book in order to get into the Dail. He remembered that there was a Testament on the table, and recalled putting it aside and saying to the officer: 'You must remember, I am taking no Oath.'

He admitted that there might have been some form of oath or promise written across the top of the page which he signed, but added that he deliberately did not read it, but simply signed the book, 'as you would sign an autograph album'.

And so, on August 12, when de Valera took the Oath and he and his party entered the Dail, their arrival in Leinster House was greeted by the Labour Party with a no-confidence vote in the Government which resulted in a tie and was defeated by the casting vote of the speaker; it would have been carried but for the absence of the Sligo deputy, Alderman John Jinks of the National League, detained against his will, according to popular rumour, by another Sligo man, R.M. (Bertie) Smyllie, editor of the *Irish Times* and a staunch Cosgrave supporter. There has never been any concrete evidence of Smyllie's part in what is known as the Jinks Affair; my own view is that Smyllie had far too much respect for the democratic process to connive in any attempt to undermine it, though it is quite possible that the three Sligo-men – they were drinking with another Cosgrave supporter, Major Bryan Cooper – were enjoying themselves so much discussing the possible effects of a no-confidence vote on the country that Jinks forgot all about his own situation until it was too late for him to have any say in the matter.

In Belfast, two days before Christmas, workmen repairing the floor of the Belvoir Hall Public Elementary School found 55,000 rounds of rifle ammunition, five bayonets, 16 Mills bombs and a grenade, all carefully oiled and packed 'against the day', as they say in Northern Ireland.

1928

JAPAN OCCUPIES SHANTUNG: SALAZAR FINANCE MINISTER IN PORTUGAL: VOTING AGE FOR WOMEN IN BRITAIN REDUCED TO 21: CROATS WITHDRAW FROM YUGOSLAV PARLIAMENT: CHIANG KAI-SHEK BECOMES PRESIDENT OF CHINA: ALEXANDER FLEMING DISCOVERS PENICILLIN

Abbey Rejects O'Casey

Early in 1928 President Cosgrave left for a tour of the United States and Canada with his Minister for Defence, Desmond FitzGerald, father of Garret FitzGerald, a future Taoiseach.

Glenstal Abbey, former home of Sir Charles Barrington, was consecrated as a Benedictine Abbey on January 19, and on January 22 the Minister for Agriculture announced the formation of a new Credit Corporation Bank to advance money to farmers to enable them to buy machinery and modernise their methods.

There was an exhibition of ballet at the Abbey Theatre on January 30 by the Abbey School of Ballet, directed by a young woman from Blessington, Co Wicklow, called Edris Stannus. Later, as Ninette de Valois, she became director of the Sadlers Wells and subsequently of the Royal Ballet in London and the person primarily responsible for the revival of ballet in the United Kingdom.

James MacNeill was installed as second Governor-General at Leinster House on February 1. About ten days later, President Cosgrave returned from his North American tour, and enjoyed a civic welcome in Dublin with fireworks at Nelson's Pillar in O'Connell Street, illuminations in all the shop windows and a salute of nineteen guns. There was a similarly lavish reception for de Valera's home-coming from his fund-raising trip to the States to secure capital for the launch of a Fianna Fail newspaper. The dark days of austerity seemed at last to be coming to an end.

A writ was issued on March 18 to fill the seat in North Dublin won by James Larkin (Communist) who, although elected, was

104

not permitted to take his seat, since he was an undischarged bankrupt.

Tipperary Tim, a horse bought for fifty guineas (£52.50) at the Dublin Bloodstock Sales in 1919, won the British Grand National on March 30 at 100/1.

The Irish Army Air Corps gave leave on April 6 to Commandant James Fitzmaurice to accompany Captain Kohl and Baron von Huenfeld on the first successful east-west trans-Atlantic crossing in a Junkers monoplane, the *Bremen*.

A special train chartered by the Irish Land Commission conveyed four migrant families comprising 25 people of all ages, 110 cattle, 241 sheep and lambs, 360 fowl, 14 pigs and six horses from one of the Congested Districts on the Dingle Peninsula in Co Kerry to a newly-divided estate of fertile land in Co Offaly on April 17.

In Limerick, on April 22, a committee was formed to set up a second sugar-beet factory and Henry Ford, on a visit to Europe, said on April 24 that he favoured the immediate abolition of tariffs on motor cars and would be prepared to give a virtual monopoly of the new Ford models for the European market to the Cork assembly plant if duties on motor cars between the Free State and the United Kingdom were abolished.

The rejection by the Abbey Theatre directors of Sean O'Casey's *The Silver Tassie*, a satire on the Great War, caused a sensation after the huge popular success of O'Casey's three previous plays.

The Liffey Tunnel was nearing completion; by now it was 820 feet long and had cost £35,000 to date. Like so many earlier attempts to build a tunnel under the English Channel, the project was eventually dropped.

On August 18, in view of the fact that the Free State had done nothing to remove tariffs on motor cars, but had instead insisted on imposing new tariffs on goods vehicles, the Ford Motor Company announced that their European market motor cars would be built at a new factory under construction at Dagenham in Essex, and that the Cork factory would manufacture tractors for the European market, as well as assembling Ford cars for the Free State. Later, the Cork assembly plant became the principal European headquarters for tractors.

The Dublin Gate Theatre opened in the Abbey Theatre's tiny rehearsal theatre, the Peacock, on October 19 with the first performance in Dublin of Ibsen's *Peer Gynt* with Hilton Edwards in the title role and settings by his partner, Micheal MacLiammoir, later to become and to remain, almost until his death in 1978, aged 79, Ireland's principal juvenile lead.

The next day it was announced that the Free State was to have a Volunteer Defence Force. The Minister for Defence told the Dail that their policy was eventually to reduce the regular army to 5,000 men, who would act as instructors for the Reserve and the new Volunteer Force.

A collection of library books, including works by Arnold Bennett, Victor Hugo and George Bernard Shaw were burned in Co Galway on October 30 on the advice of the Catholic Bishop of Tuam, to whom the local library had entrusted the task of censorship. During the year, James Joyce had published sections of *Finnegan's Wake* under the title of *Anna Livia Plurabelle*, Lennox Robinson's comedy *The Far-off Hills* was the big Abbey Theatre hit and Oscar Wilde's *Salome* had its first production by the Gate Theatre in Dublin.

1929

KING ALEXANDER I DISSOLVES CROAT PARTY IN YUGOSLAVIA: FASCISTS 'WIN' SINGLE-PARTY ELECTION IN ITALY: INDEPENDENT VATICAN CITY ESTABLISHED: IRAQ-IRAN TREATY: ARABS ATTACK JEWS IN PALESTINE: WALL STREET CRASH: FIRST FLIGHT OVER SOUTH POLE

Evil Literature Banned

Just to remind de Valera that other people were still keeping faith with the ideals he had thrown out of the window, Mary MacSwiney (sister of the Lord Mayor of Cork who had died on hunger strike) and 16 others met in the Rotunda on January 21, sitting as 'the real Dail Eireann', and passed the first reading of a Constitution of the Republic of Ireland Bill. De Valera himself was arrested at Goraghwood on the border in Co Armagh on February 5 and taken to Belfast Jail for infringing an order prohibiting him from entering Northern Ireland. On February 8 he was sentenced to one month's imprisonment. President Cosgrave made representations to the Northern Ireland Government, asking for a remission of de Valera's sentence, but as de Valera refused to give any undertaking not to attempt to re-enter Northern Ireland, he was obliged to serve a token sentence.

On February 28, readers of the Free State newspapers were somewhat puzzled to learn that the Government had assigned £5,000 for what was described as a 'secret invention', with no further details supplied. On June 17, further details of the mystery were unveiled; it was an electrical invention by a Mr James J. Drum, a UCD graduate, which, it was claimed, would revolutionise rail transport in Ireland, if not all over the world. It was in fact a new type of storage battery which would enable locomotives powered by batteries to haul passenger and goods trains and it was shortly to be tried out by the Great Southern Railway Company.

But to return to earlier events that year, the Free State Government offered Charlemont House to the City of Dublin as a Municipal Gallery of Modern Art on March 6. This magnificent Georgian mansion in Parnell Square had been built for the first Earl of Charlemont, Commander-in-Chief of the Irish National Volunteers, in the days of Grattan's Parliament, and more recently had been the headquarters of the Registrar-General.

The report of a Parliamentary Joint Committee on the Betting Acts was published on May 24; it recommended prohibited hours for betting shops (they were to be open only from 9 am to 3 pm and between 5 and 7 pm), no bets of less than one shilling (5p) to be allowed, no bets to be taken from people under 18 years of age or from men in receipt of 'Home Assistance', or Income Support as it is now called, and no winnings to be paid out until the next day.

According to a Department of Industry and Commerce report on June 8, the Free State now came second to Argentina in the supply of cattle and beef to the UK and second only to Denmark in the supply of eggs; and the adverse trade balance had fallen by £3,759,000 since 1924.

There was a ceremonial re-opening of the General Post Office in Dublin on June 11 – it had been out of use for 13 years since the Easter Rising of 1916 – and on July 2, President Cosgrave opened the intake gates at Porteen, Co Limerick, to initiate the operation of the Shannon Scheme.

The first publication featured in the Free State's first list of censored publications was a magazine known as *Health and Strength*, banned on August 28. It contained extremely blurred photographs, all taken at a very discreet distance, of naturists, or nudists, as they were then more frequently known, with their private parts air-brushed out to a bland, discreet and (literally) sexless shadowy area between the legs.

A Fox film unit arrived in Ireland at the end of the month to start work on a film starring the Irish tenor John McCormack, said to be under contract for £100,000 a year.

Early in November, the Gaelic League decided to expel members who attended 'foreign jazz dances'. The airship R101, captained by an Irish pilot, Flight-Lieutenant Irwin, flew over Dublin and Belfast on its trials. Indeed, I well remember watching it from my bedroom window in Sandymount as a small child, as it hung seemingly motionless above the city, streamlined and utterly immaculate in its silver trim.

Denis Johnston's *The Old Lady Says No* had its first production at the Gate Theatre in Dublin; it had been turned down by the Abbey Theatre, and specifically by Lady Gregory herself, hence the title.

1930–1940

❧

Ties With Monarchy Severed

At the start of the Thirties, the seven-year-old Irish Free State was a UK dominion with a British-appointed Governor-General who had to sign all legislation on behalf of the king of England before it could become law. By the end of the decade, the country had become, for all practical purposes, a sovereign independent republic with a new constitution, a president elected by the people, and all ties with the British monarchy severed.

By September 1931, de Valera had raised, mainly in the States, enough money to start his own newspaper, the *Irish Press*, and through this newspaper he had promised that if elected, he would do away with the Oath of Allegiance and the Governor-General and would urge Britain to return the three ports retained by the British armed forces under the terms of the Treaty. He accused the Cosgrave administration of over-expenditure, failure to exploit Irish resources, and failure to drive a better bargain over the border. Then, as a final master stroke, he raised the matter of the Land Annuities.

The Land Annuities were the half-yearly mortgage repayments made by Ireland's (relatively) new peasant proprietors for the farms for which they had previously paid rent to absentee landlords in England. The money was paid to the Irish

Government, which passed it on to the British Government, and it was used to pay off the holders of the original stock in the public share issue raised early in the century to end the Land War by buying the land from the absentee landlords.

De Valera now argued that since the land in question was sovereign Irish territory, the British Government had no right to the money. This argument held an immediate appeal for the Irish farmers who assumed that in future they would not have to make any more mortgage payments for their land. De Valera did not disillusion them on this score until he was safely in power. His own idea was that the annuities – worth about £3,000,000 a year – would continue to be paid, but into the Irish Treasury. There was, to be fair, a precedent for this; the annuities collected from the farmers in the North now went to Stormont and not to the British Government.

But in the long run what really brought down the Cosgrave Government was its methods of dealing with the frequent IRA raids and reprisals which continued to plague the country. In 1931, exasperated at the way IRA gunmen had been literally getting away with murder because of the natural reluctance of juries to find members of the IRA guilty of anything, Cosgrave set up a Military Tribunal to try such cases, with the power to impose the death penalty. De Valera made a good deal of political capital out of this tyrannical and unconstitutional action, and in a general election in February 1932, Fianna Fail won 72 seats as against Cosgrave's 57, and, with Labour's support, took over the Government.

With a single-mindedness which was always one of his great strengths, de Valera immediately set about implementing all the promises he had made. Within a few days he had suspended the Military Tribunal and inside a fortnight he had informed the British Government that the Oath of Allegiance to the British Crown was being abolished as an irrelevant relic of medievalism. At the same time he announced that he proposed to withhold the Land Annuities.

The British weren't greatly bothered by de Valera's abolition of the Oath, but the annuities, being a matter of hard cash rather than mere courtesy, were a different matter altogether. Penal tariffs were imposed on all imports from the Free State, to recover the amount of money the annuities had previously brought in. De Valera in turn slapped prohibitive tariffs on British imports, and the resultant struggle, which went on for nearly five years, was known as the Economic War.

De Valera next dismissed the Governor-General, and replaced him with a retired shopkeeper from Maynooth called Daniel Buckley, a former anti-Treaty politician, who was installed in a small suburban house in South Dublin where his only duty was to affix his signature, on the king's behalf, to Acts passed by the Irish Parliament. The splendid Viceregal Lodge in Phoenix Park was left vacant and Mr de Valera himself took over the business of receiving envoys from foreign countries.

There was another general election in February 1933 in which Fianna Fail won 77 seats in the Dail, as against Cosgrave's 48. Aided perhaps by the confusion into which Cosgrave and his supporters had temporarily fallen, dumbstruck at finding themselves still out of office, de Valera was able to abolish the Senate in its original form and put through parliament a number of piecemeal amendments to the Constitution to prepare the way for a new one on which he was already working.

In 1936 he took advantage of the abdication of Edward VIII to rush through an External Relations Bill which removed the Crown from the Constitution, and a few months later he abolished the office of Governor-General altogether, and in a new constitution published in April 1937, tackled the question of a new name for the Free State by finding a semantic formula which would serve for the whole country if by any miracle the Six Northern Counties could be regained and would, in the meantime, convey a vague general impression that a far greater measure of sovereign independence had been gained than was really the case.

The whole country, including that part of it not at the moment under Irish jurisdiction, was to be known as Ireland (Eire in Irish after a pre-Celtic Irish Queen). Not surprisingly this infuriated the Northern Unionists and totally confused the world's media which insisted on calling the Free State Eire (usually pronounced Air on the radio) to distinguish it from the island of Ireland which also included the Six Counties of Northern Ireland. This explicit territorial claim to the Six Counties of Northern Ireland contained in Articles 2 and 3 of de Valera's 1937 Constitution (see Appendix 2, page 353) still poses a major obstacle in the Republic's relationships with the Ulster Unionists.

De Valera's constitution set up a President (Uachtaran) as Head of State to sign all legislation and deal with diplomatic matters; he was to be elected every seven years by popular vote. The Dail remained largely unchanged, though the President of the Executive Council (the Premier) was now to be known as an Taoiseach (the chief) and his deputy an Tanaiste (the second) and the Constitution provided for a more representative Senate.

It acknowledged the special position of the Catholic Church as the religion of the majority of the population and recognised the family as the natural and fundamental unit of society and, to protect that, unit ruled out any provision for divorce.

The people voted in a plebiscite on the Constitution and in a general election on the same day. On the Constitution, the voting was close: 39 per cent for and 30 per cent against it, though 31 per cent of the electorate did not even bother to record their views. In the general election, de Valera lost his majority of one; the speaker now held the casting vote.

The British Government greeted the 1937 Constitution with a statement to the effect that the adoption of the name Eire did not in any way affect Northern Ireland's position as an integral part of the United Kingdom.

Early in January 1938 de Valera announced a meeting in London between representatives of the two Governments 'to settle outstanding questions'. Nervous that Partition was going to be one of them, the Northern Ireland Prime Minister sprang a surprise election in which the Unionists won 41 out of the 52 seats, a result which ruled out any prospect of bargaining over the border.

On the other issues, de Valera did surprisingly well. The Economic War was ended with an agreement which brought the two countries closer than they had ever been. The dispute over the Land Annuities was settled by a payment to Britain of a lump sum of £10,000,000, and de Valera agreed to reduce some of the tariffs on imports to allow British goods into the country on reasonably competitive terms while still affording a measure of protection to the new native industries. For her part, Britain agreed to remove all tariffs on Irish agricultural produce and to withdraw her forces from the three Treaty ports, Cork Harbour, Berehaven and Lough Swilly.

During the summer of 1938, Dr Douglas Hyde, a Protestant and a prominent figure in the language revival movement, became the first President of Ireland by general agreement between all the political parties. It was widely felt that this was a better notion than holding an election for President, which might have revived the old civil war bitterness.

Then, suddenly, in December 1938, the IRA served an ultimatum on the British Home Secretary, demanding the instant withdrawal of all troops from Northern Ireland within four days and threatening reprisals if the British Government failed to comply. This action was a direct result of de Valera's failure to secure any more concrete concessions on the Partition issue.

The reprisals took the form of time bombs left in letter boxes and warehouses, railway station left-luggage departments and cinemas. Plans to disrupt English life by blowing up public utilities like gas and electricity power stations fell through, as did an attempt by the young Brendan Behan, among others, to blow up the *Queen Mary* liner in dry dock in Liverpool.

The amount of damage done to life and property was not great – though there was an explosion in Coventry which killed five people, wounded more than fifty and did thousands of pounds' worth of damage – but the publicity that these exploits received in the British press did the Irish cause an incalculable amount of harm. Yet curiously enough, Irish people living in England were less often required to explain this indefensible campaign of violence than they were called upon to defend Ireland's neutrality in the war, which was a natural and obvious outcome of the separatist policy the Irish nationalists had been pursuing since 1916, and a proof to the entire world that Irish independence had finally been achieved.

1930

GANDHI BEGINS CIVIL DISOBEDIENCE CAMPAIGN: RAS
TAFARI BECOMES EMPEROR HAILE SELASSIE OF ABYSSINIA:
NAZIS WIN SEATS IN GERMANY: CONSTANTINOPLE BECOMES
ISTANBUL: R101 CRASH: FRANCE BUILDS MAGINOT
LINE: FIRST MAN-MADE FABRICS MANUFACTURED

First Irish Sweepstake

Early in 1930 the details of a Census taken in 1926 were published. They revealed that the proportion of 'unmarried persons of marriageable age' was higher in the Irish Free State than in any other country for which statistics were available, and that such marriages as were taking place were mostly occurring relatively late in life. The proportion of unmarried males in the total under-30 age group was 80 per cent, and in the 23–45 group, 45 per cent. Of all females in the 25–30 age group, 62 per cent were unmarried as against 41 per cent in England and Wales and 23 per cent in the United States. What it all boiled down to was the fact that girls born in Ireland had far less chance of finding husbands than girls born almost anywhere else.

In the Dail in February, Sean Lemass, Fianna Fail's shadow Minister for Industry and Commerce – later to become the founding father of Aer Lingus, Ireland's international airline – protested against a bill to protect wild birds on the extraordinary grounds that 'it would deprive certain classes of people of their livelihood – ie, those persons who caught birds and sold them.'

'We must,' he added, 'keep the interests of human beings before those of wild birds.' He was probably thinking along the same lines when he made the decision to deprive the greatest collection of wild birds in Ireland of their traditional sanctuary at Rineanna (in Gaelic, literally and very curiously, the gathering place of the birds) by siting Europe's first international trans-Atlantic duty-free airport there, when it became clear that flying boats and Foynes were both obsolete.

In February too, a bill was introduced in Dail Eireann to provide for the organisation of a big sweepstake, the proceeds of which would go to the Dublin hospitals to save them from bankruptcy. Obviously, because this was the Irish Sweep, it was tied to horse-racing; you drew, not a prize, but a horse in one of the classic races and you had to wait until the race was run to see whether you'd won a fortune, which gave the whole business an added frisson. The sweep was opposed by many people including President Cosgrave himself and the Protestant Archbishop of Dublin as well as by some of the Protestant Dublin hospitals which refused to accept contributions from anything as venal as a lottery.

The first Irish Hospitals Sweepstake was launched in Dublin in July. Prizes were based on a draw for horses in the November Handicap; and the first prize of £204,764 was shared by three Belfast men who drew the winning horse, Glorious Devon.

In March came the Lenten Pastorals. The ban on Catholics attending Trinity College, Dublin, was to remain; evil literature was denounced as an even greater danger to the country than strong drink; and there were warnings about belonging to oath-bound secret societies and attempts to overthrow the present Government of Ireland, a clear reference to the still recalcitrant republicans. These warnings were reinforced with a rider that the present Government had clearly been accepted as legitimate by the Pope, since he had sent a Papal Nuncio to the Free State to represent the Vatican in Ireland.

On March 4, Harland and Wolff's shipyards in Belfast launched the motor vessel *Innisfallen* for the Cork–Fishguard route, for many years the main link between the thousands of exiles from Cork and Kerry living in Southern England and Wales and their homeland.

The Dublin Gate Theatre moved into new premises in the Rotunda from the Abbey's rehearsal theatre, the tiny Peacock, on March 7. Patrons of that period (and indeed right through and after the war) will remember that during sudden dark silences at climactic moments in deep tragedies, it was impossible to ignore the soothing strains of saxophones drifting up from the dance band in the ballroom below. Gate Theatre guest actors in those early days included the young James Mason and the even younger Orson Welles.

In May, the first fruits of the earnest endeavours of the Censorship Board were announced. Thirteen books were banned, including *Point Counterpoint* by Aldous Huxley, *The Well of Loneliness* by Radclyffe Hall (both for indecency) and *Married Love* by Marie Stopes (for advocating contraception).

The new Baby Austin was launched in Dublin on July 8, price £178, ready to drive away, and created a great deal of interest. Motor racing was one of the big attractions in Dublin that summer and nobody who attended one of those early motor car races in Phoenix Park will ever forget the unmistakable stench of scorching castor oil. Captain Malcolm Campbell, holder of the world speed record (218 mph), made the fastest time ever recorded in a practice run: 87.7 mph in a Mercedes.

Senator Alfred (Alfie) Byrne was elected Lord Mayor of Dublin on October 14 for the first time. He was to be re-elected nine times and became, with his dapper bowler hat and his neat moustache, one of the best-known characters in Dublin. He usually wore a cut-away morning coat with a gold watch-chain adorning his grey vest, and sometimes pale grey spats (if anybody remembers what they were) over his socks.

The Minister for Industry and Commerce hinted in November that he was about to ask for another £25,000 for the further development of the Drumm battery train.

The Irish tenor John McCormack appeared in *Song of My Heart*, a film which also introduced a young actress from Killiney, Co Dublin, named Maureen O'Sullivan, later to become mate to several screen Tarzans, and mother of the Hollywood actress Mia Farrow in real life.

And on December 1, the Mayo Library Committee refused to appoint a Miss Dunbar Harrison as librarian on two grounds: her lack of knowledge of the Irish language and the fact that she was a Protestant. It later transpired that she was a fluent Irish speaker and a Gaelic scholar, albeit a Protestant one, educated at Trinity College, Dublin. To its credit, the Government insisted on her appointment.

1931

KING ALFONSO FLEES IN SPANISH REVOLUTION: FINAN-
CIAL COLLAPSE IN AUSTRIA AND GERMANY: RIOTS
IN LONDON AND GLASGOW OVER ECONOMY MEASURES:
BRITAIN ABANDONS GOLD STANDARD: BRAZIL DESTROYS
SURPLUS COFFEE: ICI PRODUCES PETROL FROM COAL

The Drumm Disaster

The subscriptions, if you could put it that way, to the 1931 Irish
Sweepstakes Draws made it the biggest lottery in the world,
with a turnover of nearly £3,000,000. The hospitals received
about a third of this total and the rules were changed to divide
the prize money into units so that people who drew the winning
horse could not receive more than £30,000. This was done to
obviate the sort of disasters which later so often happened in
England when the Football Pools jackpot prizes reached astro-
nomic proportions and people with no experience of handling
large sums of money became millionaires overnight. Collections
were held in the Protestant churches for the eight hospitals
which still resolutely declined on moral grounds to share the
proceeds of this bonanza.

On January 13, the degree of Doctor of Science was conferred
upon Mr James Drumm, notwithstanding the indisputable fact
that his Drumm battery train had so far made only one timid
excursion from Inchicore to Hazelhatch, a dozen miles or so
apart, at a faltering and reluctant average speed of 22 mph.

In April the Gaelic League condemned the now
Government-approved appointment of Letitia Dunbar
Harrison, the Protestant librarian in Co Mayo, as 'one of the
worst things done since Cromwell's day'.

On April 20, after the medical profession had repeatedly
expressed anxiety over the Government's delay in introducing
new legislation to control the conditions under which milk was
sold to the public, the Medical Officer of Health for Dublin City
pressed for legislation for clean milk. A personal footnote, from

memory: in Sandymount, where I lived as a child, the milk always arrived in large metal churns carried in a sort of trap, drawn by a pony. The churns all had taps on them, and the milk, frequently containing very visible hairs, human or bovine, was poured from the tap into a pewter pint or quart measure and then poured into the clients' own jugs, and the amount specified was always augmented by a tilly (an Anglicisation of the Gaelic word tuileadh, a drop more).

On June 8, the first civil aerodrome in the Free State was opened at Finglas to be the headquarters of Iona Airways, a small air-taxi company, and on August 15 the Irish Aero Club held a pageant at Baldonnel which was attended by 15,000, an indication of the growing interest in aviation in Ireland. Lord Mayor Alfie Byrne gave a public lead by taking a short 'flip' over Dublin.

The first issue of the long-awaited Fianna Fail newspaper, the *Irish Press*, appeared on September 5 and sold 200,000 copies and on October 5 the Four Courts opened for business again for the first time since the buildings were shelled by the army of the Provisional Government of the Free State in 1922.

The day fixed for the first ceremonial run of the long-awaited Drumm battery train was December 1; full of dignitaries and VIPs, it managed to make it as far as Bray, about 12 miles from the city centre, but failed to accomplish the return journey, obliging the dignitaries to return on an ordinary steam train.

The text of yet another new Road Transport Bill was published on December 11. It aimed, among other things, to eliminate the multiplicity of small, privately-owned buses which had been aggravating Dublin's traffic problems almost from the time of the invention of the internal combustion engine. Another personal note from memory: in my childhood, in the Sandymount area, there were several competing one-man bus services with such unlikely names as the Carmel Line (navy blue) and the Queen Bee (pale blue) which, whenever trade was slack, used to leave the main roads and go crawling around the residential building estates touting for business and, like the Mammy Wagons of Ghana, would deliver each and every passenger to his precise final destination, however long that might take.

The Moon in the Yellow River by Denis Johnston was the big Abbey hit of the year and Micheal MacLiammoir made his first appearance as Hamlet in the Gate Theatre.

On December 3, a party of Dublin businessmen prominent in flying circles sought the permission of the Government to develop a derelict British military aerodrome near Swords – it was called Collinstown and is today's Dublin Airport – and set up a company, known as Aer Lingus, to develop air transport in Ireland.

1932

JAPANESE REACH GREAT WALL OF CHINA: MOSLEY FORMS FASCIST PARTY IN ENGLAND: BAN ON NAZI STORMTROOPERS LIFTED: SALAZAR SETS UP FASCIST REGIME IN PORTUGAL: MAHATMA GANDHI ARRESTED: FIRST AUTOBAHN OPENED IN GERMANY: LINDBERGH'S INFANT SON KIDNAPPED

Governor-General Goes

On January 10 the Dail was dissolved and the subsequent election campaign was complicated by the emergence of the Blueshirt movement. This was during the time of Mussolini's Blackshirts and Hitler's Brownshirts, and although the Irish people are far too independent to tolerate for long anything that smacks of fascism, the appearance of the Blueshirts on the political scene caused some uneasiness.

It came about in this way. To discourage the IRA from interfering with election meetings, Cosgrave's supporters set up a friendly association of right-wing ex-officers and men of the Free State army to act as a vigilante force, and they adopted a blue shirt as a sort of uniform.

There were scuffles at election meetings and rowdy gatherings reminiscent of the Nazi rallies which made many people fear that the Blueshirts might be planning to attempt to overthrow the Government and replace it with a military dictatorship.

Nevertheless de Valera had won his first, tenuous overall majority. He was elected President of the Executive Council and immediately declared himself also Minister for External Affairs, a portfolio roughly equivalent to that of the British Foreign Secretary.

His Government introduced what was known as the 'hairshirt' budget in May; it raised income tax to 5s in the £, imposed a 1½d tax on all imported newspapers and periodicals, 33 per cent on gramophone records and 50 per cent on wireless sets. Also, just before the budget, the Government had imposed a 60 per cent duty on all imported clothing and new duties of 75 per cent on all imported private motor cars.

These measures were not at this stage part of the Economic War mentioned above, because Britain did not impose any of the punitive taxes until July. They were simply an attempt to try to redress the imbalance of payments by discouraging people from spending money on costly imported luxuries. A man of devastating austerity, whose own idea of relaxation was the study of higher mathematics, de Valera could not understand why any Irishman should hanker after any form of entertainment more sophisticated and debauched than a group of jolly lads and comely lasses dancing the jig at the village crossroads where the refreshments would be strictly limited to cups of tea and griddle scones smothered in Irish creamery butter.

Despite the hair-shirt budget, and the general down-market image of the new administration, de Valera's *Irish Press* announced on June 18 that full evening dress – white tie and tails — would be worn for a reception in Dublin Castle for the Papal legate who was visiting Ireland for the Eucharistic Congress.

And when, on June 20, Cardinal Lorenzo Laurie arrived in Dublin, there was nothing in the least austere about his reception. Guns boomed out salvos from the pier at Kingstown to match those which had greeted Victoria's Royal Yacht, and the

120

cardinal's carriage was escorted into town by the Free State Hussars, a cavalry corps dressed in pale blue uniforms with gold frogging and black Hungarian shakos, like the chorus in *The Student Prince*.

The Free State Hussars immediately became the butt of much typical Dublin abuse from people who could not see any very close connection between the reality of contaminated milk and thousands of people living in one-room tenements in the slums, on the one hand, and the fantasy of these extravagant trappings of a vanished empire on the other.

The Eucharistic Congress was held in Ireland that year to mark the 1,500th anniversary of St Patrick's return to Ireland as a bishop to preach Christianity to the savage Celts among whom he had spent his youth as a slave. It opened on June 22 with midnight mass in all the city churches.

By now the Economic War had started in earnest. One reflection of the harsh reality of the situation: at Navan Fair on July 19, only one beast was on offer. On August 3, de Valera established an Emergency Fund of £2,000,000 for trade and industry, to open up markets abroad for Irish products, to support new industries and generally to cover expenses arising out of what he called 'the emergency', a favourite word of his.

On his dismissal, Governor-General James MacNeill vacated the Viceregal Lodge on November 2, and it remained vacant until de Valera decided that it was to become the house of the President of Ireland in 1937.

Dublin publicans were warned by the IRA to boycott British beers, notably Bass, and a few days later the Army Old Comrades Association announced that members of their 'army' would safely escort consignments of Bass to the pubs.

The Co Wexford Bee-keepers Association proposed that the name of George Bernard Shaw be removed from its list of associate members for what they described as blasphemy in his book, *The Adventures of a Black Girl in Her Search for God*, which had been published earlier in the year. There was a warm welcome for the Olympic gold medallists, Dr Pat O'Callaghan (hammer-thrower) and R.M. Tisdall (400-metre hurdler) on their return from the Los Angeles Olympic Games.

In Scotland, Dublin-born Kaye Don reached 119 miles an hour in the speedboat *Miss England II* on Loch Lomond.

In Ireland, with his play *Things That Are Caesar's*, which was produced at the Abbey Theatre, Paul Vincent Carroll became the first Irish dramatist to take an overtly anti-clerical line; he returned to the theme in several subsequent plays, notably *Shadow and Substance*, produced a year or so later, about a young girl who imagined that she saw visions of the Virgin Mary, and the subsequent struggle between reason and superstition represented by the school-master and the local parish priest.

1933

HITLER BECOMES CHANCELLOR OF GERMANY: ROOSEVELT INTRODUCES NEW DEAL: POLAND OCCUPIES DANZIG: PERSECUTION OF JEWS IN GERMANY: CANADA AND US ABANDON GOLD STANDARD: UNREST IN PALESTINE: REICHSTAG FIRE: OXFORD UNION AGAINST FIGHTING FOR COUNTRY

O'Duffy and the Blueshirts

The Dail was again dissolved at midnight on January 2, 1933 and de Valera, who was seeking a firmer mandate from the people, opened his election campaign on January 5. He appealed for order and the right of free speech throughout the campaign; his answer came the following day, at a Cumann na nGaedheal meeting in Portarlington. About 40 members of the Army Comrades Association silenced interrupters while Dr T.F. O'Higgins, President of the Association and brother of Kevin O'Higgins, the assassinated Minister for Justice, told the crowd: 'If we cannot have free speech for one side, there'll be no free speech for any side. If you want a fight, you can have plenty of it.' There were stormy scenes at another Cumann na nGaedheal meeting in Dublin on January 8, during which 50 people were injured.

Then General Eoin O'Duffy, Commissioner of the Civic Guard and a former friend of Michael Collins, weighed in; he announced that all the resources of the State were at his disposal for the maintenance of order. If any situation threatened to over-tax the Civic Guard, the army could always be used in support of the Civil Authority.

There were police baton charges at several election meetings and on polling day, January 24, shots were fired in Dalkey, Co Dublin, after a clash between rival bill-posters from the two main political parties.

Almost immediately after de Valera's victory, on February 22, he sacked General O'Duffy and appointed Colonel E. Broy as his successor as head of the Civic Guard. In July, after he had been sacked as police chief, General O'Duffy was elected Director-General of the Army Comrades Association, adopted the Blueshirt uniform officially, and gave the movement the vaguely fascist title of the National Guard.

In April de Valera and other members of his Cabinet visited bogs in the Curragh area; they were already seriously consider-ing the development of the bogs and the substitution of peat for coal in many industrial applications. And in the same month the Government decided to permit the shells of motor car bodies to be imported at a reduced rate, a concession to enable the setting up of a new industry in Dublin, mysteriously known as CKD, to provide employment; the bulk of the final assembly work to be done in Dublin. An explanation of CKD will be forthcoming.

On July 20 the text of the Free State Sugar Manufacture Bill was published; it provided for the formation of a company with capital of £2,000,000 to build and operate factories for the man-ufacture of sugar from Irish beet.

On August 10, General O'Duffy outlined his plans for remod-elling the parliamentary system of the Irish Free State; he advocated election to the Dail by professional, constitutional and vocational groups rather than by popular, democratic vote. The following day the Minister for Justice banned Sunday's Blueshirt Parade as 'likely to interfere with law and order'.

What made the situation doubly dangerous was the fact that for a time it looked as if the Blueshirt movement had the full support of Cosgrave and the pro-Treaty deputies. In September 1933, Cosgrave's Cumann na nGaedheal Party and a new, basically pro-British Centre Party in the Dail, headed by James Dillon, son of John Dillon, the last leader of the Irish Nationalist Parliamentary Party, and Frank McDermott, who represented the wealthier farmers party, launched themselves as a new United Ireland Party,with General O'Duffy as President and William Cosgrave as Vice-President and parliamentary leader. This meant that the new party had an alternative para-military force with which to oppose the official army/police force – a potentially sinister situation.

On October 23 Colonel Charles Lindbergh visited the Free State to examine possible terminals for projected trans-Atlantic air routes.

1934

HITLER BECOMES FUHRER: BALDWIN INCREASES RAF STRENGTH: DRIVING TESTS IN BRITAIN: NAZI PURGE IN GERMANY: GERMANY SIGNS TEN-YEAR NON-AGGRESSION PACT WITH POLAND: GANDHI WITHDRAWS FROM CONGRESS: ANTI-FASCIST DEMONSTRATIONS IN LONDON: QUEEN MARY LAUNCHED

Republic 'A Sham'

On New Year's Eve, soldiers and police were on duty as General O'Duffy addressed a large open-air meeting in Clonmel. He declared that the Government had lost the Economic War and that the Republic was a 'sham'. In Mohill, Co Cavan, on January 1, over 3,000 young Blueshirts held a meeting to protest against the introduction of 'jazz dancing' into Ireland and on January 7, Civic Guards were stoned after a baton charge on youths who tried to create a disturbance during another Blueshirt meeting.

On January 22, the *Irish Times* reported that a section of the Civic Guard was receiving instruction in the use of arms. The men were to be known as the Special Guards, or the S-Branch, but Dubliners soon found a better name for them; they were christened 'the Broy Harriers' after Colonel Broy, the new Commissioner and, of course, with a cross-reference to the Bray Harriers, the famous hunting pack from Bray, Co Wicklow.

The Blueshirts paraded in strength at Swinford, Co Mayo, on February 4, and General O'Duffy boasted: 'I said I would come back to Mayo before long and speak in a blue shirt and here I am.'

In February a convention of the United Ireland Party in the Mansion House elected General O'Duffy President and outlined its aims: the reunification of Ireland's 32 counties and an end to sectarianism.

There was rioting and shots were fired when Cosgrave attended a United Ireland meeting at Dundalk, and a procession of Blueshirts a mile long marched into Kanturk, Co Mayo, to greet General O'Duffy when he arrived to address a meeting there.

And on March 4, just a week after the Dail had passed a bill to ban political parties from wearing blue shirts or any other quasi-military uniforms, the largest meeting ever held in Galway assembled to join the Blueshirts in hearing O'Duffy claim: 'Our movement has long passed the stage when Government intimidation could put it down.'

On March 21 the Senate rejected the bill to ban the wearing of blue shirts and on the next day Mr de Valera introduced a bill to abolish the Senate. In a protest against this move, General O'Duffy, heading a procession of massed bands and armies of men and women in blue shirts, arrived in Carrickmackross on March 21 to address a meeting attacking the Government. Neither the police nor the military attempted to block this protest. Almost immediately, the instinctive Irish feeling for democracy reasserted itself; the more intelligent members of the United Ireland Party decided that it was about time to give up its hopeless attempts to save General O'Duffy from his own stupidities and support for the Blueshirts dwindled; in a surprisingly short time, it disappeared without a trace.

On one front, things were looking up a bit. Following the end of Prohibition in America, it was announced that an unlimited quantity of Irish whiskey would be allowed into the United States for blending purposes.

On January 16, the Government set up an official Publicity Bureau for the supply of accurate information to the home and foreign press, and on January 30 a Local Government Inquiry in the City Hall, investigating the compulsory purchase of areas in Townsend Street for slum clearance, found that eleven families comprising 53 people lived in one single tenement house in Dublin.

More details of the attempt to provide employment in Ireland by reducing the duties on car bodies and starting a new form of car assembly in Ireland known as CKD were revealed on March 16. The idea was that cars manufactured on assembly lines in England and elsewhere would be 'completely knocked down' (CKD) and then reassembled in Ireland, a process which even entailed the destruction with a sledge-hammer of the windscreen so that it could be replaced with one made of Irish glass, fitted by Irish workers. Up to a point, it made sense; the scheme certainly provided employment. The only snag was that cars knocked down and remanufactured in such a labour-intensive way were so expensive that few people could afford to buy them.

On June 28 the Dail, despite all the breakdowns and other grievous disappointments, decided to vote yet another £10,000 for additional research into the Drumm battery train project. Yet another list of tariffs to protect new Irish industries was published; the items covered included plaster statues, bootlaces, buttons, combs and razor blades.

The newspapers went on strike in Ireland in July for over two months, and in September an Irish Wireless and Gramophone Exhibition was held in Dublin – it was claimed that there were now 54,000 licensed listeners in the Dublin area. In the same month, General O'Duffy resigned from the presidency of the United Ireland Party and was succeeded by

Commandant Cronin, who had just been fined one penny for negligent driving in Maryborough. O'Duffy didn't, however, altogether disappear from the scene. He later led a small contingent of Blueshirts to the Spanish Civil War to fight for Franco, and it will come as no surprise to anyone to learn that another contingent of Irishmen under Frank Ryan also went to Spain to fight on the Republican side, with the International Brigade.

On December 19, the Government introduced a new Citizenship Bill which would make anybody born after December 6, 1922 an Irish citizen automatically; naturalisation would require five years' residence in the country. It also contained provisions for bestowing Irish citizenship on foreigners making substantial investments in Ireland, provisions which led to accusations of corruption and nepotism in the Nineties.

The Irish Government refused permission for the exiled Leon Trotsky to reside in the Free State; Robert O'Flaherty, the film director, made a remarkable documentary about the Aran islands, *Man of Aran*, and a new writer called Sam Beckett, who had been James Joyce's secretary, published a novel called *More Pricks Than Kicks*.

Incidentally, James Joyce's great novel, *Ulysses*, appeared for the first time in the United States in an unlimited edition, published by Random House in December, 1934 and was immediately banned. It had been on sale in Britain in an unlimited edition, published by Shakespeare and Company, Paris, from January 1924, and in 1933 the Egoist Press had printed a limited edition of 500 numbered copies, of which 499 were seized by HM Customs authorities.

1935

SAAR VOTES TO JOIN GERMANY: STRESA CONFERENCE
ESTABLISHES COMMON FRONT AGAINST GERMANY: CROATS
BOYCOTT YUGOSLAV PARLIAMENT: SWASTIKA NOW OFFICIAL
FLAG OF GERMANY: COMPULSORY MILITARY SERVICE IN GER-
MANY: PERSIA BECOMES IRAN: GEORGE II SILVER JUBILEE

Catholics Attacked in Belfast

The first indication of a move towards a truce in the Economic
War came on January 3, 1935 with a 'gentlemen's agreement'
between Britain and the Free State under which the Free State
agreed to import mainly British coal and in return Britain agreed
to increase the cattle quota. The London newspapers revealed
on February 7 that King George V had taken the initiative in the
coal-cattle pact in an attempt to heal the rift between the two
countries before his Silver Jubilee on May 6.

On January 9, the first aluminium factory in the Free State
was opened at Nenagh, Co Tipperary, and despite the 'gentleman's agreement' to take British coal, the Government
published advertisements on January 18 urging the people to
burn Irish turf instead of British coal.

For the greater part of March, more than 4,000 workers in
the tram and bus services were on strike, and the Government
provided army lorries to take people to their work.

In May a Select Committee was appointed to inquire into
gold-mining prospects in Co Wicklow.

There was rioting in Belfast throughout July. It started on
July 2, when three men were wounded as shots were fired at an
Orange Order procession, and by the end of the month when
things had calmed down, and a reckoning was made, there had
been 141 arrests, damage to shops and houses amounted to
£70,000, and 265 Catholic families had been driven from their
homes.

The Minister for Industry and Commerce who had, towards

the end of July, introduced a supplementary estimate of £22,240 for the development of Ireland's turf production along industrial lines, opened Arklow Potteries on July 29. They were to employ 500 people, manufacturing Irish tableware; and on the same day there was a banquet to mark the opening of the Irish Dunlop Rubber Company at Cork, a factory established to manufacture tyres for the Irish motor industry. It was to employ 600 people and the tyres would not cost more than about 15 per cent more than the imported equivalent.

The first American-style cocktail bar, the Buttery in the cellars of the Royal Hibernian Hotel, opened on August 2 with George Buller, former cocktail-shaker from the liner *Empress of Britain*, employed to shake (or stir) the Martinis. George Buller was still mixing Martinis and other cocktails when I left Ireland for Fleet Street in September 1959 and was there on my frequent return visits to Dublin making both regulars and returned empties – as revisiting emigrants are called in Ireland – extremely welcome until well into the Sixties.

A factory to produce processed meat was opened in Roscrea, Co Tipperary, on August 13. In August, too, the Abbey Theatre finally got around to staging *The Silver Tassie* and the *Irish Times* commented that O'Casey had 'at last over-reached himself'.

At the end of the month a new tannery was opened at Portlaw in Co Wexford to provide Irish leather for a future shoe-making industry and Kilkenny Castle, historic home of the Butler family, was closed and its contents auctioned. It later became the headquarters of Ireland's industrial design centre.

On November 9, 19 Donegal islanders were drowned when their curragh – a frail craft made of laths and tarred canvas and built to a design that hadn't changed in ten centuries – struck a rock returning to Aranmore.

The curragh continued to be used in Donegal and the Aran Islands until long after World War Two, and drownings remained a very common occurrence. It was just such a tragedy that had formed the basis of J.M. Synge's *Riders to the Sea* and the very distinctive Aran sweaters, worn by the fishermen and knitted from oiled wool, had a practical use, too; there was a different pattern and combination of stitches for each family, to assist in identifying bodies which had been in the sea for so long that no other form of identification was possible.

Before the end of the year a site in the River Shannon estuary near Foynes, Co Limerick, had been chosen as a base for a series of trans-Atlantic flights by flying boats, to be made early in 1936.

On December 19, a new Solus Teoranta (Light, Ltd) factory in Bray, Co Dublin, was opened to provide Irish electric light bulbs for the Free State.

John Ford's film version of Liam O'Flaherty's *The Informer* was released during the year and was a great success in Ireland.

1936

DEATH OF GEORGE V: ABDICATION OF EDWARD VIII: GERMANY OCCUPIES DEMILITARISED RHINELAND: ARAB HIGH COMMITTEE FORMED TO UNITE ARABS AGAINST JEWISH CLAIMS: ABYSSINIA ANNEXED BY ITALY: SPANISH CIVIL WAR STARTS: CRYSTAL PALACE DESTROYED BY FIRE

First Aer Lingus Flight

On January 11, 1936, the RUC were given powers to arrest cattle smugglers. Then, as now, the border was constantly being used to circumvent regulations, and the British Customs reckoned that they were losing £500,000 a year in duties on cattle smuggled into Northern Ireland from the Free State and then exported to England as cattle raised in Northern Ireland.

The slowing-down of the Economic War seemed to be continuing, with increased quotas of fat cattle and bacon going to Britain, and reduced duties on both sides, and on February 17 a new Irish Trade Pact with Britain removed many more tariffs. A boot and shoe factory was opened in Killarney in February to provide employment for 250 workers and to utilise the produce of the tannery the Government had set up in Portlaw.

A new bill was introduced to make the use of turf compulsory:

coal dealers were to be required to include a proportion of Irish turf with every order of imported coal.

Trans-Atlantic air travel came a step nearer on February 23, when a £34,000 pier and deep water harbour at Foynes, Co Limerick, was opened as a future base for seaplanes and flying boats.

On March 26, passengers on the mailboat crossing the Irish Sea saw the 80,733-ton *Queen Mary*, the largest liner ever built, on her trials, and on April 24 the Irish Tourist Association reported that tourists had spent £4,250,000 in Ireland in 1935. The Dail introduced a bill on April 29 to give pensions to those members of the Connaught Rangers who had mutinied in India in 1920 as a protest against British repression in Ireland.

Aer Lingus, at this stage still a private company, bought its first plane, a five-seater de Havilland Dragon, for £2,400 from the Blackpool and West Coast Airline in England and the entire Aer Lingus staff of twelve turned out to see it off on its inaugural flight to Bristol on May 27. It carried a full complement of five passengers and pilot and, flying at 130 mph, arrived on schedule.

Johnny Maher, a former Air Corps mechanic who became Aer Lingus's first chief mechanic, told me many years later that there had been no spares apart from a handful of spark plugs and a few split pins. 'There wasn't even a spare wheel,' he added.

'Johnny Maher's biscuit box' – when he took delivery of those few spares from the Blackpool engineer who had come over with the plane, he put them into a tin biscuit box for safe keeping – became Aer Lingus jargon for the spare parts division. By 1965, it was a huge building on the edge of Dublin Airport, carrying about £20,000,000 worth of spares. It is now a subsidiary of Aer Lingus, servicing aircraft all over the world.

In a sense, Aer Lingus grew out of the old Army Air Corps, formed soon after the British left Ireland; its first pilots and mechanics had all been in the Army Air Corps. When the Royal Flying Corps (the precursor of the RAF) flew out of Baldonnel Aerodrome after the Treaty was ratified in 1922, two of their planes were unable to take off. They were immediately impounded and with another plane which had been 'intercepted' somewhere down the country, were used to form the nucleus of the Irish Army Air Corps. A fourth plane, known as 'The Big Fellow', soon joined them.

'The Big Fellow' really was a big fellow, compared with most of the planes of its day; a Martinside Passenger Aircraft, Mark II, it seated four passengers in a small cabin, and had an open cockpit for the pilot. But it was not given its nickname because of its size. It had been bought in Britain during the period of the Treaty talks, fitted with floats, and stationed in Southampton Water, where it was held in readiness to fly Michael Collins back to Dublin should the Treaty talks fail. It was thought at the time that the British might attempt to capture Collins if the talks broke down, and arrangements had been made to smuggle the Big Fellow, as he was called, down to his namesake in Southampton.

Vice-Admiral Henry Boyd Somerville, an old man of 73 who had been assisting young unemployed Irishmen to join the Royal Navy, was found shot dead in his house in Castletownsend, Co Cork, on March 24. Beside his body was a piece of paper with the words: 'This English agent has sent 52 Irishmen to the English forces during the past seven weeks.' On June 8, an inquest found that the bullet wounds had been inflicted 'by unknown persons' and on June 19, the IRA was again declared an unlawful body – it had first been declared unlawful by the Cosgrave Government of 1931 – and the annual march to Bodenstown in honour of Wolfe Tone was banned. The IRA has constantly been banned as an illegal organisation in Ireland since, though never, curiously, in the UK.

On July 3, an Air Navigation and Transport Bill was circulated; it was designed to set up a £1,000,000 semi-state company to develop air transport in the Free State around the existing company, Aer Lingus. Phoenix Park and Sandymount Strand were both considered as possible sites for new airports, but in July, an inter-departmental committee which had been examining the alternatives came out strongly in favour of the old military aerodrome at Collinstown on the Santry–Swords road, already being used by the Aer Lingus/West Coast air service for their flights to Bristol.

A housing inquiry in Dublin heard evidence of dreadful

conditions of poverty in Marrowbone Lane, which had been included in a Slums Clearance Order; the Dublin Medical Officer of Health told the meeting about one room, occupied by a grandmother, father, mother and three children with no light; another house had, he said, five families of 25 persons occupying six rooms in appalling conditions; and six families totalling 33 people living in six rooms.

On December 1, Dr Isaac Herzog, Chief Rabbi of Dublin, was appointed Chief Rabbi of Palestine, and on December 10 Edward VIII abdicated and was succeeded by his brother, George VI. De Valera took advantage of the confusion over the abdication to sever all remaining ties with the monarchy.

The popular Dublin comedian Jimmy O'Dea and his straight man, Harry O'Donovan, celebrated the tenth anniversary of their partnership with Jimmy O'Dea's traditional Christmas pantomime performance as Dame Biddy Mulligan, the Pride of the Coombe.

1937

POLAND SIGNS AGREEMENT WITH DANZIG: MAGINOT LINE EXTENDED: ALL-INDIA PARTY DEMANDS INDEPENDENCE: MOSLEM RISING IN ALBANIA: COMMISSION ON PALESTINE RECOMMENDS SEPARATE ARAB AND JEWISH STATES: SPANISH REBELS DESTROY GUERNICA: HINDENBURG DISASTER

Free State Becomes Eire

The year 1937 began on an up-beat note with the announcement on January 6 of a £2,200,000 employment scheme to include new water-works, sewage, roads, land reclamation and the development of turf and mineral resources.

For the Blueshirts it was, like the previous couple of years, a pretty down-beat one. A force of 600 of them had assembled at Passage East, Co Waterford, to await a ship that was being sent to take them to Spain, to join Generals Franco and O'Duffy; it failed to arrive and they had to go home, take off their uniforms and resume their ordinary lives.

Following an international non-intervention ban on volunteers from other countries becoming involved in the Spanish Civil War, de Valera introduced a bill in January to prohibit any further Free State citizens from participating in that particular conflict.

On February 25, the Imperial Airways flying boat *Cambria* arrived at Shannon for trans-Atlantic trials. Foynes Radio Station was ready to go into operation and 100 men were at work levelling an area at Rineanna near Limerick to be used as a site for trans-Atlantic aeroplanes, though commercial passenger land planes capable of making the crossing were not yet available. The aim was to establish the Free State as the first international junction for air traffic between Europe and North America.

Thousands of Dubliners travelled to Belfast on July 28 for a ten-hour visit to the Northern Ireland capital by George VI and Queen Elizabeth. On the same day armed men destroyed 30 customs huts and stations along the border, a bridge to the north of Dundalk was blown up, and trains between Dublin and Belfast were held up for several hours.

James Larkin returned as a delegate to the TUC Congress after a long interval (due to a combination of jail, absence in America and disbarment as an undischarged bankrupt) but as soon as he entered the Town Hall in Dundalk where the congress was being held, he walked out again, as a protest against the Japanese-made table-cloths on the tables.

The decision to try out the first automatic traffic lights in Dublin, at the junction of Merrion Square and Clare Street, cost the Government an additional £63 in customs duty on the equipment which they themselves had imposed and which for technical reasons couldn't be removed. In August, too, a crowd of 44,000 spectators at the Royal Dublin Society's show-grounds in Ballsbridge saw the Irish Army Jumping Team become the outright winners of the Aga Khan Trophy, having won it for the third year in succession.

A new set of by-laws for the control of traffic was issued on

September 7; they included detailed rules on right of way, over-taking, traffic signals and parking, but in deference to a country where horse-drawn vehicles and herds of cattle still represented a continuing hazard, they also included provisions covering 'pedestrians and animals (driven or led)'.

On September 30, the accounts for the Free State were published: during the financial year ended March 31, 1937, total revenue was £31,035,000 of which £10,016,000 (roughly one-third) came solely from customs duties imposed on imported goods, mainly from Britain.

On October 8, Maureen FitzSimons won the annual Dawn Beauty contest, run by a leading manufacturer of cosmetics; she later became much better known as Maureen O'Hara, the Hollywood film star.

On December 9, the Department of Industry and Commerce announced the building of a new international airport at Collinstown, Co Dublin, and on December 29, the day de Valera's new Constitution came into force, the Republicans flew a black flag from the Sinn Fein headquarters in Dublin.

1938

GERMAN TROOPS ENTER AUSTRIA: BRITAIN RECOGNISES ITALIAN SOVEREIGNTY OVER ETHIOPIA: GERMANY OCCUPIES SUDETENLAND: CHAMBERLAIN VISITS HITLER AT BERCHTES-GADEN: BRITISH REGISTER FOR WAR SERVICE: GENERAL FRANCO BEGINS MAIN OFFENSIVE: MUNICH CRISIS

Sean T. Wields Famous Horsewhip

Dublin's popular Lord Mayor Alfie Byrne greatly fancied his chances of being elected President of Ireland but withdrew immediately when the Government and Opposition adopted Cardinal McRory's suggestion to agree on a candidate, to avoid the unpleasantness that an election for the Presidency might arouse. Douglas Hyde was duly installed with fairly modest splendour in St Patrick's Hall in Dublin Castle on June 25, following a 21-gun salute from the esplanade of Collins's Barracks in Dublin, and he moved into the very splendid old Viceregal Lodge in Phoenix Park, rechristened Arus an Uachtarain (the house of the president).

Perhaps inspired by the fact that Ireland now had a Gaelic playwright as President, the Abbey directors passed a resolution that plays in Irish would become a regular feature of the theatre's productions and a £50 prize was offered for the best play in Irish.

War was now clearly imminent, and early in 1938 the St John Ambulance Brigade reported that 200 of its members had now become proficient in air raid precautions. Yet another factory designed to reduce Ireland's dependence on imported commodities was opened: Irish Wire Products Ltd, in Limerick, to manufacture nails, screws and wire products for the Irish market.

King George VI and Queen Elizabeth paid a visit to the £20,000 Irish pavilion at the Glasgow International Exhibition on May 3, and while he was there, the king asked J.W. Dulanty, the Irish High Commissioner, to tell him the correct pronunciation of the word 'Eirc' (for the record, it's Aireh).

The first pipes were laid on May 21 for a new water supply for Dublin, to be based on the flooding of a valley at Poulaphuca (the Fairy's Waterfall) near Blessington; the contract for the construction of a hydro-electric barrage had already gone to a British firm of contractors. Two days later, two new Irish cement factories were set up, one in Drogheda, Co Louth, and one in Limerick.

During the election campaign which opened on May 27, de Valera's deputy, Sean T. O'Kelly, distinguished himself with the remark: 'In the last six years, look how we horse-whipped John Bull every time. We wiped her right, left, and centre and with God's help, we shall do the same again.' Sean T. O'Kelly never again appeared in caricature in Ireland's humorous magazine *Dublin Opinion* without a horse-whip in his hand.

The 1936 Census had revealed that in the ten years since

1926, the population of Dublin City had increased by 81,271 to 468,105; the total population of the Irish State was now 2,968,420.

An American aviator, Douglas (Wrong Way) Corrigan, landed in Baldonnel after a solo journey across the Atlantic from New York. He had been refused permission to make the flight, and claimed when he landed that he was under the impression that he had been heading westwards, towards Los Angeles.

The Patrick Pearse Gaelic Athletic Association in Derry demanded on December 4 that the GAA Congress remove the name of Douglas Hyde, founder of the Gaelic League and President of Ireland, from its list of patrons following the President's attendance at a 'foreign' game, an Irish-Polish association football match.

The tenor John McCormack gave a farewell performance before his retirement in the Theatre Royal, Dublin. M.J. Farrell (Molly Keane) had a great West End success with her play, *Spring Meeting,* and the Dublin theatres were flourishing. The Gate reopened – after refurbishment – with Shaw's *Don Juan in Hell* and in the Gaiety, Gwen Ffrangcon Davies appeared in Ibsen's *A Doll's House,* while a series of celebrity concerts in the Theatre Royal included a recital by the 21-year-old Yehudi Menuhin.

The Censorship Board also had a good year, banning books by Ernest Hemingway, Graham Greene, Thomas Wolfe, Alberto Moravia, Beverley Nichols, Stella Gibbons and H.E. Bates.

1939

FRANCO GOVERNMENT RECOGNISED BY BRITAIN AND
FRANCE: GERMAN TROOPS OCCUPY BOHEMIA AND MORAVIA:
ITALY INVADES ALBANIA: CONSCRIPTION IN BRITAIN:
GERMAN INVASION OF POLAND BEGINS WORLD WAR II:
DISCOVERY OF NUCLEAR FISSION: POLYTHENE PRODUCED

Flann and Finnegan

Although, as mentioned in the introduction to the Thirties, the year began with an outbreak of IRA violence in London and the British provinces, life in Ireland went on more or less as normal. The Irish Sweepstake operation moved out to new premises opposite the RDS show grounds in Ballsbridge, Co Dublin, and two Irish books of particular interest were published, James Joyce's *Finnegan's Wake* and Flann O'Brien's *At Swim-Two-Birds*. Of the former, the *Irish Times* commented: '. . . in the ultimate view, although he had no more to say after *Ulysses*, in *Finnegan's Wake* he went on saying it.'

Of the latter, Graham Greene wrote: '. . . you have, (a) the narrator writing a book about a man called Trellis who is, (b) writing a book about certain characters who, (c) are turning the tables on Trellis by writing about him. It is a wild fantastic magnificently comic notion, but looking back afterwards one realises that by no other method could [the main literary traditions of Ireland] the realistic, the legendary and the novelette have been worked together.' The book introduces us to one distinctly unusual character thus: 'There was nothing unusual in the appearance of Mr John Furriskey but actually he had one distinction that is rarely encountered – he was born at the age of twenty-five and entered the world with a memory but without a personal experience to account for it. His teeth were well-formed but stained by tobacco, with two molars filled and a cavity threatened in the left canine. His knowledge of Physics was moderate and extended to Boyle's Law and the Parallelogram of Forces.'

Flann O'Brien was the pen-name of an Irish civil servant, Briain O Nuallain; the following year he started to write a column in Irish and English in the *Irish Times* as Myles na gCopaleen (when he started writing for English newspapers he simplified it to Myles na Gopaleen).

On February 12, the Department of External Affairs formally recognised General Franco's Government in Spain and on February 14, the Government voted an extra £1,250,000 for defence: the strength of the army was to be increased and Air Raid Precaution plans speeded up. De Valera, in Rome for the coronation of Pope Pius XII, called on Mussolini and had lunch with Count Ciano, the Italian Foreign Secretary. On his way home, he paid a courtesy visit to Chequers and had a two-hour chat with Premier Chamberlain.

The text of a new bill to help the tourist industry and to promote Ireland as a tourist centre was published. All hotels and guest houses were to be registered, a tourist board of five members was to be set up to supervise the building of new hotels, and to provide or assist in maintaining amenities and services, training facilities, guide books, time-tables and other tourist literature.

The Minister for the Co-ordination of Defensive Measures gave details, on June 7, of Ireland's air raid precautions: street lights were to be obscured, factories camouflaged, air raid shelters built and 'non-essential' civilians evacuated from the cities.

Sean Russell, Chief of Staff of the IRA, had been detained in Detroit for overstaying his visitor's visa on June 6; on June 8, after a threat by members of the House of Representatives to boycott the projected Royal Visit to America, he was released on a $1,000 bond.

Dublin's first female Lord Mayor, Mrs Tom Clarke, widow of the executed signatory of the 1916 proclamation, was elected, and a regular trans-Atlantic air service was inaugurated on June 28 when the Pan-Am flying boat *Yankee Clipper* carried 29 passengers and the mail from Port Botwood, Newfoundland to Foynes, and then carried on to Southampton.

On August 23, the Haulbowline Steel Works in Co Cork were officially opened to provide Irish steel for Irish industry, and on

August 30, the MV *Innisfallen* was blacked out on a journey to Rosslare. On September 1, Dublin, Waterford and other cities were partially blacked out, the Defence Forces were called up and both houses of the Oireachtas summoned. Three hundred children evacuated from Britain arrived in Waterford and Wexford on September 2, hundreds of Irish travelled home from London, and on September 3, shortly after Chamberlain declared war on Germany, the Government announced that Ireland would remain neutral. Trade with Britain would be maintained and provision was being made for the censorship of post and, if necessary, newspapers; as well as compulsory tillage to reduce Ireland's dependence on imported grain.

The reality of the war was brought home very quickly to the Irish people when, on September 4, the SS *Athenia*, en route to Canada with 1,400 people on board, was torpedoed by a German submarine off the west coast of Ireland, and the 450 survivors were landed at Galway. By September 7 trenches were being dug in the Dublin parks, and there were warnings against hoarding food.

The British Government had not been represented in Ireland since de Valera had sacked the Governor-General and taken over his functions during the confusion following the abdication of King Edward VIII in 1937. But on September 27, 1939, it was announced in the Commons that Sir John Maffey had been appointed British Representative to Eire with special powers to negotiate on trade, economic and political relations.

On October 28, the £2,500,000 oil refinery at Alexandra Basin in the Dublin docks was ready to begin operations; 36,000 gallons for home consumption would be produced from January 1, 1940. Very little of that, however, would go to Ireland's motorists: it had been announced, as early as October 16, that from October 31 petrol rationing would be introduced for all private cars. And from that same day the Government required all non-Irish citizens who arrived in Ireland from Great Britain or elsewhere to register with the Civic Guard. The Order did not, however, apply to people from Northern Ireland who were treated in every way as Irish citizens.

Tea was almost as important a daily necessity to the Irish as constant supplies of strong drink and there was a sigh of relief when, on November 20, the Control Committee of the British Ministry of Food allocated 2,000,000 lbs of tea to Ireland following representations by J.W. Dulanty, Irish High Commissioner in London.

Christmas fare included Irish whiskey at 16s–18s 6d a bottle, a 1929 Pommard at 2s 6d a bottle, gin for 14s 6d a bottle and champagne at 13s 8d–16s.

Then on Christmas Eve the army's Magazine Fort in Phoenix Park was raided by fifty armed IRA men in lorries who got away with 1,000,000 rounds of ammunition. It seemed that despite all the measures taken against them both in Ireland and the UK, the IRA were still very much a force with which to be reckoned.

1940–1950

❦

The Emergency

The repercussions of what appeared to be an alarming revival of
IRA activity towards the end of 1939 preoccupied the
Government during the early stages of the Emergency, as the
war was always called in Ireland. Initially, de Valera's principal
worry was that the Government might be pressed by its British
neighbours into taking a far tougher line with the IRA at a time
when almost the state's entire supply of ammunition – over a
million rounds of it – had been stolen by the IRA in their raid on
the Magazine Fort, the Irish army arsenal in Phoenix Park, just
before Christmas, 1939.

Although most of the ammunition was eventually recovered
and a number of men were arrested and imprisoned for their
part in the raid, the Government remained extremely uneasy
about the menace that the IRA posed to Ireland's neutrality,
especially when German agents started to converge on Ireland
from U-boats and by parachute as well as via more conventional
forms of transport.

In May 1940, shortly after the Germans had invaded Holland,
Belgium and Luxembourg, and at a time when the British Army
was preparing to evacuate Dunkirk, the Civic Guards found a
used parachute, a wireless transmitter, some German medals

and a sum of $20,000 in a house in Templeogue, near Dublin. The full significance of this find did not emerge until after the Emergency; it was part of a German plan – though it may have owed more to secret service adventurism than official German policy – to invade Ireland, set up a Quisling government in Dublin, and use the island as a base for attacking England from the rear; Iseult Stuart, Maude Gonne MacBride's daughter, appeared to be involved.

On June 6, 1940, the Government, paralysed by fear of an IRA coup of some sort, introduced legislation to set up a Military Tribunal to deal with the IRA in a far firmer fashion than any judge or jury would ever dare to do. Three officers, sitting in an upstairs room in Collins' Barracks, not unlike a school class-room, dealt with the wild-eyed young men hauled before them with brisk and business-like detachment. As a young reporter I frequently covered this court – it was known as the Special Criminal Court to give it some semblance of legality – and I'm afraid I regarded it merely as a dead easy day's work. There was usually a scuffle as the young men in mackintoshes were dragged in, and usually another scuffle as they were hauled out, some to be shot, more to be interned or imprisoned, but it was a doddle for the reporters because the prisoners did not attempt to defend themselves or offer any evidence beyond a formal state-ment, usually in Irish, to the effect that they did not recognise the competence of the court to try them. I'm ashamed to admit that it didn't impinge on me at the time that these men were motivated by the same ideals as all the patriots who had gone before them and that their sacrifice, sealed in that dreary, dusty upstairs room in a former British barracks now renamed after Michael Collins, was every bit as significant, from their own point of view, as Patrick Pearse's or Robert Emmet's.

With my colleagues from the *Irish Press* and *Independent*, and sometimes with the prosecuting counsel, I happily played poker while men of my own age spat defiance at the puppet court, and I'm ashamed to add that we sometimes even resented the inter-ruptions when we were called in to hear the sentences.

But the IRA kept up the pressure. Money was constantly stolen from banks and post offices to finance their activities.

Policemen were attacked and in some cases killed. The police were kept busy on house-to-house searches and surprise attacks on IRA camps in the mountains.

Ireland's neutrality tended to widen the gulf between the Six Counties of Northern Ireland and the rest of the country, though 50,000 citizens of the Irish State volunteered for service in the British armed forces during the war and when Belfast was heavily bombed on April 16, 1941 and again on May 5 – about 650 people were killed – de Valera immediately ordered 13 units of the Dublin fire brigade to be sent across the border to help out. 'They are our own people, after all,' he said.

Throughout the war years, de Valera was obliged to use all his innate diplomacy to steer a safe course through a sea of problems. In 1941, when the question of introducing conscription in Northern Ireland cropped up yet again, he said on May 26 that the Six Counties of Northern Ireland were a part of Ireland and that 'it would be an outrage for them [the Nationalists in Northern Ireland] to be forced to fight for Britain.' Churchill wisely decided that to extend conscription to Northern Ireland would probably be more trouble than it would be worth.

Apart from the political niceties of remaining neutral, there was the problem of securing food and fuel and other essentials for a small nation, still so new that it was only beginning to sort out its own internal problems, an island at that, situated on the edge of the war zone with, at the outbreak of war, only a token defence force, liable to be cut off from all supplies, with no shipping, no mineral resources and no bargaining power other than the force of Irish-American opinion, and in no position to survive a long-drawn-out war, even as a neutral. It is enormously to the credit of de Valera and to his energetic and efficient deputy and Minister for Supplies, Sean Lemass, that the country emerged from the war intact, and even in a position to send aid to starving Europe.

So far as ordinary life in neutral Ireland during the war was concerned, tea, sugar and fuel were all soon rationed, and private motoring had ceased to exist by 1942; even doctors and priests used pedal cycles and all over the country horse-drawn vehicles were resurrected and put into service again. Only one train a day ran on the provincial lines, often hours late as a result of inferior coal. To offset the lack of fuel for cooking, community kitchens were set up in various centres in Dublin with free food vouchers for the unemployed and their dependants and for old age pensioners.

The period of austerity which followed the return to peace in Britain was reflected in Ireland and delayed the Government's plans for the further industrialisation of the country.

At a general election in 1948 de Valera was returned with a big majority, but no longer a clear overall one. The opposition parties included Cosgrave's old Cumann na nGaedheal pro-Treaty Sinn Feiners, now known as Fine Gael (it means the Irish race), and led by General Mulcahy, who had succeeded Michael Collins as Commander-in-Chief of the Free State Army, as well as a new Republican Party under Sean MacBride known as Clann na Poblachta (the Clan of the Republic). The latter stood for a social radicalism quite new to Ireland as well as a return to the old notion of implacable republicanism. That Cosgrave's supporters, who for years had gone to absurd lengths to maintain the Oath of Allegiance and the connection with the Commonwealth, should join forces with a party dedicated to more extremist Republican ideals than even de Valera's own is curious enough; that the Labour party and the few Independents and Farmers in the Dail should unite with them to solemnise this most unnatural marriage is even stranger. But they all had one thing in common: a passionate desire to get de Valera out and themselves in, which they proceeded to do, choosing as Taoiseach the former Attorney-General, John Costello, a man who had not been actively involved in the Civil War in any way.

And the strangest thing of all was the ultimate fruit of this most unholy alliance, the Interparty Government: its declaration of the Irish Republic on Easter Monday, 1949.

Costello's completely unexpected assertion of Ireland's republican status brought about no changes in Ireland. Irish citizens could still live and work in the UK and British citizens could do the same in the Republic. Questions relating to Ireland continued to be dealt with by the Commonwealth Office, the currency remained tied to sterling and Irish travellers, arriving at British ports, found that they were still treated, willy-nilly, as British subjects.

Heaven knows why Costello did it; possibly because he had been snubbed by Lord Alexander at a dinner in Canada where the announcement was first made; possibly because as a barrister he had seen too many young lives sacrificed for the myth of the Republic and decided to give them their republic in name, to destroy the magic of the myth; possibly because he wanted to make a mark on Ireland's history.

Costello's declaration of the Republic was greeted in Westminster with the Ireland Act, 1949, a new and explicit guarantee to Northern Ireland that it would remain a part of the UK and that it 'would never cease to be a part of His Majesty's Dominions and the United Kingdom without the consent of the Parliament of Northern Ireland'.

The response to the new Republic from the Northern Ireland premier, Sir Basil Brooke, had a classic simplicity. 'There is only one prime minister here,' he said, 'and his name is not John Costello.'

1940

FINLAND SIGNS TREATY WITH USSR: GERMANY INVADES NORWAY AND DENMARK: LOW COUNTRIES INVADED: CHURCHILL HEADS NATIONAL GOVERNMENT: HOME GUARD FORMED IN BRITAIN: DUNKIRK EVACUATED: FALL OF FRANCE: ROYAL NAVY SINKS FRENCH FLEET: BATTLE OF BRITAIN

Irish Trade in Credit

The war came a little closer to Ireland when, on February 7, the B + I MV *Munster* was sunk off the British coast; all on board were saved. The British Army camp at Ballykinlar, Co Down was raided on February 11; this camp had been so often raided in the past by IRA parties intent on replenishing their arms and ammunition – and so many British soldiers stationed there had been convicted of selling rifles and ammunition to the IRA – that it had become known in IRA circles as 'the stores'.

In February a number of IRA prisoners in Mountjoy Jail went on hunger strike in a protest against being treated as ordinary criminals and not as political prisoners. In the past, Irish governments had always given in to hunger strikers, understandably perhaps, in view of the fact that Terence MacSwiney's death in Brixton Jail, after a fast of 74 days, had been one of the contributory factors in changing world opinion about the Irish struggle for independence. But this time de Valera allowed two men to die and the hunger strike was called off.

That there was a certain amount of anti-British feeling in Ireland at this period is unquestionable. Many Republicans felt that another of England's difficulties might well provide Ireland with another opportunity to make a fresh bid for full freedom, (the unification of the country). Also there was a strong reaction in Ireland to the execution of Peter Barnes and James McCormick in Birmingham Jail on February 2, 1940. They had been convicted of murder as accessories under the British rule of 'common purpose', in connection with the Coventry bomb explosions the previous year, despite the fact that Barnes had not even been in Coventry on the day of the explosions. In Dublin, on the day they were hanged, all theatres and cinemas closed, all sporting fixtures were cancelled and flags flew at half-mast.

In March, Minister for Supplies Sean Lemass expressed his appreciation of Britain's consideration in regard to the supply of scarce commodities to Ireland. At the same time, he immediately set about trying to make Ireland as independent as possible from any help from outside sources. A compulsory tillage programme was introduced which, before the end of the war, had doubled the acreage under crops. A new Electricity Bill provided an additional £4,000,000 for the Electricity Supply Board which included £800,000 for the development of a turf-burning power station at Clonsast in the Bog of Allen.

In March, too, the text was published of de Valera's new bill to establish an Institute of Advanced Studies in the Irish language and in the field of theoretical physics. It was motivated by two factors: his own interest in higher mathematics as well as the Irish language and the fortuitous presence in Ireland of Professor Erwin Scroedinger, Einstein's successor in the field of quantum physics, a refugee from Nazi Germany.

In April, Aer Lingus took delivery of the first of a fleet of new Douglas DC3 air liners, each seating 21 passengers; and from June, travel permits were required for visits to Northern Ireland.

In August a Minerals Bill, giving the Government the right to take over and develop all inefficiently-worked mines in Ireland was introduced, and the High School, a private Protestant boys' school in Harcourt Street, Dublin, became Dublin's first air raid station.

Dublin, Dun Laoghaire and Cork, as well as Bantry Bay and Lough Swilly were declared 'controlled ports', in which all shipping would be directed by the defence forces, specifically the new Marine Inscription Service, the naval branch of the part-time Local Defence Force.

At this period the new Marine Service boasted only one sea-going vessel, the British gun-boat *Helga*, which had shelled rebel strongholds from the Liffey in 1916. Renamed the *Muirchu* (sea-hound) it was basically a fishery protection vessel about 150 feet long, armed with one piece of light artillery.

In October, Germany accepted the responsibility for a bomb that had fallen at Campanile in Waterford in August, killing three girls. An unidentified plane dropped high explosives and incendiary bombs on the Vale of Clara in Co Wicklow on October 27 and on November 1 a Japanese liner, the *Husimi Maru*, en route from Lisbon to Tokyo, put in to Galway Bay to embark 170 Japanese nationals from Great Britain.

On October 9, all former Abbey Theatre records were broken when George Shields's comedy *The Rugged Path* opened for a tenth week to packed houses. In October, too, a new Irish monthly magazine appeared and provided a badly-needed forum for Irish writers during a period when most of the English literary reviews had closed down or had been reduced in size to a couple of pages; it was *The Bell*, edited by Sean O'Faolain, and the first issue contained articles by Frank O'Connor, Jack Yeats, painter brother of the poet W.B., Elizabeth Bowen, Brinsley McNamara and Flann O'Brien. When the then editor of the *Irish Times* asked me to review it, I put it to him that *The Bell*'s editor, Sean O'Faolain, might quite justifiably be insulted if his first issue was reviewed by a raw and inexperienced boy just out of school. Smyllie grinned at me and replied: 'If this magazine survives for a decade, Mr Gray, sir, which I very much doubt, it will be your generation and not mine who will be reading it. So go ahead and tell us what you think of it.' It lasted, intermittently, until 1955.

Irish trade was in credit for the first time since the state was founded in 1922. The credit balance of £45,641 reflected the inability of Irish people to spend any money on imported goods (since almost nothing that was not essential was imported) far more than any dynamic improvement in Ireland's economy; it also reflected Britain's desperate need of Ireland's agricultural produce.

On December 18, the mailboat *Cambria* was bombed and machine-gunned by a German plane, 40 minutes out of Dun Laoghaire harbour with 50 passengers on board. Two days later bombs fell in Sandycove, Co Dublin, injuring three people, and a farmer was injured by a bomb which fell from a plane at Carrickmacross, Co Monaghan. These events occurred at a time when the blitz on England was at its height and when about 4,000 people were being killed every night in air raids all over Britain; they would be hardly worth recording apart from the fact that Ireland was a neutral country.

By this time anti-aircraft batteries around the Irish coast were being manned by amateur, part-time artillerymen, members of the Local Defence Force set up earlier in that year. I was one of them and my considered view of our activities was that we were far more of a danger to ourselves and one another than we were to any marauding aircraft. My commanding officer was Tom O'Higgins, nephew of Kevin O'Higgins who had been assassinated in 1927; he was later to challenge de Valera in an election for the presidency and to come within an ace of beating him.

1941

LEND-LEASE BILL SIGNED: WAVELL ADVANCES ON BENG-
HAZI: GERMANY INVADES RUSSIA: ROMMEL ATTACKS
TOBRUK: BRITISH EVACUATE GREECE: RUDOLF HESS
LANDS IN SCOTLAND: GERMANS INVADE CRETE: BISMARCK
SUNK: JAPANESE BOMB PEARL HARBOR: US ENTERS WAR

Bombs Fall on Neutral Ireland

Unidentified bombs fell on a house in Co Carlow on January 2, killing three women and injuring two men. Two houses were destroyed by bombs in Dublin and other bombs fell on Meath, Carlow, Kildare and Wicklow. More bombs fell on Dublin on January 3; the Jewish synagogue was damaged, three people were injured and Eire lodged a protest against Germany.

A Government Order issued on January 8 made it an offence to display road signs, so that to add to the complications of the dim-out (Ireland never had a total black-out), and the general inadequacy of road-signs in Ireland, there was the added fact that, from February 1, all discernible road signs were removed or obscured.

In March, 1941, the Government announced the formation of a semi-state company, Irish Shipping, Ltd, to acquire and operate ships for the importation of essential goods. Their first acquisition was a Greek vessel which had been discovered lying almost derelict in the Spanish port of Aviles since the Civil War. Renamed the *Irish Poplar*, she became the first ship in Ireland's mercantile marine service. By the end of the war the company had acquired 15 vessels.

On May 31, German bombers, thinking they were over Belfast, or perhaps deflected from Belfast by British radar, dropped a couple of land mines on the North Strand district of Dublin, killing 28 and leaving 2,500 homeless; I was one of the first reporters on the scene and I found it a searing, unforgettable experience, watching all those dust-grey corpses streaked

151

with purple blood being carried out of the collapsed houses. One of the houses had an open piano clinging to the wall of a third-floor room, except that there was no floor, and no room – it hung there as if suspended from a picture hook, an unforgettable sight. It wouldn't, perhaps, be such a big deal these days, when we're all inured to the horrors of war on television, but in those days newspapers never printed pictures of dead bodies, and I found the whole experience shattering.

On June 16, when the Rosslare–Fishguard steamer was hit by bombs, 25 people were killed.

The Dail learnt on July 1 that 30,000 workers were now engaged in cutting 100,000 tons of turf a week. And despite the current lack of any form of transport, road or rail, 20,000 people managed to make it for the annual pilgrimage to Ireland's holy mountain, Croagh Patrick, climbing the final stages in traditional style, in bare feet.

On August 23, a £2,000,000 subsidy to keep bread and flour prices at their current level was announced. The harvest would yield 290,000 tons out of the total requirement of 350,000 tons, and while there was no prospect yet of a whiter loaf, there would be enough all-wheaten flour to maintain supplies of bread of some sort for a year. On August 27, Clondalkin paper mills bought 8,000 tons of straw to use in paper manufacture in place of wood pulp.

Another of Irish Shipping's early acquisitions, the *Irish Elm*, arrived in Dublin Port on September 4 with a cargo of grain from America, the first since the outbreak of war.

Then came the extraordinary, and at the time baffling, business of Stephen Hayes. On the morning of September 8, a half-crazed man with shackles around his ankles staggered into the police station at Rathmines with a garbled story that he had been chained and tortured in a house nearby from which he had just managed to escape. He was held in custody while the Guards went to investigate.

He turned out to be Stephen Hayes, the notorious IRA Chief of Staff, and claimed that he had been held in captivity in various places for two months, beaten, interrogated, starved, prevented from sleeping and tried and condemned as a traitor by an IRA court martial, most of whose members were unknown to him. After his trial he was confined in a house in Rathmines, his legs shackled together, and was forced to write his confession, stating that he had been acting on behalf of the Irish Government, and that he had arranged the Coventry bomb explosions and others in order to discredit the IRA.

If Hayes had been working for the Irish Government, which seems highly unlikely, they chose a strange way to reward him; for on June 19, 1942, the Special Criminal Court (the tribunal of army officers) sentenced him to five years penal servitude for maintaining 'an illegal force'. It was yet another proof, if any were needed, of the extremely fissiparous nature of the IRA; subsequent history has furnished countless other examples of the tendency of this body, like most Irish institutions, to go on splitting almost indefinitely. Brendan Behan put his finger on it years later, when, after a rare, unanimous decision on some point at an IRA meeting, he remarked: 'You don't mean to say you're all agreed on this? How the fuck is anyone going to know we're Republicans if we don't have a split?'

In any case, nothing that happened in those days was really surprising. One of the men involved in the Hayes affair was Larry de Lacey, who worked as a sub-editor on the *Irish Times* when I joined the newspaper first. I found a loaded revolver in the subs' lavatory one night; it had fallen out of Larry de Lacey's pocket. As I came out of the toilet holding this terrifying object nervously at arm's length, Larry took it from me quietly and slipped it back into his hip pocket. And not a word about the entire affair was ever said by him or by any of the other five or six people in the room.

By the end of September matches had been rationed and the Guild of Goodwill had opened a restaurant in Pearse Street, Dublin, which offered a two-course 'dinner' for 9d. In October, fuel boilers were installed in the kitchens of the Mansion House, Dublin, capable of supplying up to 40,000 hot meals per day, and four other similar centres had been planned. The Government announced on November 29 that it proposed to set up turf camps where the unemployed would be housed and fed in return for digging turf to fuel Ireland's fireplaces.

John Betjeman, then working as press attaché to Sir John

Maffey, the British Representative in Eire, wrote a poem to celebrate the 70th anniversary of the Gaiety Theatre; it was read at a gala performance in the theatre by the actor Anew MacMaster.

1942

FALL OF SINGAPORE: QUISLING BECOMES PREMIER OF NORWAY: HEAVY AIR RAIDS ON MALTA: ANGLO-SOVIET ALLIANCE: 1,000-BOMBER RAID ON BREMEN: AMERICANS LAND IN GUADALCANAL: GERMAN TROOPS REACH STALINGRAD: BATTLE OF EL ALAMEIN: GERMANS LAUNCH V2

Enter the Glimmer Man

As the new year opened, those few Dubliners able to secure enough petrol to take the car out on Sunday afternoon, and who happened to drive through Phoenix Park, noticed something unusual. The main road straight through the park – the road which had been the 'long straight' in so many pre-war Grand Prix motor races – was banked on either side with sods of turf, placed there as a reserve for the city. Dubliners soon found a name for it: the New Bog road.

From March 3 gas was rationed in Dublin, and theoretically very effectively, to the extent that the supply was cut off between 8.30 am and 11.30 am; from 1.30 pm to 5 pm, and from 10.30 pm until 7 am the next morning. But even this draconian measure didn't defeat the Irish housewife, who soon discovered, by the simple process of trial and error, that even if the gas was switched off at the mains, enough was left trickling through the pipes to enable anyone to boil a kettle or even heat up a can of baked beans. It took a long time, but it worked. The residual gas left in the pipes when the supply was officially turned off was known as 'the glimmer' and it gave birth to a new profession, 'the glimmer man', a Gas Board official whose job it was to prowl around the city during periods when the gas was supposed to be turned off and catch housewives in the act of using the glimmer.

On March 24 it was announced that rationing was to begin in May. Already 3,000,000 ration books had been printed, and it had been decided that the Government would fix the price of all rationed commodities.

Private motoring was banned from April 30 and one immediate effect was that the price of second-hand bicycles soared from a few shillings to £10–£15 in Dublin, which doesn't sound a lot but at this period my salary in the *Irish Times* as junior leader writer and reporter was 48s (about £2.40) a week. There was no coal whatever for domestic use; such imports as Ireland was able to grab were barely enough to keep industry going.

By this time, too, there were 4,500 air raid precaution wardens in Dublin and air raid shelters capable of accommodating 64,000 people. Ireland had developed an offbeat but highly profitable trade in the export of £1,000,000 worth of wild rabbits a year, an industry which also afforded employment for people capable of skinning, chilling and packaging the animals.

Dublin car parks were now converted to cycle parks but nothing had really changed. There still were dances every night of the week, and full dress dances at that; the women wore long evening gowns, and the men white tie and tails, though most of the couples arrived at the ballrooms (the Gresham, the Metropole, Clery's, the Hibernian, the Shelbourne) on bicycles, the men pedalling with their coat tails turned in on the saddle and with bicycle clips on their trouser legs, and the girls with their long dresses tucked neatly under them, sitting on the crossbar.

The style of dancing closely followed the British and American pattern – mainly quicksteps, slow foxtrots, waltzes, an occasional tango or rhumba, though in Ireland the dances always featured a few Paul Joneses (which gave everybody a chance to dance for a few moments with a total stranger at a period when dancing offered opportunities for far closer and more intimate physical contact than it does today) and at least one Irish set dance, The Walls of Limerick, or The Siege of Ennis.

The biggest event of the Dublin season was the annual Zoo Dance, held in a huge marquee in the Zoological Gardens, in Phoenix Park, Dublin in mid-summer, with a meal and drinks served in other marquees, an arrangement which lent itself ideally to casual, extra-marital encounters between the tents.

Incidentally, reporters working for the Dublin newspapers were expected to provide themselves with dinner jackets and tails. A small allowance was made for laundry, as evening dress was obligatory for reporters attending many functions, although they might well find themselves obliged to wait outside for the list of names.

A committee of inquiry into the use of Irish as a teaching medium for all other subjects including mathematics found on April 27 that National School teachers were of the opinion that such a policy was educationally unsound when the children came from English-speaking homes, which almost all of them did.

The Government paid no attention at all to this report and for a long time afterwards continued to force teachers whose first language was English to attempt to pass on, in Irish, to pupils who were as uncomfortable speaking the language as they were, whatever rudiments of other subjects such as history and geography, science and mathematics as they themselves had managed to pick up. That Irish children educated in this way were able to hold their own against children educated by the normal process in their own language speaks volumes for the adaptability of the Irish race.

This was a period during which people began to fend for themselves. Thousands of Dubliners bought or rented patches of bog in the Dublin mountains, and spent their week-ends digging and stacking turf to keep the home fires burning. Plots in many of the city parks were made available for people who had no gardens in which to grow their own vegetables and when the deer in Phoenix Park became a nuisance, trampling up the plots and eating the vegetables, a policy of culling was decided upon, and many Irish people tasted venison for the first time.

The first American GIs began to arrive in Northern Ireland; and when de Valera complained that the Irish Government had not been consulted either by the United States or Britain in regard to the landing of American troops in Northern Ireland, Roosevelt's reply was brief and to the point – a cable which simply said: 'Really?'

1943

CHURCHILL AND ROOSEVELT MEET AT CASABLANCA: RUSSIAN VICTORY AT STALINGRAD: GERMANS SURRENDER IN NORTH AFRICA: RAF BOMBS RUHR DAMS: ALLIES LAND IN SICILY: FALL OF MUSSOLINI: RUSSIANS TAKE KIEV: CHURCHILL, ROOSEVELT AND STALIN MEET AT TEHERAN

Sexes Segregated in Cinema

The problems of personal transportation in Eire during the Emergency were again emphasised by a police report early in January 1943 which stated that, during the year 1942, over 3,000 bicycles had been stolen in Dublin. New bicycles were totally unobtainable, and second-hand bicycles were scarce and expensive, so it is not surprising perhaps that many people solved their own problem by helping themselves to bicycles from the many cycle parks all over the city; the only surprising thing about the report is that the figure was not a great deal higher. Incidentally, on July 9, three lawyers, Mac O'Rahilly, Sean MacBride and J.P. Tyrell solved their own personal transport problems in a novel fashion by travelling from Dun Laoghaire to attend the Wicklow Circuit Court in Mac O'Rahilly's 17-foot racing yacht. In a small sailing boat, it was a journey that could take anything from three hours to a whole day, according to the vagaries of the weather.

Throughout the entire period of the Troubles and during the first twenty years of its existence as a separate state, first as the Free State and then as Eire, there had been relatively little genuine, professional crime in Ireland and almost no non-political murders. But Bernard Kirwan was sentenced to death on February 5 for the murder of his brother-in-law in November 1941, after a 17-day trial, one of the longest and most complex in Irish criminal history. And when he was executed in June, an English hangman had to be brought over to do the job. Oddly, there had never been any problem of finding Irish firing squads ready and willing to execute their former comrades, but there'd never been an Irish hangman. Maybe the gun was respected as one of the instruments of Irish freedom and the rope despised as a relic of British misrule.

Even during the war, despite all the shortages, a number of films were made in Ireland. The absence of barrage balloons, fighter and bomber aircraft and other signs of war as well as the country's general tranquillity made it ideal for filming – to say nothing of the availability to film crews of large and succulent steaks, prawns, lobsters, fresh salmon and other delicacies almost forgotten in Britain. In May, 1943, the actor Laurence Olivier arrived in Dublin looking for possible locations for a film he was contemplating based on Shakespeare's *Henry V*; he found his Agincourt just outside Dublin, on the estates of Lord Powerscourt at Enniskerry, Co Wicklow.

On May 3 it was announced that the Government was to buy the National Stud at Tully, Co Kildare, still owned by the British Government . It was built on a site laid out at the turn of the century by a brilliant if eccentric Englishman called Lord Wavertree, who arranged the stalls in such a way that all the horses in the stud could gaze at the stars in their courses. Ireland, which then was and still is one of the great horse-breeding countries of the world, boasted, in the Forties, the final surviving seashore race-meeting in the UK at Laytown, Co Meath, 40 miles north of Dublin, where the only permanent structure connected with the annual one-day meeting was a con-crete gentlemen's convenience. Laytown races dated back to the 1890s but the Curragh race-course – where racing took place, and still does, on 30 days in the year – dates back, it is said, to the days of St Brigid who, when told that she could have as much land as she could cover with her cloak, spread it out to cover the whole of Kildare.

Another Irish Shipping acquisition, the *Irish Oak*, was torpedoed and sunk on May 20; the crew were picked up and landed safely in Cork. And another general election on June 22 left de Valera still in power; among those elected was Liam Cosgrave, son of William T. Cosgrave.

In September the Department of Industry and Commerce report on employment admitted that large-scale emigration (to the British armed forces and wartime factories) had partly, though only temporarily, solved Eire's unemployment problem.

What amounted to the nationalisation of the railway companies came on October 15 when it was announced that a new company was to be formed to replace the old Great Southern Railway, and that the Government was to hold £16,000,000 of the £20,000,000 stock.

In October, a cinema in Clones, Co Monaghan, introduced a new regulation which enforced segregated seating of the sexes, men on one side of the aisle and women on the other, though married couples were permitted to sit together. It was not necessary to produce a wedding certificate. Age and a general appearance of respectability were given more consideration by the cinema staff than such things as wedding rings, which could easily have been borrowed for the occasion.

On November 9, *The Times* of London reported that Foynes was now the busiest flying boat junction in Europe, which probably wasn't such a big deal in the middle of a war that had totally engulfed Europe, had spread all over the Pacific, across the Mediterranean into North Africa and right across the Atlantic. The new terminal at Foynes could now provide accommodation for 15 flying boats.

George Bernard Shaw decided on November 30 that henceforth he would insist on royalties in kind from a projected American broadcast version of *Pygmalion*; he wanted to be paid with chocolates, jam, fruit and coal from America, instead of dollars.

On December 14, it was announced that Dublin was to have its first mass radiography unit, and bus queueing became compulsory on December 22 if there were more than five passengers waiting at a bus stop. Although the British appear to enjoy queuing, the Irish never took any more kindly to the concept than the French did, until the exigencies of the supermarket check-out system made it inevitable.

On Christmas Day, 1943, gas was available (officially) only from 7.30 am to 2.30 pm and from 6 pm to 7 pm. If anybody attempted to heat a drop of water to make a whiskey toddy outside these hours, it was a matter between himself and the 'glimmer man'.

1944

ALLIES REACH MONTE CASSINO: PAYE INTRODUCED IN UK: DAYLIGHT AIR RAIDS ON BERLIN: D-DAY LANDINGS IN NORMANDY: FIRST FLYING BOMB ATTACKS ON LONDON: GENERAL TOJO RESIGNS IN JAPAN: POLISH RISING IN WARSAW: DE GAULLE ENTERS PARIS WITH ALLIED ARMIES

Permanent Waves Rationed

On January 1, legislation to provide for the compulsory acquisition of the Dublin United Tramways Co was introduced; the DUTC, which also ran Dublin's buses, was to be added to the now nationalised Great Southern Railway Company to form the core of an integrated national transport monopoly to be known as Coras Iompair Eireann (the organisation of the carriage of Ireland).

Johnstown Castle, Co Wexford, former seat of the Esmonde family, dating back to the thirteenth century, was offered to the nation for use as an agricultural college on January 20.

On January 30 Harry O'Donovan, the comedian, attacked the payment of artists by Radio Eireann. It was no better than Outdoor Relief, he said; musicians were only paid 2s (10p) an hour.

In the run-up to D-day, after an American request to the Irish Government to expel the German and Japanese diplomats in

Dublin was turned down by de Valera, Britain banned all travel to and from Ireland 'for military reasons'. The border between Eire and Northern Ireland was closed from March 15, and on April 5 Britain withdrew almost all telephone services to all parts of Ireland and banned the export to Eire of British newspapers. On April 17, it was announced that Britain was to censor all diplomatic bags; official couriers were banned from leaving Britain, and the High Commissioner for Eire in London was forbidden to travel.

Railway services were cut down to two trains per week to provincial towns and the few remaining dining cars were withdrawn from service. The RDS Spring Show was abandoned and Radio Eireann programmes curtailed to save power.

When, on May 10, the Government was defeated by one vote on a motion in relation to the bill to nationalise the Great Southern Railway, a general election was announced for May 30; de Valera's overall majority was considerably reduced but he still had three seats over the combined total of all the other parties in the Dail.

On June 9, the Electricity Supply Board announced further cuts. Cinemas were to reduce their programmes to one film per day; double-decker buses were to replace trams on all routes, and permanent waves were to be 'rationed'.

Back in May the Dublin City Medical Officer of Health had reported a sharp increase in the incidence of VD; and on August 6 the Bishop of Galway deplored the arrival of undesirable persons, including prostitutes, in Galway for the annual race week.

On December 10 the actor Wilfrid Brambell took over from Jimmy O'Dea in the annual Christmas pantomime at the Gaiety Theatre and a few months later gave up his job as a clerk in the *Irish Field*, a sporting newspaper published by the *Irish Times*, for a career which was to end with one of the most popular comedy soap characters on British television, Steptoe, Senior, of *Steptoe and Son*.

1945

YALTA CONFERENCE: BRITISH REACH RHINE: RUSSIANS IN
BERLIN: MUSSOLINI KILLED BY PARTISANS: HITLER DIES
IN BUNKER: KEITEL SURRENDERS NEAR BERLIN: ATOM
BOMBS DROPPED: JAPAN SURRENDERS: DEATH OF PRESI-
DENT ROOSEVELT: GENERAL MACARTHUR ENTERS MANILA

Trans-Atlantic Service Starts

At the beginning of the year, President Douglas Hyde informed
de Valera that he would not be seeking re-election and in May
Sean T. O'Kelly was nominated as the Fianna Fail candidate
and was duly elected.

Although the war was now clearly coming to an end, the shortages continued. The butter ration was reduced in January by
another 2oz to 6oz per person per week (which in these days of
extreme sensitivity to the dangers of cholesterol does not seem
unduly penitential), and a shortage of what is known as 'edible
fat' closed all of Dublin's fish and chip shops for four days a
week from February. In March it was announced that the solid
fuel ration (mostly turf) for the two months beginning April 1
would be reduced from two tons to one. And this was at a time
when central heating was unknown in Ireland outside of the
luxury hotels and some of the smarter office blocks. The tea
ration was down to half an ounce a week and a form of tea made
from dried dandelion leaves was on sale, as well as ersatz coffee,
made, it was said, from rhubarb.

Protests against relics of the British regime continued south of
the border; on January 22 the head was sawn off the equestrian
statue of General Gough in Phoenix Park. And early in
February, the Irish Government managed to secure an agreement that all east-bound air traffic from the United States would
stop at Rineanna, the land base near Foynes, already being
described as Shannon Airport.

On April 24 Thomas MacMahon, a 40-year-old farmer from

Kilrush, Co Clare, was found not guilty of murdering his mother-in-law in January 1944 by pouring petrol over her and setting her alight. An interesting personal sidelight. This was his second trial; he had been found guilty and had been sentenced to death in November 1944 but won a re-trial on appeal against the judge's summing-up. I had reported both trials for the *Irish Times* and had been fascinated at how different the same basic set of facts looked when presented by the same barristers before a different judge and jury. It confirmed me in a view formed during two years' reporting of the criminal courts – a view which I have since found very little reason to revise – that justice is very largely a matter of luck, like everything else in this unjust world.

On March 8, the Government announced a £3,500,000 hydro-electric scheme for the River Erne, to be operated in co-operation with the Northern Ireland Government, and on March 26 the final scene in the saga of the Drumm battery train was played out when the company, whose activities had been suspended for the previous five years, went into voluntary liquidation, though the single Drumm train which had been built continued in intermittent service on the Harcourt Street–Bray line. It was neither as fast nor as reliable as the regular steam trains.

On May 2, on the very day Von Keitel surrendered to the Russians, de Valera called on the German Minister, Edouard Hempel, to express his condolences on the death of Adolf Hitler. No doubt this was perfectly proper behaviour for the premier of a neutral state, but a lot of people felt that he ought to have let protocol go by the board in the circumstances; by this time there was not much doubt in anybody's mind that the world was not going to be a poorer place without the presence of Adolf Hitler.

The German Embassy in Dublin was vacated by the Embassy staff five days after Mr de Valera's visit; in September the furnishings realised £1,760 at an auction in Belfast.

VE Day (May 8) was marked in Dublin by a series of small celebrations some of which turned into riots during which the windows were broken in Jammet's restaurant. Trinity students flew a Union Jack from the roof of the college and burned the Irish tricolour, and there were scenes of disorder all over the city. A party of students from the National University carried a Union Jack to College Green and burnt it there under the eyes of the TCD students still standing guard over the Union Jack on the roof of the college; the National University students included Charles J. Haughey, the future leader of Fianna Fail and Taoiseach.

In Germany on May 29 William Joyce (Lord Haw-Haw of the 'Jairmany Calling' wartime broadcasts to Britain) was arrested near the Dutch border. Born in New York, of an Irish father, he had been educated at the Jesuit School in Galway. He was found guilty of treason and was hanged in the Tower of London on January 3, 1946.

On June 18, Sean T. O'Kelly was inaugurated as President with great pomp and circumstance at a formal ceremony in the former Throne Room in Dublin Castle, and in July it was announced that the sugar ration was to be cut again to release supplies for distribution in Europe.

In July, John F. Kennedy, son of the former US Ambassador to Britain, and future President of the USA, spent some time in Dublin doing a series of interviews for the Hearst newspapers.

Fifty of the 200-odd Germans interned in Ireland requested permission to stay on in Ireland. The request was turned down on August 4 and on August 13, 254 internees left for Germany; nine had broken their parole and disappeared. Some of them contrived to stay on in Ireland and later reappeared to become useful and respected members of the population.

On September 18, the first trans-Atlantic land plane landed at Rineanna as Pan-Am opened the battle of the Atlantic with a proving flight in a Douglas DC4 Skymaster aircraft which had crossed the ocean in 9 hours 29 minutes.

On October 21, the last American Export Airlines flying boat left Gander for Foynes, and three days later American Export Airlines inaugurated a regular service, using DC4 Skymaster aeroplanes, to Rineanna, now officially known as Shannon Airport, and from there on to London and the continent. By November 9 the Aer Lingus Dublin–London route was resumed, using Douglas DC3 Dakota aircraft. The fare was £6 10s (£6.50) one way.

Five hundred tons of raisins arrived in Dublin Port on November 22 in good time for Christmas and by December, oranges were on sale again for the first time since before the war in Henry Street, Dublin, at 2d and 3d each.

On December 15, the details of a new Turf Bill were released. The Turf Development Board was to be dissolved and a new state-controlled company, Bord na Mona (Board of the Turf), was to be set up with a capital of £3–4,000,000 to extend turf production and to concentrate on machine-won turf.

Petrol was again available for private motoring from November, and just before Christmas there were queues for the first fully fashioned silk stockings to be seen in Dublin since before the war. Aer Lingus advertised for air hostesses and received over 400 applications.

The Abbey Theatre put on its first pantomime; only the fact that it was entirely in Irish allowed the Abbey to indulge in such a frivolous and popular form of entertainment and permit some of its leading ladies to appear in tights; it was a huge success and ran for 43 performances.

1946

COMMUNIST CONSTITUTION IN YUGOSLAVIA: NUREMBERG TRIALS: PERON PRESIDENT OF ARGENTINA: FRANCE RECOGNISES VIETNAM: GOLD COAST BECOMES GHANA WITH MAJORITY OF AFRICANS IN LEGISLATURE: FIRST UN GENERAL ASSEMBLY IN NEW YORK: BRITISH NATIONAL HEALTH ACT

Teachers Strike for Six Months

Two subjects dominated the first half of the year 1946; one was education – Dublin's National School teachers were on strike for more than six months of the year – and the other was the rapid development of air travel, now that the war was over. An air mail service was inaugurated between Eire and Great Britain on January 15, and the Statistical Abstract, published at the same time, revealed that even during the war years, and despite all the restrictions on travelling between the two countries, the number of people who flew to and from Britain annually had reached 15,000 by 1943.

The fact that the first post-war International Air Conference was held in Dublin seemed to indicate that the rest of the world acknowledged Ireland's unique position at the cross-roads of the trans-Atlantic air routes. In March, the Government acquired land for a new town to serve Shannon International Airport. And throughout 1946, air development remained in the news as work started on the building of a new 200-foot-wide runway at Collinstown, as air agreements were signed between Ireland and the UK, France and the United States.

The first Aer Lingus air hostesses proved an instant success with the passengers. A service to Le Bourget, Paris was inaugurated in June, run jointly by Aer Lingus and Air France, and although the foreign travel allowance fixed on June 8 at £75 in any one year was far from generous, a great many Irish people went to France to see it again.

The Dublin teachers went on strike in March for better wages and conditions; they were supported both by the parents and by the teachers in the country. On October 5, thousands of parents took part in a protest march organised by the Irish National Teachers' Organisation, against the Government's refusal even to discuss the question of wages unless the teachers first went back to work.

Then the Catholic Church weighed in, on the side, as usual, of the Establishment. The Catholic Archbishop of Dublin appealed to the teachers to go back to work, regardless of the rights or wrongs of the situation, for the sake of the children. And on October 30, the teachers decided to do just that, and returned to work without having achieved anything.

Two snippets to indicate that if the war had changed the rest of the world, it hadn't changed Ireland very much. On May 6 an advertisement appeared in the *Irish Times*: Wanted, gentleman (Protestant) to help two ladies, house, garden, car, no maid, salary £6 a month. And Kilcroney Country Club amended its rules under pressure from the clergy to ban gambling and insist that women wear bathing wraps at all times outside of the swimming pool.

Rubber hot water bottles, nylon toothbrushes and American lipsticks were on sale in Dublin from May 21 for the first time since the war. Author Liam O'Flaherty – who was then living in Paris – advocated horse-whipping or the removal from the electoral register of all those people in Eire who refused to speak Irish, an extraordinary piece of extra-territorial impertinence which quite rightly was ignored by the Government. On July 6 a new Republican party appeared on the Irish political scene: it was known as Clann na Poblachta and its leader was Sean MacBride, son of Maud Gonne MacBride.

Sir Alexander Fleming, the discoverer of penicillin, received an honorary degree from TCD on July 3, the first Ford cars to be assembled after the war were completed in Ford's assembly plant in their Cork factory and Morris 8 HP saloons went on sale again at £270 plus £75 15s purchase tax.

In October, the German People's Car, the Volkswagen – arguably the best popular car ever made – became available to members of the Occupation Forces for £75. The Ford V8 was at that time selling in Ireland for £505, ex-Cork, with a tax of £16 a year and petrol consumption of 22 miles per gallon. The Volkswagen did near to 50 miles per gallon. Incidentally, the Volkswagen concession for Ireland went several years later to a well-known Dublin character, Stephen O'Flaherty, who at this period was selling pre-war German Adlers.

O'Flaherty, who wanted to get into the car dealership business after the war, had somehow discovered that on the outbreak of war, the Irish customs had impounded about 50 Adler motor cars (they can still be seen in old German films, stylised eagles spreading their wings across their radiators). These cars had arrived in Dublin in a CKD (completely knocked down) condition for re-assembly in Ireland, as was the custom, and O'Flaherty figured that the Germans, being a thorough and careful race, would almost certainly have included all the essential bits and pieces plus many spares, and would probably have taken precautions to see that they didn't rust. So he made a bid for these cars, sight unseen, after the war, and because the customs people wanted to get shut of them, he got them for peanuts. He was right about the cars; Ireland was the only country in the world where brand-new Adlers were flashing along the roads at a time when the Allies had forced the Adler factory to redirect its energies to sewing machines and typewriters. They were brilliant cars, years ahead of their time, the first with front wheel drive, the first with the gear change on the steering column. I had one. I've never had a better car since.

O'Flaherty became so convinced of the excellence of German mechanical products that he bid for the Volkswagen Beetle and secured the concession for the UK as well as Ireland. He later sold it, it goes without saying, at an enormous profit, and died a millionaire.

Paul Vincent Carroll's *The Righteous Are Bold* had a four-month record-breaking run at the Abbey Theatre and the Arts Theatre in Belfast was founded by Hubert and Dorothy Wilmot.

1947

BRITISH COAL INDUSTRY NATIONALISED: MARSHALL ANNOUNCES EUROPEAN AID RECOVERY PROGRAMME: INDIAN INDEPENDENCE AND PARTITION: BENELUX CUSTOMS UNION: PARTITION OF PALESTINE: PRINCESS ELIZABETH MARRIES PRINCE PHILIP MOUNTBATTEN: FIRST SUPERSONIC FLIGHT

Austerity Unlimited

For a time immediately after the war, things were a great deal worse in Ireland than they had been at any time during the war.

On New Year's Day it was announced that sugar production was down by 30,000 tons as a result partly of the strike of workers in the sugar industry, and partly of the poor harvest. On

January 4, the Government was forced to ration bread to 4½lbs of flour or 6lbs of bread per person per week.

Food of all sorts was scarce, far scarcer than it had been during the war and a lot dearer, too. And after only a couple of months of near-normal service, CIE, the new state-run transport monopoly, was forced to cut mainline services to four days a week because of the coal shortage.

The fuel shortage now started to affect industry also. Imports of coal from Britain had dropped alarmingly; and by February the Hammond Lane Foundry had been forced to close down, throwing 200 out of work. To make matters worse, the bad weather had caused transport disruptions and most of the 1946 turf harvest, spread out on the surface of the bogs to disperse its moisture content, was under several inches of water.

By February 11, the Government had cancelled all permits to buy coal; such coal as was available was reserved for vital industries and services, and by mid-February CIE was talking about cutting passenger and goods services down to three days a week; the Dublin Gas Company was warning of even more severe rationing, and Dublin fuel merchants were refusing to guarantee even the current month's fuel ration. A reflection of the times: a Mrs Gertrude Gahan of Crumlin was sent to jail for one month for stealing from the Dublin Gas Company a quantity of gas valued at between 2s and 3s (10p and 15p) by by-passing the meter with the aid of a bicycle tube. The Gas Company announced that it was doubling its force of 'glimmer men', who were now empowered to cut all supplies from 'gas pirates'.

Cattle trains were cancelled from February 19, and an export trade worth £156,000,000 was endangered. Fords of Cork laid off 150 workers and went down to a four-day week. Things were so bad that on February 16 the Catholic Archbishop of Dublin, Dr McQuaid, not a man given to encouraging indulgence or indeed any human weakness, granted his flock total dispensation from all Lenten fasting laws and practices, because he felt it was dangerous for under-nourished people to fast.

In February, CIE announced that it was possible that all passenger services in Ireland would close down unless further supplies of coal arrived from England, and the Electricity Supply

Board warned its customers that all domestic supplies of electrical current might have to cease very soon. The United States came to the rescue, notifying the Government that they had allocated 34,000 tons of coal to Eire.

On January 22, a British naval corvette, purchased by the Government for the new Marine Service, had arrived in Dublin Port under her new name *Macha* (after an ancient Celtic war goddess). In January, too, a film called *Hungry Hill* with Siobhan McKenna, at that time the leading Abbey actress, was previewed in London; later in the year another Irish film, *Odd Man Out*, with James Mason, Kathleen Ryan (a new Irish discovery) and Abbey actor F.J. McCormick was released.

A bill to make Shannon the first customs-free airport in the world was introduced in the Dail on January 28, a few days after a team of Aer Lingus personnel left for the US to learn how to operate the new Lockheed Constellation airliner.

In February official figures revealed that remittance money had totalled £6,000,000 in 1946; £4,664,000 of that sum from Great Britain.

On March 18, the Government announced that three Liberty ships had been purchased to bring 20,000 tons of Peruvian sugar and other essential supplies to Ireland; by now even firewood was on ration.

On June 5 the first Vickers Viking arrived at Dublin Airport carrying the Aer Lingus shamrock insignia, and later in June a second corvette purchased from the British, and renamed *Maev* (after a redoubtable Connemara Celtic queen in Irish mythology), went on show at Dun Laoghaire. In September Ireland's first Constellation, the St Brigid, arrived at Shannon to form the nucleus of a trans-Atlantic fleet.

On July 30, the Soviet Union blocked Ireland's application for entry to the UN on the grounds that Ireland had not helped the Allies to lay the foundations of that organisation. There was a strong feeling in Ireland that Russia's real objection to Ireland was that, as a Catholic country, she could always be relied upon to oppose the Communist bloc.

On October 1, Dubliners received their first coal rations since 1941; the coal turned out to be mostly very low-grade slack which would not burn at all unless used with plenty of dry wood and good turf. I remember one consignment of turf delivered at this period which was so wet that we had to hang the sods from the clothes line (in string bags) to dry it out a bit before it would burn at all.

By November, Britain was prepared to send more coal to Eire: Aer Lingus had inaugurated a new Dublin–Rome service (fares £33 single and £58 return) and Italy had made a gift of a 36-ton marble Pietà in gratitude for the relief sent to Italy from Ireland during the war.

The first ball-point Biro pen available in Dublin went on sale in November for 45s (£2.25) and on December 17 the Irish Turf Board (Bord na Mona) decided to try out Danish-manufactured machines for automatically harvesting turf.

1948

BRITISH RAILWAYS NATIONALISED: GANDHI ASSASSINATED: CHIANG KAI-SHEK DICTATOR OF CHINA: OEEC SET UP IN PARIS: BRITISH MANDATE IN PALESTINE ENDS: BERLIN BLOCKADE: REPUBLIC PROCLAIMED IN NORTH KOREA: UN DECLARATION ON HUMAN RIGHTS: MINDSZENTY ARRESTED

Attempt to Unseat King

The longest court case in Irish legal history, at least until then, came to an end on March 10, 1948. The hearing of the Foyle and Bann Fisheries case in the Dublin High Court took 48 days and the pleadings filled a 300-page volume, but in fact the dispute had been going on for hundreds of years and the legal arguments involved documents going back to the time of the Magna Carta and required resort to the ancient Brehon Laws of Celtic Ireland long before that again.

The action concerned the fishing rights of a branch stream – a tributary of the River Bann – running through territory which now found itself south of the border.

From Queen Anne's time, the fishing rights to this stream had always been regarded as the private property of the Society of Governors and Assistants of the New Plantation in London, popularly known as the Irish Society. In other words by that cartel of financiers, City Guilds and other adventurers which had undertaken to replant areas of Ulster with loyal Lowland Scots after the treasonable flight of the Earls of Tyrone and Tyrconnell in 1607 and had in the process turned the ancient city of Derry into Londonderry.

Not unnaturally, the local fishermen had never accepted this claim and had continued to fish the river on the sane and sensible grounds that since it was an Irish river the fishing rights belonged to the Irish. And when a native government took over the 26 counties of what was then the Free State, the Free State Attorney-General weighed in on the side of the local fishermen in what was, after all, no more than a dispute as to whether the fishing rights were private or public property.

The 80 Donegal fishermen (and the Attorney-General) argued that the Statute of Queen Anne which had bestowed the fishing rights on the Irish Society was inconsistent with the Constitution and therefore void, and among the interesting points that emerged during the legal discussions was the suggestion, made by Professor Theodore Moody of TCD, that King George VI had no valid right to the throne of England since the Convention Parliament which had offered the crown to William and Mary when James II absconded was an emergency one, not elected by the people, and therefore never legally convened. However, although the Foy and Bann Fisheries case did not succeed in unseating King George VI, it did settle the ownership of the fishing rights in favour of the locals.

For most of the people who lived there during that period, 1948 was the year when things started to return to normal. Gas rationing ended on January 15 and, on the same day, clothes rationing ended after six years.

Ireland was, ironically, a beneficiary under the Marshall Aid plan – ironically, because the plan was designed to aid the countries devastated by the war – and received economic aid from the States to the value of £19,750,000, some of it in the form of cotton, electrical equipment, lorries, petrol, coal and farm machinery.

By May, bread and flour rationing had ended and by August four of seven new ships ordered by Irish Shipping, Ltd had been launched. The Church appeared to have survived the war unchanged; two Catholic priests wealthy enough to have been able to afford to ride to hounds with the famous Galway Blazers had the temerity to object to the choice of 'a divorced person' (Mrs Mollie O'Rorke) as Joint Master.

When the results of the general election were announced on February 7, and it became clear that de Valera no longer had an overall majority, nobody – least of all Mr de Valera himself – believed that the utterly diverse Opposition parties could ever cobble together a coalition, but they did.

Ireland won the Rugby Union Triple Crown for the first time in half a century by beating Wales by six points to three in Belfast. I'll never forget the shattering roar that followed the final whistle. In those days, every alternate 'home' Irish match was played in Belfast and even the bitterest of Orangemen shouted, 'Come on, Ireland' to a team that included Catholic nationalists as well as Protestant Unionists. In fact, the only organisations which never recognised the existence of the border were the Rugby Football Union and the Church; both Catholic and Protestant headquarters of the Christian Church are situated in Armagh, where the respective Primates of All Ireland have their Sees.

A number of liberal Dublin citizens felt it necessary to found, on March 23, the Irish Association of Civil Liberties to keep an eye on the Government.

There were queues for English-made nylons, selling for 12s 6d a pair in the Dublin shops in May; these were the first nylons seen in Ireland, apart from a few pairs presented to Irish girls by American GIs stationed in Belfast in return for the pleasure of their company.

In July, Dr Noel Browne, the new and dynamic Minister for Health in the Coalition which was always known as the Inter-

Party Government – a reflection of the deep distrust of coalitions implanted in the Irish mind by de Valera – announced a £15,000,000 health programme of which about one-third was to be spent on tackling the problem of TB. Noel Browne, a consumptive himself, had never been inside the Dail before he became a Government Minister but one of his first actions, as soon as he was appointed, was to liquidate all the Health Department's assets (around £20,000,000 in investments), take a mortgage out on the next £10,000,000 which could be expected to accrue from the Hospitals Sweepstake, and embark on a massive programme to enlarge and improve existing sanatoria and build new ones. He succeeded in almost completely wiping out TB, with the help, it is only realistic to add, of new drugs never previously available.

In July the British Labour Prime Minister, Clement Attlee, on holiday in Ireland with his wife, signed a new four-year Anglo-Irish Trade Agreement giving Irish agricultural and industrial produce free entry into the British market, while still protecting some new native Irish industries by tariffs and other means.

The corvette *Macha* of the new Irish Naval Service (as the Marine Service had now become) left Dun Laoghaire on a voyage to the South of France to bring back the body of the poet W.B. Yeats – who had died in France in 1939 – for burial 'under bare Ben Bulben's head' in Co Sligo, as he had specifically requested in a poem. It was, and still is, widely believed that the French had long since forgotten where Yeats was buried but being a polite people were reluctant to disappoint the Irish delegation sent to Menton to recover the remains of their great poet (and being realistic enough, too, as the French are, to know that a corpse was unlikely to realise that it was the wrong one, or that it had been buried in the wrong place) had dug up some unfortunate French peasant and delivered him with pomp and circumstance to the Irish navy.

A major triumph for Irish enterprise was the announcement on August 26 that electricity generated from turf would be available for the first time before the end of the year. This on top of the news in June that the Turf Board had achieved a surplus of £10,600 in its first year of operation.

When, early in November, a shop in Donnybrook, Co Dublin, was burnt down and a woman killed and a small boy badly injured in a blaze caused by fireworks, the Irish Government very rightly and properly banned the sale of fireworks for private use, a ban which is still in force. Only professionally organised firework displays are permitted in Ireland and nobody has been injured by fireworks since.

It was the year the 'New Look' hit Dublin and ankle-length skirts became fashionable, the year Ireland acquired its first holiday camp, Butlin's at Mosney, Co Meath, in July.

Evie Hone's great stained-glass East window, depicting both the crucifixion and the Last Supper, for Eton College chapel in Berkshire, was unveiled, and President Sean T. O'Kelly signed the bill turning Eire into the Republic of Ireland.

1949:

NORTH ATLANTIC TREATY SIGNED IN WASHINGTON: COUNCIL OF EUROPE SET UP: GERMAN FEDERAL REPUBLIC ESTABLISHED: CHINESE COMMUNISTS DRIVE NATIONALISTS OFF MAINLAND: UN WARNS OF DANGER OF CIVIL WAR IN KOREA: APARTHEID IN SOUTH AFRICA: BERLIN AIRLIFT

Arm Now to Take North

At the beginning of January the Irish Hierarchy sent a letter of protest to the Hungarian Government, calling for Cardinal Mindszenty's immediate release from detention. The Hungarian Government did not deign to reply.

The first white flour since the early days of the war went on sale in Dublin in January, and in February the Government set up an Industrial Development Authority to investigate areas of possible industrial development, and to examine the effects of Ireland's protectionist policies.

Complaints about the treatment of passengers on the Dun Laoghaire–Holyhead mail boats continued to pour in; in February a British MP complained of people being treated at Holyhead 'like Irish cattle'. (Why Irish cattle, one wonders: were British cattle given preferential treatment?)

In March the Government leased the Chief Secretary's Lodge in Phoenix Park, which had been vacant since 1923, to the American Government to be used as a home for the US Ambassador to Ireland.

The first post-war motor car to be seen in Ireland was the Austin A40 which had appeared in 1948; much more popular with Irish drivers was the Morris Minor which went on sale in April, 1949, for £397. Trans-Atlantic flying was still a luxurious way of travelling; on April 4, the latest state-of-the-art airliner, the 71-ton, double-deck, Pan-Am strato-cruiser, arrived at Shannon Airport. It had a downstairs lounge bar, where travellers could stretch their legs and get acquainted, if they could manage to do so without tripping over all the air hostesses. The ratio of passengers to crew was 34 to 25.

In Washington, Sean MacBride told reporters that Ireland would not join NATO (the North Atlantic Treaty Organisation) until the British cleared out of Northern Ireland. The Northern Ireland Government, for its part, banned all meetings to celebrate Costello's declaration of the Republic, mentioned above, and the Executive Commission of the International Olympic Games Committee decided that in future athletes from Northern Ireland would be considered as being members of the British sports associations.

Visitors to Dublin that spring included Pandit Nehru, the Indian Prime Minister, and the Liquat Ali Khan, Prime Minister of Pakistan. Sean MacBride, who, as early as that, had suggested a form of European Parliament based in Strasbourg, represented Ireland at a meeting in London with the five Brussels Treaty powers (the Benelux countries, France and West Germany) and the three Scandinavian countries to carry the idea further.

The Ireland Bill, 1949, containing the specific guarantee to Northern Ireland mentioned above, was published on May 3; leaders of all the Irish political parties protested to Britain about it, and de Valera described it as 'the final act of aggression'. On May 10, the Dail unanimously passed a resolution calling on the British Government and people to 'end the present occupation of our six north-eastern counties'. Another Union Jack was burnt outside Trinity College, Dublin, and the leaders of all the main parties stood on the same platform in O'Connell Street at a mass rally to protest against the bill.

On May 16, at Westminster, MPs voted 345 to 21 to keep the Northern Ireland guarantee in the Ireland Bill, and on the next day, in the Republic, posters urging the Irish people to 'Arm Now to Take the North' were torn down by the Civic Guards.

Four British Parliamentary Secretaries who voted against the Ireland Bill were dismissed on May 18 and a fifth resigned, anticipating dismissal. For the record, they were: J.P. Mallalieu (Food); F. Beswick (Air); R.J. Mellish (Admiralty); G.H.R. Rodgers (Supply) and W.R. Blythe (Civil Aviation).

On May 19, the Unionist Party won every seat it contested in the Belfast Corporation Municipal Elections, and on the second reading of the Ireland Bill in the Lords on May 23, Lord Killanin said that by leaving the Commonwealth Costello had locked the door on Partition, and the British Government's guarantee to the Six Counties was like taking the key out of the lock and throwing it away.

Tourist earnings were £35,000,000 in 1948 as against £18,000,000 in 1946, but the chief of the travel section of the European Co-operative Administration, a Colonel Theodore Pozzy, who had come to Ireland as part of a drive to attract more tourists, said on departing that he would not advise too much publicity in the United States until the standard of the hotels had been raised a bit. A few days later the Hotel and Restaurant Federation decided to establish a staff-training scheme.

Still smarting from the guarantee to Northern Ireland, the Government decided on June 16 to set up an Irish News Agency to supply Irish news to media abroad; its main purpose would be to ventilate the Government's feelings about Partition.

The first meeting of the Council of Europe in Strasbourg on August 8 was attended by an Irish delegation which included Sean MacBride and towards the end of August it was announced that Conor Cruise O'Brien had been appointed to take charge of the Information Section of the Department of External Affairs, the department which would control the Irish News Agency.

During the year the Censorship Board had banned George Orwell's *1984* as well as a report by a Royal Commission on population in the UK because it contained references to contraception.

1950–1960

❧

A Plan For Prosperity

Despite the astonishing display of ineptitude represented by the Inter-Party Government's declaration of the Republic of Ireland in 1949, the Costello Coalition remained in office for nearly three years until they were brought down by the Hierarchy's refusal to entertain even the most elementary form of socialised medicine, and Dr Noel Browne was forced to resign.

At the subsequent general election in 1951, the Republican party, Clann na Poblachta, was almost wiped out. When Noel Browne and a couple of fellow-dissidents from that party joined with the Independents in voting against Costello, de Valera managed to get enough votes to form a government, his seventh since 1932, but it was an unsatisfactory compromise and for the next four years the country lurched along in the doldrums.

Another election in 1954 put another Inter-Party Coalition Government back in, again under Costello. There was still a grave balance of payments problem despite the credit that Ireland had built up by supplying Britain with farm produce during the war, unemployment had passed the 90,000 mark and the annual emigration total varied between 30,000 and 50,000 (some say the true total was nearer 80,000 in the late Fifties) every year.

A coalition government composed of elements which had almost nothing in common, apart from their deep dislike of de Valera, could not possibly hope to cope courageously with all the problems that faced the country, though the young and able Minister for Finance, Gerard Sweetman, was already encouraging a bright top civil servant, Ken Whitaker, to draw up a comprehensive plan for economic recovery.

In February, 1957, after a no-confidence motion, the Dail was again dissolved and at the age of 75 de Valera fought his last campaign, and one of his most vigorous. He got his majority: 78 seats, nine over all others in the Dail.

Now, for the first time, a new breed of young men began to make their presence felt in Dail Eireann. They were all too young to have been involved in the Civil War, and too realistic to allow themselves to get bogged down in past history. It was clear to them that Ireland had achieved as much, politically, as was likely for some considerable time; the thing to do now was to forget about politics for a while and get down to the job of putting the country on a sound basis economically.

Sean Lemass – often described at the time as managing director of Eire, Teo (Ireland, Ltd) – took over from Eamon de Valera in 1959. The bright young men in the Dail were now sure of a sympathetic hearing and the managerial revolution was almost complete.

But de Valera did not leave the political scene without one final appeal to 'the people'. He had been proposed as President in succession to Sean T. O'Kelly and was opposed by General Sean McEoin, one of the legendary freedom fighters of the War of Independence and a staunch pro-Treaty, Cosgrave man. At the same time, Fianna Fail tried to get rid of the system of proportional representation which had resulted in the two Coalition Governments.

Both issues were put in a referendum simultaneously; not only that, but the question on proportional representation was so worded that voting Yes didn't mean yes, you were in favour of proportional representation, it meant yes, you were in favour of abolishing it.

This enabled the Fianna Fail propaganda to be both

After the Act of Union, many of the former homes of the Irish MPs and their followers in the Dublin Georgian squares degenerated into slums. An inquiry into the capital's housing in the period just before World War One revealed that more than 21,000 families were living in insanitary conditions in Dublin tenements.
Topham Picturepoint.

Evictions continued well into the first decade of this century. Widespread use of the boycott led to a series of Land Acts which turned the Irish tenant farmers into peasant proprietors.
Illustrated London News.

Maud Gonne was an ardent nationalist, married to Major John McBride, who led an Irish brigade against the British in the Boer War. The poet W. B. Yeats was in love with her all his life; she was his Cathleen Ni Houlihan, the personification of Ireland.
National Museum of Ireland.

The statue of Charles Steward Parnell, inexplicably wearing two overcoats, was erec by the Irish Nationalist Parliamentary Party commemorate their lost leader. He was depo after his marriage to Kitty O'Shea followin, a celebrated divorce case.
Hulton Deutsch.

Michael Collins (left), legendary Head of Intelligence of the Irish Republican Army
during the War of Independence and Commander-in-Chief of the Irish Free
State army during the Civil War, with his second-in-command,
General Richard Mulcahy.
Topham Picturepoint.

J W Alcock and A W Brown crash-landed in a field in Galway after
the first non-stop trans-Atlantic air crossing in 1919.
Topham Picturepoint.

The first scheduled flights, operated by American troop transport planes like the
Douglas DC4 Skymaster, began to arrive at the new international air terminal
near Limerick - today's Shannon Airport - after 1946.
Hulton Deutsch.

The Orange Order's Derry Apprentice Boys March (to commemorate the closing of Derry's gates in the face of James II's army) in August, 1969, started a series of prolonged riots which ultimately led to the deployment of the first British troops in Northern Ireland later that year.
Hulton Deutsch.

On May 16, 1976, Tim Severin set out with a crew of five in an oxhide-covered replica of the boat of Brendan the Navigator, to prove that it was possible that the Irish saint could have crossed the Atlantic in such a craft, nine centuries before Columbus 'discovered' the New World.
Hulton Deutsch.

Jack Charlton (Saint Jack to the Irish), manager of the Irish football team and hero of the 1994 World Cup in the US, greeted on his return by Albert Reynolds (centre) and Dick Spring (left). The Irish won their first match in New York before a crowd which included 15,000 Irish followers who had flown over specially for the match (including Taoiseach Albert Reynolds and most of the Cabinet).
Press Association.

Charles Haughey, intermittently Taoiseach and leader of the Opposition during the eighties, at the helm of his motor yacht en route from mainland Ireland to his private retreat of Inishvickillane.
Irish Press.

Five people died and ninety-one were injured when a thirty-pound bomb exploded outside Harrods department store in Knightsbridge, London during the Christmas shopping rush on Saturday December 17, 1983.
Syndication International.

In June 1963, US President John F. Kennedy
paid a visit to Ireland. Here he is seen with
President Eamon de Valera at Arus an
Uachtarain, in Phoenix Park, Dublin.
In May 1993, Ireland's first woman president,
Mary Robinson (inset, bottom right),
had tea with Queen Elizabeth II,
the first meeting between the British
and Irish heads of state for
seventy-one years.
Main picture: Popperfoto.
Inset: Hulton Deutsch

extremely simple and extremely misleading. 'VOTE YES AND DE VALERA', the posters urged, thereby implying – to people who didn't examine the issue too closely – that only in this way could they secure for Dev the signal honour he so richly deserved of becoming Ireland's First Citizen and Head of State for the declining years of his life.

But the people were quick enough to spot that there was a bit of over-simplification here designed to deprive them of a system of voting which they felt had afforded them some measure of protection against the dangers of political dictatorship.

The result was unequivocal: it was NO AND DE VALERA by an overwhelming majority on both counts. Proportional representation was retained and de Valera moved into the sumptuous surroundings of the Viceregal Lodge, while the young men of the Fianna Fail Party got out the Whitaker Plan again and took another look at it.

The main idea behind the plan was simple enough: that public money should be diverted, for the time being anyway, away from hospitals, sanatoria and social services and concentrated on productive investment – investment that would be likely to lead to increased production for export.

Whitaker had been quick to see the flaw in the earlier approach to industrialisation. Such factories as had been built in the new Irish State were intended to make Ireland self-sufficient, as far as possible, in consumer goods. But, as the Irish market was a small and dwindling one, they never offered very much in the way of employment and could never produce goods able to compete, either in price or in quality, with the imported equivalent.

There had been a slight revival in Irish industrial activity during the Emergency, when the shortage of imported goods made it possible for Irish industrialists to sell almost anything they turned out, but as soon as the post-war austerity period was over, it became increasingly clear that any plans for further industrial expansion must be export-orientated. This was the conclusion initially reached by Whitaker.

The keystone of his plan was an attempt to attract foreign capital and industrial expertise to the Republic by offering grants and loans to firms prepared to transfer some of their man-ufacturing capacity to Ireland and by allowing them a tax-free holiday. It was true that the profits from any new enterprises Ireland might be able to attract in this way would leave the country, but the wages paid to the workers and all the money spent on power, transportation and other infrastructural services would help the economy along in all sorts of ways. It was also hoped that the expertise which these foreign industrialists would bring to Ireland might spread to some of the older Irish industries.

Allied with this attempt to attract foreign investment there was to be a big drive to make the older Irish industries more competitive. The plan envisaged the gradual removal of import quotas and a progressive scaling down of the protective tariffs – some of them still as high as 60 per cent – behind which Irish industry had been huddling for years. Some of the more pro-gressive Irish firms had already realised the way the wind was blowing and had been concentrating on increasing their own efficiency and on building up their own export markets. To enable the other, less progressive, ones to meet the challenge any form of common market would bring, the Government set up councils to advise on mergers and the rationalisation of pro-duction and marketing and to discuss ways of increasing productivity with both managements and unions. Money was also made available for grants to enable these firms to increase their efficiency, initially at any rate, at the expense of the state.

The first programme for economic expansion was experi-mental in its approach and modest in its targets. It covered the years from 1959 to 1963 and envisaged an annual growth in the Gross National Product of 2½ per cent a year. It is doubtful if this meant a great deal to the average Irishman at this stage, but the plan did give the impression that the Government knew what it was doing, and that in itself was a very welcome change.

At long last, it seemed, the rot had been stopped and the Republic had a Government that was looking forward into the future and not back on the past.

Somewhere in Simla . . .

The decade began on a cheerful note with the publication on
January 1 of the Trade Statistics for the first 11 months of 1949;
they recorded a £12,000,000 increase in exports to Britain and
Northern Ireland, mainly food products. Aer Lingus claimed
another record year, with 13,000 more passengers than 1948's
total of 193,000 and in fewer planes; Aer Lingus had by now settled on a standardised version of the DC3 Douglas Dakota,
carrying 24 passengers, one of the safest and most versatile
planes ever built.

Premier Costello left for Rome, to be received by the Pope on
January 13 in celebrations connected with the first post-war
Holy Year. Marshall Aid to the tune of $45,000,000 for the fiscal
Year 1949–50 was allocated to the Republic of Ireland on
January 17, and a contract was signed for a £1,000,000, 488-bed
sanatorium for Glanmire, Co Cork; later in the month Dr Noel
Browne opened two new 40-bed units at the Royal National
Hospital for Consumption in Newcastle, Co Wicklow. But the
past was not yet entirely forgotten: over 10,000 people attended
the unveiling by President Sean T. O'Kelly of a monument at
Soloheadbeg Cross to commemorate the ambush in January,
1919, when two members of the RIC were shot dead in the first
incident of the War of Independence.

At the end of January, initiating the building of a sub-regional
250-bed sanatorium at Ardkeen, Co Waterford, Noel Browne
announced that his short-term programme to provide 2,000 beds
for TB patients had now been completed. And although he
went on opening new sanatoria throughout the year, he was

already working on a new project which was to bring him into sharp conflict with the religious establishment. But first he clashed with the medical establishment when he publicly deplored the attitude of the Irish Medical Association whose members believed that nothing in the way of improved health services should be introduced unless it first had the unqualified approval of that association.

On February 2, Eamon Andrews, the Irish radio commentator and Theatre Royal quiz compere, was invited by the BBC to join the 'Ignorance Is Bliss' TV team, and became the first of a long line of Irish TV personalities who dominated British radio and TV for nearly fifty years; others included Terry Wogan, Gay Byrne, Brian Inglis, Frank Delaney, Anthony Clare, Gloria Hunniford and Henry Kelly.

It was a sign that the end of austerity was at hand when the emergency dumps of sodden turf which had lined the main road through Phoenix Park for years gradually began to disappear as it was sold off at £1 a ton, to be replaced by low-grade American coal which also, eventually, had to be sold off.

Premier Costello told the Fine Gael Ard Fheis (annual conference) on February 14 that while the use of force to end Partition had been rejected, the Government still intended to raise the Partition question as an international issue at every available opportunity.

Announcing that the new Industrial Development Authority was to undertake an exhaustive survey of industry in Ireland, Dan Morrissey, the Inter-Party Government's Minister for Industry and Commerce, told the Dail that in 1926 only 102,000 people in Ireland had been engaged in industry and the services; now the figure was 200,000, an increase of over 90 per cent.

Predictably, there was a good deal of resistance from some industries at any suggestion of an investigation into their affairs. Fifty traders protested that a clause in the bill setting up the Industrial Authority forced them to give evidence and information about their financial status, claiming that the whole thing savoured of the Star Chamber and would give the IDA greater powers than even Hitler or Stalin had ever possessed.

After a series of strikes (shipping, trains and buses), caused principally by growing differences between British Unions with a continuing membership in Ireland and the new Irish Unions which had been gradually replacing them, it was decided in August that the NUR (National Union of Railwaymen, one of the largest British Unions) was to withdraw from Ireland, presenting the country with a sum of money to enable its 10,000 Irish members, North and South, to establish their own unions.

The first hint that the Irish might have been a shade overoptimistic about the importance of Shannon as the hub of all future trans-Atlantic air travel came early in August, when BOAC decided to dismiss its entire staff at Shannon. All the company's operational and meteorological work would in future be done in London, and traffic handling would be done by Aer Lingus staff. The trans-Atlantic schedule was cut to two flights per month via Shannon; all other BOAC flights would overfly Shannon.

CIE's city bus station, the prestigious new bus station designed by Michael Scott to be an example of Ireland's new architectural flair, was handed over to the Department of Social Welfare, which elected to use it as an office building, in effect Dublin's principal labour exchange. The widely-held view in Dublin was that the decision was aimed as a snub for the de Valera Government which had commissioned it.

On August 11, Irish delegates to the Council of Europe at Strasbourg created a scene by raising the Partition issue yet again during an important motion by Churchill, who was trying to create a European army. Three days later, after 19 years in Kilmainham, the headquarters of the Civic Guard were moved to Phoenix Park, near McKee army barracks, which looks as if it should have been built in India, as indeed it should; the story goes that some idiot in the British Civil Service got the plans mixed up and that there is a stern granite, slated building, ideally suited to the rigours of the Irish winter climate, somewhere in Simla.

Ireland's transportation systems were going through a bad period. As early as March, CIE, the Republican transport monopoly, announced losses of £1,205,476, while the Great Northern Railway Company, still based on Belfast, reported losses of £91,497 for the year. In August the Northern Ireland Government decided that it would not buy out that part of the GNR company operating in Northern Ireland; and the shareholders called on the Chairman, Lord Glenavy, to close the company down altogether, to avoid further losses. In the Republic, the Grand Canal company, which had operated the barge traffic on Ireland's canals, was wound up after 178 years and its assets were nationalised under a Transport Bill designed to nationalise all transportation in the Republic.

There was a draft agreement during the year between the Ministry for Industry and Commerce in the Republic and the Northern Ireland Ministry of Finance to share the costs of establishing the proposed River Erne hydro-electric scheme.

In September, the Irish Government announced that it proposed to borrow £15,000,000 to finance housing, electricity, land reclamation, re-afforestation and other development schemes; this brought Ireland's total borrowing up to £156,000,000, a sum which represented a national debt of £52 for every man, woman and child in the Republic, quite a tall order at a time when teachers were earning a maximum of about £500 a year.

Three young Dublin architectural students – Tony Jacob, Des Dalton and Sean Kenny – sailed an old 36-foot gaff-rigged cutter called the *Ituna* from Dun Laoghaire, 6,000 miles across the Atlantic via Brest, Bermuda and New York, to join Frank Lloyd Wright's architectural school in Wisconsin. Sean Kenny subsequently became a well-known theatrical designer.

1951

NORTH KOREAN AND CHINESE TAKE SEOUL: LES SIX SIGN
PARIS TREATY: BEVANITE REVOLT SPLITS BRITISH LABOUR
PARTY: BURGESS AND MACLEAN FLEE TO USSR: KING
ABDULLAH OF JORDAN ASSASSINATED: PERON RE-ELECTED
PRESIDENT OF ARGENTINA: ATOMIC ELECTRIC POWER

Republic Ruled from Maynooth

The year 1951 began with a situation with which the Irish were
to become all too familiar over the next couple of decades; the
bank officials were on strike and all the banks were closed. In
any industrialised, or semi-industrialised country, a bank strike
would be regarded as a major crisis and would not be permitted
to continue for more than a couple of days; in Ireland, it didn't
seem to make much difference. People wrote cheques on the
backs of envelopes and on odd scraps of paper, which were
cashed by the local grocer or publican. In this and in subsequent bank strikes, a lot of people lost a lot of money when the
banks opened again and the envelopes and scraps of stamped
paper started to bounce, but in the meantime life went on and
people continued to spend as if there was still plenty of money
around.

On January 9 it was announced that the Governments of
Northern Ireland and the Republic had agreed to purchase the
GNR; the shareholders would be compensated in cash, and the
railway run by a joint board. Dealings in GNR stock were immediately suspended and the 10,000 shareholders were not at all
pleased at the price they were offered: £3,900,000 (later
increased to £4,500,000) for the lot – tracks, locomotives, rolling
stock, signal boxes, stations, buffets and all.

When the price of coal jumped from £6 14s (£6.70) to £8 5s
(£8.25) a ton – it went up another £1 in March – the Government
announced yet another new national campaign to increase turf
production, and by the end of the month railwaymen had joined

the bank officials on strike, Money had to be freighted by air to Dublin to large firms experiencing difficulties in laying their hands on enough cash to pay their staffs.

It was perhaps typical of this particular period in Ireland that when Premier Costello intervened in the bank strike on January 22, it continued, regardless; on the other hand, when Archbishop McQuaid took a hand in sorting out the transport strike on January 22, the men went back to work straight away. Fares went up immediately to recover £1,000,000 lost on wage increases. Towards the end of the month the bank workers accepted a recommendation by a Banking Arbitration Tribunal, and eventually went back to work after nearly a month.

The Bishops' Lenten Pastorals, which warned that social security 'always brings danger', should have been a warning to Dr Noel Browne, but on March 6 he announced the details of his Mother and Child healthcare scheme. Basically, it did no more than offer to provide free maternity and post-natal care both for mother and child, without any conditions and without a means test.

The scheme had already been bitterly opposed by the medical profession, just as Bevan's National Health plan was initially opposed by the doctors in Britain, and perhaps it was the sinister proximity of the new, Godless, welfare state, just across the water, which proved too much for the bishops. The Catholic Hierarchy sent a letter to Costello, informing him that Noel Browne's proposals were contrary to Catholic moral teaching. They believed the health of both mother and child alike to be a matter for the individual (ie, the father) and always provided that that particular individual had been fully counselled by the Church, his right to act (or fail to act) in furtherance of the health of mother and child was not a matter which could safely be abrogated by the state. Furthermore, they deeply disapproved of any welfare scheme which might encourage local medical officers to discuss gynaecological matters with Catholic women, since those discussions might even include references to the dread topics of contraception and abortion.

Nobody was a bit surprised when Costello caved in instantly; the Cosgrave pro-Treaty Sinn Feiners and subsequently the Cumann na nGaedheal and Fine Gael parties had all been staunch, almost abject Catholics. It was said that Cosgrave could not bring himself to pass a Catholic church without nipping in for a short session of prayer, and it is certainly true that his entire party and all its successors walked in far greater fear of Mother Church than did de Valera and his followers, many of whom had risked and survived the worst punishment the church could possibly prescribe, at any rate on this side of the grave: excommunication. What was a bit more surprising was that the leader of Noel Browne's radical Republican Party, Sean MacBride, should cave in equally easily.

By April 8, before his scheme had even been discussed in the Dail, Noel Browne was forced to resign and the Northern Ireland Attorney-General was warning the Belfast Orange Lodge that the parliament of Eire might well sit in Dublin but the real rulers of the country sat in Maynooth.

The Dail was dissolved on May 4, and in the general election that followed Fianna Fail was returned with an overall majority of two seats. One of the new Fianna Fail government's first decisions was to restore the Store Street building to its original purpose as a central bus station.

Television was seen in Ireland for the first time on the stand at the RDS Dublin Spring Show; the British Home Office refused to return Casement's remains to Ireland; and the fuel shortage became so acute that the Government offered holidays with pay to any students prepared to spend their vacations digging turf. The Abbey Theatre was burnt to the ground on July 17 and the Abbey Players moved first to the Rupert Guinness Hall and then to the Queen's, an old variety theatre in Pearse Street.

When the Belfast Arts Theatre brought Jean Paul Sartre's *Huis Clos* to Dublin, they were requested by the governors of the Royal Irish Academy – where the performances were given – to remove the name of the author from all publicity and programmes on the grounds that he was known to have religious beliefs which might prove offensive to Irish audiences. A producer called Felix Mendelssohn cancelled a tour of the Republic by his Hawaiian serenaders and accompanying hula-hula dancers because of advance objections from the clergy to 'lightly-clad girls'.

Irish TV enthusiasts attempting to filch British programmes from the ether with aerials on masts as tall and as elaborately stayed as those of the *Cutty Sark*, reported that reception from the new Holme Moss transmitting station near Manchester had proved 'disappointing', and 16 paintings by Jack B. Yeats at the Victor Waddington Galleries in Dublin were sold for £6,580 within 24 hours of the opening of the exhibition. A gala performance of Balfe's *The Rose of Castille* in the old Theatre Royal, Wexford, marked the opening of the first Wexford Festival. Orson Welles was picketed as a Communist by the Catholic Cinema and Theatre Patrons Association when he turned up in Dublin to see Maura Laverty's play *Tolka Row*.

Professor Walton, a fellow of Trinity College, Dublin, shared the Nobel Prize for Physics with Sir John Cockcroft, Director of Britain's Atomic Energy Establishment at Harwell.

As the year ended, the upturned, 6,700-ton American Liberty ship the *Flying Enterprise* was still afloat 300 miles off the south-west coast of Ireland with only Captain Carlson on board.

During the year, two new Irish cultural institutions had come into existence, An Chomhairle Ealaion (the Arts Council) and Comhaltas Ceoiltoiri Eireann (Brotherhood of the Musicians of Ireland), a society formed to foster interest in traditional music.

1952

ACCESSION OF ELIZABETH II: FIRST CONTRACEPTIVE
TABLET: CHURCHILL ANNOUNCES BRITAIN HAS ATOM
BOMB: KING FAROUK OF EGYPT ABDICATES: INDIA'S
FIRST NATIONAL ELECTIONS: EUROPEAN DEFENCE
COMMUNITY FORMED IN PARIS: HUSSEIN KING OF JORDAN

Two Lord Mayors for Derry

When, in November 1950, Aer Lingus had been awarded the Cumberbatch Trophy for an unblemished air safety record, many people felt it was only a matter of time until the company had a serious accident. And on January 10, 1952, came the company's first fatal crash. An Aer Lingus Dakota, the *St Kevin*, crashed on Moel Siabod in the Welsh mountains en route from Northolt to Dublin; and all 23 people on board were killed.

A census of the population published in January indicated that the number of women emigrating annually had increased by 44 per cent since 1936. A so-called 'fertility inquiry' in connection with the census which was published later in the year revealed a tendency towards smaller families – by Irish standards, that is. Of the total of married women, it was found that 17.4 per cent had no children, 27.1 per cent had one or two, 32 per cent had three, 18.7 per cent had six to nine and 4.8 per cent had ten or more.

The new Irish Tourist Board began a campaign to entice Irish emigrants to return to Ireland for their holidays. Tourism had earned £32,000,000 in 1950.

President Sean T. O'Kelly, by now 70, was unopposed and was re-elected President of Ireland in a one-minute ceremony in the Custom House, Dublin on May 16. The mortality rate from TB was now down to 0.78 per 1,000 of the population, the lowest figure ever recorded.

On May 30, Alderman Eddie McAteer (Anti-Partitionist) was defeated by eleven votes to seven by Alderman Samuel Orr

(Unionist) in the elections for Mayor of Derry City. Alderman McAteer nevertheless insisted on occupying the Mayoral Throne alongside Alderman Orr on the grounds that he had equal right to the position which had been denied to him 'because of gerrymandering and trickery'. Expanding on the point, he explained that the 32,000 Nationalists in the Derry area could only send eight representatives to the Corporation while, as a result of gerrymandering of the constituencies, the 18,000 Unionists were represented by twelve members.

In June, the Taoiseach Sean Lemass turned the first sod in a series of archaeological excavations of the area around the Hill of Tara in Co Meath and, in October, the remains of 112 Stone Age crannogs (lake dwellings built on piles) were discovered during excavations at Lough Gara in Co Westmeath.

Walter Macken's *Home is the Hero* ended a 20-week run at the Abbey Theatre (still playing in the Queen's) and Brendan Behan made his first mark as a writer with two plays, *Moving Out* and *The Garden Party*, both broadcast by Radio Eireann. One of the films of the year was *The Quiet Man*, based on the novel by Maurice Walsh, starring Maureen O'Hara and John Wayne and filmed partly in Ireland.

Alterations were made to the Carlisle Pier in Dun Laoghaire to improve facilities for tourists coming to Ireland by boat; but despite the expenditure by the Government of £25,000 on the pier, and by CIE of £3,000 on refurbishing the buffet at Dun Laoghaire station, passengers still complained that they were being treated like cattle, both in Holyhead and Dun Laoghaire.

On July 30, the Government published a White Paper on new and extended health services to be provided by the local authorities; lower income groups would get full medical, hospital and specialist services free; and maternity cases, all children under six weeks old and all National School children would receive free hospital and specialist services.

A report on the Irish News Agency was issued on November 25: in the period between March 1950 and March 1952, it had cost £70,738 against a gross revenue of £4,523. The Government granted it a further subsidy of £38,500 to keep it going.

Legislation to make adoption easier was passed, the Irish Management Institute was founded and the first poteen case to come before the courts in 30 years was heard in Co Wexford. Brendan Francis Behan, describing himself as a journalist, was fined £15 at Lewes Court, Sussex, for entering Britain at Newhaven (from Dieppe) while under order of prohibition, and was deported to the Republic.

The Electricity Supply Board reported that it had drawn up contracts with a French firm to construct power stations for a hydro-electric scheme for the River Lee; 3,500 acres of Co Cork would be flooded.

1953

EISENHOWER INAUGURATED US PRESIDENT: DEATH OF JOSEPH STALIN: HAMMERSKJOLD ELECTED SECRETARY-GENERAL OF UN: KENYATTA CONVICTED OF MANAGING MAU MAU: ROSENBURGS EXECUTED AS SPIES: ARMISTICE IN KOREA: EVEREST CONQUERED BY HILLARY AND TENZING

Strike on Here

By 1953, Downey's pub in Dun Laoghaire had become famous all over the world as the pub with the longest strike ever recorded: it had been picketed for over 14 years by members of the Irish National Union of Grocers', Vintners' and Allied Trades' Assistants who were protesting against the employment by the proprietor, James Downey, of non-union labour. The pickets were frequently changed during the 14-odd years of the strike, but they all remained on extremely good terms with Downey and his non-union assistants, who always sent out cups of tea for them and sometimes invited them in for a free drink in bad weather. In the bar, the proprietor displayed postcards from all over the world from people who had visited the pub and were wondering how the strike was going.

On May 30, James Downey died and later the pub was taken over by his brother-in-law. On November 27, the pub opened under the new management and with a new staff, all members of the union. The picket was finally called off after the longest strike in trade union history: 14 years, 8 months and 24 days, but the pickets were not allowed to leave without a final drink on the house.

From April 5, Ireland was At Home to the World for three weeks after the President had opened the first Tostal (pageant). This was a concept which had been dreamed up by the Tourist Board the previous year, in an effort to bring more foreign tourists to Ireland, though nobody knew what it was supposed to commemorate.

Initially it consisted of nothing more than would have been on offer anyway in the theatres, restaurants and hotels in Dublin and throughout the country. The only concession made by the Government to celebrate the occasion was the provision of a 'Bowl of Light', a vulgar construction of Perspex with integral flickering lighting, designed to adorn O'Connell Bridge. The Bowl of Light was universally known in Dublin as 'The Thing' and was quickly and quite rightly uprooted from its moorings and flung into the Liffey by discerning architectural and engineering students of UCD.

But although the Tostal died the death after the first few years, the idea of festivals as a way of promoting tourism in Ireland lived on and now there is an oyster festival in Galway, a beer festival in Kilkenny, a film festival in Cork, a theatre festival in Dublin and a festival for something, somewhere, every day in the week and every week in the year. Of all the festivals, the most successful has probably been the Rose of Tralee competition, now in its 35th year and still going strong. For the last 20 or 25 years it has been broadcast by RTE (Ireland's radio and television network) over two nights with Gay Byrne interviewing some 30 to 35 prospective Tralee roses from all over the world. The only condition is that they must have had an Irish parent or grandparent, or an Irish great-grand-parent or some equally tenuous connection with the ould sod, which allows for the possibility of a contest between a San Francisco rose, a

Melbourne rose, a Dublin rose and a Galway rose, as well as at least one rose from Germany.

On January 31, the MV *Princess Victoria* sank near the Copeland Islands at the entrance to Belfast Lough; only 44 survived out of the 372 people on board in Ireland's worst peace-time sea disaster.

In February Ireland's National Stud paid £25,000, then a world record price, for the Aga Khan's unbeaten Tulyar. The capital of the National Stud was doubled on February 13 to £500,000. Although stud fees were astronomical, local farmers with likely mares were allowed to put their names in a hat, and the winner acquired the services of Tulyar for a nominal sum.

On March 23, the Minister for Posts and Telegraphs Erskine Childers announced a new campaign to encourage savings: the Government, he said, required £600,000 for industrial and agricultural development and added that the only way this could be obtained was through the savings of the people.

On April 1953, Madame Maud Gonne MacBride died at Roebuck, Co Dublin, aged 88. The Blasket Islands, the most westerly inhabited islands in Europe, were evacuated during the year and the inhabitants re-settled on the mainland. Dublin cinema proprietors decided not to show the film of the Coronation of Queen Elizabeth II because of the risk of damage to their own premises and on June 9, books were burned in Northern Ireland in a protest organised by the Revd Ian Paisley against 'modernism'.

In July, fashion buyers from England and America attended Sybil Connolly's spectacular and much publicised show at Dunsany Castle, which included some striking adaptations of traditional Irish costumes that brilliantly utilised Irish tweeds. And a Dublin dentist, Dr Jimmy Mooney, won the Edinburgh Cup for the International Dragon Class yacht races at Cultra, Co Down, competing against, among others, the Duke of Edinburgh.

The tiny Pike Theatre was founded by Alan Simpson and Carolyn Swift in a Dublin mews, and Sam Beckett published two books, *L'Innommable*, in French, and *Watt* in English.

On September 1, Taoiseach de Valera left for a holiday in

Lourdes, Fatima and San Sebastian, and on his way back was a guest of Sir Winston Churchill at 10, Downing Street.

In October, the Allenwood peat-fired power station in Co Kildare, the largest in Europe, was opened, and the new bus station, known in Dublin as the Busarus, was opened by Sean Lemass.

1954

NASSER PREMIER OF EGYPT: FALL OF DIEN BIEN PHU: MALENKOV ELECTED PRESIDENT OF USSR: TERRORISM IN ALGERIA: COMMUNISTS OCCUPY HANOI: US HYDROGEN BOMB TESTS AT BIKINI ATOLL: FIRST VERTICAL TAKE-OFF AIR-CRAFT: BANNISTER RUNS MILE IN UNDER FOUR MINUTES

Kildare Street Club in Retreat

Early in the year it was announced that under the provisions of the new Health Act, 1954, and the Maternity and Child Regulations, 1954, surgical, midwifery and hospital and specialist services would be provided 'free of cost for the majority of women, with small contributions for the balance'. Provision was also made for dental, ophthalmic and aural services for children up to the age of 16.

From August 1, there would no longer be a 'poor man's' health code, either: a new permanent card would replace the old system by which a 'blue card' – a sign of reduced circumstances – had to be produced every time a 'poor' family required medical care.

When Fine Gael won a couple of by-elections in Louth and Cork City, Taoiseach de Valera announced an early general election, and dissolved the Dail on April 24.

During the election campaign, that last bastion of the West British in Dublin, the Kildare Street Club (at the bottom of Kildare Street, overlooking the Trinity College cricket pitch, where the reassuring clunk of leather upon willow could still be heard) was forced to sell part of its premises in an effort to keep afloat; it was one of the many signs of the times.

On April 17, President O'Kelly opened the second Tostal with the Pageant of St Patrick, the most ambitious open-air pageant ever staged in Dublin. It was a dismal failure.

When the votes in the general election were counted, Noel Browne lost his seat on the first count. The final strength of the parties came out at 65 for de Valera's Fianna Fail against 82 others, and once again John Costello was elected Taoiseach of an Inter-Party Coalition Government.

On June 20 the President of Sinn Fein, Geroid O Broin, told a Wolfe Tone commemorative service at Bodenstown that the arms taken in a raid on Armagh (on June 12 when 15 men dressed in British Army uniforms had stolen 300 rifles and automatic weapons from the military barracks at Armagh) would be used against the British forces in Northern Ireland.

The Dublin Brigade of the IRA pressed for the removal of Nelson's Pillar in June and called for the erection there instead of a memorial to the men of 1916.

In July the American film director John Huston arrived in Ireland to film Melville's *Moby-Dick* in Youghal, Co Cork. Canned beer went on sale for the first time at the RDS Horse Show in Ballsbridge in August, and in September the first oyster festival opened at Clarenbridge, Co Galway with oysters priced at 6s (30p) a dozen.

In October, the tourist allowance was raised from £50 to £100, a plaque was affixed to Oscar Wilde's birthplace in Merrion Square, Dublin and a new play by Brendan Behan, *The Quare Fella* (a jail drama about a man on Death Row),had its first production at the tiny Pike Theatre.

In December, architect Michael Scott bought the Martello Tower at Sandycove, the location of the first scene in James Joyce's *Ulysses*, for £4,700; later he turned it into a Joyce Museum.

1955

BULGANIN SUCCEEDS MALENKOV AS PRESIDENT OF USSR:
TREATY FOR EUROPEAN UNITY RATIFIED: EDEN SUCCEEDS
CHURCHILL: BRITAIN SUBMITS DISPUTE WITH ARGENTINE
OVER FALKLANDS TO INTERNATIONAL COURT: POLIO VAC-
CINE DISCOVERED BY SALK: WEST GERMANY JOINS NATO

Don't Talk Through Your Hat

Shortly before he became Taoiseach of an Inter-Party Coalition
Government for the second time, John Costello gave an interview to the *Yorkshire Post* in which he claimed that he was
prepared to meet the Prime Minister of Northern Ireland, Lord
Brookeborough (formerly Sir Basil Brooke) at any time to discuss matters of common concern.

Reluctant to let Costello steal the limelight again, de Valera
immediately gave his own views on the matter to the *Yorkshire
Post*, endorsing the idea of North-South talks and giving the
project his own (totally unsolicited) blessing.

Bryan Maginess, Acting Premier of Northern Ireland during
Lord Brookeborough's protracted visit to the US and Canada,
was quick to reply. He was agreeable that the talks should take
place, he said, but only on certain conditions: there was to be no
discussion of Partition and the constitutional position of
Northern Ireland must be accepted as final before any talks
could take place.

And that ended the matter; on the following day, February 18,
Taoiseach Costello declared that Maginess's conditions for the
North-South talks were 'impossible of acceptance by an Irish
Government'.

On February 15, geologists urged the Government to start
drilling for oil in West Clare where, according to a TCD survey,
there were considerable deposits of oil and natural gas. This
would hardly be worth mentioning if it were not for the fact
that after repeated nudgings from dozens of geologists, the

Irish did eventually find rich veins of natural gas off the southern coast of Ireland and there have been some proven finds of oil in that part of the Atlantic which washes the western coast of Ireland, though most of it is too deep to be worked in sufficient quantities to make it viable for the moment. Other geologists, pressing the Government to dig for gold and precious metals in Wicklow, Tynagh and elsewhere, did eventually succeed in establishing Ireland as the leading supplier of lead and zinc in Europe.

Tony O'Reilly, later to become one of the most highly-paid businessmen in the world (as chief executive of the Heinz Corporation) made the news in January 1955 when, at 18 years of age, he was capped to play for Ireland after only six games in senior Rugby.

The bank officials had become restive again, and the banks were open for only two hours every day from January 24 because of curtailed hours being worked by officials pending settlement of current disputes.

On February 28 over 1,200 people queued for the 400 gallery seats in the Gaiety Theatre to see Sean O'Casey's new play *The Bishop's Bonfire*; all the other seats had been booked months in advance. There were disturbances in the theatre and riots in the streets outside, with many people who could not possibly have seen either the script or the play carrying placards denouncing it as a blasphemy.

In March Dublin dockers, like dockers around the world, opposed a plan to introduce drive-on, drive-off freight lorries to accelerate cargo handling. A horse called Quare Times, ridden by Pat Taaffe, was trainer Vincent O'Brien's third successive Grand National winner on March 26.

In April the Municipal Gallery of Modern Art declined the offer of Rouault's *Christ and the Soldier* for a second time – it remained in Maynooth College, the seminary, where apparently neither the priests nor the clerical students were upset by its irreverent modernism. Dublin's Municipal Gallery of Modern Art also turned down a gift of one of Henry Moore's reclining figures.

Sinn Fein reappeared on the political scene when Unionists

won ten of the 12 Northern Ireland seats in the British general election of May 27; the other two were won by Sinn Fein candidates both serving jail sentences. Donegal lobsters were exported to France for the first time in June at 43s (£2.15) a dozen and a Dail Committee on Procedure and Privileges circulated a list of useful phrases in Irish for deputies to use in the Chamber; these included Mar dhea! (Says you!) and Abair e! (Hear, hear!) as well as approximations for 'Don't be talking through your hat', 'Sit down' and 'Talk sense'.

In July the Government announced that a new oil refinery would be built at Whitegate, Co Cork where the harbour offered docking facilities for the new super-tankers.

BBC television programmes broadcast from the new Divis transmitter in Northern Ireland were clearly received along the east coast of Ireland and led to a sharp increase in the sale of TV sets in Dublin. By the end of September the *Irish Times* had started to publish regular reviews of BBC television. In November the first successful television test transmission was made from the Republic; the event covered was the Amateur Boxing Association Tournament on November 15.

On September 11, the National Ploughing Association announced that it would provide a dowry of £500 for young women who could prove that they could plough, provided that they also married before the age of 25, and settled on the land.

One of the first of the foreign-owned factories, a German Faber-Castell plant to manufacture pencils, was opened in Fermoy, Co Cork in September, and Ireland became a full member of the United Nations in December.

On October 15, a request by the Archbishop of Dublin, the Most Revd Dr McQuaid, that a match arranged between the Republic of Ireland and Yugoslavia for October 19 should be abandoned in view of the imprisonment of Archbishop Stepinac, was supported by many of the Catholic organisations in Dublin. Despite this, and despite representations from the Department of Justice, the Football Association of Ireland decided to go ahead with the match anyway.

It was then learned that President O'Kelly would not be attending the match. The Football Association countered this by reporting that the demand for tickets was, nevertheless, very heavy. Next the Army No 1 Band was withdrawn, and no substitute band seemed to be willing to take its place. The Yugoslav Ambassador to London expressed regret at the intolerance revealed by the entire affair.

On October 18 it was announced that the Irish team's trainer, Civic Guard Dick Hearns, had withdrawn his support and assistance from the team. It was perhaps a sign of the changing times that all these attempts to sabotage the match failed completely, and a capacity crowd of 21,400 watched Yugoslavia beat Ireland at Dalymount Park while Christopher Gore Grimes of the Association of Civil Liberties argued at a technical students' debate that the attendance of over 21,000 people at the match proved that 'this was no longer a clerical state'.

During the year, the Pike Theatre staged the first production in Ireland of Sam Beckett's *Waiting for Godot*, a curiously bleak piece of theatre about two tramps, Vladimir and Estragon, who are waiting, in what may or may not be the right place, on what may or may not be the right day, for someone they think they remember as called Godot, who may or may not have promised to meet them. What Godot intends to do, or is expected to do for them, is never made clear – indeed neither of them is all that clear about meeting Godot – and the play, if you could call it that, contains the most nihilist exchange in the entire history of Franco-Anglo-Irish drama. After their endless, desultory dialogue has been briefly interrupted by two other characters, Lucky and his slave, Pozzo, Vladimir cheerfully remarks: 'That passed the time.'

Estragon's dour reply? 'It would have passed in any case.' There is not much that anybody can add to that.

1956

USSR TANKS INVADE HUNGARY AFTER HUNGARIAN RISING:
SUEZ CRISIS: PAKISTAN BECOMES ISLAMIC REPUBLIC:
ARCHBISHOP MAKARIOS DEPORTED TO SEYCHELLES: ISRAELI
TROOPS INVADE SINAI: RELEASE OF CARDINAL MINDSZENTY:
TRANS-ATLANTIC TELEPHONE SERVICE INAUGURATED

Let's All Buy Killarney

The Irish Censorship Board marked the new year by banning *Molloy*, by Sam Beckett, *The Quiet American* by Graham Greene and *Lolita* by Vladimir Nabokov. *Picture Post* was also banned because of some 'suggestive' pictures it had carried of the film star, Anita Ekberg.

The Government offered tax concessions to firms interested in developing mineral resources in Ireland; as an added inducement it was promised that there would be no tax on profits for the first five years.

In June, the Trustees of the Estate of the 7th Earl of Kenmare put 8,300 acres of the most beautiful landscape in Ireland, if not the world, on the market, including two of Killarney's famous lakes and fells. I was editor of the *Times Pictorial*, a weekly tabloid run by the *Irish Times* Group, at the time, and we ran a campaign under the slogan 'Let's All Buy Killarney'. Our idea had been to start a fund and let the Irish people buy the estate and employ the Tourist Board to run it for them. But before we could get anything organised it was clear that negotiations for its sale were already well advanced and in August it was announced that it was to be sold to an American millionaire. The lakes have since been handed back to the State.

On January 26, the *Irish Times* reported a new boom in ballroom dancing; the newspaper estimated that 4,500 Dublin people went dancing every night. The Dublin Gate Theatre players left for a tour of Egypt on February 20, and on the same day in Detroit, Robert Monteith died, aged 77; he had been one of the two men who landed on Banna Strand with Roger Casement from a German submarine in 1916.

In April the Mining Corporation of Ireland started to drill for copper in Co Meath and for lead, zinc and silver in Co Monaghan. A new village of 104 houses for turf workers was opened in Kilcormac, Co Offaly and in London, one of the Lane pictures, *Jour d'Eté* by Berthe Morrisot, was stolen in broad daylight from the Tate Gallery by a member of the National Students' Council, who simply took it off the wall, wrapped it in a sheet of brown paper he had brought in with him, and walked out of the gallery with the painting under his arm, both as a protest at the British refusal to acknowledge that the paintings had been intended for Ireland, and as a demonstration of the poor care and attention they were receiving in British hands. Five days later, after the protest had made world headlines, the picture was handed in to the Irish Embassy in London in perfect condition.

On May 1, for the first time since the establishment of the Royal National Hospital for Consumption at Newcastle, Co Wicklow in 1896, the annual general meeting learned that they now had some empty beds. And in May, too, the Dublin Corporation decided to accept the offer by the Friends of the National Collection of the Rouault *Christ and the Soldier* and a Henry Moore *Reclining Figure* which the Municipal Gallery had previously turned down.

On May 17, the 33,000-ton liner *America* arrived in Cobh dressed overall in honour of the Tostal which was celebrated this year with the Pageant of Cuchulain in Croke Park, another disastrous piece of proof, if any were needed, that unlike their next-door neighbours, the Irish have no flair for pageantry.

On June 1, provisional figures for the latest census, taken on April 8/9, 1956, revealed the population at 2,894,822, the lowest ever recorded. Net emigration between 1951 and 1956 averaged 40,079 a year.

Louis (Satchmo) Armstrong gave two concerts in Dalymount Park, Dublin. Cork had its first film festival and over in London, at the Theatre Royal, Stratford East, Brendan Behan's play *The Quare Fella* was produced by Joan Littlewood.

More importantly, perhaps, T. Kenneth Whitaker (39) was appointed Secretary to the Department of Finance on May 29. Towards the end of June, Councillor Robert Briscoe, TD, became the first Jewish Lord Mayor of Dublin, and F.H. Boland, former Irish Ambassador to the Court of St James in London, became the Republic's first permanent representative at the United Nations in New York. Dr C.S. (Tod) Andrews, Managing Director of Bord na Mona, left for Russia to study the peat industry there. Russia, being plagued, like Ireland, with millions of acres of the unpromising material, had developed some sophisticated new techniques for utilising it.

In September President O'Kelly unveiled, in Wexford, a statue to Commodore John Barry, an Irish emigrant who had founded the American Navy, and Garret FitzGerald, later to be Taosieach of Ireland, was appointed Assistant Commercial Manager of Aer Lingus in October. In October, too, there was a highly organised attack on the border posts by the IRA in a campaign code-named 'Operation Harvest', master-minded by Thomas MacCurtain, son of the Lord Mayor of Cork who had been murdered in front of his family by the British forces of law and order in March 1920.

The Government announced a new plan for health insurance always referred to as 'the voluntary'; it was an attempt to provide a semi-state contributory system of Medicare for the better-off to supplement the free, means-tested scheme now available to the lower-paid.

On December 2, Ronnie Delaney became an Irish hero when he won a Gold Medal at the Olympic Games in Melbourne, Australia, running 1,500 metres in a record-breaking 3 minutes 41.2 seconds.

1957

MACMILLAN SUCCEEDS EDEN: ISRAELI TROOPS WITHDRAW
FROM SINAI BUT REMAIN IN GAZA STRIP: GHANA BECOMES
INDEPENDENT STATE: ROME TREATY FOR COMMON MARKET:
MAKARIOS RELEASED: NEHRU FORMS NEW INDIAN CON-
GRESS MOVEMENT: WOLFENDEN REPORT ON HOMOSEXUALITY

Solutions to Border Problem?

Petrol rationing was re-introduced in January, following the Anglo-French attack on Egypt over the Suez Canal, and refugees continued to arrive in Ireland from Hungary, after the suppression by the Russian tanks of the rising the previous year. The first 180 refugees had arrived in October, 1956.

There was hardly a day, throughout the year, when the papers didn't report trouble of some kind on or near the border. Police and customs huts, bridges and railway lines, even drill halls used by the RUC were constantly being blown up, and a continuous stream of men kept coming before the courts, North and South, charged with offences against the state.

The Taoiseach, John Costello, possibly making a second effort to achieve a slight measure of immortality before finally quitting the political scene, came up with his own 'federal' solution to the border question at the Fine Gael Ard Fheis on February 5. He proposed to *allow* (the italics are mine) the continuation of a separate legislature for the Six Counties, or for a smaller area containing a homogeneous majority of those opposed to reunion. The powers over the Six Counties currently reserved by the British Government would then be transferred to a democratically-elected Parliament for All Ireland.

On March 3, another 'federal' solution came from an unexpected quarter; Cardinal Dalton, Primate of All Ireland, proposed that each of the Six Counties of Northern Ireland should be allowed to choose between Dublin and Belfast for the administration of all local affairs. If the North then agreed to accept federation with the Republic, Ireland could rejoin the

Commonwealth as an independent republic with the same status as India, and would then be in a position to offer its naval bases to NATO.

Needless to say, neither of these suggestions found a very warm welcome in Northern Ireland. Replying to Costello's proposal, the Northern Ireland Minister of Home Affairs, W.W.B. Topping, said: 'We are asked to exchange our position as a member of the greatest company in the world, with branches everywhere . . . for a subordinate position in a company with a doubtful past and an even more dubious future.'

At the 27th National Ploughing Championships, held in Boyle, Co Roscommon, in February, it was announced that this was the last championship in which horse-drawn ploughs would be eligible.

At a general election in March, de Valera was returned with a majority of 25; Sean MacBride lost his seat, but Dr Noel Browne, who stood as an independent, was elected. One of the first actions of this new government was to 'run down' the activities of the ill-fated Irish News Agency and by the middle of July it had ceased to exist.

The Hungarian refugees – a group of about 200 was housed at Knockalisheen army camp, Co Limerick – went on hunger strike to draw attention to their anxiety to get out of Ireland and off to America or Canada.

Dublin's first international theatre festival opened on May 8, as part of the Tostal attractions. And on May 12, Alan Simpson produced Tennessee Williams's play *The Rose Tattoo* in his tiny Pike Theatre as his contribution to the festival.

On May 21, he had a visit from the police who warned him that he was breaking the law and that he would be liable for arrest if he didn't take the play off immediately. The play was not banned; in fact it was openly on sale in Dublin, and its choice had been approved by the festival council, and so he paid no attention.

On May 23 he was arrested, jailed overnight in the Bridewell prison and charged under an old Victorian law, a relic of the British rule, with 'having produced for gain an indecent or profane performance'. It was the production on stage of a condom which made it in the eyes of the law indecent and profane.

The proceedings dragged on for nearly a year. The police witnesses claimed privilege and refused to reveal who was behind the prosecution; and although in the end it was found that there was no case against Simpson, he was not awarded costs, and the Pike Theatre never really recovered. A large part of the bill for costs was subscribed by Simpson's supporters, among them John Osborne, Sean O'Casey, Peter Hall, John Gielgud and Wolf Mankowitz.

In Northern Ireland a bill was passed in June to prevent members of illegal organisations from going forward as candidates for election to Stormont. In the Republic, 63 members of Sinn Fein were arrested in a swoop on July 7, and the next day an internment camp was set up in the Curragh to accommodate them, and 200 additional Civic Guards were sent to police the border. By August all roads to the North of Ireland were sealed off; only approved routes manned by customs, RUC and Civic Guards remained open. The RUC (Royal Ulster Constabulary) had replaced the RIC in Northern Ireland from 1922.

In August, too, Louis Elliman, Director of Dublin Film and Television Productions, Ltd formed a new company to build and run Ardmore Studios (Ireland) Ltd at Bray, Co Wicklow, to make films in Ireland and promote an Irish film industry.

In September, 20 of the Hungarian refugees still interned in Knockalisheen army camp absconded and entered the UK illegally, and in October signals from the first Russian earth satellite Sputnik were picked up in Dublin. I saw it clearly, from Sandymount Strand, winking its way across the stupendous cyclorama of Dublin Bay; ironically, or perhaps prophetically, my small son Michael, who was with me, couldn't see what I was making all the fuss about. I say ironically because he now works as editor for CBS Television News in Tokyo and uses satellites as regularly and as casually as I use the telephone.

As the year ended, 40 men were released from Belfast Jail on parole; the internees at the Curragh elected to stay there rather than give any undertaking to be of good behaviour, and other prisoners in Mountjoy went on hunger strike in protest against the rejection of their claim to be treated as political prisoners. The Northern Ireland Government reckoned that the 'disturbances' during the year had cost the state at least £1,000,000.

1958

EGYPT AND SUDAN PROCLAIM UNITED ARAB REPUBLIC: BRUSSELS WORLD EXHIBITION: KRUSHCHEV SUCCEEDS BULGANIN: CASTRO REVOLUTION IN CUBA: EMERGENCY IN ADEN: DE GAULLE TAKES OVER IN FRANCE: EXECUTION OF IMRE NAGY IN HUNGARY: RACE RIOTS IN NOTTING HILL

Irish Speak Out at UN

During the early, heady days of UN membership, the Irish delegates, understandably, wanted to make their presence felt in the assembly, and the Irish newspapers, equally naturally, reported their interventions in every debate in considerable detail. Indeed, it is probably not much of an exaggeration to say that whenever an Irish delegate got up on his hind legs to say a few words in the General Assembly, or put down a motion for discussion, the Irish newspapers usually gave him a headline.

Throughout 1958, Minister for External Affairs Frank Aiken and the Irish delegates concentrated on a few key issues: the suggestion that both the Russian and the Western forces should withdraw, step by step, from Central Europe; a proposal that the nuclear 'club' should be limited to those countries which already possessed atomic weapons and that members of that club should refuse to share nuclear technology, even with their allies, as a first step towards total nuclear disarmament; the argument that the admission of Communist China to the United Nations should at least be discussed despite China's deplorable behaviour in Tibet; and firm opposition to partition as the solution to any political problem in Cyprus or elsewhere.

On February 11 the Archbishop of Dublin, the Most Revd Dr McQuaid, announced that he was withdrawing his permission for religious services to be held to inaugurate An Tostal, 1958, because the drama programme included a play by Sean O'Casey and a dramatisation of James Joyce's *Ulysses*. Three days later the Dublin Tostal Council announced that they were dropping O'Casey's *The Drums of Father Ned*, and *Bloomsday* by Alan McClelland from the programme. Later in the year O'Casey banned all performances of all his plays in Ireland until further notice.

The dancing boom continued. The most popular venue in Dublin was the Gresham Hotel, where for 8s 6d (45p) you could dance every Saturday night in evening dress from 8 pm to midnight. During the week, you could also dance in the Gresham and the Metropole and Shelbourne, if you could lay your hands on a pair of tickets for the countless staff dances which were held there between 9 pm and 2 or 3 am every week-night.

A course in television techniques opened in February at the Institute of Science and Technology in Kevin Street, Dublin (always known in Dublin as the Kevin Street Tech), and in March Mr Justice George D. Murnaghan was appointed Chairman of a Commission to consider the establishment of a national television service and to make recommendations on the subject to the Government.

On March 20, the Minister for Justice informed the Dail that there were still 131 men interned in the Curragh Camp for political offences. In Belmullet, Co Mayo, fear of the wrath of the little people stopped all work on a drainage project when 20 men downed tools rather than dig up a rath, a circular mound in the centre of a field, believed to be a dwelling place inhabited by fairies. On the same day, radar was installed at Dublin Airport, and on April 28 came the departure from Dublin of the first flight to the US by Aer Lingus Super Constellation *Padraig*.

The ban on married women teachers was revoked by Minister for Education Jack Lynch, and by October over 250 married women had taken up permanent employment as National School teachers. On June 24 Irish Army officers joined a United Nations patrol for the first time on the Lebanon border, and on the same day, Dr Frances Moran, Regius Professor of Law, became the first woman member of the Governing Board of Trinity College, Dublin.

In July, the Dublin dentist, Dr A.J. Mooney, won the Duke of Edinburgh Cup in the International Dragon class yacht races at Cultra, Co Down, for the second time, and sailed back to Dun Laoghaire with the cup wrapped in a spare sweater and stowed in the bow of his boat.

Dr C.S. (Tod) Andrews, who had made such a success of managing the Turf Board, was appointed Chairman of CIE, the transport monopoly, with powers very similar to those subsequently given to Dr Beeching in Britain. He was handed a pretty straightforward brief: to provide a reasonable, efficient and economic transport system and to see that it paid its way within five years.

A plant to produce electrical power from milled peat – the first to be built outside Russia – was opened at Forbane, Co Offaly, by Sean Lemass, Minister for Industry and Commerce, on September 15. On September 25, the actress Glynis Johns arrived in Ireland to appear with James Cagney in *Shake Hands with the Devil*, the first film to be made at Ardmore Studios and on location in Ireland. And on the last day of the month, the last GNR train arrived from Howth; from midnight, all GNR trains operating within the Republic became CIE property, and all services north of the border came under the Ulster Transport Authority.

In October the first report of the Voluntary Health Insurance Board revealed that it now had 16,000 subscribers, representing 52,000 people. Canadian mining experts arrived for the official opening of St Patrick's copper mines at Avoca, Co Wicklow, leased by the State to a subsidiary of Consolidated Mogul Mines, Ltd, and it was announced that the Department of Industry and Commerce was negotiating with several American oil companies for the rights to explore for oil and natural gas in the Republic and the seas around it.

The Irish delegation to the United Nations drew the attention of that organisation to the fact that Ireland could provide experienced administrators who, with their non-colonial background, would almost certainly prove more acceptable to emergent nations than administrators from former imperial powers.

On October 29 the Government announced a bill to amend the Constitution and substitute the single member constituency straight majority vote for the system of proportional representation which had been used ever since the state was founded. But by November 17 pressure in the Dail had forced them to introduce legislation for a referendum on the issue in 1959.

Dublin's first shopping arcade, Creation House, off Grafton Street, was opened in October at the height of the hula hoop craze which had spread to Ireland from England during the summer. The Censorship Board banned 23 books, including Brendan Behan's *Borstal Boy* in November, and on the last day of the year, the last train ran from Harcourt Street to Bray; Tod Andrews had decided to close the line and substitute a bus service.

1959

CASTRO BECOMES PREMIER OF CUBA: EFTA ESTABLISHED: DALAI LAMA ESCAPES TO INDIA: FIRST MEETING OF EUROPEAN COURT OF HUMAN RIGHTS: ALASKA BECOMES 49TH US STATE: UN CONDEMNS APARTHEID: EMERGENCY IN SOUTHERN RHODESIA: FIRST HOVERCRAFT CROSSES CHANNEL

Drive for Economic Expansion

On January 5, Sean Lemass, Minister for Industry and Commerce, announced that an agreement had been made with the Messman Rinehart Oil Group of Texas to explore the Republic for oil and natural gas over a period of ten years. A few days later it was announced that the Government had signed an agreement with the Verolme United Shipyards of Holland, completing the purchase of Cork Dockyards from Irish Shipping, Ltd, and launching a £5,000,000 ship-building business in Cork Harbour.

Knockalisheen camp closed on January 7, after 24 months' occupation by Hungarian refugees; the last nine had left the camp towards the end of 1958.

In February the Trade Union Congress and the Congress of Irish Unions agreed to merge as the Irish Congress of Trade Unions after a split of 14 years. The last of the internees were released from the Curragh camp by mid-March, despite a protest from the British Prime Minister Harold Macmillan. Ireland's first cattle-breeding and research station was set up at Moorepark, Co Cork by the Mitchelstown Cooperative Agriculture Society and Aer Lingus ordered three trans-Atlantic 707 jet airliners from Boeing.

On April 3 the Government decided to accept the advice of a Commission on Income Tax and introduced the British Pay As You Earn system. Brendan Behan's *The Hostage* was playing to packed houses at the Théatre des Nations in Paris, and copies of the 'black' diaries of Sir Roger Casement, published in Paris, were seized and held by the Dublin Customs.

The Government allocated £250,000 towards the rebuilding of the Abbey Theatre, destroyed by fire in 1951, Radio Eireann banned some of the songs from the musical comedy *Gigi* as 'unsuitable' for Irish ears, and the first cargo of oil was unloaded at the new refinery at Whitegate, Co Cork.

The architect Michael Scott received the Royal Institute of Architects' gold medal for his design for the Busarus, the central bus station. Gael Linn (Irish Reign or Lifetime), an energetic and progressive language revival movement founded in 1953 had received a small (£3,250) grant from the Department of Education to enable it to make films in Irish and in June it produced the first of a series of Irish weekly newsreels known as *Amharc Eireann* (*View of Ireland*). George Morrison, an independent film producer, made a successful documentary, *Mise Eire* (*I am Ireland*). A Commission on University Accommodation recommended a new £8,000,000 building programme to transfer UCD from the city centre to Belfield, in Stillorgan, a few miles outside Dublin.

After the referendum which said Yes to de Valera as President and No to the abolition of proportional representation, de Valera was inaugurated President in the Throne Room, St Patrick's Hall, Dublin Castle on June 25 and his deputy, Sean Lemass, became Taoiseach.

A permanent Anglo-Irish Trade Committee was established on July 13 to examine economic questions and improve trade between the two countries. The first helicopters to be seen in Ireland were imported from the United States by a new Shannon-based company, Irish Helicopters, Ltd, in July.

Erskine Childers became Minister for the new Department of Transport and Power on July 23. In July, too, the British Government announced that the Casement diaries would be made available to scholars and historians.

In August, a Government survey on the first year of the phosphate subsidy scheme, part of the five-year economic programme, had brought an increase of 25 per cent in the use of fertilisers by farmers. A small 'pilot' fish processing plant to can Irish mackerel for the American market was opened in Dunmore East, Co Waterford; Johnstown Castle in Co Wexford was taken over by the Agricultural Institute and the TB Sanatorium in Ballinrobe, Co Mayo, was taken over by the Agricultural Institute for use as a sheep research centre.

In September the Revd Ian Paisley of the Free Presbyterian Church of Ulster was fined £5 for disorderly conduct at a public meeting in Ballymena, and Sean Lemass officially opened the £12,000,000 oil refinery at Whitegate.

The Gaiety Theatre was packed on September 28 for the first night of *Posterity Be Damned* by Dominic Behan, Brendan's young brother, and a dramatised version of Donleavy's *The Ginger Man*, with Richard Harris, in the same theatre, was withdrawn after three days because the producer and author refused to make cuts demanded by the theatre management.

The most ambitious technical course – a full four-month training programme for pilots for the new Boeing 707 jet airliners – was launched by the City of Dublin Vocational Education Committee, and the Lee hydro-electric scheme was opened at Inniscara, Co Cork on September 30.

In October, the foreign travel allowance was increased by £150 to £250 a year, General Mulcahy resigned the leadership of the Fine Gael party and John A. Costello resigned as leader of the Opposition in the Dail; James Dillon, son of the last leader of the Irish Nationalist Parliamentary Party, took over in both capacities.

In October, too, a Government-sponsored board took over the management of greyhound racing in Ireland. The Irish have always been a great betting people, and for those not affluent enough to follow the horses, greyhounds always provided an acceptable alternative. Coursing (trials of dogs, usually greyhounds, set on a released hare) had always been popular in Ireland, but in 1927 the first greyhound track as such was opened in Ireland at Shelbourne Park, Ringsend. From 1928, the Easter Cup, the Greyhound Grand National, to commemorate the Easter Rising, was always held there. The most famous Irish greyhound, Mick the Miller, won his first race on April 28, 1928 and his last in 1931; in 1935 he had a part in a Gainsborough film, *Wild Boy*. Greyhound racing was equally popular in Northern Ireland where the first greyhound track, at Celtic Park in Belfast, was also opened in 1927.

In November, the Taoiseach told the Dail that Britain had at last agreed to the return of the Lane pictures, no big deal really since the National Gallery in London has more good pictures in storage than it could ever hope to show in a year of Holy Thursdays.

December saw the passing-out parade of the first 12 Ban Gardai (Women Civic Guards) at the depot in Phoenix Park, and 47 Irish horses being exported to Amsterdam for slaughter for human consumption died on board ship during a storm.

1960–1970

❦

When the Going was Good

For the Irish, the swinging Sixties were the Golden Years, the first years of plenty, the period when the Republic established an unmistakable and perfectly valid national identity in its own right, no longer largely dependent on or even automatically associated with Britain.

The Whitaker Plan appeared to be working like a dream. By 1963, at the end of the first five-year period, the Government was able to announce that instead of the projected 2½ per cent annual growth in Gross Domestic Product, a rate of over 4½ per cent had been achieved, and that industrial exports had doubled.

And nobody suspected that this was government propaganda because you only had to look around you to see the evidence of the new prosperity on all sides: brand new cars parked outside spanking new double-garaged, four-bedroom detached houses; shining new tractors and trailers parked alongside brightly painted new barns and outbuildings; shops and department stores bursting with a greater variety of consumer goods than the Irish had ever clapped eyes on before.

During the period about 200 new factories had been built and 27,000 new jobs created in industry and the services. For the first time since 1923 the population decline had been halted, and then reversed, and emigration was down to around the 20,000 a year mark, as some emigrants were tempted to return to the Emerald Isle.

The range of products being manufactured in Irish factories set up by foreign investors was impressive. They included plastic piping (Dutch); wood veneers (British); greeting cards (American); pencils and ball-point pens (German); pianos (Dutch); cranes (German); chewing gum (American); cutlery (German); ships (Dutch); aeroplane parts (French); and sewing machines (Japanese).

In these days of universal and almost obsessive privatisation and demoniacal denationalisation, it is perhaps worth noting that what then looked like the Irish economical miracle could only have been achieved with the aid of the state-sponsored bodies, which were initially set up to provide essential services and utilities not likely to prove profitable enough to attract private investment. The provision of power by harnessing the rivers was one; the development of a sugar beet industry and the industrialisation of turf production were others. These state-sponsored companies were run exactly like public companies, except that they were answerable, not to a board of directors, but to the Government Minister responsible. They were financed by the taxpayers, by floating public loans or by commercial loans from Irish and foreign banks, backed by Government guarantees. In general they were non-profit-making, and the Government was happy enough if they paid their way. Often their activities were interdependent and inter-related; for example, the Electricity Supply Board bought turf from the Turf Board and sold power to CIE, the state-sponsored transport monopoly.

By 1970 there were 43 of them responsible for such diverse activities as the provision and distribution of fertilisers and cement; the organisation of the bloodstock and greyhound industries; the processing, sale and distribution of Irish agricultural produce and the development and financing of the new Irish industries as well as the marketing of their output.

Between them, the state-sponsored companies set up by the

Irish Government to promote, develop and market Irish industrial produce, and the foreign industries attracted to Ireland by the Whitaker Plan, managed to export an extraordinarily diverse collection of products to some of the most unlikely corners of the world including turf briquettes (to Norway); razor blades (to Russia); transistor radios (to Switzerland); musical instruments (to Germany, of all places); scientific instruments (to the United States); tyres and tubes (to Turkey) and sewing machines (to Panama).

Encouraged by the success of the First Programme, Sean Lemass then embarked on a much more ambitious and far-reaching plan, covering the years from 1963 to 1970. Towards the end of the decade what Lemass and his supporters confidently referred to as a 'levelling off' in the economic miracle seemed to be occurring. The planned capital investment had to be cut from £103,000,000 to £100,000,000 and, in order to meet even that target, the Government had to borrow £22,500,000 from Irish banks, $20,000,000 from New York banks, and float a new national loan for £25,000,000. The servicing and repayment of these loans was costing the taxpayer £35,000,000 a year by the end of the decade.

Eventually, in July 1967, the Second Programme was abandoned altogether in favour of a more flexible Third Programme covering the years up to 1972.

Among the aims of the Second Programme had been the provision of better facilities for education and training, badly needed in a country where the system, apart from the introduction of compulsory Irish, had hardly changed at all from the turn of the century and which was still based on Dickensian National Schools run by the churches offering a basic education between the ages of six and 14.

The secondary schools were also largely controlled by the Churches – many of their teachers were priests and nuns – and all charged fees, though there were a small number of free scholarship places available to children bright enough to pass competitive examinations. In addition, a small state-supported vocational sector provided technical education for nominal fees.

In 1963, the Lemass Government embarked on a programme

of providing a whole range of state-supported comprehensive schools, mostly co-educational, in areas where privately-owned educational facilities were clearly inadequate, thus for the first time making secondary education an integral part of the mass education system.

In 1967 the abolition of all fees in the vocational schools was announced, with a state subsidy for all secondary schools willing to waive charges to pupils, as well as a free bus service to and from school for pupils who lived more than three miles away from their nearest secondary school. The enormous cost of providing free education on this scale added greatly to the Government's problems in balancing the books, but Lemass and his Ministers regarded it as a worthwhile investment for the future.

On the international scene, too, the Sixties were a good time for the Irish. With F.H. Boland, an Irish diplomat, installed as President of the United Nations Assembly in New York, and Conor Cruise O'Brien in Katanga as UN representative, not to mention Irish soldiers fighting and dying in the UN force in the Congo and fifty officers and men serving with another UN force in Cyprus, the Republic's separate and distinct identity was established on the world scene as never before.

When, in 1965, Lemass went to Stormont Castle to meet Captain Terence O'Neill, the new Prime Minister of Northern Ireland – previously the premiers of the two parts of the country had never met nor indeed even acknowledged each other's existence – it seemed that a solution to the border problem might be close.

But the meeting between the two premiers was deeply resented by many diehard Protestant Unionists, among them the Revd Ian Paisley of the Free Presbyterian Church of Ulster, who became the principal spokesman for the Protestant working-class youth and the petty bourgeoisie. The trouble wasn't purely or even primarily a religious matter; it was basically about jobs and houses. The young Ulster Protestants feared Catholic integration because there were simply not enough jobs to go around; if they were lucky enough to be in work themselves, it was because so many of their Catholic counterparts were unemployed, and they wanted that situation to continue for as long as humanly possible. The small shopkeepers and the factory owners had survived by keeping their wage bills low, which they could do because of the high rate of unemployment among the Catholic workers; they also got preferential building grants, rate reductions, government contracts and so on from the Unionist Councils as well as council houses, and these perquisites of Protestantism now also seemed to be threatened by O'Neill's liberalism.

So far as Northern Ireland's Catholics were concerned, O'Neill's new liberal attitude actually did far more harm than good, since he raised expectations which he could not possibly have hoped to fulfil.

The situation was further complicated by the emergence, towards the end of the decade, of NICRA, the Northern Ireland Civil Rights Association. The first civil rights demonstration was sparked off by a successful squatting protest organised by Austin Currie, Nationalist MP for Co Tyrone. He had been trying to get a council house in Caledon for a Catholic family in bad need of accommodation; the local council wanted to let it instead to the unmarried, 19-year-old-secretary of a Unionist politician.

Currie's squat-in at the house in June 1968 and the publicity the whole affair received in the press and on radio and television, led to a civil rights march at Dungannon in August. It was peaceful, and the police didn't intervene.

This march in turn led to another, bigger one, in October 1968, in Derry. It was banned by the Northern Ireland Minister for Home Affairs, William Craig, but the Civil Rights Association decided to go ahead with their protest march anyway. When the 3,000 unarmed marchers reached the Loyalist area of Derry, they found the road blocked by RUC men armed with batons and riot shields and supported by water cannon. Without warning, the police baton-charged the marchers and turned the water cannon on them. An official inquiry later admitted that the police had 'used their batons indiscriminately' and with 'needless violence'. Ninety-six people, including two Labour MPs, received injuries which required hospital treatment.

Make no mistake about it, this is the precise point at which the current Northern Ireland troubles started – everything that happened subsequently came under the headings of action and reaction, reprisal and counter-reprisal – and you don't have to be an expert on Irish history or indeed on anything else to be able to say who was primarily responsible.

1960

KENNEDY ELECTED US PRESIDENT: MASSACRE AT SHARPEVILLE: AGADIR EARTHQUAKE: BLACK SIT-IN CAM-PAIGN AT US LUNCH COUNTERS: AMERICAN U2 SHOT DOWN BY USSR: KARIBA DAM OPENED: EICHMANN ARRESTED: MAKARIOS PRESIDENT OF CYPRUS: PACEMAKER FOR HEART DEVELOPED

No More Bonafides

The year began with big demonstrations in the Dublin docks as another cargo of horses destined for slaughter on the continent for human consumption was loaded; several photographers were injured. It was, after all, less than a month since forty-seven horses had died on board a ship bound for Amsterdam, with thundering repercussions in the British tabloid press.

In response to all this pressure, the Government later in the year established an Irish horse abattoir in Straffan, Co Kildare, so that the very profitable export of horse-meat for human consumption on the Continent could be continued without subjecting the horses to the rigours of a sea voyage before slaughter.

In April it was announced that a new town was to be built at Shannon Free Airport to house the families of those employed in the new factories in the customs-free industrial zone, and Dr C.S. Andrews was able to report that CIE losses for the year had been cut by over £700,000 to £1,000,000.

At the Irish Sugar Company's factory in Mallow, Co Cork, work started on Ireland's first commercial accelerated freeze-drying plant. A committee of voluntary workers rented Kilmainham Jail from the Government for a nominal rent of ls (5p) a year for five years and converted it into a historical museum. A cemetery for German servicemen who died in Ireland during the two world wars was nearing completion at Glencree, Co Wicklow.

In June, the first scheduled jet airliner – a Pan-Am DC8 – landed at Shannon from Detroit and Pye (Ireland) Ltd began work on a £105,000 transmitter on Mount Kippure in Co Wicklow for the Irish television service, now slated to start in May 1961; in the meantime, a nine-person authority to control the television service had been appointed.

A list of 35 books banned in June included Edna O'Brien's first novel, *The Country Girls*; 30,000 people attended the first large-scale Fleadh Ceoil (literally, feast of music, but in fact a week of folk singing, dancing, storytelling and general carousing) which was held in Boyle, Co Roscommon and became a pattern for future music festivals; in Sligo, a 27-foot cabin cruiser which had been ordered by Lord Louis Mountbatten was launched. It was to be fitted out in time for his annual visit to his Irish home, Classiebawn Castle, Mullaghmore, Co Sligo.

The world trend towards lighter types of lager beer was reflected in the decision of Arthur Guinness, Son & Co to produce a Guinness lager; Harp went on sale in July at ls 6d a bottle. More importantly, for drinking men, on July 4 a new Intoxicating Liquor Bill became law. Widely known as 'the liquor bill', it was a measure designed to extend legal drinking hours until 11.30 pm in the summer, and 11 pm in the winter; it was introduced largely for the benefit of the tourist trade, but it sealed the fate of the bona fide houses, a uniquely Irish institution which had enabled anybody lucky enough to own a car to drink right through the night provided he could establish that he was a 'bona fide' traveller, more than five miles away from home.

In July, Charlie Chaplin and his wife Oonagh and family spent a holiday touring Ireland, and the 32nd Infantry Brigade left Baldonnel to fly out to the Congo for service with the UN forces there.

On August 17, the 33rd Infantry Battalion left for Katanga and on September 20 F.H. Boland, formerly Irish Ambassador to the Court of St James in London, was elected President of the 15th UN Assembly in New York.

The 14th annual report of Bord na Mona, the Turf Board, recorded a surplus of £1,000,000 in September and Brendan Behan left for New York to attend the opening of *The Hostage* on Broadway, pledging that he would drink only soda water, 'a good drink, invented in Dublin', a pledge he was not, alas, to keep.

In October, Taoiseach Sean Lemass opened the Verolme Shipbuilding Yards in Cork Harbour.

On November 9, ten Irish soldiers were killed in a Baluba ambush in Northern Katanga; they were remembered along with victims of both world wars at Remembrance Day services in Ireland on November 13. Their funeral cortège took an hour to pass through Dublin on November 22nd, and the word 'baluba' entered Dublin jargon as a general, all-purpose term of opprobrium and abuse.

The first Aer Lingus Boeing jet *Padraig* arrived at Dublin Airport on November 18, after a record trans-Atlantic crossing from New York to Shannon in four hours 57 minutes.

In December, legislation was introduced to set up a Dairy Marketing Board known as Bord Bainne (Milk Board) to find markets abroad for Irish dairy produce, and an £8,000,000 factory was established to produce powdered milk for export to South America.

1961

US SEVERS RELATIONS WITH CUBA: PATRICE LUMUMBA
KILLED: ARMY REVOLT IN ALGERIA: TRIAL OF SPY
GEORGE BLAKE: CND DEMONSTRATIONS IN BRITAIN:
GAGARIN FIRST MAN IN SPACE: SOUTH AFRICA LEAVES
COMMONWEALTH: BERLIN WALL SEALS EAST–WEST BORDER

A Royal Visit

On the first day of the new year, Princess Margaret and her new
husband Anthony Armstrong-Jones came to Ireland to stay with
his mother, the Countess of Rosse, in Birr Castle, Co Offaly.
They must have liked it, because they came back to Ireland
again several times in the following years.

The Irish sent the *Book of Kells* to London for a loan exhibition and the first twenty of the Lane pictures arrived in Dublin
from the National Gallery in London for exhibition in Ireland.
The new ritual in the vernacular was tried out in some Catholic
Churches – much to the disgust of many older Irish Catholics,
who felt that this fruit of the second Vatican Council would
weaken rather than strengthen Irish Catholicism, which
depended to some extent, as Catholicism did everywhere, on
the mystery and universality surrounding the Latin form of the
ritual of the Mass.

There was a fire at the Red Bank restaurant in Dublin where
their famous Dublin Bay prawns no longer came from Dublin
Bay, even then already hopelessly polluted, but from the Red
Bank in Galway Bay, and Scandinavian designers were invited
by Coras Trachtala (literally, 'trading organisation', one of the
state-sponsored companies set up under the Whitaker Plan) to
advise on the development of a distinctive Irish design for
industry; for years, the best designs sponsored by the Irish
Industrial Design Centre in Kilkenny were unashamedly
Scandinavian in concept, though none the worse for that.

After five years of intensive litigation, Dublin dockers were still refusing to handle container traffic, and in the Congo Irish troops took over the control of the airport at Elizabethville.

Irish freeze-dried vegetables were on show for the first time at the RDS Spring Show in May; Minister for Justice Charles Haughey used a helicopter for the first serious traffic survey of Dublin, and a new company, Poteen Ireland, Ltd, was registered to make legal poteen in Kilkelly, Co Mayo for export. Brendan Behan was fined $300 in Toronto for assaulting a policeman.

On May 28, Conor Cruise O'Brien left for New York to take up duty as a special representative of the Secretary-General of the United Nations in the Congo, and the next day the Irish Government bought *Asgard*, the yacht which Erskine Childers had used to run arms into Howth for the Irish Volunteers. It was subsequently converted for use as an Irish naval service training vessel.

Garret FitzGerald, a future Premier, was appointed economics consultant to the Federation of Irish Industries on June 9; and the Dublin International Festival of Music and the Arts had to be held out of doors in Croke Park, Dublin, the Gaelic sports stadium, because all the theatres and cinemas in Dublin were in the middle of a five-week strike.

In June, too, the Department of Agriculture expressed an interest in experiments which were being carried out at Knocklally, using peat moss as a soil compost; the officials must have been impressed by what they saw because by July 3, a new processing plant to produce the moss on an industrial scale had been commissioned in Drogheda, Co Meath.

On July 12, Ireland joined UNESCO (the United Nations Educational, Scientific and Cultural Organisation). Towards the end of the month a contract was signed for the rebuilding of Liberty Hall, the HQ of the Transport and General Workers' Union on the Liffey, from which Connolly's Citizen Army had set out on Easter Monday 1916 with Patrick Pearse's Volunteers to march on the GPO; it was to be Dublin's first skyscraper, albeit fairly modest, at 27 storeys.

In August, the first consignment of refrigerated horse-meat left Straffan for Belgium and Bord Failte reported 1960 as the best year ever for tourism with receipts at over £42,000,000. In addition, the TB figures were the lowest on record; a total of 32 TB hospitals had been closed in the past few years. On the other hand, VD and other sex-related diseases were up, alcoholism was on the increase, and drugs were beginning to prove a bit of a problem.

A general election gave the Fianna Fail Party three seats short of an overall majority but, with a little help from his friends in other parties, Lemass was able to form a Government with his son-in-law, Charles Haughey, again as Minister for Justice.

A footnote: before I left Ireland in September 1959 for Fleet Street, I had been briefly employed by Charlie as a sort of public relations officer, to help him shape his speeches, advise him on the best time to make a speech from the back benches and so on. I knew as little then about public relations as he did about politics, but we were both learning; I suggested he should buy a yacht so that if his name didn't appear in the Dail debates or the political commentaries, at least it would appear in another context in the sporting pages. He didn't exactly follow my advice; he bought a horse instead and never looked back.

On September 13 an extension to St Vincent's Hospital at Elm Park (on part of the course of a very smart golf club just outside Dublin) was opened, and Cork International Airport opened three days later. Gael Linn introduced *Teach-Yourself-Irish* records in November and the Government revived the Special Criminal Court, basically a military tribunal, to try cases involving members of illegal organisations who had been plotting against the state.

On December 13, a ban on handling container traffic which had been in force for five and a half years was lifted by the unions, the Censorship Board lifted the ban on Frank O'Connor's *Kings, Lords and Commons*, which included a translation of Bryan Merriman's *The Midnight Court*, and at the end of the year it was announced that Irish bank notes would no longer bear the insulting legend: 'Payable to the bearer on demand in London'.

1962

BEN BELLA PREMIER OF ALGERIA: THALIDOMIDE DISAS-
TER: EICHMANN HANGED IN ISRAEL: RUSSIA REMOVES
MISSILES FROM CUBA: ANTI-OAS RIOTS IN PARIS:
OLIVIER FORMS MINISTRY IN MALTA: BRITAIN AND
IRELAND APPLY TO JOIN EEC: ALGERIAN INDEPENDENCE

The Great Stamp Fraud

On January 1, 1962, Ireland joined the Security Council of the United Nations. A new air service was inaugurated by Curragh Air Services, Ltd, for the transport of brood mares between Dublin and Cambridge, headquarters of the British bloodstock industry.

A strike at Ballina School made history because the protest was *against* the appointment of a cleric as head-master. A report by the Department of Social Welfare and the Department of Industry and Commerce indicated unemployment at its lowest level since 1939, and on January 26, Dr Paul Singer, a Viennese-born naturalised British subject, was acquitted after the longest trial (for fraud) in the history of the Irish state. The fraud arose out of the soliciting of investments in stamp collections.

One of the problems during the trial had been that no disinterested jury could be summoned; everybody on the jury list seemed to have had some money invested in Shanahan's stamp auctions. When he was finally released on January 24, after 47 days on trial, Singer told reporters: 'Nobody has lost any money yet, because the stamps have not yet been sold off, and when they have been sold, nobody will lose any money. In fact there may even be a little [in it] for myself.'

By the time the liquidation proceedings began in the High Court, Dr Singer had left the country and could not be traced. In effect, the £280,000 realised on the sale of the stamps in 1965 was nowhere near enough to pay the 9,000 claims by investors and creditors, totalling nearly £2,000,000.

On February 26 the IRA announced the termination of the campaign of resistance to the British occupation, launched in December, 1956, and 29 men detained under the Offences Against the State Acts were released from Mountjoy Jail following the statement.

On April 20, the Government reported that exports had reached a record level of £180,300,000 for the year; apart from some discontent among the farmers, who had been marching in protest against low incomes and high rates, things had never looked better for the Irish Republic.

In June, Larkspur, trained by Vincent O'Brien, won the Derby; Taoiseach Sean Lemass turned the first sod at the site of the new UCD building at Belfield in Stillorgan; Dr C.S. Andrews announced that he proposed to close down 23 branch lines and substitute road transport; and Aer Lingus reported an 80 per cent increase on the 1961 figures, including a substantial increase in trans-Atlantic traffic. A sign of the general prosperity: the Dublin jeweller, Desmond West, bought the biggest teak motor-yacht built in the British Isles since the war, for £70,000.

Sylvia Beach, the Paris publisher of James Joyce's *Ulysses*, visited Dublin in June at a time when Ireland's best-known actor, Peter O'Toole, from Galway, was playing Lawrence of Arabia in David Lean's film of that name.

In July a Canadian mining company claimed to have struck silver in the Tynagh Mines near Loughrea, Co Galway, which eventually became the biggest supplier of lead and zinc in the European Community.

In October, Irish butter (under the brand name Kerrygold) was launched on world markets by Tony O'Reilly, former rugby international, now in charge of marketing in Bord Bainne, the Irish Dairy Produce Marketing Board. He once told me that he travelled 100,000 miles a year trying to find markets for Irish butter. In 1962, he discovered that Ireland was importing a minute amount of pollard for pig feeding from Russia, and immediately hopped on a plane for Moscow, determined to talk the Russians into a bit of reciprocal trade in Irish butter. 'It took me three days to convince them that I didn't come from Iceland,' he said, 'and I still haven't sold them any butter yet, but at least they now know the difference between Ireland and Iceland, and that's a step in the right direction.'

Sean O'Casey lifted the unilateral five-year-old ban on any performances of his plays in Ireland and drilling for oil started in Kilkee, Co Clare.

In the Republic, three more television transmitters were brought into operation in counties Sligo, Cork and Carlow, and 15,000 emigrants were expected home for Christmas.

1963

TSHOMBE ACCEPTS UN PLAN FOR SECESSION OF KATANGA: BEECHING REPORT ON BRITISH RAILWAYS: PHILBY ESCAPES TO RUSSIA: FRANCE LEAVES NATO: BRITAIN REFUSED COMMON MARKET ENTRY: RACE RIOTS IN ALABAMA: KENNEDY ASSASSINATED: ARMY COUP IN VIETNAM

Tumultuous Rising Trial

In January, the Committee on Industrial Organisation reported on the CKD (completely knocked down) car assembly business: it saw no prospect beyond four years for the industry, which then employed about 2,500. In January, too, CIE put on show a new 950 hp diesel locomotive, announcing that 36 similar locomotives had been ordered from the US at a cost of £2,500,000. British Rail and the B + I Company announced increased accommodation for cars; extra cranes had been built on Dun Laoghaire pier to load the cars. It's hard to believe it, but as comparatively recently as 1963 cars were still loaded onto boats by crane.

The Government Information Bureau reported a rush for prospecting licences in Ireland; over 50 had been issued since April, 1962, mainly to Canadian companies.

Mushrooms were now the most important Irish horticultural

export; two and a half tons a day were being flown to Britain at this period.

Monsieur Potez, the French light aircraft manufacturer, who had set up a factory in Baldonnel with Government aid, extended his empire in Ireland when a factory to manufacture oil heaters was opened in Galway; it would offer employment to 700 workers, M. Potez said. Two days later he flew from Galway to Baldonnel in a prototype Potez 840 aircraft, which, he claimed, was soon to be manufactured in his factory at Baldonnel.

By this time – just over a year after the dockers had lifted their ban on container traffic – between 900 and 1,000 containers were leaving Dublin Port every week.

On February 6, the Government decided to apply for membership of GATT (the General Agreement on Tariffs and Trade) to which 37 nations were already signatories and on the same day a UN Commission on International Trade classed Ireland with Spain and Greece as 'under-developed' countries. Lemass protested to the United Nations at this slur on the Republic.

Then came two of those hilarious cases which enliven the normally deadly dull processes of the law. On February 18, the Supreme Court dismissed the appeal of a Tralee commercial traveller, sentenced to two years' imprisonment for sending threatening letters under the Tumultuous Rising (Ireland) Act of 1831; he had argued that this Act was repugnant to Ireland's 1922 and 1937 Constitutions and had been implicitly repealed by subsequent legislation.

The Supreme Court decided that there was nothing in the 1831 Act which disclosed discrimination and that it was not therefore repugnant to the Constitution, though the original, earlier Tumultuous Rising Acts of 1776, 1786, 1787 and 1800, did refer specifically (and disparagingly) to 'Papists'.

On March 18 another prosecution, brought under the original White Boys Acts of the same period, against three men for forcible entry, was claimed by the defence to be unconstitutional since, among other things, it specified 'transport to America' as a possible punishment. The prosecution replied that the Act had been passed by an all-Irish Parliament, was still on the Statute Book and was a perfectly good law, adding that the prosecution could equally have been brought under an Act of Richard III, passed 300 years before the 1786 Act. The judge directed the jury to find the men not guilty and they were discharged.

The car of the year was the new Ford Zodiac with heater and demister (these now standard amenities were then still so rare as to qualify for mention in advertisements); it cost £1,085, ex-works in Cork.

In March, Lord Brookeborough resigned as Premier of Northern Ireland and was succeeded by Captain Terence O'Neill, ex-Guardsman, old Etonian and the first liberal (with a small 'l') Unionist to hold the post. O'Neill could trace his ancestry back to Niall of the Nine Hostages, one of the High Kings of Celtic Ireland, which gave him a far purer pedigree than President de Valera or any single member of the Government of the period.

In May, a new peat-operated power station opened in Co Mayo and the Minister for Education, Dr Hillery, announced plans for the first of the revolutionary changes in the educational system, mentioned above, including comprehensive, co-educational schools. The new Intercontinental Hotel in Ballsbridge opened in what had been the botanical gardens of Trinity College, and Edna O'Brien was back in Dublin working on the script of a film based on her book *The Country Girls*, which was being shot at Ardmore and on location in Dublin, with Peter Finch and Rita Tushingham; it was released under the title *The Girl With Green Eyes*.

A Fleadh Ceoil in Mullingar in June attracted 60,000 visitors and participants, and towards the end of June President John F. Kennedy paid a three-day visit to Ireland.

On July 24, four men were arrested at an IRA training camp in the Knockmealdown Mountains; when questioned they explained that the purpose of the training camp was the 'revival of the campaign of direct action' in Northern Ireland.

In August Ireland won the Aga Khan trophy at the RDS Horse Show for the first time in 14 years, the Government's second Programme for Economic Expansion was published, and

Prince Rainier and Princess Grace arrived to spend a holiday in Ireland at Carton House, Co Kildare. A 603-foot, 30,000-ton ship, the largest ever built in the Republic, was launched at the Verolme Dockyards in Cork Harbour, and Sean Lemass proposed talks at any level with the Government of Northern Ireland, without any preconditions.

In September, Bord Bainne ordered a special wrapping in Arabic for Kerrygold butter for the Near East market and Sean MacBride was appointed Chairman of Amnesty International at Koenigswinter, Germany.

Newcastle TB Sanatorium closed in October for lack of business and in the *Irish Times* a family living in Ballybrack, Co Dublin advertised for a cook-housekeeper (nursemaid and parlourmaid employed – such style, in 1963), offering £5 a week wages.

In November, as everybody remembers, John F. Kennedy was assassinated in Dallas, Texas. Possibly because he had visited Ireland as recently as June 1963, possibly because he was a Catholic whose family had emigrated from Ireland, his death was celebrated in many Irish homes as 'the saddest day'; for many years afterwards his photograph appeared, with that of the current Pope, beside the statue of the Virgin Mary on Irish mantelpieces. And not only in Ireland, indeed; we once spent a night unexpectedly in a tiny hotel in the Catholic part of Switzerland, near Brig, and encountered the same strange triptych.

At a Beatles concert in the Adelphi Cinema, Dublin, there were twelve arrests; cars were overturned outside the cinema and many people were treated in hospital for fractured limbs and minor injuries. John Jameson introduced a new brand of Irish whiskey, Crested Ten, the Irish National Stud bought Miralgo for £85,000, the Irish Army Air Service acquired two air-sea rescue helicopters, and Jacobs, the Dublin biscuit manufacturers, made their first television awards: one went to Gay Byrne as outstanding personality of the year (he's still presenting *The Late, Late Show*, on British as well as Irish television, every week 30 years later, and it's still about the best talk show around).

1964

CHINA EXPLODES ATOMIC BOMB: IAN SMITH PREMIER OF
RHODESIA: BRITAIN LAUNCHES BLUESTREAK: TANZANIA
FOUNDED: NELSON MANDELA SENTENCED TO LIFE IMPRIS-
ONMENT: MARTIN LUTHER KING WINS NOBEL PEACE PRIZE:
US CIVIL RIGHTS BILL: FALL OF NIKITA KHRUSHCHEV

First Driving Tests

On the first day of the new year, Brendan Behan, back in
Dublin, was found unconscious and was taken to the Meath
Hospital, suffering from pneumonia. The film director John
Huston became an Irish citizen on January 3, and on the same
day the Clancy Brothers – the first of a long line of Irish groups
which were to top the pop charts for many years – returned from
a highly successful tour of the United States. The Government
decided on January 14 to dispose of St Patrick's Copper Mines at
Avoca and the oldest yacht club in the world, the Royal Cork,
founded in 1720, put its premises up for sale.

On January 30, a ten-man delegation headed by Eddie
McAteer, a Northern Ireland Nationalist, met the Liberal leader,
Jo Grimond, to discuss discrimination in Northern Ireland. On
the same day the Revd Ian Paisley threatened a monster
demonstration if a Catholic priest, invited to speak in a
Presbyterian Church in Belfast as part of the general ecumenical
movement, dared to accept the invitation.

A pamphlet called *Facts About Ireland*, published by the
Department of External Affairs on March 3, caused a controversy
in the Dail when Fine Gael deputies, quite understandably,
objected to the omission of any mention of the parts played by
Michael Collins, Kevin O'Higgins and Arthur Griffith in Ireland's
struggle for freedom.

The new traffic regulations which turned Dublin into an
initially confusing city of one-way streets – Charlie Haughey's
very largely successful attempt to solve what otherwise looked
like becoming a permanent traffic jam – came into force on

March 18, as did the mandatory test for a driving licence.

Brendan Behan died on March 20, aged 41; two of the Beatles, John Lennon and George Harrison, were on holiday at Dromoland Castle luxury hotel and were paying £77 a week (outrageously expensive at that time) for the privilege. Arkle, trained by Tom Dreaper and ridden by Pat Taaffe, won the Cheltenham Gold Cup for the first of three successive years, as well as that year's Irish Grand National at Fairyhouse.

An OECD report on the Irish economy recorded a 4 per cent growth for 1963 and took an optimistic view of Ireland's future. The Irish Sugar Company landed a £1,000,000 contract for refining sugar for Great Britain, and the Dail agreed to accede to U Thant's request for more Irish troops for the UN peace-keeping mission in Cyprus. On April 15 Charles Haughey defended the practice of telephone tapping and told the Dail that when necessary information could not be obtained in any other way, telephone communications might legally be intercepted under a warrant from the Minister for Justice (his good self).

At the end of March, the results of the 1961 Census were published: this census, which included questions about religious faith, revealed that the proportion of Catholics in the Republic was now 94.9 per cent as against 3.7 per cent Church of Ireland, 0.7 per cent Presbyterians, 0.2 per cent Methodists, 0.1 per cent Jews, and 0.2 per cent others.

On April 9, the Kilkenny Beer Festival, the loudest, longest and most unruly of all the Irish festivals, was inaugurated. On April 24, Ireland's first international fashion fair attracted buyers and fashion writers from 70 countries, and property prices hit the roof, with a record price: £27,750 for a house in Burlington Road, Dublin.

An order by the Minister for Agriculture on May 16, banning the export of all horses over five years old other than bloodstock or riding ponies, put a final end to the export of horses to the continent for slaughter for human consumption, and on May 18 the opening of the Fleadh Ceoil in Clones, Co Monaghan attracted 70,000; on the same day, the last of the Irish troops left the Congo.

Towards the end of June, in an effort to get the best of both worlds, the Irish whiskey distillers decided to manufacture an Irish 'Scotch' for tourists who found the straight Irish malt whiskey too fierce for their taste; the result, CDC's (the Cork Distillery Company's) Hewitt's, was soon selling well at 1d or 3d a glass less than real Scotch.

In July, another 400 troops were sent to Cyprus, and the Government produced a second edition of *Facts About Ireland* which made some amends by including photographs of Arthur Griffith, Michael Collins and Madame Markievicz.

With a baffling lack of consistency, a Government which was striving to attract foreign investment to Ireland in, among other things, an Irish film industry, allowed its film censor to ban the film version of Edna O'Brien's *The Girl With Green Eyes* at the very moment when scenes for another Ardmore-location Irish film were being shot in the streets of Dublin; this was *Young Cassidy*, based on the life of Sean O'Casey.

Ronan O'Rahilly, proprietor of the highly successful pirate station Radio Caroline, broadcasting from a ship moored in the North Sea just off the English coast, returned to his native Dublin on July 17, to set up a company to canvas advertisements for Irish goods for his radio station.

A third Infantry group left for Cyprus on August 5, bringing the total of Irish troops in the UN Peace Force up to 1,000.

Bord Failte reported another record year; tourist spending was up 8 per cent to £56,800,000. The Chief Medical Officer of Dublin attacked food hygiene standards; the country was still in the Molly Malone age of wheelbarrows and old prams, he said. The General Statistics Office reported that 233,617 man days had been lost in 1963 because of industrial disputes, and in Trim, Co Meath, a grandmother of 44 gave birth to her 21st child.

On August 28 a restriction order prevented the Revd Ian Paisley from going into the Catholic Divis area to protest against the showing of a tricolour in the window of the headquarters of a republican organisation; the RUC went in instead, smashed a number of windows, seized the flag and started a series of riots that went on until October 2, during which buses were burnt, shops looted, and 50 civilians and 12 police were injured.

From Ireland, during the year, had come assorted evoked and

reconstructed portraits of selected personalities painted by the artist, Louis le Brocquy as well as Brian Friel's play *Philadelphia, Here I Come*, which was a huge success on Broadway and in the West End of London as well as in Dublin.

1965

DEATH OF WINSTON CHURCHILL: MALCOLM X ASSASSI-
NATED: MARTIN LUTHER KING LEADS CIVIL RIGHTS MARCH
TO MONTGOMERY: US OFFENSIVE IN VIETNAM: INDIA-
PAKISTAN WAR: RHODESIAN UDI DECLARATION: BP STRIKES
OIL IN NORTH SEA: TSHOMBE DISMISSED IN CONGO

Hands Across the Border

Princess Margaret and Lord Snowdon arrived on January 3 for another ten-day private visit to his mother at Birr, Co Offaly and were not frightened away by an explosion at an ESB transformer in nearby Abbeyleix; and on January 7, the Rolling Stones received a deafening reception at two performances in the Adelphi Cinema, Dublin.

Richard Burton and Elizabeth Taylor came to Dublin in January; he was starring in the film *The Spy Who Came in from the Cold*, made in Ardmore Studios with location shots in parts of Dublin which could easily be disguised to resemble East Berlin.

A White Paper on Irish showed that the Government were at long last becoming realistic about the prospects of reviving the national language; it announced that students who failed in Irish in the Schools Leaving Certificate would be given a second opportunity to take the examination.

On January 15, the Revd Ian Paisley protested against the idea of any meeting between Sean Lemass and the Northern Ireland premier, Captain O'Neill. But he was too late; the meeting mentioned above had already taken place at Stormont the previous day.

On February 2, for the first time, the Northern Ireland Nationalists under Eddie McAteer became the official opposition at Stormont. By February 9, Captain O'Neill had returned Lemass's visit to Belfast by visiting him in Leinster House in Dublin; he had told the Northern Ireland Parliament that the initiative for the first meeting had come from him – though it is still widely believed in Ireland that it had come from Lemass – and he had added that the British Government had not been told about it until Lemass was safely on the road from Dublin to Belfast. When I interviewed him in 1965, he told me that it had been 'a real James Bond operation . . . if there'd been a leak, we'd have had trees felled by the IRA all along the road from Dublin to Belfast, and all the extremists in the North lining the avenue all the way out to Stormont.'

On February 2, too, the Government took over the B + I line from Coast Lines for £3,600,000 and on February 11 they paid about £2,500 for a continuing interest in the copyright of *A Soldier's Song*, written by Peadar Kearney, an uncle of Brendan Behan's, and adopted in 1924 as the Irish national anthem – probably the dreariest one in the whole European Community, with the possible exception of *God Save the Queen*.

Gestures of friendship abounded at this period. On February 12 Charles Haughey, who had taken over the portfolio of Agriculture in a cabinet reshuffle, invited the Northern Ireland Minister for Agriculture, Harry West, to stay with him in Dublin, and in March Harry West returned to Dublin to address the Council of the National Farmers' Association, becoming in the process the first Northern Ireland Government minister ever to address a public meeting in the Republic.

At long last, the remains of Roger Casement were returned to Ireland by the British Government; they lay in state in the Pro-Cathedral in Dublin for five days before a state funeral in Glasnevin Cemetery on March 1.

To mark the elevation of Cardinal Conway, 45 prisoners were released from Mountjoy Jail, including ten serving sentences in connection with the explosion which had occurred during Princess Margaret's visit to Birr earlier in the year.

At the annual St Patrick's Day Banquet in London Harold

Wilson, the first British Prime Minister to attend the function since 1911, suggested a new series of talks about Northern Ireland and the Republic in London, and in April Erskine Childers, Minister for Transport and Power, announced the setting-up of joint committees on cross-border tourism in Dublin and Belfast.

After a general election narrowly won by Fianna Fail – Lemass was re-elected Taoiseach by a majority of only five – James Dillon resigned the leadership of the Fine Gael Party and was succeeded by Liam Cosgrave, son of William T. Cosgrave. Lemass retired in 1966 and was succeeded by Jack Lynch.

The first drive-on car-ferry ever seen in Ireland arrived for the Rosslare-Fishguard service in May. Early in August another drive-on ferry arrived for the Dun Laoghaire–Holyhead crossing and before the end of the summer had carried twice as many cars as had been carried in the whole of the previous year.

Dublin booksellers decided not to stock Edna O'Brien's *August is a Wicked Month*, although it had not been banned, and other Irish books of the year included *The Dark*, by John McGahern, William Trevor's *The Boarding House* and Brian Moore's *The Emperor of Ice Cream*.

The new Minister for Education asked for an additional £2,121,887 for his department; it was the Government's policy to build 100 new schools a year, and make major improvements to another 50 existing schools, as part of the Second Programme for Industrial Development, mentioned above.

Gortrum Mines, Co Tipperary, reported copper ore deposits of 4,500,000 tons which would produce a net profit of $10,000,000 after mining costs, and three Coca Cola bottling plants were opened in Dublin, Cork and Tuam, Co Galway.

In October, Northgate Base Metals opened a mine at Tynagh near Galway, to work lead-zinc and copper-silver deposits and in November the Silvermines Lead and Zinc Co announced that Consolidated Mogul Mines of Toronto were raising £7,000,000 for mine developments in Co Tipperary. Earlier in the year, the activities of the Rio Tinto company, mining for minerals at Keel, Co Longford, were hampered for a time by the fact that they couldn't succeed in getting a single telephone connection to the mine site.

In 1965, and again in 1966, Ireland topped the International Labour Office's annual international strike tables, and throughout the decade was never very far from the top. Initially, one of the attractions of Ireland for foreign investors had been the large and adaptable work force prepared to accept moderate wages, but that situation didn't last for very long. After years of chronic unemployment, when men were often forced to take severe cuts in their wages in order to hold down their jobs, the first whiff of prosperity had proved a heady brew and the trouble was that the worst strikes were always in sectors most likely to discourage and disillusion the new investors in the Irish industrial miracle: the bank clerks, the telephone operators, the dockers, the transport workers . . .

As the year ended, the telephone workers had been on strike for 12 weeks, a strike of workers in the bakery business meant that Dublin had had no bread for three weeks, Jacobs' biscuit factory was also closed because of a strike, the building workers' unions had served strike notice on more than a dozen firms, and a gas strike seemed imminent.

1966

US CALL-UP FOR MILITARY SERVICE: AGREEMENT BETWEEN INDIA AND PAKISTAN AT TASHKENT: US POLARIS FLEET COMPLETED: CULTURAL REVOLUTION IN CHINA: ART MASTERPIECES LOST IN FLOODS IN FLORENCE: AFRICAN STATES BREAK OFF RELATIONS WITH BRITAIN

Nelson's Pillar For Sale

The year 1966 was the 50th anniversary of the 1916 Easter Rising, and the authorities on both sides of the border waited apprehensively to see what form the celebrations would take.

In Dublin, they took the rather dramatic form of an explosion which not merely removed Nelson from the top of his pillar in O'Connell Street, but scattered the major part of his column all over the centre of the city. The Irish Army removed the remainder of the column – affectionately known in Dublin as 'The Stump' – about a week later.

The traders of Moore Street (Dublin's main street market parallel to O'Connell Street) immediately started to stock fragments of the true pillar, more than enough, somebody calculated, to build a pyramid even bigger than the one at Cheops. Obtaining supplies was no problem. The column had been made of granite, a type of stone of which the Dublin and Wicklow mountain ranges are largely composed.

The disappearance of the pillar posed a bit of a problem for CIE. For years, most of the city tram and subsequently bus services terminated at the pillar, which was well known and was marked on every street map. The decision to re-christen the area An Lar (the centre) was logical enough but it caused endless confusion among the tourists who couldn't find An Lar in any of the street maps, or on any of the road signs.

In January, the 1916 Jubilee Committee told the Abbey Theatre that they would like to see plays presented which emphasised the heroism of the Easter Rising martyrs, which, they argued, O'Casey's plays emphatically did not.

In February, Radio Eireann became RTE (Radio Telefis Eireann); John McGahern lost his teaching post at Clontarf National School because of 'indecencies' in his novel *The Dark*, which although officially banned by the censor was freely available to the blind in its Braille version, which was not subject to censorship.

Due to the property boom, two very different institutions closed for business in March: the Dolphin Hotel, in Essex Street, Dublin, an old-fashioned steak house much frequented by the racing set, and the Sacred Heart Convent in Leeson Street, one of Dublin's better girls' schools.

The Revd Ian Paisley flew to Rome on the same plane as the Archbishop of Canterbury to protest at the latter's visit to the Pope, but was refused permission to leave the airport and was obliged to return to London. Henry Potez arrived from France to visit his aircraft factory at Baldonnel, which so far had not even produced one plane, and Gerry Fitt (Republican Labour) won a seat from the Unionists in a by-election in West Belfast.

Then, in April, came the official celebrations of 1916. Kapitan Raimund Weisbach, who had brought submarine *U19* to the coast of Co Kerry with Casement on board, attended a commemoration ceremony at Banna Strand on April 8.

On April 10, President de Valera inspected a Guard of Honour outside the GPO, no doubt finding, as everybody else did, that O'Connell Street looked strangely naked without the pillar. The following day he opened a 1916 Garden of Remembrance in Parnell Square. Northern Ireland celebrated the occasion by sealing the border for north-bound traffic from 9 pm, and the Revd Ian Paisley led his followers to Ulster Hall, 'to give thanks,' as he himself put it, 'for the defeat of the 1916 Rising'.

The Irish banks closed yet again on May 5 as 3,400 junior clerks went on strike for an additional 7 per cent on top of the tenth-round national wage increase. Most of them migrated to England where they worked as waiters and waitresses, barmen and barmaids, until the strike ended. A few days later the ESB workers also went on strike and the Government requested consumers to curtail their use of electricity as far as possible.

In June, the Hierarchy decided that mixed marriages would henceforward enjoy the same blessing from the Church as marriages between Catholics, and the Maynooth seminary announced that it was opening its courses to nuns, as well as to the laity; St Patrick's College was to be developed as a Centre for Higher Studies, as part of the general drive to improve educational facilities in Ireland.

Just how urgently they needed to be improved was highlighted by the report of an OECD commission of statisticians, economists and educationalists, set up in 1963 to examine Irish educational facilities. Their findings, published under the title *Investment in Education*, made extremely depressing reading. Less than half of all National Schools had piped water or modern sanitation and more than 57 per cent of the boys and 49 per cent of the girls left school without any record of having taken the Primary Certificate examination or even of having completed their schooling.

President de Valera was inaugurated President on June 25 for a second term, having been re-elected by the skin of his teeth. He had been opposed by Tom O'Higgins, the barrister nephew of Kevin O'Higgins who, according to Garret FitzGerald's autobiography, came to within one-half of one per cent of defeating him.

Three whiskey distilleries – Powers, Jamesons and Cork Distillers – decided to merge that summer as the United Distillers of Ireland. The rebuilt Abbey Theatre reopened on July 18 with a dramatisation of its own history, *Recall the Years*, and the Revd Ian Paisley was sent to jail on the following day for refusing to pay any fine or enter bail for creating a disturbance outside the General Assembly in Belfast on January 6.

Discontent among the farmers at poor prices for agricultural produce and the reluctance of the Minister for Agriculture, Charles Haughey, to listen to their arguments, boiled over in October. Richard Deasey, President of the National Farmers' Association, spent the night of October 19 sitting on the steps of Leinster House as a protest against Haughey's refusal to see him; the next day farmers vandalised Haughey's car and threatened to ban any hunt with which Haughey or any member of his family attempted to ride.

Tony O'Reilly, who as general manager of the Milk Board had put Kerrygold on the map of Europe as a distinctive Irish product, became Managing Director of the Irish Sugar Company (which included Erin Foods, the Irish free-dried food processors).

On December 19, the new Premier Jack Lynch met Harold Wilson in London for talks about their respective applications for entry to the European Economic Community.

1967

INDIRA GANDHI PREMIER OF INDIA: REAGAN SWORN IN AS
GOVERNOR OF CALIFORNIA: SIX-DAY WAR BETWEEN ISRAEL
AND ARAB STATES: OLIVIER ORDERS BRITONS OUT OF
MALTA: NIGERIA-BIAFRA CIVIL WAR: 2000,000 PROTEST
IN US AGAINST VIETNAM WAR: DEATH OF CHE GUEVARA

Protests by Farmers

On January 1, Coras Trachtala reported that exports had been up
by 11 per cent in 1966. The farmers' quarrel with the
Department of Agriculture had not been solved by the appointment of a new Minister; on January 9, there was chaos on the
roads as 35,000 farmers used 15,000 farm vehicles (including
combined reapers and harvesters) to block all trunk roads in
support of the Farmers' Rights Campaign.

On January 12 Film Studios of Ireland, Ltd took over
Ardmore Studios, in the hands of the Official Receiver since
1963. On January 22, the Minister for Industry and Commerce
told the Irish Mining and Quarrying Society that the value of
exported metal ore had risen from £70,000 in 1965 to £2,400,000
in 1966 and that Ireland could be well on the way to becoming
one of Europe's leading zinc-lead producers.

Senator Margaret Pearse donated the demesne and house of
St Enda's – Patrick Pearse's old school – to the nation on
February 1 and on February 23, the National Farmers'
Association rejected membership of a National Agricultural
Council proposed by the Government. By this time there were
32 farmers in jail for non-payment of rates in protest against the
Government's handling of agricultural matters, and six more
were jailed on February 24. On February 27, after the Civic
Guards had been involved in scuffles with 300 more farmers,
there were 12 further arrests.

On February 1, NICRA (the Northern Ireland Civil Rights
Association) was founded. Based on the National Council for

Civil Liberties in Britain, it included in its aims one man, one vote in local elections to replace the property/company vote; the disbanding of the B-Specials, an armed, part-time auxiliary force attached to the RUC; the allocation of all public-sector housing on a fair points system; and the repeal of the Special Powers Acts.

On March 2, the Government turned down yet another request from the United States to be allowed to land planes at Dublin Airport without the mandatory stopover at Shannon, and the Dail heard on March 7 that 55.2 per cent of the people who had taken a driving test in the last six months had failed to qualify.

On March 30, it was announced that Jammet's restaurant on Nassau Street at the bottom of Grafton Street, established in 1900 by Lord Cadogan's chef and arguably one of the best restaurants in the British Isles, had been sold, and would no longer be a restaurant.

Erin Foods, the Irish freeze-dried food processing company, merged with Heinz and its 57 varieties to form a joint company on April 3, and on April 11, Charles Haughey's first budget as Minister for Finance allowed medical expenses to be set off against tax; increased children's allowances and pensions; and gave free travel and electricity to pensioners.

The Minister for Education, Donagh O'Malley, announced a plan to unite the Universities in Dublin into one, with two constituent colleges (it was one way to get around the ban on Catholics attending Trinity College) and the Minister for Justice, Brian Lenihan, announced changes in the law affecting book censorship. Books banned before 1947 would be automatically released from censorship and appeals against censorship could be made at any time.

In May, the United Kingdom and Ireland applied together to join the EEC and, for the second time, General de Gaulle said No to Britain; a decision on Ireland's application was deferred.

Premier Lynch received a delegation from the National Farmers' Association on June 1, when the Government agreed to mitigate all outstanding fines and farmers in jail were released.

At a press conference in Dublin, Syntex Pharmaceuticals announced that an average of 3 per cent of women aged between 16 and 45 were now on the pill in Ireland as against 10 per cent in Britain. At this period, Irish doctors were cheerfully prescribing the pill to young women – not to exercise any form of contraceptive birth control, but purely to ensure regular menstruation, so that they could use the 'safe period' system of family limitation approved by the Church. When I pointed out to one young Dublin housewife that once she was on the pill, she didn't need to use the safe system or any other, to avoid conception, she replied piously: 'Well, that's as may be. But the reason I'm taking the pill is purely to regularise my periods, so that I can use the safe period, as recommended by the Church.' You can't argue against that kind of logic.

The Fleadh Ceoil at Enniscorthy, Co Wexford was reckoned to have brought £250,000 to the town, a sum which, even allowing for a fair share of broken windows and other casual damage, must have represented a considerable profit. On June 15, Mrs Jacqueline Kennedy, widow of John F. Kennedy, came to Ireland for a five-week holiday with her children.

On June 31, the Government Information Bureau announced that 93 per cent of all Irish secondary schools had opted for the Government's projected 'free education' scheme.

In a reversal of everything that had gone before, a Russian team of peat experts came to Ireland in August to study Bord na Mona's methods of 'winning' (harvesting) and drying turf and the highly successful turf-burning power stations built on the bogs.

On October 2, Minister for Transport and Power Erskine Childers signed an agreement with the Northern Ireland Minister of Commerce, to link up cross-border electricity supplies, and on the same day Coras Trachtala opened an office in Jamaica to handle Irish exports to the Caribbean countries and South America. Irish Shipping and Normandy Ferries announced a joint ferry service between Cork and Le Havre, to start in June 1968, and memorials to Wolfe Tone and W.B. Yeats were unveiled in St Stephen's Green.

Ireland devalued its currency by 14.3 per cent following the

British devaluation of the £ sterling on November 18, and on December 11 Jack Lynch met Northern Ireland Premier Captain O'Neill for the first time at Stormont; the Revd Ian Paisley celebrated the occasion by pelting Lynch's car with snowballs.

1968

RIOTS IN WARSAW: JOHNSON SENDS 500,000 MORE TROOPS TO VIETNAM: FIRST POLARIS MISSILE TESTS: MARTIN LUTHER KING SHOT: STUDENT RIOTS IN PARIS: RUSSIAN TANKS SENT IN TO CRUSH PRAGUE SPRING: ROBERT KENNEDY ASSASSINATED: NIXON ELECTED US PRESIDENT

The Education Explosion

In January, Premier O'Neill returned Jack Lynch's visit; they discussed tourism, tariffs, the metric system and the best precautions against foot and mouth disease, at that period ravaging Great Britain's cattle. The Irish Government announced that exports in 1967 had reached the record level of over £283,000,000; it emerged later in the year that the new Shannon Free Airport Industrial Development Co had contributed very nearly one-tenth of that total.

In February, a world-wide survey of psychiatric illness found Ireland at the top of the league with 10.82 per cent of the population affected. The figure for the US was 5.65 per cent and, for the UK, 5.34 per cent. Japan was at the bottom of the list with only 0.64 per cent.

Around this period Irish clothes, and particularly those made from Irish tweed, were selling well all round the world. In March Donald Davies of Enniskerry opened a boutique in Paris; he was, he said, now exporting 85 per cent of his woollen garments.

The Tenth Infantry Battalion left for service with the United Nations Forces in Cyprus, and on March 24, an Aer Lingus

Viscount Aircraft crashed in St George's Channel on a flight between Cork and London, killing 61 people. It is generally believed in Ireland that the cause, which was never officially revealed, was a guided missile fired from Valley, in North Wales, during an RAF training exercise.

The sudden collapse and death of Donagh O'Malley, Minister for Education, on March 10, was followed on March 26 by the announcement that Brian Lenihan was taking over the portfolio. Throughout the year, profound changes continued to be made in the Irish educational system, which put the department's bill for the year up to a record £49,000,000. In January, Avoca School in Blackrock and Kingstown Grammar School were amalgamated as part of a plan to rationalise Protestant education. In July, the Government clarified its plans for the universities – the National University of Ireland was to be dissolved and UCD and TCD amalgamated as the University of Dublin with Cork and Galway as separate universities – and in August a Higher Educational Authority was set up to prepare a blueprint for the plan.

Charles Haughey's second budget on April 23 increased pensions for OAPs, as well as maternity and unemployment benefits, and allowed pensioners free radio and TV licences.

A new car ferry terminal in Dublin Port was completed and handed over to the Port and Docks Board in May, to handle a new car ferry service between Dublin and Liverpool; in November, the MV *Leinster*, a car ferry, was launched in the Cork shipyards for the service. In May, too, the Bishop of Galway, the Revd Michael Browne, attacked Trinity College, Dublin, as 'a centre of atheism and Communist propaganda'. A new Criminal Justice Bill was introduced which repealed more than 120 old British Acts, and made majority jury verdicts legal.

On June 6, the proceedings of the Dail and Senate were interrupted as a mark of respect to Robert Kennedy, who had been assassinated in Los Angeles the previous day, and on June 10 TCD decided to allow women to become eligible as Provost, Fellows and Foundation Scholars. Phelim O'Neill, a Northern Ireland MP, was expelled from the Orange Order for attending a community service in a Catholic church.

In May, a receiver was appointed to take over the subsidiary Potez factory in Galway built to manufacture oil heaters; to date, M. Potez had cost the Government £530,000. Despite this, and despite the fact that the Potez aircraft factory at Baldonnel had still not yet produced one single aircraft, the Government poured another £258,000 into the project on June 25, only to learn a month later that the Baldonnel factory had been closed down following a phone call from Paris.

The first shipment of 2,500 tons of lead and zinc left Mogul Silvermines, Co Tipperary, for Hanover, Germany, in July. President de Valera attended, for the first time, the annual commemorative mass for Michael Collins in Dublin Castle. Mrs Jack Lynch launched the 312,000-ton *Universe Ireland*, the largest tanker ever built, at Yokohama, Japan. A monument to Roger Casement was unveiled at Banna strand, Tralee, Co Kerry and a bust of the poet W.B. Yeats was unveiled in Sandymount Green. He had been born in a house in Sandymount Avenue, and we believed that he had lived for a period in Sandymount Castle, a Victorian Gothic folly in which we'd had a flat when we were first married. When ghostly voices started to emanate from the geyser in the bathroom, we immediately assumed that this was as a result of the poet's tampering with the spirit world while in residence there. We later learned that it was not W.B. Yeats, but his father, the painter John B. Yeats, who had lived for a period in Sandymount Castle, and as he never tampered with anything less material than his own paintings, I daresay we have to assume that the ghosts in the geyser were subjective.

The full text of the papal encyclical Humanae Vitae – in which the Pope gave his followers the benefit of his views on birth control – was published in the *Irish Times* on August 2, and produced a heated follow-up of controversial correspondence.

In September, the nitrogen fertiliser plant was officially opened at Arklow, Co Wicklow, and a £500,000 factory for turning potatoes into Tayto crisps was opened at Coolock, Co Dublin. The last house in Fitzwilliam Square to be used as a one-family residence was vacated; it had been the home of a Dublin doctor and family since 1920. St Grellan's National

School at Ballinasloe switched to teaching other subjects in English, after struggling for 25 years to try to teach 'through the medium', and a census report indicated that the population in 1966 at 2,484,775 was higher than it had ever been since 1841.

The crucial outbreak of violence in the recent (and indeed current) Northern Ireland Troubles, during the second civil rights march in Northern Ireland to Derry on October 5, 1968, was followed in Belfast by the foundation of the People's Democracy movement by Bernadette Devlin, Eamonn McCann and Michael Farrell, and in Dublin by a civil rights demonstration in the course of which petrol bombs were thrown at the British Embassy.

Right from the start of the Troubles, the media coverage overwhelmingly favoured the civil rights cause, and this perhaps made the militant Protestants feel that their position of privilege in relation to jobs and houses was now possibly in jeopardy.

Some pressure from Britain brought reforms – Derry was promised 1,200 new jobs and 960 new houses by 1981 – but the Civil Rights Association regarded this as too little and too late. A few days after these minimal reforms had been announced, William Craig, Minister for Home Affairs, made a militant speech which included the unfortunate sentence: 'We must face reality: where you have a Catholic majority, you have a lower standard of democracy.'

The Revd Ian Paisley revealed that he held the same doctorate as Billy Graham, from the Bob Jones University in Greenville, South Carolina. TCD Historical Society ended its ban on women in December and Tony O'Reilly resigned from Erin Foods to join the Heinz company in Great Britain as Managing Director.

Seamus Heaney, then 29, won the Somerset Maugham award for his first book of poems, *Death of a Naturalist*, and other Irish books of the year included J.P. Donleavy's *The Beastly Beatitudes of Balthazar B* and Brian Moore's *I am Mary Dunne*.

1969

VATICAN DROPS ST CHRISTOPHER AND 30 OTHER SAINTS
FROM LITURGICAL CALENDAR: INVESTITURE OF PRINCE OF
WALES: FRANCE WITHDRAWS FROM NATO: NEIL ARMSTRONG
FIRST MAN ON MOON: MARY JO KOPECHNE DROWNED IN
KENNEDY CAR: FAMINE IN BIAFRA: HO CHI MINH DIES

Troubles Flare in North

Towards the end of 1968, the Northern Ireland Premier Terence
O'Neill made a television appeal for an end to the violence; and
when the new People's Democracy movement attempted to
hold a protest march from Belfast to Derry on January 1, the
RUC made no attempt to protect what was a perfectly legitimate march from attacks by militant Protestants who
intercepted it at several points along the route, injuring a great
many people and at one point driving the protest marchers,
which included several young women, into a river at Burntollet
and pelting them with stones.

During the weekend that followed, RUC men invaded the
Catholic Bogside area of Derry, batoning men, women and children in the streets and even in their own homes.

A deputation of citizens from the Derry Bogside area went to
London to protest to Prime Minister Harold Wilson about the
behaviour of the RUC and the B-Specials and the Revd Ian
Paisley led a protest at St Paul's Cathedral in London against a
visit by Cardinal Heenan to preach there.

In despair, O'Neill called a general election; he took only 47
per cent of the poll as against 39 per cent for the Revd Ian
Paisley, and 14 per cent for Michael Farrell, one of the leaders of
the People's Democracy.

Bernadette Devlin, an undergraduate at Queen's University
and a founder member of the People's Democracy movement,
was elected as a Westminster MP in a by-election, and her
maiden speech in the House of Commons on April 22, 1969

made headlines right round the world. 'If the British troops are sent in,' she said, 'I should not like to be either the mother or sister of any unfortunate soldier stationed there.' She took her seat on her 22nd birthday, the youngest woman ever to be elected to Westminster and the youngest MP for 50 years.

In May, Dublin Corporation adopted a plan for a new bridge over the Liffey below Butt Bridge; Taoiseach Lynch officially opened the £10,000,000 Bantry Bay oil terminal; and Gulf Oil began preparations to drill for oil in the Irish Sea off the Isle of Man.

Haughey's third budget on May 7 announced complete freedom from income tax for all painters, sculptors, writers and composers living and working in Ireland, regardless of nationality. It was intended to make Ireland a haven for creative artists, but it didn't really work. Although several top-earning writers like Frederick Forsyth and Richard Condon moved to Ireland to avoid tax, they found, as generations of Irish writers had found before them, that they couldn't work in Ireland; for one reason or another, it was too distracting. It was far easier, they eventually decided, to live and work elsewhere and pay the tax.

General de Gaulle spent a holiday in Co Kerry in May, a car ferry across the mouth of the River Shannon between Tarbert in Co Kerry, and Killimer in Co Clare, was opened on May 29, and on June 16 a drugs treatment and advisory clinic in Jervis Street Hospital was opened by Charles Haughey.

In Dublin, TCD reported that applications from Catholics for places at the University had increased by 40 per cent since 1968.

When, in April, an electricity plant at Castlereagh was blown up and the provisions of the Special Powers Acts (to which Premier Wilson had strongly objected, on the grounds that they contravened the Human Rights Convention which Britain had signed) were invoked, O'Neill realised that he could no longer maintain order in the province and resigned. He was succeeded by Major James Chichester Clark.

The next flash-point was the annual march of the Derry Apprentice Boys on August 12. To prevent a recurrence of the

RUC invasion of January, the residents of the Bogside area began to erect barricades and to manufacture petrol bombs from milk bottles and petrol drained from parked cars. When the RUC approached the area, the residents bombarded them with stones and petrol bombs. The RUC replied with CS gas.

A 'Free Derry' was proclaimed and various flags including the Irish tricolour (banned in Northern Ireland since 1921) and the Plough and the Stars of James Connolly's Workers' Republic were flown from the tallest buildings in the area. Bernadette Devlin, MP, was later singled out and jailed for six months for her part in the Bogside Rising.

In Derry, it proved possible for the Catholics to hold out against the RUC because they were concentrated in one area, which became a 'No Go' area (the first of many), into which the RUC and military did not dare to venture. In Belfast, the Catholic ghetto area of the Falls Road and the poor Protestant quarter of the Shankill Road run parallel to one another, with a narrow no-man's-land in between them. The Catholics in Belfast now began to build barricades to protect themselves against the reprisals they knew would surely follow, even commandeering double-deck buses for the purpose. By Thursday, August 14, street fighting had broken out; six people were killed and 87 injured in the shooting before it could be contained.

These incidents were followed by the arrival of the first reinforcements of British troops in the province to augment the token Ulster standing garrison of 2,500. The troops set up 'peace' lines of corrugated iron and barbed wire between the Protestant and Catholic ghetto areas and started to patrol them, carrying automatic weapons. The scene was set for a repetition of what had happened all over Ireland in 1919.

On September 11 the Cameron Commission report on the Northern Ireland disturbances blamed Stormont for much of the Catholic discontent and the police for contributing to the disorder, and a month later the Hunt Report recommended that the RUC be relieved of all military duties, and the armed, part-time B-Specials phased out. A White Paper, published on November 12, suggested a new Northern Ireland security force of 6,000 to take over from the B-Specials in the light of the report. This force, to be known as the Ulster Defence Regiment, would be under the control of the British Army, not the RUC.

Towards the end of the year, Sam Beckett was awarded the Nobel Prize for Literature; his reaction was to grunt the one word 'catastrophe' and abscond to Tunisia where, according to the *Independent*, 'he led a paranoid, briefly peripatetic existence, moving from hotel to hotel, encased in anonymity.'

1970–1980

❦

Back into the Red Again

Once the reforms recommended in the Hunt and Cameron Commissions had been accepted, everybody in Britain confidently assumed that the grievances of the civil rights demonstrators in Northern Ireland would be redressed, and that Ulster's troubles were now over. The Ulster Catholics knew better; not only could the Stormont Government not be trusted to put the reforms into effect, but if they even attempted to do so, they would meet with intractable opposition from the militant Ulster Protestants.

The Paisleyite movement continued to grow in strength and in popularity. The disbanded B-Specials were encouraged to form amateur shooting clubs so that they could keep their marksmanship up to scratch, and it came as no surprise to the Northern Catholics to learn that the battalion commanders in the new, 'impartial' Ulster Defence Regiment all turned out to be ex-B-Specials.

In order to protect themselves from attacks by Protestants and the Protestant police, the Catholic nationalists in Ulster began to equip themselves with arms supplied by the IRA and by well-wishers in the Republic and elsewhere. By now, there had been yet another split within the ranks of the IRA. One section was against direct armed intervention in Ulster at this stage; another section, known as the IRA 'Provisionals', had already started to send in snipers and explosives experts to attack the troops sent there primarily to protect the Catholic nationalist minority. In these circumstances, it was inevitable that the friendly relationship which had initially existed between the nationalists and the British soldiers could not be maintained, and the first open battle between them occurred in April 1970, during riots in the Ballymurphy area of Belfast when the troops used tear gas against nationalist youths.

When the violence escalated, the army imposed a curfew, and, as the months passed, the troubles settled into that deadly pattern which became so numbingly familiar on our TV screens, night after night after night: British armoured cars and personnel carriers prowling around the seedy back streets; soldiers and police in riot gear, carrying shields and batons and CS gas guns; gangs of Belfast and Derry citizens, many of them no more than schoolchildren, hurling stones and petrol bombs at the police; and homes and pubs and shops and factories all going up in flames.

In 1971 it looked for a time as if the troubles were about to spread across the border and involve the Republic; two members of the Irish Government were charged with involvement in an attempt to run guns into Ireland for use against the forces of law and order in the North.

And throughout the decade every attempt at an initiative, assembly, convention or forum put forward by the British to solve the problem was almost immediately boycotted by one or other of the factions in Northern Ireland.

Irish Premier Jack Lynch had talks with British Premier Edward Heath at Chequers; Harold Wilson, the Labour leader, put up his own 12-point peace plan which included a Council of Ireland, the first move towards what became known as the Dublin dimension, and there were tripartite talks between Dublin, Ulster and the Conservative Government at Chequers which got nowhere, though the fact that Britain was now prepared even to discuss the Northern Ireland question with representatives from the Republic was something that would not have been contemplated a generation earlier.

Another increase in the armed forces came in October 1971 when three battalions – about 1,500 men – were added to the 11,900 already stationed in Ulster.

On yet another of Ireland's Bloody Sundays, January 30, 1972, 13 civilians were shot dead by paratroopers during a banned civil rights march in Derry. In reprisal, there was a bomb explosion in the paratroopers' headquarters at Aldershot which killed a priest, a gardener and five women cleaners.

They were saying then that it couldn't go on, and they are still saying it can't go on as I write this, on the day after the explosion in 1993 in Warrington, near Liverpool, in a crowded shopping centre, which injured 65 people and killed a little boy of three who was buying a Mother's Day present, and a boy of 12 who died in hospital later from his wounds.

In the meantime, the troubles had spread to England in the form of constant bomb attacks including indiscriminate pub bombings like those in Guildford and Woolwich and Birmingham, or deliberate, planned assassinations like those of Ross McWhirter, Christopher Ewart Biggs and Airey Neave. Finally, on August 27, 1979, Lord Louis Mountbatten was killed when the boat built for him locally in 1960 was blown up off the coast of Mullaghmore, in Co Sligo, where he had a summer home.

While all this was going on, the Republic was adjusting itself to membership of the European Community. After a referendum in May, 1972, in which the electorate voted to join the Community by a majority of five to one, Ireland was admitted to the EEC on January 1, 1973. Ireland did extremely well out of the CAP (Common Agricultural Policy); in general, joining the community proved very valuable to the Republic. It enhanced and underlined the state's separate identity from Britain, and when on January 1, 1974, Ireland took over the presidency of a community of nine nation states among which Great Britain was merely another member, the Irish were delirious.

Whether membership of the European Community was altogether beneficial for Ireland in the long run is debatable. It gave the Republic an enhanced credit rating, a dangerous facility for a country already heavily in the red and spending a very high percentage of its income on servicing earlier and still unpaid debts; it also probably speeded the already marked tendency of the young people to reject traditional values in favour of the new creed of relentless consumerism.

The plain truth was that by the 1970s Ireland was changing, rapidly and profoundly. De Valera's vision of a land of comely lasses and healthy lads dancing the jig at the cross-roads had given way to a society in which arrests for trading in heroin and cocaine were becoming almost as common as they were in Britain and the States, and crime of all kinds was on the increase.

In *Ireland, a Cultural and Social History, 1922–1979* (London: Fontana, 1981)Terence Brown makes the point that 'ostentatious consumption in a society enjoying a rapid rise in its living standards marked the Seventies in Ireland as in no other country in modern history. Motor cars, fitted kitchens, dish-washing machines, hi-fis, boats and foreign holidays became major preoccupations, if not passions. Supermarkets and the shopping precinct have replaced the many small shops, and the wine bar and the off-licence now cater for a middle class whose drinking habits have been influenced by package holidays and images of the good life nightly presented on the national television channels.'

Television undoubtedly contributed to the change. By 1978, 83 per cent of all Irish homes had television, 92 per cent in Dublin, 54 per cent in the far west, and most people in the east could and did watch the four British television channels as well as the two Irish ones.

Despite the economic improvements of the decade, poverty persisted. At least a quarter and possibly a third of the population lived below the poverty line.

In the mad scramble to join the consumer society, many old values inevitably went to the wall. On December 7, 1972, in yet another referendum, those who bothered to go to the polls voted overwhelmingly to delete from the Constitution the clause recognising the special position of the Catholic Church, a good thing, from most points of view, but a radical departure from traditional Irish thinking. Senator Mary Robinson's projected bill to make contraceptives easier to obtain fell by the wayside, but when a Mrs McGee took a specific case to the Supreme Court, the verdict was that it was no longer an offence under the Constitution to import contraceptives for personal use and legislation to regularise the situation became inevitable.

The Archbishop of Dublin decided during the decade that it was no longer a sin for Catholics to attend Trinity College, Dublin, either, and the Irish language was another of the casualties of the dash for affluence. In 1973, one of the first decisions made by a Fine Gael/Labour Coalition Government was to ditch the requirement that a pass in Irish was necessary before any pupil could be awarded the Leaving Certificate, and Irish was also soon dropped as a qualification for a job in the civil service.

Douglas Hyde and Patrick Pearse, among many others, must have been spinning in their graves.

1970

RHODESIA SEVERS LINKS WITH UK: BIAFRAN FORCES SURRENDER: ASWAN DAM COMPLETED: POLISH SHIPYARD RIOTS: RUSSIAN SPACECRAFT ON MOON: CAMBODIA DECLARES KHMER REPUBLIC: BP MAKES MAJOR OIL STRIKE IN NORTH SEA: GADAFFI LIBYAN PREMIER: LEAK AT WINDSCALE

The Great Arms Trial

From the start of the troubles in Northern Ireland, Taoiseach Jack Lynch found himself in a very difficult situation. The economy of the Republic was still heavily dependent on British tourism, exports to Britain and British investments. He could not very well ignore British pressures on him to get tougher with known members of the IRA who were carrying out raids in Northern Ireland and then escaping over the border to the Republic, where they often openly gave TV interviews and held press conferences; equally, he was not sufficiently strong within his own party to ignore those members of it who were patently in favour of intervention. As a result, he had to content himself with making intermittent threatening and soothing noises aimed in the general direction of Westminster.

In January, the Ulster Defence Regiment, the part-time military unit of the British Army set up to replace the disbanded B-Specials, was officially inaugurated in Belfast. The Archbishop of Dublin, the Most Reverend Dr McQuaid, opened a chapel for the Sacrament Fathers in the building which had been Dublin's famous Red Bank Restaurant, and 60,000 farm workers sought a wage increase of £3 a week. The RUC resumed patrolling the Falls Road area and the Dublin Gate Theatre was declared unsafe by Dublin Corporation because of dry rot. It was closed down.

There were baton charges outside the Royal Hibernian Hotel where the Springboks, the South African rugby team, were staying, and 60,000 people marched on Lansdowne Road to protest against the match. Dublin's first parking meters were installed on January 14 and on January 20, Northern Ireland Premier Chichester-Clark rejected any possibility of 'federal' talks either with the UK or with the Republic.

In April, Trinity College, Dublin and the National University's UCD rejected the Government's suggestion that they should merge, and on April 30 the banks closed their doors yet again, as the clerks went on strike once more.

On May 3, the Derby was won by Nijinsky, a horse trained by Vincent O'Brien, who dominated the Irish racing scene for more than a quarter of a century. A Tipperary man, with stables at Ballydoyle, 120 miles south of Dublin, he burst on the racing scene by training the winners of the Grand National at Aintree for three consecutive years between 1953 and 1955. When he switched to flat racing, he had three winners in the Grand Prix de l'Arc de Triomphe in Paris and six Derby winners, besides the Cheltenham Gold Cup and the Champion Hurdle. One of the greatest trainers of modern times, he encountered problems endemic to modern horse-racing, among them horses like Storm Bird, which were quite simply – in terms of their potential stud value – too valuable to race. Storm Bird was sold for $30,000,000 in 1981 without having run one single race.

On May 5 came the staggering news that Charles Haughey, Minister for Finance, and Neil Blaney, Minister for Agriculture and Fisheries, had been sacked by Taoiseach Jack Lynch, 'because of differences on Government policy towards Northern Ireland' and that Kevin Boland, Minister for Local Government and Social Welfare, had resigned in sympathy with them. Lynch survived the subsequent vote of no confidence by 72 votes to 64.

Then, on May 27, three men – Captain James Kelly, John Kelly of Belfast and Albert Luykx, a Belgian-born business-man – were arrested for conspiracy to import arms, and the next day Charles Haughey and Neil Blaney were also arrested and charged with being implicated in an attempt to run arms into the Republic. Before the trial started, Captain James Kelly, a former Irish Army intelligence officer, claimed that Lynch's Minister of Defence, Jim Gibbons, had known all along about the attempt to import the arms.

Neil Blaney was freed on July 2 because of insufficient evidence against him; he promptly accused the Government of tapping his phone, a charge which was indignantly denied by the Taoiseach.

During the course of the trial of the other defendants, two former ministers swore that the Republic's contingency plans had included limited incursions across the border by the Irish Army, and Minister for Defence Gibbons admitted that he had sanctioned the training of Derry citizens by the Irish Local Defence Force at an Irish Army post in Donegal. On October 23, the jury retired for two hours to consider their verdict before finding the remaining defendants not guilty.

In a general election in Great Britain in June, when Edward Heath became Prime Minister, Bernadette Devlin won her seat with an increased majority, and in August British troops used plastic bullets on rioters in Northern Ireland for the first time.

President Nixon arrived in October to visit relatives at Timahoe, Co Kildare; he was burnt in effigy outside the US Embassy in Dublin as a protest against the Vietnam War.

On November 12, Lynch went to Paris to attend a memorial

mass for General de Gaulle who had died on November 9, and on November 17 the banks, which had been closed for over six months, opened again, but only between 10 and 12.30 am.

The Irish singer Dana (Rosemary Browne) won the Eurovision Song Contest in Amsterdam with *All Kinds of Everything*, the ban on Brendan Behan's *The Borstal Boy* was lifted, and Flann O'Brien's *At Swim-Two-Birds*, originally published in 1939, but now a cult novel, was adapted for the theatre and produced at the Peacock. It had almost disappeared without trace when it first appeared, and the warehouse containing most of the copies had been bombed in the blitz.

1971

MILITARY COUP BY IDI AMIN IN UGANDA: APOLLO 14 LANDS ON MOON: OIL CRISIS: PAPA DOC DIES IN HAIITI: CIVIL WAR IN PAKISTAN: THREE RUSSIAN COSMONAUTS DIE IN SPACE: DEATH OF KHRUSHCHEV: CHINA ADMITTED TO UN: MY LAI MURDER TRIAL IN USA: ETNA ERUPTS

Customs Men Pelted with Condoms

At the Sinn Fein Ard Fheis (party conference) on January 17, it was agreed to drop the abstentionist policy and put forward candidates who would sit in parliament, though it was reaffirmed that the party's ultimate policy was to create a 32-county socialist republic, outside the European Community. The Central Statistics Office reported that receipts from tourism in 1970 had been over £100,000,000, and the banks reported that cheques totalling £7–8,000,000 had been written during the six months' strike. The Department of External Affairs changed its name to the Department of Foreign Affairs, and the Women's Liberation Movement protested at masses all over the city against the Archbishop's ruling on contraception.

Throughout the year things went from bad to worse in Northern Ireland. There were even clashes between rival factions of the IRA – the Provisionals had now been joined in Ulster by other IRA units. In March, when Lord Carrington, the British Defence Secretary, and the British Army Chief of Staff flew to Belfast to explain a new British Army security policy, Major Chichester-Clark resigned, and was succeeded by Mr Brian Faulkner.

I spent about three months, off and on, in Belfast that spring and summer, researching a book about the Orange Order, and I have one abiding memory of the period. Driving alone out into the country to call on Phelim O'Neil, the break-away liberal Unionist MP who was always in trouble with the Orange Order, I approached a cross-roads where a number of young men were casually standing around, on the look-out, it seemed, for cars. At this time cars were regularly being hi-jacked by the IRA and the Ulster paramilitaries for various purposes. The problem? Do you put your head down, jam your foot hard on the accelerator and blast your way past them, or do you drive up to them as if you suspect nothing and stop if requested. I put my head and my foot down and blasted through and nothing happened; others weren't so lucky.

Even at this period, when the violence was at its worst, ordinary, everyday life went on almost as normal, just as it had done in Southern Ireland during the worst of the troubles. And it only needed a few minutes' crack in a pub to convince you that the Irish, north and south of the border, in bad times and in good, have far more in common with each other than either of them have with the British.

On April 14 the Women's Liberation Movement held its first public meeting in the Mansion House, Dublin, and on May 23 organised a protest trip to Belfast to purchase contraceptives, having inflated them like balloons, they pelted customs officers at Connolly railway station on their triumphal return.

A British naval launch was blown up in Cork, and explosions wrecked the homes of two senior RUC men in Belfast. The increased concern for the Northern Nationalists south of the border was expressed when 10,000 ordinary people joined the

IRA Provisionals in a march to Wolfe Tone's grave at Bodenstown, near Dublin, towards the end of June. Although the IRA was an illegal organisation in the Republic at that period, its supporters openly collected funds in the Dublin streets and were not discouraged from doing so by the police.

At dawn on August 9 in Northern Ireland, 300 men were arrested by British troops who broke into their homes, with their faces blackened, and hauled them out of their beds and into custody. Faulkner announced the introduction of internment without trial under the provisions of a Special Powers Act. In the violent protests that followed, 17 people were killed and thousands of Catholic refugees crossed the border into the Republic, where army camps were hurriedly converted to house them.

The nine Stormont Opposition MPs – who had formed themselves into a united Opposition under the title of the Social Democratic and Labour Party (SDLP) under the Nationalist MP Gerry Fitt – announced a campaign of civil disobedience, including the non-payment of all rents and rates, and refused to be party to any official discussions of the problem until all the internees had been released. Eventually, in September, Faulkner agreed to tripartite talks with Taoiseach Lynch and Premier Heath.

By August, the Irish Army had opened two camps for refugees from Northern Ireland in Cork and Wicklow; according to an army spokesman there were already 4,339 refugees from the North in camps in the Republic. Jack Lynch blamed Britain for the border shootings and claimed that the British Army had made 30 incursions into Republican territory in the previous two years.

In September, a new, permanent internment camp at Long Kesh, near Lisburn, was established; internees from the prison ship, *Maidstone*, and from Crumlim Road Jail were transferred there.

Ruairi O Bradaigh was elected President of Sinn Fein at a meeting in Dublin on October 24, and the British forces put down a riot in Long Kesh prison to which 300 internees had now been moved.

Radio Telefis Eireann banned patriotic ballads like *Off to*

Dublin in the Green, *The Patriot Game* and *Today I Killed a Man I Didn't Know* on November 12, and on November 30, the Government decided to bring the case of the Northern Ireland internees before the International Court of Human Rights.

By the end of the year, it was reckoned that there were over 100 members of the Provisional IRA on active service in Northern Ireland. The official IRA declared a truce for Christmas but the shooting went on. By December 29 the total number of soldiers killed during the year had reached 43.

1972

MASSACRE OF ISRAELIS AT MUNICH OLYMPIC GAMES: NOR-
WAY VOTES AGAINST JOINING COMMON MARKET: DEATH OF
DUKE OF WINDSOR: LOD AIRPORT MASSACRE: NIXON IN
CHINA: KISSINGER MEETS LE DUC THO IN PARIS: LABOUR
GOVERNMENT IN AUSTRALIA: MINERS STRIKE IN BRITAIN

Derry's Bloody Sunday

In January the Most Revd Dr McQuaid, Archbishop of Dublin for 31 years, retired; he was succeeded by the Rt Revd Dermot Ryan. The Minister for Justice denied that other ministers' telephones had been tapped, and seven escapees from the prison ship *Maidstone* (they swam to the shore of Belfast Lough) held a press conference in the Dublin headquarters of Sinn Fein which was attended by IRA Chief of staff, Sean MacStiofan.

British paratroopers killed 13 civilians during a civil rights rally in the Bogside area of Derry on Bloody Sunday, January 30; on the following days the British Embassy in Dublin was firebombed a couple of times, then finally burnt down, and at Westminster Ms Bernadette Devlin, MP, belted Home Secretary Reginald Maudling.

By March, the Dail had learned that 18 international conferences had been cancelled as a result of the burning of the British

Embassy, and the B + I Line reported a 60 per cent drop in bookings.

By 1972 the monolithic solidity of the Ulster Unionists had started to crack under the strain. In addition to Paisley's breakaway Democratic Unionists, there were now William Craig's breakaway Vanguard Unionists and three sitting Ulster MPs left the official Unionist Party to join the Alliance, a liberal Unionist (if that is not a contradiction in terms) break-away group who were mainly supporters of O'Neill worried by the official Unionist drift towards Paisleyism.

Then, on March 10, Premier Heath came up with a new initiative which included three points: periodic plebiscites on the border issue, an immediate start to the phasing out of internment without trial, and the transfer of all responsibility for law and order to Westminster. When Faulkner told the British Premier that the Stormont Parliament would never wear these pre-conditions, Heath prorogued Stormont on March 24 and appointed William Whitelaw Secretary of State for Ireland to administer the Six Counties under direct rule from Westminster.

Craig's Vanguard movement immediately announced a two-day general strike that paralysed Belfast and most of Ulster, and Britain sent more troops to Northern Ireland, bringing the total up to 18,500.

Heath's next move was to propose an Assembly, elected by proportional representation, with a power-sharing executive (six official Unionists, one Alliance and four SDLP) led by Brian Faulkner, with Gerry Fitt of the SDLP as his deputy.

It is significant that Heath, like all the other British leaders who ever attempted to solve any aspect of the Irish Question, plumped for proportional representation as the only possible way of ensuring that the minority would get a fair proportion of the votes, though they would have nothing to do with it in their own elections. And equally significant, perhaps, that although it had been the system of election specified for both Irish parliaments in Lloyd George's Government of Ireland Act of 1921, one of the first things the Stormont Government did was to throw PR overboard and go for the first-past-the-post system which would ensure a big Unionist majority for the foreseeable future, just as it has kept the Tories in power in Britain for the last, disastrous fourteen years. (PR had been abolished for local government elections in 1922 and for elections to Stormont in 1929.) This is probably the strongest single argument in favour of the fairness of the PR system. I'm surprised that it is not used more emphatically.

Taoiseach Lynch welcomed the abolition of Stormont and Heath's decision to impose direct rule from Westminster.

On April 19, the Widgery Report blamed the NICRA march for the 13 deaths in Derry on Bloody Sunday in January; the report accepted that the first shot had been fired *at* the British troops.

In June President Gadaffi of Libya claimed that he was supplying arms to the IRA and twelve of Ireland's top industrial managers were among the 118 victims of a BEA Trident aircraft which crashed on taking off from Heathrow for a European Council meeting in Brussels.

A Marriage Bill, first circulated in July, raised the marriage age to 16; previously it had been 14 for boys and 12 for girls. In July, also, Governor Ronald Reagan spent three days in Dublin on the final stage of a European tour as special envoy for President Nixon and in August it was announced that two famous old Dublin hotels were to close, the Moira and Jury's.

This was a period during which Dublin's eating habits profoundly changed. The old restaurants, which were expensive but extremely good, like Jammet's, the Red Bank, the Royal Hibernian, the Russell, the Dolphin, the Moira and Jury's, were all closing down and were being replaced by fast-food outlets – Dublin's first Macdonald's opened in Grafton Street in May 1977 – such as Italian pizza houses, hamburger joints and American drugstore type diners. At the same time a few trendy new restaurants appeared, prospered for a time and then disappeared.

One very singular Irish institution, Bewley's Oriental Cafés – there were three of them in Dublin – continued to provide an extremely popular meeting place for all classes of the community, over a cup of extremely good coffee served with cream in a Wedgwood pot. The tables were marble-topped, and you sat in red, velvet-covered stalls or on old bentwood chairs, and the entire restaurant reeked of real coffee from the beans roasting in the window.

Taoiseach Lynch went to Munich for the Olympic Games in September and a National Institute for Higher Studies was opened in Limerick. The Pfizer Chemical Corporation opened a plant at Ringaskiddy, Co Cork which certainly was an eyesore and very possibly a source of pollution; on the other hand, it provided employment in an area where jobs were scarce and it spread a great deal of wealth in the area indirectly. On November 1, Value Added Tax was introduced to replace the old turnover and wholesale taxes.

On Citizenship Sunday, November 4, a Catholic Archbishop of Dublin attended a service in Christ Church Cathedral for the first time since the Reformation.

1973

ARAB TERRORISTS KILL 20 AT ROME AIRPORT: PAUL GETTY KIDNAPPED: YOM KIPPUR WAR IN ISRAEL: FAMINE IN ETHIOPIA: NIXON SWORN IN AS US PRESIDENT: PEACE IN VIETNAM: BEN GURION DIES: PRINCESS ANNE MARRIES MARK PHILLIPS: PERON AGAIN PRESIDENT OF ARGENTINA

Ireland in the EC

On January 1, Ireland, along with Britain and Denmark, joined the European Community, and on January 15 became a member of the European Investment Bank. The toll of deaths and injuries in Northern Ireland in 1972 was released in January: it totted up to 467 dead and 3,148 injured.

An indication of the growing menace of the drug problem in Ireland was the circulation on January 4 of the Misuse of Drugs Bill, which imposed penalties of up to 14 years and fines of up to £3,000 for drug pushing.

In January Tara Shoes, Ltd, of Kells, Co Meath, closed down

with a loss of 64 jobs, and on January 20 there was a car bomb explosion in Sackville Place, Dublin, which killed one man and injured 30.

Towards the end of January, Elizabeth McKee, the first woman detained under the Detention of Terrorists Act in Northern Ireland, was transferred to the Maze prison and it was reported that the former Provisional Commander in Anderston, Gerry Adams, was taking over from Sean MacStiofan as Provisional IRA Chief of Staff.

On February 5 came the sudden dissolution of the Dail; an election was to be held in five weeks, before the 18-year-olds were due to get the vote. The two main opposition parties decided to face Fianna Fail as a Coalition.

On March 14, after a Fianna Fail defeat, a Coalition Government was formed with Liam Cosgrave as Taoiseach, Brendan Corish (Labour) as Tanaiste and Minister for Health and Garret FitzGerald (Fine Gael) as Minister for Foreign Affairs. In a border poll, held on March 8, more than 57 per cent of the Northern Ireland electorate had voted to remain part of the UK. Most nationalists boycotted the poll.

On March 16, Tony O'Reilly, ex-rugby football star and chief executive of Heinz, UK, paid £1,095,000 to take over Independent Newspapers.

Six men were arrested when the Irish Naval Service intercepted a Cypriot boat, the *Claudia*, carrying arms, off the Irish coast, near Waterford. In Northern Ireland, William Craig of the Vanguard Party and the Revd Ian Paisley's Democratic Unionists decided to form a coalition known as the Vanguard Unionist Progressive Party to challenge the official Unionists in the forthcoming elections.

Obligatory Irish was dropped from examinations in the Republic from April 5, Sean MacStiofan was released from the Curragh Camp, and it was reported that more than half the total active strength of the SAS Paratroop Regiment was now in Northern Ireland.

On May 14 the Irish Minister for Defence ordered two new battalions to join the border control, increasing the number of Irish troops there to 1,040.

On May 23 the first Guinness official strike over pay for 215 years occurred, and if I have relatively little social history of this particular period to offer, the plain truth is that the people, like the newspapers, North and South of the border alike, were totally preoccupied at this period with the Troubles in the North and the prospect, which then seemed imminent, that they were about to spread across the border into the Republic.

On June 4, Aldergrove Airport near Belfast was hit by a Russian hand-launched missile; by now the IRA were getting their hands on some highly sophisticated weapons.

Eamon de Valera retired as President on June 24 and was succeeded by Erskine Childers. A new ESB power station at Turlough Hill in the Wicklow Mountains above Glendalough, using the pump storage system, came on stream on July 14.

More guns and ammunition were seized at Dublin docks on July 16, and on July 19 the British Army arrested 18 Provisionals in Northern Ireland, including Gerry Adams. On the last day of July came the opening of the new Northern Ireland power-sharing assembly at Stormont.

On August 3, the Northern Ireland Community Relations Commission reported that between 30,000 and 60,000 people had been forced to leave their homes in Belfast during the previous three and a half years, as a result of intimidation.

Letter bombs caused injuries in London and Washington, and the verdict in the inquest into the deaths of the 13 people killed in Derry on Bloody Sunday, 1972, accused the British paratroopers of 'sheer, unadulterated murder'.

British Prime Minister Edward Heath had a meeting with Taoiseach Cosgrave at Casement Airport at Baldonnel, near Dublin, on September 17, to discuss the proposed Council of Ireland, planned to bring a Dublin dimension into matters of mutual concern such as tourism, power and transport, and there were further car bombings in England.

Yet another example of the IRA's increasing use of modern technology came on October 31, when three Provisional IRA prisoners were snatched by helicopter from the exercise yard of Mountjoy Jail in the centre of Dublin and in full view of the police and warders.

In November, eight people were found guilty at Winchester Crown Court of offences in connection with London bombings; they included two young girls, the Price sisters, Dolors and Marion, who were sentenced to life imprisonment.

On December 2, Francis Pym replaced William Whitelaw as British Secretary of State for Northern Ireland, and on December 6 the question of a Council of Ireland was given priority during the first day's talks at Sunningdale, but the only agreement that was reached was an agreement to try again next year. On the same day, £15,500 was paid for the Jack B. Yeats painting which used to hang in the front room in Jammet's restaurant.

The worst spate of bombing in Central London since March hit Pentonville prison, Horseferry House, Westminster, and a Post Office Sorting Office; more than 60 people were wounded.

On December 19, the Price sisters, serving life sentences in Brixton Jail, were said to be in a weak condition as a result of hunger striking and forced feeding. On December 19, too, the ban on the importation of contraceptives was dropped; the decision made in the Supreme Court on Mrs McGee's appeal was that the ban on contraceptives was unconstitutional.

A new development on December 28 was the kidnapping outside his own home of Herr Thomas Niedermayer, the German honorary consul in Belfast. He was still missing when the year ended.

During the year, the Freedom of the City of Dublin had been conferred on actors Hilton Edwards and Micheal MacLiammoir of the Dublin Gate Theatre; the Irish Government bought Ardmore Film Studios for £390,000; the Abbey Theatre celebrated its 75th anniversary with a performance of M.J. Molloy's *The King of Friday's Men*, and *The Freedom of the City*, Brian Friel's play about Derry's Bloody Sunday, was a great success at the Royal Court Theatre in London.

1974

WINTER OF DISCONTENT IN BRITAIN: ARMY SEIZES POWER
IN PORTUGAL: NIXON RESIGNS: FORD TAKES OVER:
ERLICHMAN AND DEAN JAILED AFTER WATERGATE TRIAL:
TURKS CUT CYPRUS NORTH OF NICOSIA: BADER
MEINHOFF TRIAL: YITZHAK RABIN PREMIER OF ISRAEL

End of NI Assembly

On the first day of the New Year, Brian Faulkner, former
Premier of the Northern Ireland Government, reoccupied his
old office at Stormont as head of the executive of the new
Northern Ireland Assembly. But not for long. On January 4, the
Ulster Unionist Council, the governing body of the Unionist
Party, rejected the All-Ireland Council by 427 votes to 377 and
before the end of the month, Ian Paisley had denounced the
agreement. His Democratic Unionists, as well as the official
Unionists and the Vanguard Party, withdrew from the Assembly,
determined to have no further truck with power-sharing in any
shape or form.

The kidnapped Dr Niedermayer was still missing. The IRA
had seized another helicopter on January 24 and had bombed a
field in Strabane with milk churns filled with explosives and
there had been a number of appeals to the British Government
to let the Price sisters die or transfer them to a prison in
Northern Ireland. There doesn't appear to be any connection
between these very diverse happenings, but a link was later to
emerge.

On February 2, the former British Home Secretary, Reginald
Maudling, was injured by a letter bomb in London. As a result of
the OPEC oil crisis, the price of petrol was increased by 9p a gallon to 50p and the National Prices Commission reported that
cars were at least 25 per cent more expensive in Dublin than in
Belfast or London, due largely to excise duty and VAT.

After the winter of discontent came the collapse of the Heath

Government and the general election of March 1974. The Anti-Sunningdale Loyalists won 11 of the 12 Northern Ireland seats in the elections and decided to form a separate party, the United Ulster Unionist Coalition (UUUC), determined to resist any further attempt at power-sharing and, even more important, any notion of collaboration with Dublin. Harold Wilson took over as British Prime Minister on March 4 and Merlyn Rees was appointed Secretary of State for Northern Ireland.

Connradh na Ghaelige (the Gaelic League) attacked the Minister for Post and Telegraphs, Conor Cruise O'Brien, for his proposal that BBC television should be transmitted in Ireland by RTE and demanded a second Irish channel. The text of a new bill to control the importation, sale and manufacture of contraceptives was published; it prohibited the purchase of contraceptives, except by married people.

In April, the Archbishop of Dublin, the Most Revd Dr Ryan, handed Merrion Square back to the people of Dublin to be used as a public park: the project to build a Catholic cathedral in the square had finally been dropped. Paintings worth millions were stolen from the home of millionaire Sir Alfred Beit in Blessington, Co Wicklow.

On May 1, the Government repealed the 20-year tax-free holiday on profits made from mining in Ireland and introduced a bill enabling them to tax such profits and use the revenue to develop Irish industry; the following day Marathon Petroleum, Ireland, Ltd announced a find of natural gas in the sea off Kinsale with reserves for at least 20 years.

On May 3, the thieves who had stolen the Beit paintings offered to return them if the Price sisters were transferred to a jail in Northern Ireland, and the next day some paintings from the collection, worth about £6,000,000, were found by the Civic Guards in a cottage in Glandore, Co Cork; a Dr Rose Dugdale, daughter of an English millionaire, was detained in connection with the theft.

The final death-blow to the power-sharing Assembly came in May, when Brian Faulkner broke with Paisley's Democratic Unionists and the Vanguard Party to try to reform the old Unionist Party as a pro-Assembly party, but it was too late. The

Ulster Workers Council had already declared a General Strike against the whole idea of power-sharing. It started on May 15, and went on until the Executive was broken up and the Assembly prorogued at the end of the month. By this time, Rees had authorised the use of British troops to control the distribution of fuel and operate the power stations and the Irish Government had recalled 300 troops from UN service in the Middle East to augment border controls. There were four car bomb explosions in the Republic on May 27, three at rush hour in Dublin and one in Monaghan. The bombs killed 27 and injured over 100 people, six of whom died later from their injuries.

On June 7, the Price sisters abandoned their hunger strike after 205 days, but that wasn't the end of the story by any means. Dr Rose Dugdale was charged on June 19 with hijacking a helicopter in Co Donegal for use in the milk churn bombing incident, and on June 25, she was sentenced to nine years for receiving paintings stolen from Sir Alfred Beit. The full details never came out, because all hearings of the case were censored by the Irish Government.

In July, the Department of Foreign Affairs reported that Ireland had achieved a net profit of £46,000,000 at the end of its first year as a member of the European Community. The Government's Contraceptive Bill was defeated in the Dail by 75 votes to 60; Taoiseach Cosgrave was among those who voted against it. And a bomb in the Tower of London killed one woman and injured 35, mostly foreign tourists.

On July 4, 1974, the British Labour Government had published a White Paper announcing yet another initiative, a Constitutional Convention to decide what form of government would prove 'most likely to command the most wide-spread acceptance throughout the whole country'.

In August the Women's Liberation Movement invaded that ultimate male sanctuary, the Forty Foot bathing place at Sandycove, Co Dublin, where, for as long as anybody could remember, men and boys had dived naked from the rocks to swim in the Irish Sea. They were now joined, willy-nilly, by the ladies. The foundation stone of a new Church of Our Lady

Queen of Ireland (to accommodate 10,000) was laid at Knock, Co Mayo, on the site of one of the last recorded sightings of the Virgin Mary in 1879, and the Irish Union of School Students reported that corporal punishment was still being used in 84 per cent of Irish secondary schools.

Kenneth Littlejohn, an Englishman, was sentenced to penal servitude for 20 years by the Special Criminal Court (Military Tribunal) in Dublin in August for his part in a £67,000-raid on the Allied Irish Bank's Grafton Street branch in October 1971, and his brother Keith was sentenced to 15 years for the same offence.

During the course of an appeal in the High Court, which was dismissed, it came out in the evidence that the Littlejohns had been working as undercover agents for British Intelligence. Kenneth Littlejohn said that he had been informed that the raid was one of a number of operations intended to give the impression that there had been a large increase in the activities of illegal organisations in the Republic, and so hasten the progress through the Dail of anti-terrorist legislation, which, the British felt, was taking too long. He had been, he added, regularly reminded that if he were arrested in the Republic, any knowledge of him would be immediately denied by the British Government.

In September, Enoch Powell was adopted as a highly unlikely official Unionist candidate for South Down and prisoners at the Maze in Long Kesh refused to take any food as a protest against conditions in the jail; a riot there, the following month, spread to other prisons in the North. At one stage the Governor of the jail was being held hostage by the prisoners in Armagh.

Five died and over 50 people were injured on October 5 in the pub bombings in Guildford, Surrey, a town surrounded by military camps, barracks, and other MOD establishments, and a popular watering hole for soldiers off duty.

In October, T.F. O'Higgins was nominated Chief Justice and there was an oil spill in Bantry Bay which halted all operations on Whiddy Island as Gulf Oil fought a slick along 22 miles of the most beautiful and most unspoilt coastline in Europe, the biggest ever spill in the history of Gulf Oil.

In November, President Erskine Childers collapsed at a dinner and died later in the Mater hospital in Dublin. He was succeeded by Cearbhall O Dalaigh, a lawyer who had been Attorney-General in several Fianna Fail governments as well as Ireland's representative at the European Court of Justice. On October 22 James Molyneaux was elected leader of the Ulster Unionist MPs at Westminster, a position which he still holds.

On November 4, Powerscourt House, one of the most gracious and best-known big houses, at Enniskerry, about 16 miles from Dublin – once the seat of an Elizabethan, Anglo-Irish aristocratic family, and at that time the home of the Slazengers, the sports equipment manufacturers – was destroyed by fire.

On November 7, one person was killed and 28 injured in an IRA bomb explosion in a pub in Woolwich, London, and on November 21, bombs in Birmingham killed 17 people and injured 182; two of the injured victims died in hospital the following day.

In December, a baby was born to Dr Rose Dugdale in Limerick prison, the Price sisters were moved to Durham Jail, the Minister of Education announced that there would be no University merger, and the Provisional IRA announced a ceasefire from midnight on December 22.

Sean MacBride shared the Nobel Peace Prize with the former Japanese premier, Eisaku Sato, the Irish Government decided that the Great Hall of UCD in Earlsfort Terrace would in future be used as a 900-seat concert hall, and a new drink arrived on the market, Bailey's 'traditional' Irish Cream, made from surplus Irish cream, chocolate and whiskey. It was an immediate popular success all over the world, particularly with women, probably because it has a bland, sweetish taste while packing quite a punch. It is now demanded – and supplied – even in such remote corners of the world as the Café des Treize Vents in Herepian in the Languedoc.

1975

BALCOMBE STREET SIEGE IN LONDON; MARGARET THATCHER BECOMES LEADER OF CONSERVATIVE PARTY: LOME CONVENTION SIGNED IN TOGOLAND: SAIGON BECOMES HO CHI MINH CITY: WAR IN ANGOLA: DEATH OF ARISTOTLE ONASSIS: JUAN CARLOS I KING OF SPAIN

Trouble at Maze Prison

On January 1, Ireland took over Presidency of the European Council of Ministers and the next day, the Provisional IRA announced a two-week extension of their Christmas cease-fire. It ended at midnight on January 16.

On January 8, the Republic claimed oil and gas exploration rights over 15,000 square miles of the North Atlantic and on January 27, the Europa Hotel in Belfast was hit by bombs for the 27th time since it opened, only two and a half years earlier.

On January 23, a National Gas Board was established to distribute natural gas and build an £18,000,000 pipeline between Dublin, Cork, Waterford and Limerick.

On February 9, the IRA council announced an indefinite cease-fire from February 10, in Northern Ireland and Great Britain, and on February 12, the Catholic Church appointed a press officer in Dublin; it was perhaps the most striking indication of the changing times that the Catholic Church felt itself in need of a PRO to state its case

Airey Neave was appointed Conservative Shadow Cabinet spokesman on Northern Ireland on February 18, and, in view of the cease-fire, 80 detainees out of 496 were released from Long Kesh.

On March 7 the Freedom of the City of Dublin was conferred on Eamon de Valera and John A. Costello, and there was an EC summit at Dublin Castle. On March 18, the Price sisters were transferred from Durham Jail to Armagh, and on April 2 the IRA exploded a 20-pound bomb in Belfast City, the first bomb in seven weeks, as a warning against truce violations by the British army.

On April 3, 70 workers in a bankrupt piano factory on the Shannon Industrial Estate (one of the first of the new industrial enterprises to collapse) were being offered pianos in lieu of wages. The worst weekend's violence in Northern Ireland for months left ten dead and over 75 injured. A few days later Merlyn Rees announced that 39 people had died and 490 had been injured in Northern Ireland in the first three months of 1975.

An Irish parliamentary delegation to Libya failed to elicit any assurance from Colonel Gadaffi that no further arms would be supplied to the IRA, and the Labour Government's effort to end the stalemate – the suggestion of a Constitutional Convention to make recommendations on the Irish Question – bit the dust. Although all the parties represented in the Convention submitted proposals, only the loyalist majority proposal was ever submitted to the British Government and it, predictably, sought full parliamentary powers for a Unionist-dominated Stormont with no interference of any kind from Westminster. In the hope of breaking the deadlock, the Labour Government extended the life of the Convention and referred its report back for reconsideration. The British underestimated Ulster recalcitrance then, as they had done in 1913, and as they have done ever since.

On May 15 the Dail was told that 54 industrial undertakings had closed between February 1974 and February 1975, and that Ireland still had the highest proportion of its workforce (23.4 per cent) engaged in agriculture in the whole Community.

On July 22, Irish farmers learned that they were to get a £17,000,000 boost to their incomes following an EEC decision to devalue the Green £ by 5 per cent, and on July 31, three members of the Miami Showband and two UVF (Ulster Volunteer Force) men were blown up by a UVF bomb on the main Dublin-Belfast road, while the band was returning from a concert in Northern Ireland. The UVF was among the first of a number of new Unionist paramilitary organisations to emerge at this period.

On August 15, six men known as the Birmingham Six were

jailed for life at Lancaster Crown Court for their part in the Birmingham bombings, and on September 16, three men and a woman (the Guildford Four) appeared on 11 charges in connection with the bombing of pubs in Guildford, Surrey, and Woolwich. On August 29, Eamon de Valera died in a Co Dublin nursing home, aged 92, and was buried, with full state honours, on September 2.

A contract for the Kinsale pipeline was signed with the British Gas Corporation on September 22, and on October 3, the kidnappers of Dr Tiede Herrema, a Dutch businessman who had disappeared on that day, threatened to kill him if Dr Rose Dugdale and two other prisoners were not released; by October 8, over 4,000 Gardai were involved in the search for the Herrema kidnappers, who turned out to be Marion Coyle (22), and Eddie Gallagher, an IRA man. They suddenly found themselves surrounded by press, army and police at Monastrevan, Co Kildare, on October 21 and eventually surrendered on November 7, because they couldn't take the pressure themselves. Dr Herrema was perfectly healthy, and even Marion Coyle was in far better shape than Eddie Gallagher when the siege ended. On November 7 also, the Kildare Street Club and the University Club amalgamated, another sign of the times.

On November 27 Ross MacWhirter, publisher and TV personality and co-author with his brother Norris of the *Guinness Book of Records*, was shot dead at his home in Enfield, Middlesex. He had been a well-known right-wing member of the British Civil Liberties movement and had never made any secret of his opposition to the IRA.

On December 7, four IRA Provisionals held two Londoners hostage in their Balcombe Street flat for five days. During the year, Margaret Thatcher succeeded Edward Heath as the leader of the Conservative Party in Britain, and Lord Lucan, an Irish peer, disappeared in curious circumstances.

1976

ANGOLA EXECUTES MERCENARIES: COUP IN LEBANON: MIL-
ITARY JUNTA TAKES OVER IN ARGENTINA: CALLAGHAN
BECOMES BRITISH PREMIER: SOWETO RIOTS: ISRAELI
HIJACK RESCUE AT ENTEBBE: WAR IN ETHIOPIA: CARTER US
PRESIDENT: MAO TSE TUNG DIES: CONCORDE IN SERVICE

President O'Dalaigh Resigns

The year began with the ordination of the first woman priest in
the Presbyterian Church at Larne, Co Antrim – not that so papish
an expression as that of priest would ever be used by any Larne
Presbyterian – and the announcement that the budget deficit in
the Republic had reached an all-time record of £258,900,000. On
January 22, the Central Bank reported that foreign borrowings
had hit the £560,000,000 mark. Not only was the budget deficit
the highest ever; unemployment in the Republic at 116,000 was
higher than it had been since 1940.

The Municipal Gallery of Modern Art in Parnell Square,
Dublin, was renamed the Hugh Lane Gallery of Modern Art in
January and the Government published a list of structures to be
preserved in the Dublin area; they included the Martello towers
(built by the British to protect the coast against a possible invasion by Napoleon), and the Grand Canal Hotel at Portobello
Lock, as well as the GPO, the Royal Hospital at Kilmainham
and the Wellington Monument in Phoenix Park.

Dr Herrema, perhaps understandably, left Ireland to take a
post in his native Holland, and on February 12 Frank Stagg, a
member of the Provisional IRA, died in Wakefield Jail after 60
days on hunger strike.

On March 11 Eddie Gallagher was sentenced to 20 years
imprisonment and Marion Coyle to 15 years for kidnapping and
imprisoning Dr Herrema. On April 1, Princess Grace of Monaco
bought the Co Mayo cottage from which her grandfather had
emigrated to America a century earlier and on April 25, 10,000

people defied a Government ban and marched through Dublin to celebrate the 60th anniversary of the Easter Rising.

Some 500 British troops were withdrawn from Northern Ireland and replaced by military police in May, women were called for jury service for the first time in the Republic, and the Chairman of the Irish Gay Rights Movement called for an investigation into the position of homosexuals in Ireland. Nine prisoners tunnelled their way out of the Maze prison on May 5 and on the same day an Irish Army patrol arrested eight SAS paratroopers, caught on the wrong side of the border in Co Louth; they were released on bail and disappeared over the border into Northern Ireland.

The bank clerks went on strike again on June 29 for eight weeks until Sept 6, and an economic survey on June 30 reported inflation at 18 per cent and unemployment at 130,000.

On July 12, Ireland learned that it was to have 15 seats in the 410-seat European Parliament. On July 21, Christopher Ewart-Biggs, the new British Ambassador to Ireland – he had only just presented his credentials to the President – was murdered outside the embassy residence,.

The Department of Agriculture reported that the income of the average farmer had increased by 32 per cent in 1975, and the prisoners at the Maze found a new way of protesting about conditions in the jail; they threw 673 cooked meals over the compound walls.

A new Women's Peace Movement started in Belfast. On August 13, thousands attended the funeral of three children killed by a hijacked car in Belfast and the following day a peace march was led through the city by the aunt of one of the deceased children, Mairead Corrigan, and her friend, Mrs Betty Williams; they followed it up with another peace rally a week later, which attracted an enormous amount of media attention.

The Department of Foreign Affairs reported on August 24 that European Community grants and subsidies had amounted to £121,000,000 in 1975, and on August 26 the European Commission on Human Rights found the British Government guilty of using torture in the interrogation of internees in Northern Ireland in 1971.

A pub and a cinema in Lower Abbey Street, Dublin were bombed in protest against the Irish Government's decision to declare a state of emergency and introduce emergency powers. Using a guillotine motion to curtail discussion of the measure in the Dail, an Emergency Powers Bill was rushed through on September 10, and passed by 63 votes to 56. The President wasn't too happy about this, and decided to consult the Council of State as to whether it was unconstitutional, an action which was bitterly resented by the Government. When, on October 15, the Supreme Court found that the bill was perfectly constitutional, Minister for Defence Donegan referred to the President as 'a thundering disgrace'. In his autobiography, *All in a Life*, Garret FitzGerald suggests that this word 'thundering' is normally used in Ireland as a euphemisim for something a great deal stronger, probably what my grandchildren call the f-word.

On October 22, President Cearbhall O Dalaigh resigned and was replaced by Dr Patrick Hillery, the Irish Finance Commissioner to the European Community. As the Fianna Fail Minister for External Affairs, he had been largely responsible for the conduct of the negotiations which had led to Ireland's accession to the EEC. He was returned unopposed and was inaugurated on December 3.

A European Trades Union conference on November 19 took the view that the low proportion of Irish married women among the total of female workers was evidence of discrimination. For the record, at this particular period, only 13.5 per cent of the female workers in Ireland were married women, as compared with 67.2 per cent in Britain, 62 per cent in France and 59 per cent in West Germany.

On November 4 the Government announced that it found the EEC offer of $5,000,000 to improve the 'catastrophic' state of the Irish economy extremely disappointing.

In December a family planning booklet, published by the Fertility Guidance Company and widely circulated for four years, was suddenly banned as 'indecent and obscene'. Just before Christmas, the Government admitted that inflation had reached 20 per cent and the Provisional IRA announced an unofficial cease-fire.

The Women's Peace Movement continued to grow in strength, and when it was discovered that it was too late to put the names of the two ladies behind the movement forward for the Nobel Peace Prize, the Norwegian people collected £200,000 as a People's Peace Prize for Mairead Corrigan and Mrs Betty Williams, who were presented with the cheque by King Olaf on November 30. On December 12 they were presented with the Carl von Ossiettzy medal for Peace in West Germany.

1977

MOLUCCAN TERRORISTS HIJACK TRAIN IN HOLLAND: GANG OF FOUR EXPELLED FROM CHINESE COMMUNIST PARTY: SILVER JUBILEE OF QUEEN ELIZABETH II: FAMINE IN GHANA: STEVE BIKO DIES IN SOUTH AFRICAN JAIL: 574 DIE IN AIR CRASH IN CANARIES: MAKARIOS DIES IN CYPRUS

Waiting for the Big Bonanza

At midnight on the last day of 1976, the Irish unilaterally declared a new 200-mile fishing zone. The first victim of violence in Northern Ireland in 1977 was a 16-month-old baby, and there were five knee-cappings, a particularly nasty form of punishment devised by the IRA to deter defectors, traitors and informers and encourage all the others. A new wealth tax, levied on all incomes over the first £100,000, had yielded £6,500,000 in 1976, the Government announced.

On Feb 8 Britain undertook, at Strasbourg, not to use interrogation methods which had been found to constitute torture by the International Court, and the *Irish Times* published a series of articles on police brutality in the Republic. On March 7, the eight British soldiers still on bail for having strayed across the border in May 1976 appeared before the Special Criminal Court

281

in Dublin. They were fined £100 each for possession of arms without licences, and released.

And in Belfast on February 11, 26 members of the UDF (the Ulster Defence Force, another new Protestant paramilitary organisation) were sentenced to a total of 700 years' imprisonment for their parts in a campaign of bombing and armed robbery in East Antrim.

At the end of March Marathon and Esso decided to drop drilling for oil in Irish waters, but on April 1, Shell and Agip began prospecting off Loop Head, Co Clare and later in the year, in October, the first off-shore oil rig arrived in Dublin Bay. So certain were the Irish at this period of finding oil somewhere in the seas around their coast, that there was a widely-believed story circulating among the journalists that successive Irish Ministers for Finance were now preparing two budgets every year; one based on the assumption that they would have found considerable oil reserves in time for Budget Day and another, based on the assumption that they would not.

On June 6 Tim Severin reached Newfoundland from Crosshaven, Co Cork, in a reproduction of Saint Brendan's leather-covered curragh, after a year at sea designed to prove that it was possible that the Irish really had discovered the New World before the Portuguese and the Spanish.

In June, too, Fianna Fail had an unexpected general election victory with 75 seats as against Fine Gael's 37 and Labour's 17; Jack Lynch became Taoiseach of the 21st Dail with George Colley as his deputy, and Charles Haughey, forgiven for his alleged involvement in the Arms Plot, became Minister for Health and Social Welfare.

In August, Belfast rioters clashed with the RUC and British troops as security was tightened up for the Queen's Jubilee visit to Ulster, and on August 9 five Belfast women paraded in Dublin wearing only blankets and demanding political status for Republicans and Socialists in Northern Ireland's jails. Why they decided to make this protest in front of Dublin's GPO, instead of in Belfast or Westminster, has never been clear.

On August 10, Mairead Corrigan and her Women's Peace Movement colleagues were received by Queen Elizabeth on board the Royal Yacht. Before the end of the month, in the first detailed breakdown of their finances, the movement revealed that it had not yet provided any money whatever for the community from the £200,000 donated by the people of Norway; £75,000 had been 'disbursed', as they quaintly put it, on the movement's headquarters and on helping people to escape from paramilitary organisations.

There was a key policy change on power-sharing in the Social Democratic and Labour Party (SDLP) in Northern Ireland, with more emphasis placed on an all-Ireland political context, the so-called 'Dublin dimension'. Naturally this increased the fury of the Northern Ireland Unionists who always feared the Dublin dimension more than anything else. One member of the Stormont Government put it to me very forcibly in 1965 when I was researching a book on the Irish Question: 'We've got to accept that the Ulsterman is basically unattractive, both to the southern English and to the southern Irish. The southern English get on far better with the southern Irish than they do with us. And so we're always terrified that the English are going to do a deal with the Dublin Government behind our backs.'

In September, Amnesty International called on the Irish Government to hold an inquiry into Garda brutality, Charles Haughey announced free phone rental for pensioners, and on October 10, Ulster's Peace Women, Mairead Corrigan and Mrs Betty Williams, were awarded the Nobel Peace Prize (worth approximately $167,000).

Alcan, the international aluminium consortium, decided in November to build a plant on a site in the Shannon estuary; the Irish Industrial Authority agreed to provide £16,750,000 towards this development over a nine-year period from 1978. Ferenko, the Dutch steel cord factory in Limerick, which had laid off 1,000 workers in November, was wound up finally on December 20, and the Standard Pressed Steel Company in Galway closed down with a loss of 230 jobs.

VAT was extended to a wide range of items and services, among them livestock sales at marts, auctioneers' fees, artificial insemination and entrance to the Dublin Zoological Gardens.

1978

JOHN PAUL II BECOMES THIRD POPE IN ONE YEAR: WAR IN
LEBANON: MURDER OF ALDO MORO BY RED BRIGADE: PEACE
PRIZE FOR BEGIN AND SADAT: JONESTOWN MASS SUICIDE:
GOLDA MEIR DIES: IRAN DEMONSTRATIONS AGAINST SHAH:
THE TIMES CLOSES DOWN: AMOCO CADIZ OIL SPILL

Well Woman Centre Opens

On January 1, domestic rates were abolished. A faith healer called Finbarr Nolan, who had attracted huge crowds of disciples and a great deal of media publicity by curing all sorts of complaints through the simple process of the laying on of his hands (minimum treatment, three visits and fairly pricey), went bankrupt and surrendered his passport to the High Court. A new family planning operation, known as the Well Woman Centre, opened in Dublin on January 17 and was immediately picketed by Mna na hEireann (the women of Ireland), a violently anti-contraceptive outfit.

On January 18 Britain was found guilty of inhuman treatment – during an in-depth interrogation of 14 internees in Northern Ireland – by the European Court at Strasbourg. In August 1971, 12 Northern Ireland internees had been taken to a special interrogation centre in Ballykelly Camp in Co Derry. There they were medically examined, photographed naked, dressed in boiler suits and hooded. They were then taken into a large room, where they were spread-eagled against the wall, while 'white noise' was piped into the room from a tape recorder. Periods of interrogation interrupted this procedure, and for the first 24 hours they were refused food – later, they were offered bread and water every six hours. They were prevented from sleeping and kept standing against the wall, with their hands above their heads, in the 'search' position. The Court of Human Rights, composed of 17 judges, found Britain guilty of 'degrading and inhuman treatment'.

On January 24, Eddie Gallagher – who with Marion Coyle had kidnapped and held the Dutch businessman Tiede Herrema hostage – married Dr Rose Dugdale, mother of his child, in Limerick Jail.

The Wealth Tax – 1 per cent on all sums over £100,000 in 1974 terms (which would roughly correspond with £500,000 today), imposed by Garret FitzGerald's Fine Gael Government – was abolished in the Budget on February 1, and on February 5 the first Hare Krishna temple in Ireland was opened in Phoenix Park. The Hierarchy reasserted its view that although contraception was wrong, it didn't follow that the State was bound to prohibit the sale and distribution of contraceptives.

On May 1, the Northern Ireland Office denied that prisoners who refused to wash or empty their chamber pot were being hosed down and disinfected in what was known as the 'dirty protest' at Long Kesh, though any reasonable person might have wondered why they shouldn't have been, and on May 17, Minister for Health Haughey opened a new centre for alcoholism, deploring, as if it came as any surprise to him, as a former drinking man, that £1,250,000 per day was being spent on drink in the Republic.

On June 1, Irish novelist Paul Smith, author of *The Countrywoman*, won a $7,000 award made by the Irish-American Foundation and Hugh Leonard's play *Da* won a Tony award, the New York stage equivalent of a Hollywood Oscar.

On June 19, an Enniskillen woman was fined £1,000 for growing poppies for opium in her back garden, and in July the Government announced stiffer penalties for drunken drivers although the limit in Ireland was still 100 mg as against 80 mg in most other European countries. On July 24, the Pioneer Total Abstinence Society reported a 50 per cent drop in membership over the past 20 years.

On August 1, Archbishop Fiach, Primate of All Ireland, compared the H-blocks to the slums of Calcutta; there was an oil find off Loop Head in Co Clare, and Ireland's first natural gas was pumped ashore from the Kinsale gas fields. Irish farm incomes were up again (by 31 per cent) according to the

Agricultural Institute, and thousands arrived at Carnsore Point in Co Wexford to protest against the Government's proposals to build a nuclear power plant there.

In September Ireland applied for £650,000,000 from the EEC to enable her to join the European Monetary System, and Aer Lingus, after several years of losses, or at best breaking even, made a profit of £4,500,000.

A second Irish television channel, RTE 2, opened on November 2. On November 9, the Irish rock group *Thin Lizzy* topped the *Melody Maker*'s poll, and at the end of November the first shop selling contraceptives across the counter opened in Dublin.

1979

MARGARET THATCHER BECOMES FIRST WOMAN PM OF BRITAIN: SALT II AGREEMENT SIGNED: BHUTTO HANGED IN KASHMIR: PALIMONY CASE AGAINST LEE MARVIN: 18 DROWN IN FASTNET YACHT RACE: POL POT GUILTY OF MURDER OF 3,000,000 CAMBODIANS: FALL OF IDI AMIN

Pope Visits Ireland

In January, Bord Failte figures showed that the tourist total for 1978 had topped 2,000,000 for the first time, and two days later the Government announced the most ambitious economic plan in the state's history. It aimed to wipe out unemployment completely by 1983, to achieve a further 6½ per cent increase in the GDP and a fall in inflation to 5 per cent. The Irish Industrial Authority planned to provide 30,000 new jobs within the current year.

Fifty people were killed when the French tanker *Betelgeuse* exploded at Whiddy Island oil terminal on January 8. In Dublin and Cork almost a million commuters were walking to work – or taking a lift from an army lorry – during a fortnight-long strike by bus drivers. To add to the general discomfort, the postal services had also been on strike for a fortnight, and by the middle of the month it was beginning to look as if the telephone services would be affected. The B + I took delivery of a new luxury car ferry for the Dublin–Liverpool route; the ship had been built in the Verolme Dockyards in Cork Harbour.

On January 9, the bus-drivers went back to work, and the post office workers returned to deal with a fortnight's backlog of mail, only to strike again on February 18; they were seeking a wage increase of 37 per cent.

The budget, on February 7, increased pensions by 16 per cent and freed 40,000 people from paying any tax at all, by abolishing the lowest rate and raising personal allowances. University fees were increased by 25 per cent and at UCD the college authorities removed a contraceptive vending machine which had been installed by the students.

The Fianna Fail Ard Fheis on February 23 called for restraint in wage claims; 'When we see claims for 40 per cent and 50 per cent it is clear that people have lost all touch with reality,' one speaker remarked.

Airey Neave, the Conservative Northern Ireland Shadow Secretary, was murdered as he left the House of Commons car park on March 30 and, on the same day, the Republic broke the sterling link and joined the EMS (European Monetary System). The Irish pound, always previously interchangeable with sterling, became the punt, and English visitors to Ireland had to provide themselves with Eurocheques or some other form of international currency. In bars and restaurants English money was accepted, but at par, despite the fact that for most of this period the Irish punt was worth about 10 per cent less than the £ sterling.

The President of the IMA (Irish Medical Association) told the association's annual congress on April 18 that more than 7,000 Irish women had joined what he called 'the abortion trail' to Britain in 1978. The Catholic Guild of Pharmacists decided on April 29 not to sell contraceptives.

Humphrey Atkins was appointed Secretary of State for

Northern Ireland after a Westminster general election in which William Craig lost his seat, and Margaret Thatcher became Britain's first woman Prime Minister. Thirty people were arrested in the Republic on May 9 after violent clashes between the police and postal workers, now on strike for ten weeks, and on May 10 Taoiseach Jack Lynch became the first head of Government to call on Mrs Thatcher at No 10 Downing Street.

In June, Aer Lingus appointed its first woman pilot, Grainne Cronin (in October CIE employed women bus drivers and conductors for the first time), traffic wardens first appeared in the Dublin streets, and the President unveiled an eloquent statue to James Larkin (by Oisin Kelly) in O'Connell Street. In June, too, Aer Lingus acquired a controlling interest in the Hotel Commodore on the Boulevard Haussman in Paris.

On July 7 Taoiseach Jack Lynch left for Strasbourg where, as European Community President, he inaugurated a new European Parliament. Armed men got away with £50,000 in a robbery at the Bank of Ireland; the manager's wife and daughter were held hostage in a hideout in the Dublin Mountains while the robbery was taking place. A few days later, Minister for Justice Collins told the Dail that the level of armed robberies was causing considerable concern: 150 robberies netting £1,037,384 since the beginning of January, 1979, and a total of 287 robberies netting £2,196,508 in 1978.

In August, 51 Vietnamese refugees arrived in Dublin as part of a Government commitment to accept 200 boat people. On August 26, Civic Guards found a large quantity of cannabis in Kill, Co Kildare. On August 27, Lord Mountbatten's boat was blown up by the IRA, and Lord Mountbatten, his 15-year-old grandson and a 15-year-old friend were killed, as well as a 17-year-old boatman and the Dowager Lady Brabourne. A Provisional IRA landmine killed 18 British soldiers at Carlingford Lough on the same day.

On Sept 6 armed men stole £15,000 wages from a Garda patrol car, holding the driver and his companion up at gun-point, and on September 25 the Orange Order took the extreme step of writing to their arch-enemy, the Pope, complaining that the Catholic Church had not yet excommunicated the IRA.

A few days later, Pope John Paul arrived in Ireland for a three-day visit, during the course of which he made an eloquent appeal for peace: 'On my knees I beg you, turn away from violence.'

A survey carried out by the Economic and Social Research Institute and published on October 15 reported that 72 per cent of the people in the Republic were in favour of British withdrawal from Northern Ireland, and some 21 per cent emerged from the survey as being in some degree in support of the IRA.

On October 11 it was announced that driving tests for holders of provisional licences had been waived because of a backlog of 60,000 applications.

In November, for the first time since the break-away from sterling, the Irish punt briefly topped the £ sterling, the Guards seized a large consignment of arms at Dublin Docks, and in the Special Criminal Court Thomas McMahon was sentenced to life imprisonment for the murder of Lord Mountbatten.

On November 21, the British Government issued a working paper on Northern Ireland which ruled out a specific 'Dublin dimension', but emphasised the necessity of involving the minority in any attempt to shift responsibility for running the state back to Northern Ireland. At the end of November, the European Community heads of Government met in Dublin, and on December 5 Jack Lynch resigned as Taoiseach and was succeeded by Charles Haughey.

1980–1990

&

The Boss Takes Over

The decade began with two highly promising meetings between Charles Haughey and Margaret Thatcher, who looked and sounded as if they were going to be able to do business and together attempt to crack the Northern Ireland problem. By January 1982 an Anglo-Irish Intergovernmental Council had been formed as a forum for discussions between officials of the two governments. This led to the signing of the Anglo-Irish Treaty, at Hillsborough House, Co Down, on November 15, 1985, a development which pleased politicians and people in the Republic who have always felt that, as Northern Ireland happens to be a part of Ireland, they should have some say in how it is run. It did not greatly please the Unionists, however, who believe the Six Counties to be an integral part of the UK and therefore completely outside Dublin's sphere of influence.

At the beginning of the decade Charles Haughey, who had taken over from Jack Lynch in December 1979, quite obviously relished the power which had come with the job; and he immediately announced that he was going to make the North his first political priority.

Many Irish people found The Boss, as he was known in the Fianna Fail Party, a puzzling but engaging character. He had been born in Castlebar, Co Mayo, to parents both from Northern

Ireland. He was the third child of a Free State army officer who, when Haughey was three, had retired to Donnycarney, one of the less salubrious Dublin suburbs, there to bring up seven children on his army and old IRA pensions.

Haughey married Sean Lemass's daughter and, as early as 1960, had acquired Grangemore, a gracious Victorian mansion on 45 acres in Raheny, just outside Dublin, followed by a big farm in Co Meath, a string of hunters and race-horses, plus a large and powerful motor yacht to get him to and from mainland Ireland and Inishvickillane, one of the Blasket islands off the coast of Co Kerry, yet another of his subsequent acquisitions.

Towards the end of the Sixties, his town house was Abbeyville, designed by James Gandon, of Custom House fame, for the Lords Lieutenant of Ireland, standing on 250 acres of prime land in North Co Dublin. This was grandeur on a dazzling scale never before contemplated, much less achieved, by any Irish politician, and a very far cry indeed from Dev's austere vision of the Irish Dream.

The whole decade of the Eighties was dominated by political instability – five general elections within ten years, none of them decisive – and by the dire state of the economy.

As an accountant, Haughey must have known very well what had gone wrong – the country was hounded by crippling bills for the servicing and repayment of astronomical loans from all over the world – but he chose instead to seek popularity by giving the teachers, to take one example, a pay rise far bigger even than that recommended by an arbitration board, and by continuing to spend, spend, spend, like a drunken sailor.

On the international scene, he soon ran into trouble over the Falklands War when, after reluctantly going along with the rest of the European Community in supporting sanctions against the Argentinians, he suddenly allowed his Minister for Defence to accuse the British of being the aggressors. This put a fairly abrupt end to his special relationship with Margaret Thatcher.

Although he had been directly responsible for the situation which forced Garret FitzGerald, who succeeded him in June 1981, in charge of a Fine Gael/Labour coalition, to apply some drastic corrective measures, Haughey then went straight into the attack, referring to economics as 'a dismal science', describing FitzGerald's attempts to clear up the mess as 'deflationary' and 'monetarist', and talking about 'needless doom and gloom', secure in the knowledge that the FitzGerald Government was not likely to last very long. And in that he was right; FitzGerald 'goofed', as he put it himself, by allowing his Finance Minister to impose VAT on children's clothing, including footwear.

The Boss came back to power in March 1982, after a deal with the Sinn Fein Workers' Party and with Independent Socialist Tony Gregory, which committed him to a promise to create 4,000 new jobs at a cost of £4,000,000, to build 440 new houses in Gregory's Dublin constituency and to develop a 27-acre site in Dublin Port.

In October 1982, Haughey's coalition with Tony Gregory and the Workers' Party collapsed, and an election in November put the Fine Gael/Labour coalition back in power.

Garret FitzGerald now produced his own contribution to Anglo-Irish relations, the New Ireland Forum, an attempt to incorporate the views of all the various political parties, north and south of the border, on the best solution to the Northern Ireland problem, all contained within one single document.

Unfortunately, FitzGerald failed to consult the Unionists in advance on his Forum idea, with the result that none of the Unionist parties was represented at any of the Forum meetings in Dublin Castle, nor did any of them make any contribution to its final report.

During the Forum discussions, Haughey agreed to a formula which acknowledged the unitary state as 'the particular structure which the Forum would wish to see established', but which also included a federal solution and joint authority as two other possible options, essential if the Forum report was ever going to win any support from the Unionists.

However, as soon as the report was published in May 1984, Haughey immediately repudiated it, arguing that only the unitary state option could possibly bring peace to Ireland.

Throughout the decade, Garret FitzGerald – whose mother was a Northern Ireland Presbyterian – kept trying to bring about changes in the Constitution, including the removal of the ban on divorce and the specific territorial claims on the Six Counties of Northern Ireland. He wished to make the idea of eventual unity more acceptable to the Ulster Unionists, in the event that the Anglo-Irish negotiations achieved a closer rapprochement between the two sections of the country.

Also, towards the end of its second term in Government, the Fine Gael/Labour coalition had been forced to come up with some pretty radical money-raising schemes, including a national lottery (to replace the Irish Hospitals' Sweepstake with much bigger prizes, and with part of the proceeds going to sport, the arts and the national heritage, as well as to the hospitals). The new Deposit Interest Retention Tax, levied directly on interest accrued in banks and building societies by long-term deposits, a measure which could be conveniently castigated under the acronym DIRT by Haughey while in opposition, though he did nothing to abolish it when he was returned to office later because, like the lottery money, it had proved to be a nice little earner.

In January, 1987, the coalition fell apart and Haughey scraped back in with a casting vote from the speaker and became Taoiseach for the third time. O'Malley's Progressive Democrats – a break-away section of the Fianna Fail Party – had won 11 seats and Fine Gael had the lowest total (51) since 1957; not long after the election Garret FitzGerald resigned and was succeeded by Alan Dukes, an economist who had worked with the Irish Farmers' Commission in Brussels.

Haughey and his Finance Minister, Ray MacSharry, immediately cut spending across a wide range of areas, notably in the departments of Health, Social Welfare and Education. Haughey succeeded in persuading the government departments, the trades unions and the farmers to accept his plan for general overall cuts in expenditure, and talked the employers and the trades unions into a tight new wage agreement covering three years. In the wake of Thatcher's rout of the unions in Britain, the Irish union leaders found his formula acceptable: an apparent involvement in decision-making at top level in return for moderate (2.5 per cent) wage increases for their members. These measures led to a dramatic amelioration of Ireland's fiscal problems.

One of the things that the Anglo-Irish Agreement had attempted to achieve was a greater measure of co-operation between the security forces on both sides of the border. It is perhaps not surprising that many Irish people were not impressed by what passed for justice in Britain in the 1980s. Apart altogether from what looked very like a shoot-to-kill policy in Northern Ireland, and what had happened elsewhere – in Gibraltar, for example, where two unarmed men and a young woman were shot dead by the SAS *before* they had committed any offence – there was also the affair of the Guildford Four. They were eventually cleared and released in 1989, after serving 14 years for the pub bombings in Guildford and Woolwich, when public opinion forced the British Government to look again at the evidence and question the integrity of the police. The case of the Birmingham Six, also re-opened towards the end of the decade, disclosed similar irregularities.

In these circumstances, Irish judges were extremely reluctant to extradite their fellow-countrymen but tended instead to find the extradition orders flawed – as indeed, many of them were – or that there was not sufficient evidence of identity. This was a continuing cause of friction between Westminster and Dublin.

Haughey suddenly dissolved the Dail on May 25, 1989, and – following another totally indecisive election, and having given his party a firm assurance that any possibility of a coalition was completely ruled out – formed a Coalition Government with the break-away section of Fianna Fail, the Progressive Democrats, giving them two key seats in the cabinet, much to the surprise and disgust of his colleagues, whom he hadn't even bothered to consult. He argued that he had made this decision in the best interests of the nation but everybody knew that he had done it to hang on as The Boss, whatever the cost to the country, for as long as humanly possible.

That didn't prove, in the event, to be for very long.

```
                        1980

NORTH SEA OIL RIG COLLAPSE: TITO DIES: MOUNT ST
HELENS VOLCANO ERUPTS: IRANIAN EMBASSY SIEGE IN
LONDON; SANJAY GANDHI KILLED IN AIR CRASH: SHAH OF
IRAN DIES: SOLIDARITY MOVEMENT IN POLAND: JOHN
LENNON SHOT: SOVIET TROOPS IN AFGHANISTAN
```

Peace Funds Disappear

In January, a constitutional conference on the future of Northern Ireland opened at Stormont without the benefit of the presence of any of the Unionist representatives, who were still boycotting the discussions. Mrs Betty Williams, one of the founders of the Peace People movement in Northern Ireland, resigned in February and the other, Mairead Corrigan, announced later in the year that all the movement's funds, including the Nobel Peace Prize, had 'dried up'; all the money had been spent on what might loosely be described as 'administration'.

Tony O'Reilly, Chief Executive of Heinz and its 57 varieties, became Chairman of the *Irish Independent*; the trade gap reached £208,000,000; and the funeral was held of Mr Thomas Niedermayer, whose body had been found six years after his kidnap. The IRA admitted killing British officers in West Germany and the British Ambassador at The Hague.

In April a B + I jet foil crossed the Irish Sea between Dublin and Liverpool in three and a half hours, the Irish National Teachers' Organisation urged the Department of Education to change the terms of employment for teachers so that they would no longer be obliged to teach religion, and Johnny Logan won the Eurovision Song Contest for Ireland with the song, *What's Another Year?*

Marion Price was released from Armagh Jail after serving seven years of a life sentence for London bombings, and on May 21, 1980, Charles Haughey first met Margaret Thatcher, herself also in her first year in office, at 10 Downing Street, bringing her a present of an antique Irish silver teapot; by all accounts, initially they got on famously.

In June, the 800-year-old Cistercian Abbey Duiske at Graiguenamanagh, Co Kilkenny, was re-opened after 300 years, inflation topped 20 per cent for the first time since 1976, and the Irish Labour Party made the first of a number of attempts to get an all-party committee of TDs to look for a formula by which the ban on divorce could be removed from the Constitution.

The Revd Martin Smyth, head of the Orange Order, made his own distinctly unhelpful contribution to the Anglo-Irish discussions – which he refused to attend – by suggesting that Britain should annex the three counties of Ulster still part of the Republic. The Central Bank forecast nil growth for the year and the Tynagh mines closed after 15 years with a job loss of 330.

The Industrial Development Association confirmed that approximately 200,000 jobs would be lost during the year; the Central Statistics office reported that the emigration rate was now over 26,000 a year; and planning permission was granted for Ireland's first crematorium in September.

Also, in September, Monsignor James Horan of Knock, Co Mayo, who had been agitating for an international airport there to enable foreign pilgrims to visit the shrine marking the only recent appearance of Our Lady on Irish soil (on August 21, 1879), unveiled a plaque in Castlebar to commemorate the birthplace of Charles Haughey. Haughey and family attended the ceremony and on the same day it was announced that the Government had given the go-ahead for Monsignor Horan's international airport at Knock. To everybody's surprise, it has since proved quite a success, though not so much from the proceeds from pilgrims as from fares paid by building labourers commuting between their homes in the far West of Ireland and building sites in London, Liverpool, Birmingham and Manchester.

In October, Miss Mella Carroll became the first female High Court Judge in Ireland; Dr Rose Dugdale, now Mrs Gallagher, was released from Limerick Jail after serving six years of her nine-year sentence; and seven men began a hunger strike 'to the death' in Long Kesh. Later in the year other Republicans in various jails brought the total on hunger strike up to 45.

The old family firm of Pierce of Wexford, manufacturers of agricultural machinery, closed in November with the loss of 147 jobs, and the Irish Sugar Company, the Government announced, was facing a shut-down because of the closure of Erin Foods, a food processing subsidiary sold to Heinz, UK, Ltd, now under the control of Chief Executive Tony O'Reilly. The citizens of Castlebar (birth-place of Taoiseach Charles Haughey), almost to a man tenants of Lord Lucan, rejoiced in the fact that they had not paid any rent since his disappearance six years earlier, adding that they hoped he would not re-appear for one more year, when their debts would be statute-barred.

James Plunkett's novel about Dublin in the early years of the century, *Strumpet City*, was presented on Irish television; RTE also ran a series called *Sean*, based on the autobiographies of Sean O'Casey.

In December, Margaret Thatcher returned Haughey's visit and arrived in Dublin with Lord Carrington, her Foreign Secretary, who had just negotiated a successful settlement of the Rhodesian situation, and the Chancellor of the Exchequer, Geoffrey Howe, as well as the Northern Ireland Secretary of State, Humphrey Atkins; and it began to look as if a settlement of the Irish problem might not be all that far away. However, a communique later issued by Haughey gave the mistaken impression of a far closer relationship with Thatcher than had ever existed in fact, and Haughey allowed his Foreign Minister to suggest that constitutional changes had been discussed.

Margaret Thatcher never forgave Haughey and never again trusted the soft-tongued donor of the silver teapot.

1981

AMERICAN HOSTAGES RELEASED IN IRAN: GREECE JOINS
EUROPEAN COMMUNITY: REAGAN ASSASSINATION ATTEMPT:
POPE WOUNDED IN ATTEMPTED MURDER: RACE RIOTS IN BRIX-
TON AND TOXTETH: SPACE SHUTTLE COLUMBIA IN ORBIT:
SADAT KILLED: PRINCE CHARLES MARRIES LADY DIANA

The Year of the Maze Hunger Strikes

In January 1981, the news of the closing of the American GAF
vinyl factory in Mullingar, which had employed 300 people, was
not of any great importance in itself, but was symptomatic of
what had been happening increasingly in Ireland in recent years.

One possible explanation as to why so many foreign-owned
Irish factories were closing was offered by an OECD report
which appeared in January. The gross pay of the average Irish
worker had risen by 101 per cent in the four years between 1974
and 1978. Wage increases of such proportions made a nonsense of
one of the attractions which had lured foreign investors to Ireland
in the first place in the middle Sixties: 'a plentiful supply of
cheap labour' was how one Government hand-out had put it.

By the middle of January the unemployment figures totalled
120,000, the punt had dropped to £0.78, petrol was up by 30
per cent and gas by 16 per cent, though there were hopes that
when approximately £100,000,000 had been spent on piping a
natural gas find off Kinsale up to Dublin, there might be a
slight reduction.

In February the de Lorean wonder sports car made its debut
at the Belfast motor show. About 400 of the cars left the
Dunmurray factory for the States in April; so far, the British
Government had ploughed £80,000,000 into the project which
ultimately collapsed in disaster. In February, too, the Minister
for Health informed the Dail that a total of 9,000,000 condoms
had been imported into the Republic between November 1980
and January 1981.

The former speaker of the Northern Ireland House of Commons, Sir Norman Stronge, and his son were shot dead at their home on the Armagh border on January 21 and the IRA admitted responsibility, saying that it was a direct reprisal for Loyalist attacks on Nationalists in the North. By now it had become clear that most of the killings and bombings in Northern Ireland represented reprisals and counter-reprisals, mainly sectarian, as an increasing number of Protestant paramilitary terrorist organisations entered the fray.

Ever hopeful, the Government announced in January that a finance company was to be formed from the private sector to pay for part of the £100,000,000 needed to modernise the telecommunications system. Down the country in Ireland at this period, you could be the chief executive of the Irish division of the biggest multi-national corporation in the world, but you couldn't get through to the next village, much less to Tokyo or Detroit, unless you happened to be on very good terms with the local post-mistress who operated the telephone exchange.

It was not widely reported that Premier Charles Haughey was at Shannon to greet the American hostages when their plane stopped off there for refuelling, en route from Teheran to Washington.

As early as January 13, about 60 H-Block prisoners had agreed to end their 'dirty' protest as soon as they were moved to clean cells, given civilian clothing, and when other privileges such as visits, letters and parcels had been restored to them. But something went wrong. By January 28, the newspapers were reporting 'tension high' in Long Kesh after 96 prisoners had smashed up the furniture in the new cells to which they had been transferred, and were back on the 'dirty' protest, not merely refusing to use the toilets, but decorating their cells with their own waste products.

The Provisionals claimed that a number of prisoners had been assaulted during the move, and by the following day the 96 prisoners were considering a suggestion by their leader Bobby Sands that they should go on hunger strike if there was no real move from the British. On February 12, the British Government announced that it would make no compromise whatever with the prisoners.

Haughey had wanted to hold a general election as soon as possible which would give him a direct mandate from the public to run the country, but a succession of events – including a disco fire in his own constituency in Artane, Co Dublin, which killed 46 young people in horrifying circumstances, as well as the protests and hunger strikes at the Maze prison – caused the election to be postponed until June, 1981.

Aer Lingus, once the big success story among Irish companies, was now looking for £25,000,000 to cover its trading losses; the company admitted existing debts of £92,000,000.

But if faith in the new materialistic Ireland was beginning to wane a bit, faith in the more ancient sense appeared to be returning. On February 10, the Catholic Church Vocations Director announced an increase in vocations for the priesthood of 20 per cent and added that the figure would have been a lot higher if all the prospective entrants had been accepted. Possibly the Pope's recent visit to Ireland was a contributory factor, but in the late Sixties, when Ireland's industrial miracle was at its height, the number of vocations had dropped away alarmingly; now, with unemployment at an all-time high and the economy in total disarray, the Church was turning away dozens of prospective priests. An unsympathetic observer might see in these facts a tendency on the part of Irishmen to use the Church as a safe bolt-hole whenever things started to get tough in the big outside world.

Before long, the H-Block hunger strike was hitting the headlines, particularly after Bobby Sands won a by-election to the House of Commons, and died after 66 days' fasting on May 5. There were riots in Belfast in which an RUC man was killed and five people were wounded, business premises all over Ireland were closed down for the funeral, and there were riots at the British Embassy in Dublin. Sands's death was followed by that of nine other hunger strikers, but the Iron Lady did not flinch. Even people in Ireland bitterly opposed to the IRA considered Thatcher's intransigence ill-advised; not because they thought the H-block protesters should be accorded any special treatment but because they knew that every death on hunger strike brought a flood of new recruits into the IRA, particularly in the political, economic, industrial and intellectual vacuum of Northern Ireland in the early Eighties.

The first hint of a problem that was soon to become very acute came from Maynooth where a seminar on drugs was told that the Gardai had encountered as many illegal drugs in Ireland in the past year as in the previous ten, and that the Jervis Street Hospital drug addiction unit had reported a five- to ten-fold increase in the number of new cocaine and heroin addicts.

On March 5, Charles Haughey, who had already made Ireland a tax haven for writers and artists, announced a new scheme known as Aosdana (literally, poets) to provide an annual income of £4,000 a year for Irish writers and artists, to augment their meagre earnings from their chosen profession. In April, Dolors Price was released from jail on medical grounds; she had been in prison since 1975 for bombings in Britain. Later she married the Irish actor Stephen Rea and now lives for part of the year in Hollywood.

On May 1, an Aer Lingus plane with 113 people on board was hijacked for what must have been the most extraordinary motive of any hijacker before or since; when he surrendered to the French police, he confessed that he had intended to hold the passengers hostage only until the Pope had confided to him the secret of Fatima, where an apparition by the Blessed Virgin Mary upon Portuguese territory as recently as 1917 was believed by many people to have divulged a secret now known only by His Current Holiness.

In the general election on June 11, Haughey failed to get the mandate he sought – he lost a number of votes in the border area because of the hunger strike and two republican prisoners in the Maze H-block protest were elected to the Dail in the constituencies of Louth and Cavan-Monaghan. A coalition of the Fine Gael and Labour Parties, plus some Independents, elected Garret FitzGerald Taoiseach by 81 votes to 78.

The hopeless prospect that Ireland presented for school-leavers was never more graphically illustrated than by the announcement on August 7 that the Bank of Ireland had received 17,580 applications for 300 vacancies.

Inflation was up to 20 per cent by September and Ireland was rated 'the most disadvantaged area in the EEC, along with the Mezzogiorno in Italy' in one of the many economic and social reports that kept pouring out of Brussels.

On October 16, millionaire store-owner Ben Dunne was kidnapped and was returned to his family on October 22, presumably after a substantial ransom had been paid, though the amount never came out. This was the first in a long series of IRA abductions of rich businessmen for ransom purposes.

In London, IRA bombs blew the legs off a British general and killed a bomb disposal expert in a Wimpy Bar in Oxford Street. Taoiseach Garret FitzGerald met Margaret Thatcher on November 1, and agreed on the establishment of an Anglo-Irish Council, as well as an advisory committee on economic, social and cultural co-operation.

On December 23, two men from Northern Ireland were convicted in the Dublin Special Criminal Court of using firearms and of escaping from Crumlin Road Jail in Belfast. It was the first time that convictions had been made in Dublin for crimes committed in Northern Ireland. This came about as part of an agreement made during the Sunningdale talks initiated by Edward Heath in 1973, and subsequent meetings between Thatcher and Haughey and FitzGerald.

Towards the end of the year, Buck's Fizz won the Eurovision Song Contest in Dublin; it had cost the Irish Government £300,000 to stage the event and an RTE executive remarked to me that he hoped to God they would never win it again, though they did.

1982

UK GOES TO WAR OVER FALKLAND ISLANDS: ISRAELIS DRIVE
PLO FROM BEIRUT: PRINCESS GRACE OF MONACO KILLED IN
CAR CRASH: COLLAPSE OF LAKER AIRLINE: HEIR TO ENG-
LISH THRONE BORN: STATE OF EMERGENCY IN NICARAGUA:
1,800 PALESTINIAN REFUGEES KILLED AT SABRA

Goof over Children's Shoes

In January Ireland was paralysed by blizzards, and the Army Air
Corps was stretched to its limits by rescue attempts in some of
the worst weather for 50 years. A Loyalist gunman was jailed for
life, and two others for a total of 35 years for the attempted murder of Bernadette McAliskey (formerly Devlin) and her husband.
The liquidator dismissed 456 workers at the Clondalkin Paper
Mills, and on January 27, as we have seen, FitzGerald's Coalition
Government was defeated by 82 votes to 81 on Bruton's budget,
which reduced food subsidies and put VAT on children's clothing, including footwear.

The Royal Hibernian Hotel, for years one of the best in
Dublin, closed at midnight on February 11; the space it had
occupied was to be used for 'office development'.

In March amid a crescendo of closures and curtailments – the
Irish Sugar Company announced losses of £9,500,000 in its fifth
successive, loss-making year; Mogul Mines closed with a loss of
550 jobs; Fieldcrest Ireland Ltd went into receivership with 630
job losses in Kilkenny; and redundancies rose by 21 per cent –
Haughey was elected Taoiseach by 86 votes to 79.

In the meantime, a new Northern Ireland Secretary of State,
James Prior, had arrived on the scene, with another initiative
which included yet another power-sharing assembly.

In June, Patrick Cooney of Fine Gael expressed the opinion
that Fianna Fail's decision to go ahead with Knock Airport was
'beyond belief'. The airport would cost £8,000,000 to build and
would lose £800,000 a year, he predicted.

Provisional IRA nail bombs killed three bandsmen, two cav-
alrymen and several horses in London parks in July and the
Irish MEPs at Strasbourg protested when the European
Parliament passed a resolution ruling out political offences as an
obstacle to the extradition of terrorists.

In July, too, a young nurse, Bridie Gargan, was attacked in
broad daylight while she was sunbathing beside her car in
Phoenix Park. She died in hospital from her wounds and in
August it emerged that Malcolm Macarthur, the man accused of
murdering her (as well as an Offaly farmer, Donal Dunne), had
been staying in the flat of Haughey's Attorney-General, Patrick
Connolly, and had been driving around in a state car. Connolly,
who was on his way to a holiday in America, was ordered by
Haughey to return at once and explain what Macarthur had
been doing in his apartment and how a shot-gun used by
Macarthur had been found there. Not surprisingly, Connolly
disappeared from the political scene before very long.

This incident gave rise to the curious term GUBU, subsequently used to describe the many unlikely and inexplicable
events that so frequently surrounded Haughey. Originally it was
based on a phrase used by Haughey himself in his first reaction
to the arrest of Bridie Gargan's murderer in the flat of his
Attorney-General: he described the whole affair as 'grotesque,
unbelievable, bizarre and unprecedented'. Haughey's arch-
enemy in the Dail, Conor Cruise O'Brien, immediately seized
on this phrase, turned it into the acronym GUBU, and it stuck.

Gerry Fitt's house was attacked with bombs for the second
time that year; his party, the SDLP, had decided to contest elections for Prior's new Northern Ireland Assembly on an
abstentionist basis, despite an appeal from Prior to enter the
Assembly and use it for power-sharing. In October, quite understandably, Prior lost his patience when an Assembly was elected
and 30 per cent of the elected members, representing all the
Catholics who had voted, supported a total boycott of the entire
outfit, and he threatened that unless some agreement was
reached on how power was to be shared, there would be no further devolution of power from Westminster.

In September a travel tax had come into existence; if you

were Irish and wanted to go somewhere else, or if you were a visitor to Ireland, you now had to pay for the privilege of leaving the place: £3 if you were going to the continent, £2 if you were going to Britain.

After a general election following yet another Government defeat after a no-confidence motion in November, Garret FitzGerald again became Taoiseach of a Coalition Government, with the new Labour leader, Dick Spring, as his deputy. Gas from Kinsale reached Dublin for the first time, and the new Minister for Justice, Michael Noonan, ordered an inquiry into phone-tapping by the state.

Thousands of travellers were stranded when the 'Magic Bus' service – the cheapest ever way of visiting Ireland from England or vice versa – collapsed, and William Trevor's *Ballroom of Romance*, set in a dance hall in the wilds of Mayo, was a huge success on television both in Ireland and in the UK.

1983

BENIGNO AQUINO SHOT IN MANILA: BRINKS-MAT ROBBERY: US MARINES INVADE GRENADA: TWO MILLION GHANAIANS EXPELLED FROM NIGERIA: HERTZOG PRESIDENT OF ISRAEL: RUSSIANS SHOOT DOWN KOREAN JET: CRUISE MISSILES ARRIVE AT GREENHAM COMMON: GALTIERI TRIAL

The Abortion Referendum

The year began with a ban by the Government of the INLA (Irish National Liberation Army, yet another break-away IRA group) and a life sentence for Malcolm Macarthur, the murderer of Nurse Bridie Gargan. More than 120,000 Irish citizens took advantage of a new series of day trips to Wales on Sea Link ferries for a flat rate of £12.50 each, including a free litre of spirits per person.

In February, the stallion Shergar was kidnapped from the National Stud, presumably with the intention of demanding a ransom for its return, but mysteriously nothing happened and the horse was never seen again.

FitzGerald's Minister for Health, Barry Desmond, refused to have anything to do with a bill which was introduced to enable a referendum to be held on an amendment to the Constitution in relation to abortion. As early as 1981, the Pro-Life (anti-abortion) campaigners had made the point that, in the light of a US Supreme Court judgment some years earlier which had declared the American anti-abortion legislation to be unconstitutional, the Irish Government should immediately take steps to ensure that no similar judgment could ever be reached by the Irish Supreme Court.

Influenced partly by his own inherent antipathy to abortion and convinced that the majority of Irish people, North and South alike, were fundamentally against abortion, FitzGerald – while in office in 1981 – had tried to find a formula that would fit the bill, but found it extremely difficult to draft an unambiguous amendment. In 1982, Fianna Fail, back in power, came up with an amendment which caused an outcry from doctors, barristers and interested laymen who argued that the amendment left uncertain the question of which life was to be protected, and left it open to the courts to outlaw operations to save the life of the mother, then routinely carried out in all hospitals in Ireland. In 1983, FitzGerald – back in office again – appealed to the Church leaders and in August 1983 the Catholic Hierarchy came out heavily in favour of the flawed Fianna Fail amendment.

The issue wasn't put to the people until September 1983 and by that time I don't believe anybody either knew or cared greatly what it was all about. Only about half the electorate turned out and those who did voted two to one in favour of the amendment, whatever it may have meant. The Hierarchy had pronounced that 'a clear majority for the [Fianna Fail] amendment would greatly contribute to the continued protection of human life [that of the unborn child as well as that of the mother] in the laws of our country', and that was probably good enough for most of those who voted for it.

To make it even more difficult for people who could afford to pay the £3 tax (now raised to a flat rate of £5) whenever they felt like leaving Ireland, the Government in March increased the cost of passports from £20 to £30.

Gerry Fitt, leader of the SDLP, was defeated in the British general election in June by the Sinn Fein candidate, Gerry Adams, who later that year replaced Ruari O Bradaigh as President of Sinn Fein. Fitt resigned from the Party and became a life peer.

Four people were shot as the Gardai foiled an attempt to kidnap the Canadian businessman Galen Weston and his wife at their home in Roundwood, Co Wicklow: 100 bullets were fired in an exchange of shots.

In October, Minister for Energy John Bruton signed an agreement to supply Kinsale gas to Northern Ireland, local authorities introduced charges for water, sewerage and refuse collection for the first time ever in ten areas, and a corrugated iron Peace Line barrier was replaced by a 3.5 metre high wall built between Catholic and Protestant areas in Belfast.

A haul of cannabis worth £2,250,000 found in Dublin Airport in November gave some indication of the extent of the drugs problem, and in December President Hillery was inaugurated for a second term. Don Tidey, Quinnsworth Supermarket executive, kidnapped near his home in Dublin, was released in Co Longford on December 16.

On the following day, a car bomb at Harrods in Knightsbridge killed five Christmas shoppers and wounded almost 100; my wife and I were in the store when the bomb went off and I remember it not so much as an explosion, but as a sudden, sharp, frightening pressure in the chest. The reactions of the staff, who efficiently and calmly evacuated the building, and of the customers, who filed quietly down the stairs and out into the street past horribly mutilated victims, confirmed the impression I'd always had that these were not people likely to be readily panicked by any form of terrorism. By now 81 people had been killed in bomb attacks on the British mainland since the start of the troubles in Northern Ireland in 1969.

1984

BLOODLESS COUP IN NIGERIA: LAST MARINES LEAVE
BEIRUT; UK MINERS GO ON STRIKE: WPC SHOT OUTSIDE
LIBYAN EMBASSY IN LONDON: US BEIRUT EMBASSY
ATTACKED: INDIRA GANDHI MURDERED: IRA BOMB TORY
CONFERENCE IN BRIGHTON: BHOPAL GAS LEAK DISASTER

Reagan Visits Ireland

The year 1984 began with the news that the Ford motor assembly plant in Cork – which had been the first modern factory in Ireland back in the early Thirties – was to close with the loss of 800 jobs; the Hierarchy informed the New Ireland Forum that the ban on divorce must stay, regardless of its effect on future relations between the Republic and Northern Ireland, and Arthur Guinness, Son & Co reported that their alcohol-free lager Kaliber, launched in the spring of 1983, was now sold in nine out of ten pubs in Ireland and enjoyed 70 per cent of the market share.

The Central Statistics Office reported on February 21 that there had been an increasingly large repatriation of profits from overseas companies based in Ireland; in 1983 the outflow had reached £300,000,000.

The INLA (Irish National Liberation Army) leader, Dominic McGlinchy, was arrested in the Republic on March 17, and became the first republican to be handed over to the RUC, who wanted him extradited to face a charge of murder.

President Reagan came to Ireland in June, primarily to visit his relatives at Ballyporeen, Co Tipperary, though he also went to Leinster House and addressed both houses of the Oireachtas in the Dail chamber. A referendum to decide whether British citizens living in Ireland should be allowed a vote in Irish general elections decided by three to one to afford them that privilege.

On July 23, the first section of the DART (Dublin Area Rapid

Transit) was opened between Bray, Dublin City centre and Howth, and it was announced that the green Irish passport would no longer be issued after the end of the year; future Irish passports would be the small, plum-coloured European Community ones. In July, too, the first phase of a £10,000 development plan for Murphy's brewery in Cork – taken over by the Dutch firm of Heineken in April 1983 – was completed and Taoiseach Garret FitzGerald attended a summit meeting at Fontainebleau to take over the Presidency of the European Community.

The five-star Westbury Hotel, just off Grafton Street in the centre of Dublin, was opened in July; so was a new centre for rape victims in the Rotunda Hospital, the most striking testimonial to the inescapable fact that Dublin was now becoming every bit as dangerous as London or New York. On July 26, the House of Commons was informed that almost 200 prisoners in Ireland enjoyed – if that's the word – the 'political' status for which the hunger strikers had died; 101 Loyalists and 83 Republicans.

A new group known as LEARN (Life Education and Research Network) was formed to resist any divorce amendment to the Constitution. In September, Minister for Justice Michael Noonan said that the Government would not rule out dropping articles two and three of the Constitution – those making a specific territorial claim on the Six Counties of Northern Ireland – in response to a major British initiative, and the Fianna Fail Party decided that it would not co-operate with the Coalition Government in recommending a referendum on divorce.

Douglas Hurd replaced Prior as Secretary of State for Northern Ireland and an EEC report from Brussels on taxation noted that a married Irish executive with two children earning £30,000 a year would be allowed to keep only 50 per cent of his gross earnings, as against 75 per cent in Switzerland, and 65 per cent in Britain and the States.

Paisley's Democratic Unionists replied to the Forum report with a document entitled 'Ulster, the Future Assured'; it proposed devolution for Northern Ireland with majority rule (and you could almost hear Paisley adding, 'And no nonsense about power-sharing').

The IRA accepted responsibility for the explosion in the

Grand Hotel in Brighton on October 12, during the Conservative Party conference, probably intended to assassinate Thatcher, in which five people were killed and 30 injured, and two days later Mrs Thatcher ruled out any immediate initiative on Northern Ireland.

A new toll bridge across the Liffey below Butt Bridge was opened in November and Taoiseach FitzGerald went to see Mrs Thatcher at Chequers. She dismissed his Forum report but agreed to meet him again to continue discussions, and a couple of days later Douglas Hurd rejected the notion of any formal institutionalised role for the Dublin Government in Northern Ireland affairs. Copies of an unrevised official version of the Dail debates (the Irish Hansard) for November 20 were withdrawn in order to have a reference to Mrs Thatcher as the 'Britshit PM' deleted.

1985

GORBACHEV SUCCEEDS CHERNENKO AS COMMUNIST PARTY CHAIRMAN: 52 DIE IN BRADFORD CITY STADIUM FIRE: SOUTH AFRICA ABOLISHES RACIAL SEX LAWS: TIDAL WAVE KILLS 1,500 IN BANGLADESH: 40 DIE IN HEYSEL STADIUM RIOT IN BRUSSELS: FRENCH SINK GREENPEACE SHIP

The Year of the Kerry Babies

Although a number of extremely important events occurred in 1985 – the Family Planning Bill, always known as the Contraceptive Bill, the signing of the Anglo-Irish Agreement, Des O'Malley's expulsion from the Fianna Fail Party, the eventual opening of Knock Airport – for the Irish newspapers, and for the Irish public, the year was dominated by two domestic topics, one sacred and one, so to speak, profane: the moving statues and the Kerry babies.

311

I'll take the Kerry babies first, because it had all started the previous year. On April 14, 1984, a dead male infant with stab wounds had been found on the rocks at Cahirciveen, Co Kerry, by a local farmer. He reported the finding to the police and attention then switched to Tralee, and to Joanne Hayes, a young unmarried mother who was employed as a telephonist at the Tralee sports centre and was known to be having an affair with Jeremiah Locke, a married man who worked as groundsman at the centre.

In a small place like Tralee, everyone knew all about the affair. It was common knowledge that before the birth of her daughter Yvonne, Ms Hayes had had at least one miscarriage, and that she had again been very obviously pregnant until fairly recently and was widely believed to have delivered a full-term baby herself. The police immediately assumed that the Cahirciveen baby was hers and charged her with the murder of the baby on May 1, 1984. Her sister Kathleen, her brothers Ned and Mike, and her aunt, Mrs Fuller, were initially charged with collusion to conceal the birth but these charges were subsequently dropped, and a tribunal was set up to inquire into accusations that the Gardai had acted improperly.

Ms Hayes stoutly maintained that the body of her baby was buried in a field on the family farm and when her sister helped the police to locate it exactly where she had said it would be, they refused to abandon the convenient conviction that she was the mother of the Cahirciveen baby and advanced a new theory that she had had twins and had thrown one of them into the sea. When a blood test revealed that the two babies were of different blood groups, the police advanced the hypothesis that if a woman had sex with two men within a very short space of time, it would be possible for her to have twins of different blood groups, even citing a case history in West Germany in which a prostitute who had been with two GIs in the same afternoon had had two babies, one black and one white.

In the end, in October, the Tribunal decided that the baby found in a field at the Hayes farm had been born inside the farmhouse and that it had died after Joanne Hayes had put her hands to its throat to stop it crying and had hit it with a bath brush. It also decided that she was not the mother of the baby found on

Cahirciveen strand, that the Hayes family were guilty of perjury and the police guilty of resorting to 'unlikely, far-fetched and self-contradictory theories that she had given birth to twins, in an attempt to link her with the Cahirciveen baby'. After the Tribunal, all charges were dropped, presumably on the principle that the poor girl and her family had suffered enough.

Now, to the moving statues. Towards the end of July, two ladies taking a walk one evening stopped for a prayer at a grotto to Our Lady at Ballinspittle, Co Cork, and imagined that they saw the statue of the Virgin Mary move. The next weekend, 40 villagers went out to the grotto to investigate the incident and all reported that they had seen the statue – and indeed other statues in the grotto – moving. Within a week, 80 voluntary stewards had been appointed to supervise the new shrine and CIE were bussing in 1,000 people a day in special coach excursions. The Department of Applied Psychology at UCD put the phenomenon down to 'light conditions' (the statues only appeared to move at twilight); and the Hierarchy advised caution.

Nevertheless, 20,000 people visited the shrine on the Feast of the Assumption of the Virgin Mary on August 15, and there were the usual reports of miracles; a Mrs Frances Rearden, a housewife who had been totally deaf for 17 years, claimed on September 18 that she had completely recovered her hearing after one visit to Ballinspittle. I spent about 20 minutes in 1989 watching the principal statue in the grotto like a hawk and I can be certain I saw no sign of any movement; by this time it had had its face smashed in by one of the Protestant paramilitary groups from the North, and was painstakingly recreated from photographs by a master plaster sculptor.

Now, back to the real world of 1985. In January, it was reported that 60 prisoners were 'missing' from Mountjoy Jail; on January 11, the Department of Justice conceded that 59 were still 'at large'. The explanation? They had been 'let out' because of the shortage of prison accommodation and hadn't returned.

At a moment in history when unemployment had reached a record total of 225,445, or 17 per cent of the work force, it was revealed that Government Ministers' cars were costing the country £78,000 a year each, a total of nearly £2,000,000.

The Family Planning Bill, passed in February, set the age limit for buying contraceptives at 18, removed any need for a prescription, dropped the bona fide family planning qualification and allowed condoms, spermicides, etc., to be sold in chemists' shops, doctors' surgeries, family planning clinics and health centres as well as maternity and VD hospitals.

The Dail passed the Bill on February 20 by 83 votes to 80. During the debate, in which the Bill was strongly opposed by Fianna Fail, one of Haughey's brightest supporters, Dessie O'Malley, brilliantly defended FitzGerald's concept of a pluralist state, and stressed the effect a defeat for the bill would have in Northern Ireland. He was expelled from the Fianna Fail Party by Haughey and within a year had formed his own party, the Progressive Democrats,

In the meantime an unmarried Dublin Ban-Garda (woman police officer) had been disciplined for having a baby in 1984, and in April a report of the Medico-Social Research Board stated that 8 per cent of all births registered in the Republic in the third quarter of 1984 were to unmarried women and that there had been 3,026 abortions carried out in 1984 in England on women with Irish addresses.

On March 15, the Government had to step in to avert the collapse of the Insurance Corporation of Ireland, the Republic's biggest non-life insurance company, after the discovery that it had failed to make provision for commitments of £50,000,000.

Some facts about Ireland emerged from the reports which continued to pour from the European Community presses; Ireland had the highest unemployment rate in Europe, the highest birthrate (twice the EC average) and there were 700,000 people on welfare in the Republic, mainly the unemployed and the elderly. The EC also queried the legality of the Irish travel tax of £5 per departure from the country, which so far had yielded £11,000,000.

Guinness won control of Arthur Bell, the Scottish whisky distillers, after a £370,000,000 take-over bid, and on August 30, the Central Statistics Office reported that nearly £700,000,000 had left Ireland in the first three months of 1985; £279,000,000 through repatriation of profits by foreign companies and payments to foreign investors and £400,000,000 as a result of interest payments on foreign debts. These were the mysterious 'black holes' in the Irish economy, through which vast sums of money had been disappearing during the Haughey regime.

On September 3, Douglas Hurd was replaced as Northern Ireland Secretary by Tom King after a Cabinet reshuffle, and a few days later Chris Patten, an extremely popular Northern Ireland Junior Minister, was recalled to London. On September 18, King spent four hours in Dublin and announced that an Anglo-Irish Agreement would be ready for signing at the October summit, without first consulting the Northern Ireland Unionists.

On September 19, a committee of doctors at Calvary Hospital in Galway secretly signed an agreement at the instigation of Bishop Eamonn Casey (later to become famous in another context) that they would not carry out any sterilisation operations for contraceptive purposes, and accepted a ban imposed by the same bold bishop on artificial insemination by donor.

In October, a major survey sponsored by the Hierarchy showed that support among Irish Catholics for divorce had risen by 7 per cent over the previous ten years, and Senator Mary Robinson (also later to become famous in another context) urged the Government to face up to the reality of marriage breakdowns by naming a date for a referendum on divorce.

The first three commercial 'proving' flights (i.e. securing routes) from Knock Airport, Co Mayo, took place on October 25 and on November 1, Douglas Hurd, now Home Secretary, ordered an investigation into the case of the Birmingham Six.

On November 16, Margaret Thatcher and Garret FitzGerald signed the Anglo-Irish Agreement at Hillsborough, Co Down. The agreement gave the Republic a 'constant and official involvement' in Northern Ireland affairs. It infuriated the Unionists, who immediately threatened to resign their Westminster seats, and it was repudiated by Charles Haughey as being in conflict with the Constitution.

Senator Mary Robinson resigned from the Labour Party on the grounds that the Agreement did not achieve its objective of securing peace and stability in Northern Ireland and in the island as a whole, since the Unionists had not been consulted in advance. King was set upon by a Loyalist mob in Northern Ireland, and an opinion poll in the *Irish Times* showed 59 per cent of the Republic's population in favour of the agreement.

On November 23, 100,000 Loyalists paraded outside the City Hall in Belfast, burning effigies of Margaret Thatcher; on November 28, the bill accepting the Anglo-Irish Agreement was passed in the Commons by 173 votes to 47, amid shouts of 'No Surrender!' and 'Ulster Forever!' from the Revd Ian Paisley; on November 29 it came into force and was registered at the United Nations as a formal and binding agreement.

It was the year of Bob Geldof's Live Aid Concert in Wembley Stadium and another Dubliner, Terry Wogan, was voted favourite TV personality of the year. Maeve Binchy, the *Irish Times* columnist from Dalkey, Co Dublin came up with a second block-busting bestseller, *Echoes*; her first had been called *Light a Penny Candle*.

Thousands of people turned up at Dunsink Observatory to see if they could catch a glimpse of Halley's Comet. They couldn't.

1986

SPACE SHUTTLE CHALLENGER VII EXPLODES ON TAKE-OFF KILLING SEVEN: CORAZON AQUINO PRESIDENT OF PHILIPPINES: BABY DOC FLEES HAITI: CHERNOBYL DIS-ASTER: US AIR STRIKES AGAINST LIBYA: WALDHEIM AUSTRIAN PRESIDENT: BIG BANG IN CITY OF LONDON

Unionists Invade Republic

The year 1986 opened with a Unionist march in Belfast to protest against the Anglo-Irish Agreement. Guinness made a bid of £2,270,000,000 for UK Distillers towards the end of January.

In January, a purpose-built refuge for battered wives opened in Dublin, and in February a campaign for the homeless claimed that there were now 2,700 homeless people in the Republic. Suspicions began to grow that there had been, as Haughey had claimed, a deliberate shoot-to-kill policy in Northern Ireland. A report by Deputy Chief Constable John Stalker, which had been with RUC Chief Hermon since August, was known to refer to the killing of three Provos and two members of the INLA, all of them unarmed.

James Molyneux, the official Unionist leader, offered new talks on March 1, on the condition that the Anglo-Irish Agreement was first suspended; this offer was rejected by the Irish Foreign Minister on March 3, and a 24-hour strike in Northern Ireland in protest against the Agreement turned into a day of disturbances and riots during which the RUC were accused of standing idly by while hooded Loyalists intimidated motorists on their way to work.

The bishops continued to agitate against any change in the ban on divorce, though O'Malley's new Progressive Democrats (the PDs, as they were known) announced that they would back a divorce amendment and a Divorce Action group was set up in Dublin. On March 24, shots were fired in Dublin as Evelyn Greenholmes was released by the Dublin District Court for the third time as a result of defective British warrants for her extradition on various charges of terrorist offences in Britain in 1981 and 1982.

On April 11 an Irish teacher, Brian Keenan, disappeared in Beirut; it emerged later that he had been one of a group of men, which subsequently included John McCarthy and Terry Waite, who had been kidnapped and held hostage in Lebanon.

The trial of Patrick Joseph Magee, principal defendant in the IRA Brighton bombing in 1984, began at the Old Bailey on May 6 (he received eight life sentences on June 21); on May 21, paintings worth £10,000,000 were stolen from the home of millionaire Sir Alfred Beit at Blessingdon, Co Dublin; and on May 23 it was announced that the Northern Ireland Assembly was to be dissolved in June, largely because the SDLP had never taken up their seats.

In June, Bob Geldof was knighted (though he was to be

known as Mr Bob Geldof, KBE, and not Sir Bob, on account of his Irish passport) and Kilmainham Jail was handed back to the State by the committee of volunteers who had reconstructed it for use as a museum. Sir John Hermon, head of the RUC, denied any involvement in the removal of Stalker from the investigation into the alleged shoot-to-kill policy in Northern Ireland.

When the referendum on divorce was finally held on June 26, only half the electorate bothered to turn out to vote, though three nuns did vote in favour of divorce as a civil right. The result: an amendment to remove the ban on divorce from the Constitution was rejected by 935,845 votes to 538,279.

By far the most interesting event of the year was an excursion into the Republic by the deputy leader of Paisley's Democratic Unionist Party, Peter Robinson. He was arrested in Co Monaghan, on August 8, when a party of Loyalist protesters vandalised the local Garda station and attacked two Civic Guards. The purpose of this invasion into Republican territory was, Robinson explained, to expose the inadequacy of border security, though the very fact that he had been arrested so promptly proved that it wasn't so bad.

The next day he appeared on charges of unlawful assembly, malicious damage and assault in Ballybay District Court, and was remanded on bail, which the court set at £10,000, in cash, and he was obliged to remain in custody while a member of his party went to Dublin to raise the cash.

When he appeared before the court again on August 15, petrol bombs were hurled at Loyalist supporters, a dozen people were injured, including two Guards, and over 500 Guards were involved in the security operations. Robinson was remanded until October 3, when the District Justice at Ballybay tried to raise the bail from £10,000 to £50,000. Once again, Robinson was held for over four hours while his representatives went to Dublin to appeal (successfully) against the £50,000 bail. Towards the end of October, the State tried (and failed) to have the case transferred to the Special Criminal Court; Robinson told the Ballybay District Court that anything would be better than trial by twelve honest citizens of the Republic and that he would welcome trial by the Special Criminal Court. On January 16,

1987, he paid £17,500 in fines and compensation, a fairly stiff price for a failed and pretty silly public relations exercise.

In August, the RUC were called in to investigate Loyalist intimidation of Catholic workers at Short's aircraft factory in East Belfast, and it was reported that over 300 families, mainly Catholic, had been forced to flee their homes in the first six months of 1986.

The Orange Order threatened to call a strike at Short's factory if Loyalist flags, posters and other Unionist emblems were removed by the management, and on August 28, 1,000 workers walked out in protest against the removal of matter which the management considered might prove offensive to Catholic workers.

At the end of the month, possibly in an effort to appease Loyalist workers, Short's decided to fly the Union Jack every day. This move was followed on September 13 by a British Government decision to introduce legislation to make it illegal to fly the Union Jack 'provocatively' in Northern Ireland, and on September 17 Tom King announced a 'fair employment' policy for Northern Ireland, threatening firms which discriminated against people for their religious beliefs with financial sanctions, including the withdrawal of Government grants.

On October 2, FitzGerald admitted that the Government was walking a tightrope in the worst-ever Exchequer disaster. Figures that emerged a few days later put the total debt at over £20 billion, the highest in the world in relation to the size of the population.

But it wasn't all gloom. On July 25 the Jeffersen Smurfit Group completed the biggest ever purchase in their 51-year history, paying $1,200,000,000 for the Container Corporation of America. Ryanair, a relatively new air company, got the go-ahead for a new jet service between Luton, outside London, and Dublin Airport and later took over the failed London European Airways routes between Dublin and London, Brussels, Amsterdam and Rotterdam.

Guinness Peat Aviation, the world's largest and first plane-leasing company (the only successful air company in the world which had started out without any aeroplanes and with no scheduled routes) entered into a £1.5 billion contract to buy 100 Fokker aircraft, and Bord na Mona found itself obliged to buy turf briquettes from Finland because of the effects of two bad summers.

On October 25 Nazar Hindawi, a Jordanian, was sentenced to 45 years in jail for attempting to use his pregnant Irish girlfriend, Ms Anne Marie Murphy, as a human bomb by trying to get her on board an El Al plane carrying three pounds of high explosive in her hand luggage.

In Belfast, on November 15, two died and 70 were injured in riots at Loyalist demonstrations to mark the first anniversary of the Anglo-Irish Agreement. In December, the Sinn Fein Party decided to abandon their abstentionist policy and attend the Dail, and woodcock shot in Co Sligo showed signs of radiation.

The Government admitted that it was owed £717,000,000 in VAT arrears of which probably £515,000,000 was not recoverable. An Post (formerly the GPO) won the contract to run the state lottery with prizes of up to £20,000,000 a year, and in London the redoubtable Bishop Casey of Galway was banned from driving for a year and fined £200 with £100 costs for being over the legal limit.

1987

TERRY WAITE KIDNAPPED IN BEIRUT: IRANGATE INQUIRY: HERALD OF FREE ENTERPRISE CAR FERRY CAPSIZES OFF ZEEBRUGGE: KLAUS BARBIE ON TRIAL: BLACK MONDAY MARKET CRASH: KING'S CROSS UNDERGROUND FIRE: HURRICANE LASHES SOUTHERN ENGLAND

Passports For Sale

In January, those members of the staff of Dunne's Stores who had been on strike for about a year, following their refusal to handle goods from South Africa as a protest against Apartheid, returned to work. The Government complained to Israel about its army policy in Beirut; 21 Irish soldiers had been killed in Lebanon since 1978. On January 20, FitzGerald dissolved the Dail and called an election for February 17, and a publicity campaign on AIDS planned by the Government was postponed yet again until after the election. When the nominations were all in, there were 52 women standing in 14 of the 41 constituencies, the highest total ever. Haughey once again scraped in, with Ray MacSharry as his deputy and Finance Minister.

The Unionists decided to appeal to the Queen, presenting her with a petition signed by 400,000 people requesting a referendum on the Anglo-Irish Agreement. The Well Woman Centre announced that it had had to refuse counselling to nearly 500 women since a recent High Court ruling banning abortion referrals took effect.

Two former British Intelligence officers claimed in a newspaper report that the security forces in Northern Ireland had used paramilitaries to carry out assassinations and kidnappings in the Republic in the 1970s.

The first news of irregularities in the sale of Irish passports by the Irish Embassy in London came on April 13. Early in May a number of Moroccan nationals in London told the police that they had purchased Irish passports for thousands of pounds, and on May 21, Kevin McDonald, an official employed at the Embassy, was named as the man behind 60 suspicious passports which had been issued: he was discovered to be missing from his home in London.

In May, when the Government finally launched the long-promised campaign on AIDS, with a strong emphasis on monogamous sex and avoiding any explicit advice on the use of condoms, a Jesuit, the Revd Paul Lavelle, admitted that the use of condoms, while in general condemned by the Catholic Church, might be justifiable in the case of married people provided always that the purpose of using them was the avoidance of the disease AIDS, and not contraception.

The European Parliament attacked restrictions on cross-border duty-free goods between the Republic and Northern Ireland. The Revenue Commissioners had estimated that in 1986 alone £300,000,000 worth of goods (mainly drink) had crossed the border from Northern Ireland into the Republic on day trips, organised with that sole aim in view . As a result the 48-hour stop-over rule was introduced – duty-free goods could not be imported into the Republic until after a stop-over in Northern Ireland of at least 48 hours.

In the first of a series of cut-backs in health and education, a £10 hospital charge (per bed per day) was introduced for both out-patients and in-patients and cut-backs in higher education funding were made which would, the teachers claimed, lead to a loss of up to 3,000 third level places for school leavers.

At the end of May, Branson's Virgin Atlantic Airline provided a new London (Luton) to Dublin air-link for £78 return, £17 cheaper than Ryanair, and the former chairman of Guinness, Arthur Saunders, finally resigned from the Guinness Board because of criminal charges against him for unlawful share support operations during the Guinness take-over bid for UK Distillers.

On July 29, the Government decided that the farmers and the self-employed would have to pay PRSI (pay-related social insurance) amounting to approximately one-third of their income and in August an extradition order for passport clerk Kevin McDonald, now living in the Republic, was found to be defective. It was announced that Steevens Hospital, founded in 1720, would be obliged to close by the end of September because of a £2,000,000 cut-back in expenditure on health, along with the County and City Infirmary, built in 1785 in Waterford, the oldest hospital in Ireland outside Dublin City.

On August 14, Hurd ordered a police inquiry into the Guildford and Woolwich bombings and in early September 1,000,000 students (one-third of the total population) returned to schools facing unprecedented Government cut-backs on the 20th anniversary of 'free' education in Ireland; the INTO reported chaos in many schools. Bigger classes, fewer teachers and possibly a later school starting age were expected to follow a £40,000,000 cut in education funding.

When the Extradition Bill – which had been introduced by FitzGerald following the Anglo-Irish Agreement in 1986 with a stay of execution of one year – was due to come up again in

December 1987, Taoiseach Haughey was faced with a pretty daunting dilemma. He was now obliged to pilot through the Dail a measure which he had bitterly opposed and which most of the Dail members were dead against. While he was pondering the problem, outside events intervened.

First, in October, there was the kidnapping of the Dublin dentist, John O'Grady and the emergence, after his rescue by the Gardai on November 5, of the fact that two of his fingers had been hacked off and sent to his father-in-law (an extremely wealthy Dublin physician) in an effort to persuade the latter to pay a huge ransom. The kidnappers had threatened to cut Dr O'Grady up, bit by bit, until the ransom was paid.

Then there was the IRA bombing of a Remembrance Day ceremony in Enniskillen which killed eleven people including a young girl, Marie Wilson, whose father broadcast an eloquent and generously forgiving reaction to the incident. A shipment of arms for the IRA from Libya was captured on board the *Exund* off the coast of France and it came out that over £20,000,000 worth of arms had got through to the IRA in earlier consignments.

The public attitude towards terrorism suddenly seemed to harden, and Haughey was able to profit from this change to push the Extradition Bill through with certain safeguards, including approval of all extradition applications by the Irish Attorney-General.

Plans were made to merge some of the state-sponsored bodies and abolish others, and the Department of the Environment encouraged banks, building societies and insurance companies to take over mortgages normally serviced by the state's housing finance agency and by the Local Authorities under the Small Dwellings Act, in an effort to transfer between £70,000,000 and £140,000,000 from the Exchequer to the private sector.

The Irish pop group, U2, gave a weekend concert at Croke Park, Dublin, and their fans did so much damage to the pitch that a hurling final fixed for July 13 had to be cancelled. Stephen Roche of Carrick-on-Suir won the Tour de France on July 25, and Sir Alfred and Lady Beit gave 17 of their paintings worth

£17,000,000 to the Irish nation; they included a Vermeer, a Velasquez and a Gainsborough.

Johnny Logan won the Eurovision Song Contest for the second time (in Brussels) with *Hold Me Now* and John Huston, the American film director, died soon after he had completed filming one of James Joyce's short stories, *The Dead* – from the collection called *Dubliners* – on location in Ireland.

1988

166 KILLED IN FIRE ON PIPER ALPHA OIL RIG: BOMB ON TWA PLANE KILLS 276 AT LOCKERBIE: ZIA KILLED IN PLANE CRASH: MIKHAIL GORBACHEV TAKES OVER IN USSR: LATVIANS VOTE TO LOOSEN USSR TIES: US WARSHIP SHOOTS DOWN IRANIAN AIRBUS: EARTHQUAKE IN ARMENIA

Death on the Rock

The year 1988 was selected as Dublin's millennium year, the 1,000th anniversary of the founding of a Danish port and trading post, at Dyfflin (the black pool) near the mouth of the River Liffey. It was no different from any other year in that one of the first items that appeared in the *Irish Times* was the news that during the first six months of 1987, 1,850 Irish women had travelled to Britain to have abortions. The Government announced that it proposed to privatise the Irish Life Assurance Company, and Patrick Mayhew, the British Attorney-General, told the Commons that there would be no prosecutions following the Stalker/Sampson shoot-to-kill report, though there had been evidence of attempts to pervert the course of justice. An IRA arsenal discovered at Mallin Head in Co Donegal was the first of many unearthed that year; there were other arms finds in Belfast, in Portmarnock, Co Dublin (with Libyan markings), in Antrim and Belfast and later in the year in London, where a bomb factory was found in Battersea which included 150 lbs of Semtex and a consignment of Kalishnikov rifles.

By this time the Appeal Court had rejected the appeal by the Birmingham Six; their final appeal was dismissed by the House of Lords in April, to wide disappointment in Britain and Ireland.

The Anglo-Irish conference met in Belfast in February but made no further progress, and on March 6 three members of the IRA, including a young woman – believed to be on a mission to bomb a British Army march-past in Gibraltar – were shot dead on the Spanish border by the SAS.

The bodies of Mareid Farrell, Sean Savage and Danny McCann were returned to Dublin from Gibraltar and thence to Dundalk. On March 16, mourners in Milltown cemetery in Belfast were raked with gunfire: three men were killed, four seriously injured, and 70 treated in hospital. A few days later two members of the Royal Corps of Signals were killed in particularly horrific circumstances at another IRA funeral in Anderstown and the RUC resumed active policing of IRA funerals.

In April, there were fireworks in Phoenix Park to mark the launch of the State Lottery and in Northern Ireland, Congressman Joe Kennedy, son of Ted of Chappaquiddick fame, if that's the right word, found himself involved in altercations with British troops who stopped the car in which he was driving. 'Why don't you go back to your own country?' he asked them. 'This is our country,' came the reply. 'Why don't you go back to yours?'

Irish fishermen whose nets had become entangled with a British submarine off Clogher Head six years earlier were awarded £20,000 each in the Belfast High Court. Other Irish fishermen were not so happy. The imposition by the Government of a rod licence of £15 on people who had been fishing free in their own waters all their lives caused an uproar; bailiffs, who resented the legislation as much as the anglers, responded by confiscating trout from tourists who had caught them while fishing for salmon with a perfectly valid salmon licence, and anglers in the West and South closed off all the rivers and lakes in their areas from fishing of any kind, as a protest. By the end of May, the Government reckoned that the rod and line dispute had cost the country £6,000,000 in lost tourist revenue.

There was a heated controversy over a television documentary called *Death on the Rock*, screened by the BBC despite violent objections from Thatcher. It included, among other things, an eye-witness account of an SAS man standing on dead Danny McCann's chest as he pumped further bullets into him. On September 30, the inquest reached the conclusion that they had been killed lawfully.

Under manager 'Saint Jack' Charlton, the Irish football team reached the quarter finals in the European Cup in 1988 and then went on to reach the quarter finals of the World Cup in Italy in 1990 and in the United States in 1994.

On May 4, the High Court had decided that the District Court had been wrong to refuse an application for extradition in the case of former Irish Embassy official, Kevin McDonald, wanted in Britain for issuing false Irish passports, so he appealed to the Supreme Court; on July 28, the latter rejected his appeal, but instead of ordering that he should be extradited, returned the case to the District Court. It wasn't until April 10, 1989 that he was finally extradited: it is small wonder that the British found all this prevarication very irritating. The first test case brought under the new extradition arrangements in Portlaoise (against a man called McVeigh) also failed, and McVeigh was released because the judge wasn't satisfied that he was the man mentioned in the extradition order.

Knock Airport received a £1,300,000 grant from the European Community Regional Fund and on May 13, a duty-free shop at Moscow Airport was set up by a joint enterprise on the part of Aer Rianta (the Irish airports authority) and the Soviet airline Aeroflot; the entire construction and shop-fitting had been carried out by a team of Irish workers. A few days later the Lord Mayor of Moscow visited Dublin for the first time, and enjoyed a Big Mac in MacDonald's in Grafton Street.

On May 14, the Revenue Commissioners revealed that among 175 tax offenders on their list, were included three clergymen and one Civic Guard. Earlier in the year the police had reported that about 76,000 cars in the Republic were uninsured.

Eight British soldiers died in an IRA attack near Omagh on August 20. Three people with Irish addresses living in the Winchester area were jailed for 25 years by Winchester Crown Court on October 27 for conspiracy to murder Northern Ireland Secretary of State Tom King, and a Father Pat Ryan, wanted by the British police, arrived in Dublin after his extradition from Belgium was refused.

In September, a new *Irish Times*/Aer Lingus literary award was announced in New York, with an international panel of judges: it was for a work of international fiction and the prize initially was £10,000. Since it was inaugurated, additional special prizes for Irish literature and poetry have been awarded, and within the past year, Aer Lingus has dropped out and left it to the *Irish Times*. So far the main prize has never gone to an Irish writer.

1989

EMPEROR HIROHITO DIES: KHOMEINI CONFIRMS FATWA ON AUTHOR RUSHDIE: EXXON VALDEZ OIL SPILL IN ALASKA: HILLSBOROUGH STADIUM DISASTER: JACKIE MANN KID-NAPPED IN BEIRUT: TIENANMEN MASSACRE: HUNGARIANS OPEN BORDERS: BERLIN WALL DOWN: CEAUSESCU EXECUTED

Two New Universities

At the beginning of January, two new Universities were announced, one for Limerick and another for Dublin, to be achieved by upgrading two existing institutes of higher education. Fines for water pollution – an increasingly serious problem in Ireland in the Eighties – were increased from £5,000 to £25,000 with the additional possibility of a five-year jail sentence.

In February a leading Northern Ireland solicitor, Patrick Finucane, was murdered by Loyalist terrorists, an incident which caused the Irish Government to complain about a remark by a Junior Home Office Minister that some Northern Ireland solicitors seemed to be unduly sympathetic to the IRA.

On February 17, accusations were made that National Lottery funds had been used to buy computers for the Department of the Taoiseach, and on February 22 Mrs Phyllis Nolan became the first woman Superintendent of police in a force of 10,800 members, only 378 of them women.

On February 24, Fine Gael's Separation Bill was approved by the Dail after about a year of debate. All it did was grant a legal separation order by the courts after evidence of the breakdown of a normal marriage for at least a year.

Haughey dissolved the 25th Dail on May 25. The election results were typically inconclusive, and Haughey carried on as acting Taoiseach until, on July 12, after doing a deal with the PDs as mentioned above, he was again voted Taoiseach by 84 votes to 79.

Peter Brooke became Secretary of State for Northern Ireland in a cabinet reshuffle on July 25, and on September 1 Neil Kinnock and his wife escaped injuries in Dublin when their car driver had a heart attack.

The IRA bombed the Royal Marines' School of Music in Deal, Kent, on September 1, and a Jack Yeats painting was bought by Michael Smurfit for £280,000.

On September 25, Kevin McDonald, the Irish Embassy official who had been selling fake Irish passports, was sentenced to two years for conspiracy; hundreds of students demonstrated outside the Four Courts during a SPUC (Society for the Protection of the Unborn Child) protest against a hearing for committal proceedings against four student leaders for contempt of court.

What had happened was that SPUC had won an injunction to prevent Trinity students from disseminating advice to freshmen, which included information on where abortions could be obtained. The students continued to distribute their advice regardless, and when four of them were charged with contempt of court, Mary Robinson, future President of Ireland, appeared for the defence.

She argued that the question at issue was whether any group of people in one European Community state, attempting to publicise a service which was freely available in another European Community state, could be prevented from doing so by any pressure group. She emphasised that the nature of the service which was involved in this particular case (abortion) was immaterial and that the matter was one for the European Court of Justice in Luxembourg to decide.

The judge in the case, who happened also to be a woman, Ms Justice Carroll, postponed any decision and referred the whole matter to Luxembourg. She warned the society that a ruling might not come for a year or even eighteen months and that, in the meantime, no action could be taken against the Trinity students. The latter, wearing T-shirts emblazoned with the legend 'SPUC YOU', celebrated in the streets of Dublin and continued to peddle information about facilities for abortion to Trinity freshmen or, more accurately, freshwomen.

On October 24, the Guildford Four were declared innocent of the crimes for which they had served 14 years; the Court decided that the Surrey police had colluded to mislead the trial. Since then, an inquiry into the behaviour of the police has found them innocent, which makes a bit of a nonsense of the whole British judicial system; if they weren't lying and the Guildford Four weren't lying either, then who was? Or was all the fuss intended merely to confuse the issue and distract attention from what looked very like a police fit-up, as the criminals call it?

Inciting hatred against homosexuals became illegal after an amendment to the anti-incitement legislation in the Dail on November 16 and, after representations from the church authorities, Minister for Education Mrs O'Rourke agreed to substitute the phrase 'family planning' for 'contraceptive' in guidelines issued to science teachers on a training course.

The outstanding play of the year was Brian Friel's *Dancing at Lughnasa*, first produced at the Abbey Theatre in Dublin, which went on to win awards in London and New York.

Into the Nineties
❦
A Chance for Peace?

As the final decade of the twentieth century dawned, everything was looking good for Charlie Haughey and his Fianna Fail Party. With Ireland holding the EC presidency again, Haughey was back in office as President of Europe as well as Taoiseach of Ireland, and his deputy, Brian Lenihan, was odds-on favourite to succeed President Paddy Hillery when he retired at the end of his second term.

The Communist regimes of the USSR and Eastern Europe had collapsed, the Berlin Wall had been torn down and Haughey suddenly found himself in a position to help the German Chancellor, Helmut Kohl, to gain full EC backing for German reunification; his stature on the international scene had never been higher.

There had been no presidential election since 1972 (O Dalaigh and Hillery were both agreed candidates) but the Labour leader, Dick Spring, now succeeded in persuading Senator Mary Robinson to stand. She had been a member of the Labour Party, but had resigned in protest against the way in which the Anglo-Irish Agreement had been handled, without prior consultation with the Unionists. She was a successful barrister and a feminist with extremely radical and liberal views on many subjects including what the Dubliners called the Distortion Issue (divorce and abortion). Although proposed by the Labour Party, she went forward as an Independent, a strong point in her favour with many voters.

When Garret FitzGerald refused nomination, Fine Gael proposed Austin Currie, the Northern Ireland civil rights agitator and former SDLP politician, a man almost unknown in the Republic.

Right at the start of the campaign, while Mary Robinson was doing an American-style, whistle-stop tour of the country, there was a row over whether Fianna Fail had tried to put unwarranted political pressure on the then President, Dr Hillery, in January 1982. This was at the time of Garret FitzGerald's goof over VAT on children's clothing, and when his government was defeated on the budget issue FitzGerald had quite correctly gone to the President to ask for a dissolution of the Dail. At this stage Fianna Fail didn't want a general election, because they couldn't be sure of winning it.

Lenihan was asked on a TV chat show in 1990 whether it was true that Fianna Fail had tried at that time to pressure President Hillery into exercising his discretionary powers to refuse to dissolve the Dail and instead invite Haughey to form a government with the help of some of the smaller parties. Lenihan strenuously denied this, and when FitzGerald – who was on the same chat programme – said that he had been present in Arus an Uachtarain when the calls came through, Lenihan dismissed this as pure fiction and a few days later Haughey called FitzGerald a liar in the Dail.

The *Irish Times* then produced a tape of an interview with Lenihan, made by a UCD post-graduate student of politics, Jim Duffy, who was doing a thesis on the Irish Presidency. On this tape, Lenihan openly admitted that not only had he tried to persuade Hillery to refuse to dissolve the Dail at FitzGerald's request, but so also had several other senior party members.

When the PDs threatened to withdraw their support from Haughey's Government unless Lenihan resigned or was sacked, Haughey first swore that he would not dream of putting any pressure on an old friend of 30 years' standing, then did just that, and when Lenihan refused to be intimidated, sacked his old friend unceremoniously, just in the nick of time to avoid a no-confidence vote and another election he knew he couldn't win.

Lenihan survived this death blow and struggled on to fight the presidential election. Amazingly, he won 44 per cent of the votes on the first count, but when Austin Currie was eliminated and his second preferences were redistributed, Mary Robinson became the clear winner with a majority of 86,000.

It was the first time since Douglas Hyde's death that the presidency had passed out of Fianna Fail's hands, and not only that, but into the hands of a young woman, a controversial liberal, married to a Protestant, with very different ideas about the role of the President of Ireland from any of her six predecessors.

In the meantime, Haughey's deal with the unions and industrialists known as the PESP (Programme for Economic and Social Progress) was running into trouble as a result of the recession in Europe, the UK and the United States, as well as the uncertainty created by the Gulf War.

Haughey's final come-uppance came after a welter of allegations of business 'irregularities', involving, among other things, millionaire Larry Goodman's meat empire – which had supplied beef to both sides in the Iraq-Iran war, as well as to the Allied Armed Forces in Germany – the privatisation of Irish Sugar, one of the state-sponsored companies, and the fact that a private helicopter company, run by his son Ciaran, had somehow managed to get its hands on a confidential report by Irish Helicopters, a subsidiary of Aer Lingus, and Ciaran Haughey's principal competitor.

When Haughey's Finance Minister, Albert Reynolds, backed a no-confidence motion against him on November 6, 1991, Haughey immediately sacked him and insisted on an open vote rather than a secret ballot on the question of his own survival as leader of the Fianna Fail Party. Haughey always insisted on an open vote on such matters and for obvious reasons; he'd have been defeated years earlier in any secret ballot, but few people would ever risk opposing him in an open vote. In this instance he clawed back the confidence, if that's the word, of his parliamentary party, by 55 votes to 22.

By December 1991, he seemed yet again on top of the world when John Major came to Dublin for the first summit meeting between Haughey and a British prime minister for seven years.

But when Haughey's Minister for Justice tried to push through a bill to outlaw phone-tapping, and Sean Doherty – who had carried the can for Haughey over the phone-tapping scandal of a decade earlier – said on television that Haughey had been fully aware in 1982 that two journalists' phones had been tapped, and had never indicated any disapproval of the action which had been taken, Haughey found himself in much the same position as Brian Lenihan a year earlier. He initially rejected Doherty's claims as completely false, but later, under heavy pressure yet again from the PDs, he suddenly and uncharacteristically surrendered, deciding to retire, as he put it, to immerse himself in his 'bucolic pursuits'.

Still continuing to quote Shakespeare, he concluded: 'I have done the state some service. They know't, no more of that.'

He had a far better scriptwriter in 1992, when he quit the political scene, than he'd had in 1959, when he started out.

The last decade of the century will be a crucial one for Ireland. It will be a period of change; already so many things have profoundly changed. Contraceptives are now freely available, homosexuality between consenting adults is no longer an offence, women are allowed access to information about abortion and are free to go abroad for abortions, and it seems probable that the next attempt to remove the ban on divorce from the Constitution will be successful. In every walk of life, women are achieving a status they never attained in Ireland before. Not only has the Republic a woman President, but there are more women members (20) than ever before in the Dail; and in December, 1992, Mrs Justice Susan Denham became the first woman member of the Supreme Court.

The Labour Party, with an all-time high of 33 seats, now holds the balance of power and its leader, Dick Spring, is as liberal and radical in his thinking as Mary Robinson. In the financial year which ended in April 1993, the economy grew by 3 per cent, a higher growth rate than any other country in the European

Community. The Catholic Church no longer goes unquestioned and is accepting, if reluctantly, that Church and State are, and must be seen to be, separate entities.

When Reynolds, a former dance-hall proprietor, took over from Haughey, he was faced almost immediately with an enormous dilemma. The anti-abortion clause, which had been inserted into the Constitution with the full approval of the Catholic Hierarchy, backfired badly. A 14-year-old girl, who had been seduced and sexually abused – allegedly by a neighbour old enough to be her father – became pregnant and was taken to England by her parents to have an abortion. The parents contacted the police to ensure that if any DNA tests were taken, they would be acceptable as evidence in any prosecution proceedings which might later be taken against the man believed to be responsible. The Civic Guards referred the matter to 'higher authorities' and the Attorney-General ordered that the girl should be returned to Dublin.

A High Court case followed in which it was ruled that the girl, who was not named in the court, had no right to travel abroad for an abortion, since the foetus had 'an equal right to life'. There was an immediate public outcry, and the case was taken to the Supreme Court, which ruled that as the girl appeared to have suicidal tendencies, and since she had an equal right to life with the foetus, she should therefore be allowed to travel to England for the purpose of having an abortion.

The Supreme Court's decision revealed the need for a further amendment, which would require yet another referendum. This was held at the same time as the general election of November 1992 and the electorate voted overwhelmingly for the right of a pregnant woman to acquire information and to travel for the purpose of obtaining an abortion; however, there was a two-to-one defeat of a second amendment which attempted to clarify the very tricky 'right-to-life' aspect of the matter when the possible suicide of the mother was involved on the one hand, as against, on the other, the certain destruction of the foetus.

The Catholic Church demanded yet another referendum, but the Government for once ignored the Hierarchy and declared its intention to clear up the entire matter by means of new legislation which would spell out the precise circumstances in which abortion would be legal; this defiance of the Hierarchy represented a considerable step forward in the Church/State relationship.

Such a situation would have been unthinkable a few years ago. It would even have been unthinkable in 1992, were it not for the revelation in May of that year that the much-loved, highly-regarded Bishop of Galway, Eamonn Casey, had had a son some 18 years previously with a Ms Annie Murphy, the daughter of a relative who had emigrated to America. Casey had taken the girl, then in her early twenties, into his household to help her to recuperate from a disastrous marriage, and part of the treatment he administered resulted in the birth of a son. Not only that, but the bishop admitted diverting £70,669 from diocesan funds to pay for his son's upkeep and, presumably, to encourage Ms Murphy's continuing silence on the subject.

In the months that followed the breaking of the story, Bishop Casey abjectly apologised to his erstwhile flock and then disappeared without trace, while Ms Annie Murphy was busy telling all, over and over again, in newspaper stories, in a book, and on countless television chat programmes all over the world.

The fall of Eamonn Casey was a tremendous blow to the Catholic Church, one from which the Hierarchy will not readily recover. It will be difficult, in the immediate wake of the Casey affair, for the bishops to interfere in political matters, taking the high moral ground, as they have always done in the past.

But the fight is not over yet, by any means. By the middle of 1993, some of the bishops were already making noises which suggested that the Casey scandal was fading into history and indicating that, if they are to maintain any credibility, they are going to have to take a strong stand on some moral issue in the near future. That issue is most likely to be the introduction of legislation to provide for divorce in the Republic which will require yet another alteration to the Constitution and consequently, yet another referendum.

It is, perhaps, ironic that Bishop Casey, who had been as unwavering in his condemnation of contraception as the Vicar of Christ himself, should turn out to be the man who did more than anyone else to undermine the authority of the Hierarchy in Ireland.

The election which Reynolds hoped, as Haughey had hoped a decade earlier, would give him a firm personal mandate to run the Fianna Fail Party and the country for four or five years, was held in November, 1992, at the same time as the referendum on abortion.

Reynolds wound up with 68 seats as against 45 for Fine Gael, ten for the PDs and 33 for Labour (an increase of more than double Labour's total at the previous elections).

Initially Dick Spring, the Labour leader, tried to form an alliance with Fine Gael. He had to; he had been one of the most persistent and devastating critics of Fianna Fail and everything the party stood for.

When this move failed, Fianna Fail produced a policy document which embodied as much as possible of the Labour programme and played down everything else. Spring then took the biggest political gamble of his career; from his position of strength, he did a deal with Albert Reynolds which secured for the Labour Party the position of the Tanaiste (deputy), with his own staff and budget, six of the 13 cabinet posts and a disproportionately high number of junior ministries.

Spring became Tanaiste and insisted also on the portfolio of Foreign Affairs; he wanted to be in on any negotiations which might conceivably result in a re-united Ireland. To be fair, he also saw the coalition with Fianna Fail as the only sensible and practical way of getting any radical reforming legislation through the Dail. Previous experience had shown clearly that Fianna Fail would, without scruple, use the Catholic Church and any or all of the right-wing, semi-religious organisations to frustrate any Fine Gael/Labour attempts to liberalise social legislation.

On the other hand, with Fianna Fail support – and between them Fianna Fail and Labour now have an unprecedented overall majority of 38 – he knew that he could start getting things done.

The biggest single economic problem facing Ireland in the run-up to the next century is unemployment. In this respect, Ireland is no different from all the other European Community countries.

But Ireland depends to a great extent – far too much – on multi-nationals, particularly companies in the fields of electronics and pharmaceuticals. In 1992 Digital, the big Boston-based computer multi-national, rationalised its operations, closing down a plant in Galway employing 2,200, and moving part of its operation to Ayr in Scotland, which is far closer to a large population base and is also far more likely to get orders from the British Government, the Ministry of Defence, etc., than a factory in Galway. This is only one instance; but it is the sort of thing that is likely to recur. Ireland will always face an uphill battle to retain such industries, situated as it is on the outer edge of the European Community.

Agriculture has for too long been living on EC subsidies, producing beef and dairy products that nobody wants – one-third of all the European Community intervention beef is Irish – and all the signs are that the subsidies will be phased out over the next few years to comply with GATT requirements. Irish farmers will have to become more imaginative in their use of land, and work a lot harder, or the core industry of the nation will simply fade away.

Tourism will continue to be a big industry, one of the biggest, because Ireland offers an amenity increasingly difficult to find anywhere: under-population and its by-product, unlimited tourist *lebensraum*. But pollution of the rivers and lakes as a result of bad farming already threatens some of the best angling facilities in Europe. There are plenty of uncrowded golf courses still, but some of the new ones have been built in the most unspoilt scenic areas, which is no help at all in attracting non-golfing tourists. The policy of going for the top end of the tourist market has proved in the main sound, but there is a danger that some of Ireland's hotels and restaurants are pricing themselves out of every potential market. Ireland is already one of the priciest tourist spots in Europe; food and drink are outrageously expensive.

The success of Irish singers and musicians in the Eurovision Song Contest, the world-wide popularity of groups like U2, Enya, Sinead O'Connor, the Pogues, the Boomtown Rats and countless others, and the international reputation won by so many recent Irish films like *The Commitments* – scripted by Roddy Doyle, who also won the 1993 Booker award with his novel, *Paddy Clarke Ha Ha Ha* – and the Oscar-winning *My Left Foot*, have helped to enhance Ireland's individual identity; all over the European Community, particularly among young people, Ireland is now well-known for its music and actors and entertainers, as well as its writers, and that in itself would tend to attract many more young tourists, if the place was not so prohibitively expensive.

Another potential threat to the Irish tourist industry is the future (or non-future) of Aer Lingus. In deep financial trouble – the company was losing £1,000,000 a week early in 1993 – a belated plan to save the national airline was drawn up which included the shedding of some 2,000 jobs, the selling-off of many subsidiaries including a chain of international hotels and, at long last, an end to the idiotic compulsory stopover at Shannon.

The most spectacular failure so far was the virtual collapse of GPA (Guinness Peat Aviation), the international aeroplane leasing company, founded at Shannon by Tony Ryan, a former Aer Lingus employee. The jewel in Ireland's commercial crown, the company had planned to float its shares on the world's stock markets in 1991. The morning the shares were due to go on sale, the whole flotation was withdrawn. The timing was wrong, the airline industry was in trouble worldwide, and the shares were over-priced, it was said. Since then, GPA has been taken over by General Electric, the American multi-national.

Waterford Glass, another prestigious Irish industry, is just about holding on; its downfall has been caused by bad management and greedy trades unions. In any event, Waterford-type crystal glassware, indistinguishable from the real thing, can now be far more economically produced in Eastern Europe.

But all this fades into insignificance alongside the broad picture of the unemployment level – steady at around the 300,000 mark for about three years – which has led to serious crime, vandalism and drug abuse. Dublin is now among the most dangerous cities in Europe, and some tourists have been mugged and robbed within a few hours of their arrival in Dublin's fair city.

Hanging heavily over any really firm development of the tourist industry – or indeed any other industry – is the on-going mayhem in Northern Ireland. People see what they see on the TV, hear what they hear on the radio and read what they read in the newspapers and nothing will ever convince them that it doesn't apply to the whole country. It's Ireland, isn't it, where bombs keep exploding all the time?

In the autumn of 1993, there appeared to be what looked like the first glimmer of real hope. Influenced perhaps by growing evidence – from John Hume, leader of the SDLP among others – that the IRA are now genuinely seeking a cessation of hostilities, the Revd Martin Smyth, leader of the Orange Order, of all people, said on October 10 that he could see a place for Sinn Fein at the negotiating table, provided that the IRA first indicated that they were prepared to end the violence. Then came John Hume's announcement of his controversial peace talks with Gerry Adams, president of Sinn Fein, and his repeated pleas to John Major and the British Government to at least give him a hearing, on the grounds that any hope of securing a cease-fire must be better than none.

Inexplicably, immediately in the wake of this initiative, an IRA bomb exploded prematurely in a fish shop on the Shankill Road, Belfast, killing nine Protestants and the IRA man carrying it. Three days later, two Protestant gunmen fired on city sanitation workers in Catholic West Belfast killing two, and Protestant gunmen shouting 'Trick or Treat?' shot up a Hallowe'en party in a Derry pub, killing seven. And while the British were trying to make their minds up about the Hume-Adams initiative, Gerry Adams turned up at the funeral of the Shankill Road IRA bomber, and was photographed helping to carry the coffin. Once again, it would not be surprising if the British found the messages coming out of Ireland a bit confusing, to say the least of it. On the other hand, the Irish found the messages coming out of Britain pretty confusing, too.

After repeated assurances from Sir Patrick Mayhew, the Secretary of State for Northern Ireland, and from Premier John Major himself, that there would be no discussion whatever with Sinn Fein or the IRA until the violence had ceased for an appreciable and convincing period, it emerged at the end of November that discussions between the British and the IRA had in fact been going on since 1990, if not far longer.

Dick Spring, the Irish deputy premier and Foreign Minister, and Albert Reynolds, the Premier, were determined to exploit to the full what looked like the best opportunity the Republican Government has ever had to play a key role in achieving peace, and John Major put Northern Ireland at the top of his list of priorities when the new parliament opened on November 18, and this despite the fact that he had been obliged to do a deal with the Unionists at Westminster to defeat the Maastricht Tory rebels. He even specifically stated that he would not allow any one group of Unionists to veto talks on agreement.

At the beginning of December, Major went to Dublin for the first of a series of talks with Reynolds, and on Wednesday, December 15, the two premiers issued a joint statement from No 10 Downing Street, offering Sinn Fein a place at any constitutional talks which might take place, provided that the IRA suspend violence for three months from Christmas. The declaration was instantly rejected by the Revd Ian Paisley as a shameless sell-out to the rebel thugs, and in the discussions which followed at Westminster, in the press and on radio and television, everybody appeared to be under the impression that the IRA had started it all; nobody seemed to remember that it had all started with an unprovoked attack by the RUC and the armed B-Specials on a peaceful civil rights march in Derry on October 5, 1968, and the point of no return was reached when British paratroopers fired on a civil rights rally in Derry on January 30, 1972, killing 13 civilians.

Around Christmas, 1993, there seemed to be more hope of a genuine peace in Northern Ireland than at any time in the past 25 years. Feeling perhaps that some of the initiative of the joint declaration had been lost over the holiday, and upset by the renewal of violence in Northern Ireland immediately after the Christmas cease-fire expired, Albert Reynolds announced on January 11, 1994, that the ban on Sinn Fein and IRA spokesmen giving their views on Irish radio and television, which had been

341

imposed in the Seventies by Conor Cruise O'Brien, was to be lifted completely.

No similar announcement was made in Britain, where a much stranger ban existed, and still exists. Because members of Sinn Fein have been elected to the Westminster Parliament, and it would therefore appear undemocratic not to allow them the freedom of the air, men like Gerry Adams are permitted to give their views on British TV and radio, but not in their own voices. For some obscure reason which has never been adequately explained, these must be wiped out and replaced by those of actors. Since most actors are far better at putting messages across than politicians or freedom fighters, the net result of this arrangement has been that the Sinn Fein argument, such as it is, has until June 1994 been conveyed far more effectively to the people in Britain than it ever has to the people of the Republic, not that that greatly matters.

The British stubbornly continued to refuse Gerry Adams an entry visa, though Clinton allowed him to visit the United States early in 1994. He was fêted in America and interviewed ad nauseam on all the coast-to-coast talk programmes, but although the visit did a lot for Gerry Adams's personal image, and probably for his self-esteem, it didn't do much for the cause he was espousing, and it now seems as if majority American opinion (as well as majority opinion in the Republic, in Great Britain and in Northern Ireland) is firmly set against the IRA and any prospect of continuing violence.

After firing a few missiles which failed to explode – or, more probably, were never meant to explode – at Heathrow Airport, presumably to demonstrate the damage they could still do to the Establishment, if they were so minded, the IRA offered a 72-hour truce starting on Easter Tuesday, asking for 'further clarification' of the terms of the joint declaration. And when that failed to materialise, they resumed operations with a few (probably intentionally) ineffective grenades.

During a visit to Canada and the States early in April, Sir Patrick Mayhew, Secretary of State for Northern Ireland, gave what looked like a clarification designed to make it easier for the IRA; it would not be necessary, he said on April 12, for the IRA to surrender, merely to agree to a complete cessation of violence.

But apart altogether from the Reynolds/Major declaration – and many people feel that a joint declaration from Gerry Adams and the Revd Ian Paisley would carry a lot more weight – there must be some hope in the growing evidence that what the ordinary people of Ireland, North and South, most want is to be allowed to get on with their ordinary, everyday lives without any interference. And there is no doubt whatever that the British people would like to see the army pulled out of Northern Ireland as soon as possible and would welcome a final end to the horrific haemorrhage, in terms of lives (3,111 up to the date of the declaration), and money, that is the cost of providing security and economic support for the thankless Ulster statelet which, their Government has openly admitted, is no longer of any strategic, economic or political interest to Britain.

And aside from the killings and bombings on so-called mainland Britain, where an IRA mortar which exploded near Number 10, Downing Street and very nearly blew up John Major and his entire cabinet, and an IRA attempt early in 1993 to disrupt the commercial life of the city of London did millions of pounds' worth of damage, it costs Britain about £6.5 billion a year to subsidise Northern Ireland economically, and another £500 million a year to provide such security as the British Army presence affords. Even if you subtract from that total the £3.5 billion paid by the people of Northern Ireland in direct and indirect taxation, the annual bill for a statelet the British never wanted in the first place, and certainly don't want now, is pretty prohibitive for a country already hard pressed by the escalating cost of social security.

Certainly, Paisley and many of the Ulster Unionists will go on saying no, for ever and a day. What is no longer so certain is that the British will go on listening to them. As I write this, on the twenty-fifth anniversary of the arrival of the first British troop reinforcements in Belfast, it is beginning to look as if there might at last, be some slight hope now of a chance for peace.

Straws in the wind, maybe . . . but then, who would ever have thought, in November 1989, that the Berlin Wall would have come tumbling down before Christmas?

Appendix 1

Ireland Before 1800

If you know nothing about the history of Ireland before 1800, please start here:

Ireland has been inhabited since the Stone Age, and for more than 5,000 years various collections of peoples moving around the continent of Europe have wound up in Ireland and have contributed a dash or two of their national characteristics to what has since become the Irish race.

There are people in Ireland who like to think of themselves as true Gaels, direct descendants of the Gaelic Celts who came to the island around 350 BC and with their iron weapons easily defeated the earlier, bronze-armed inhabitants, a dark-haired people from what has become Northern Spain.

But most Irish people today would admit that they couldn't possibly help being a mixture of perhaps some Celtic, almost certainly some Danish, Norman, English and Scottish blood, as well as retaining, perhaps, some traces left over from those earliest settlers.

Factual Irish history doesn't begin until the Christian era, but it is possible to glean a vague picture of life in pre-Christian

Ireland from the legends and stories and epics which were passed down verbally from generation to generation and were written down by monks in the early Christian period. From them we know that the island was divided into five distinct kingdoms, under a high king ruling at Tara whose supremacy was challenged every bit as often as it was acknowledged. The people were largely nomadic; they didn't build cities or towns, though the kings and high kings lived in earthen-work settlements, surrounded by their courtiers, their poets and musicians, their lawyers and warriors.

These earlier rulers of Ireland were Gaelic Celts, whom Plato described as a tall, fair-haired race of people greatly inclined to drunkenness and much given to fighting, a description which might be considered not altogether inappropriate to their latter-day descendants. They appear to have migrated into Europe somewhere around the source of the Danube and seem to have spread their very considerable influence by peaceful infiltration as much as by forceful conquest, all over central Europe, Gaul and Spain, as well as the British Isles.

For some unknown reason, the Romans never attempted to extend their empire to include Ireland, though they knew all about it. Perhaps if they had, 400 years of straight Roman roads and strict Roman discipline might have made the Irish a bit more amenable to colonisation by the Anglo-Normans when it came, and so might have changed the course of Irish history.

But before the Normans arrived, there was Saint Patrick. A Latin-speaking Roman Christian living in Wales, he was captured and carried off to Ireland as a young boy during the course of one of the periodic raids which the Irish Celtic chieftains were constantly making on what is now idiotically known as Mainland Britain. Idiotically because England was called Anglia by the Romans and the very word Britain comes from Welsh Celtic; if anybody has any legitimate claim to Mainland Pritain, as the Welsh used to call the country, it must be the Celts, and not the mixed bag of Danes, Saxons, Angles, Jutes and Normans who came crowding in afterwards.

Saint Patrick was sold as a slave in Ireland and spent the formative years of his youth herding sheep on the slopes of a mountain in Co Antrim. Eventually he escaped to the continent, studied for the priesthood and returned to Ireland in 432, determined to preach Christianity to the pagans among whom he had spent his boyhood.

Even in his wildest dreams, Patrick himself could hardly have foreseen the fanatical zeal with which the mystical and impractical Celts took to the religion he preached. For over 1,500 years – well into the permissive Sixties – the Irish enjoyed a reputation for fervent piety unequalled in the world outside of Poland and Spain, and certainly not always shared by many of St Peter's successors in the Vatican.

Then the Vikings arrived. While the saints and scholars were busy over their books and the captains and the kings were quarrelling among themselves as usual, they all fell easy prey to the marauding bands of Scandinavian and Norwegian adventurers who were plaguing England and Northern France around the same time.

Initially the Vikings came to plunder, but they stayed on to settle, to marry Irish women, to build and fortify Ireland's first towns and to set up Ireland's first trading posts. For 200 years they occupied large areas of Ireland, mainly along the coastline, near the natural harbours. They pillaged the monastic settlements and exacted tributes from the monks in return for a guarantee not to plunder, a primitive form of protection racket. Only in Ulster, the most fiercely Celtic part of the island, were the O'Neills and O'Donnells sufficiently strong to keep them out.

Throughout the rest of the country, the Irish kings were too busy quarrelling with each other to make any concerted effort to get rid of the Danes until 1014, when a large number of the latter were driven into the sea during the course of a great battle at Clontarf, near Dublin. The survivors of this encounter were assimilated into the Irish race; the trade they had built up had proved highly useful to the Irish kings.

So the Irish once again had control of their own affairs and proceeded to restore the monasteries and seats of learning pillaged by the Vikings. It was during this period that a king called Malachy – who was later canonised – arranged the ecclesiastical division of Ireland which persists to the present day, in both the Protestant and Catholic versions of the Christian church.

By the middle of the twelfth century, England's Norman barons (descendants of Vikings who had settled in Northern France and had become the Normans), searching for new estates and fresh fields to conquer, were starting to look hungrily at Ireland's undeveloped acres, but typically, it was yet another row between a high king and a king of Leinster which led to the invasion of Ireland by the Anglo-Normans and started a war between the Irish and their next-door neighbours which isn't over yet and doesn't look as if it ever will be.

In 1166, Dermot MacMurrough, King of Leinster, defeated and banished by Rory O'Connor, the high king, travelled to England determined to avenge himself. He brought with him his beautiful daughter and offered her hand in marriage – with the additional bonus of the kingship of Leinster – to any Anglo-Norman baron prepared to lead an expeditionary force against the Irish high king and recapture Leinster. Dermot was willing to offer his former kingdom to the Normans because it was his private plan to try to take over the high kingship himself, with the assistance of the Norman troops.

A Norman expeditionary force landed at Waterford in 1170 under the command of the Earl of Pembroke, known as Strongbow. He had grown up in Wales, hence the title Pembroke, but he still spoke only French and he was in no way fitted to become an Irish king. He captured Waterford and marched on Dublin, where he married Aoife, Dermot's daughter, in Christ Church cathedral. However, just as he was about to settle in, preparatory perhaps to breaking away from England and establishing his own independent Norman monarchy in Ireland, Henry II arrived in Ireland with a strong army of knights to prevent just such an eventuality and to ensure that Ireland became part of his own kingdom which then included large areas of France as well as England and Wales.

Completely ignoring the high king and all Irish notions of sovereignty, Henry parcelled up much of the island between various of his Norman knights and a few native Irish chieftains and kings who were prepared to pay him an annual tribute.

He didn't, of course, do this without authority. Pope Adrian IV – an English pope, it is true, and the only one, but a pope nevertheless – had issued a Papal Bull bestowing the island of Ireland on Henry. He had done this because he was alarmed at the great and increasing divergence between the Church in Ireland and the rest of Christendom – Ireland alone of all the Christian nations had taken no part in the Crusades – and he probably felt that a spell of strong, stern Anglo-Norman government might help to bring the Irish Church back into line.

For a time the Norman conquerors had to fight to hold on to the lands assigned to them by the Crown, and they spread their power piecemeal, attempting to reproduce in Ireland the whole feudal structure of manors and abbeys, castles and fortresses. But gradually their presence came to be accepted by the Irish, and before long the Normans began to adopt some of the easy-going Irish customs and habits, and even the Irish language, becoming in a much-quoted phrase, probably more memorable than it is accurate, 'more Irish than the Irish themselves'.

Certainly, left to themselves, the Anglo-Norman colonists probably would have found a way of adopting their laws and customs to make them more acceptable to the Irish, but their rulers in England persisted in ignoring all Irish traditions and interests, and in running Ireland as an English colony.

Many second and third generation Anglo-Norman lords, born and brought up in Ireland, began to think of themselves not as Anglo-Normans any longer, but as Anglo-Irish, a situation which didn't at all appeal to the English monarchs who feared a line-up between these Anglo-Irish barons and the ancient Irish kings and chieftains.

Ireland's first parliament was convened towards the end of the thirteenth century. It was not elected but appointed by the Crown, and one of its first actions was to issue a series of decrees designed to prevent the colonists from assimilating with the Irish.

It needed only the Reformation to add the disastrously divisive element of religious bigotry to the gulf which had been created between the Irish and their Anglo-Norman – by now English – overlords. What had been merely a fundamental difference in race and outlook flared into fanatical hatred when Henry VIII, and to a far greater extent, some of his successors, tried to impose the reformed religion on Catholic Ireland.

The Reformation also added to the Crown's problems with the Anglo-Norman overlords, many of whom objected to the enforced religious changes every bit as much as the Irish did. Aware of this, and aware that he could no longer claim to be holding the country on the Pope's behalf since he had so signally failed to recognise the Pope's authority in other matters, Henry had the additional title 'King of Ireland' conferred on him by edict of the Irish Parliament, and made the Anglo-Norman lords and barons and Irish chieftains surrender their lands to him and receive them back, to be held by knight-service. Some of the Irish chieftains thus acquired English titles, which explains why the O'Neills of Ulster – descendants of an ancient Celtic high king – came to hold the English title of Earls of Tyrone.

The stage was now set for a succession of rebellions, insurrections, risings and other outrages, as often as not planned and master-minded by the Anglo-Norman Ascendancy, many of whom had become Anglo-Irish rather than English in their sympathies. Sometimes these risings were supported by expeditionary forces from continental Catholic countries anxious for one reason or another to get a crack at Protestant England, and they were usually followed by confiscations on a vast scale of land still in Irish hands which was then stocked with loyal English or Scots settlers, or awarded to the English soldiers who had helped to put down the risings.

The last stand of the old Gaelic Catholic aristocracy took place in Ulster, where the O'Neills of Tyrone and the O'Donnells of Tyrconnell (Donegal) held out for nine years against Elizabeth's forces with the support of some Spanish troops and the majority of the Gaelic chieftains in the rest of the country. When they were finally defeated, pardoned and reinstated in their lands, the disillusioned O'Neills and O'Donnells bought a ship and cleared out to the continent, taking with them into exile ninety-eight other Gaelic Catholic chieftains.

This Flight of the Earls, as it was called, was regarded as treason; all their lands were confiscated and the entire area of today's state of Northern Ireland was repopulated with Scottish Lowland Presbyterians and English Protestants. And it was the introduction of these settlers, utterly different in background, race, religion and character from the remainder of the population, and all concentrated in one corner of the country, which laid the foundations for the partition of Ireland 300 years later, and for the current troubles in that area.

The year 1641 saw the outbreak of another Protestant-Catholic war, during which the new Protestant settlers were subjected to some terrible atrocities; indeed much of the Ulster Protestant fear and mistrust of Catholics stems from this period. Eventually the rebellion was stamped out with zealous efficiency and terrible cruelty by Cromwell's Parliamentary Army; and it was followed by a new British policy of clearing as many Catholics as possible out of the three other provinces and herding them all into the harsh and barren wilderness of Connemara, west of the Shannon River.

Things began to look a bit more hopeful when a Catholic king, James II, came to the English throne, but he didn't last very long, and when William of Orange landed in England in 1688 to secure forever the Protestant Succession, James fled first to France and then to Ireland to raise a Catholic army to regain his throne. William followed him over with an army of 36,000 men. Naturally enough the recently-imported Scots Presbyterians and English Protestants in Ulster rallied to the Orange banner. James was finally routed at the Battle of the Boyne, and another flock of wild geese set out for service as mercenaries on the continent.

In 1795 and again in 1798, a society called the United Irishmen, led by an Ulster Protestant lawyer, Wolfe Tone, and one of the Anglo-Irish aristocrats, Lord Edward Fitzgerald, with some half-hearted French assistance, made two efforts at insurrections which were quickly quelled.

Then, in 1803, Robert Emmet, a friend of the poet Thomas Moore, with a tiny band of nationalist followers, tried to seize Dublin Castle in the most pathetic attempt at a rising of them all. The only concrete result of the affair was the killing, in the confusion, of an elderly and well-intentioned judge. Emmet was hanged, but not before he had made a speech from the dock which was to keep the spirit of rebellion alive for another generation: 'When my country takes its place among the nations of the world', he said, 'then, and not until then, let my epitaph be written.

However, in the meantime, in 1800, the British had decided that Ireland could more conveniently be run by direct rule from Westminster, the point at which this book begins.

Appendix 2

The 1937 Constitution

Herewith, for the record, is the precise phrasing of the two clauses (Nos 2 and 3) in de Valera's 1937 Constitution which imply direct, explicit and (still) continuing claim to the territory of the Six Counties of Northern Ireland:

Article 2:
The national territory consists of the whole island of Ireland, its islands and the territorial seas.

Article 3:
Pending the re-integration of the national territory, and without prejudice to the right of the Parliament and Government established by this Constitution to exercise jurisdiction over the whole of that territory, the laws enacted by that Parliament shall have the like area and extent of application as the laws of Saorstat Eirean and the like extra-territorial effect.

Appendix 3

A Glossary of Abbreviations

BBC	British Broadcasting Corporation
B + I	British and Irish Steampacket Company (a shipping line)
CIE	Coras Iompair Eireann (Ireland's transport monopoly)
DART	Dublin Area Rapid Transit (Dublin's rail network)
DIRT	Deposit Interest Retention Tax
DUP	Democratic Unionist Party (Paisley's breakaway Unionists)
DUTC	Dublin United Tramways Company
EC	European Community
EEC	European Economic Community (now the European Union)
ESB	Electricity Supply Board
FAO	Food and Agriculture Organisation (of the United Nations)
FF	Fianna Fail
FG	Fine Gael
GAA	Gaelic Athletic Association
GATT	General Agreement on Tariffs and Trade
GPO	General Post Office

ICTU	Irish Congress of Trade Unions
IDA	Industrial Development Authority
ILO	International Labour Organisation (or Office)
INLA	Irish National Liberation Organisation (a break-away Republican force)
INTO	Irish National Teachers Organisation
IRA	Irish Republican Army
LDF	Local Defence Force
LEARN	Life, Education and Research Network
LSF	Local Security Force (later LDF)
MEP	Member of the European Parliament
NATO	North Atlantic Treaty Organisation
NICRA	Northern Ireland Civil Rights Association
NUI	National University of Ireland (initially UCD, UCG and UCC)
OECD	Organisation for Economic Co-operation and Development
OPEC	Organisation of Oil Producing and Exporting Countries
OUP	Official Unionist Party
PD	People's Democracy
PD	Progressive Democrats (a breakaway Fianna Fail party)
PESP	Programme for Economic and Social Progress
PR	Proportional Representation
PRSI	Pay-related Social Insurance
RIC	Royal Irish Constabulary
RTE	Radio Telefis Eireann
RUC	Royal Ulster Constabulary
SAS	The Special Air Service (commandos) of the Royal Marines
SDLP	Social, Democratic and Labour Party (of Northern Ireland)
SPUC	Society for the Protection of the Unborn Child
TCD	Trinity College Dublin (Dublin University)
TD	Teachtaire Dala, a member of the Irish Dail or parliament
UAC	Ulster Army Council

UCC	University College, Cork (part of the National University)
UCD	University College, Dublin (part of the National University)
UCG	University College, Galway (part of the National University)
UDA	Ulster Defence Association, a Protestant Unionist organisation
UDF	Ulster Defence Force (a Unionist paramilitary force)
UDI	Unilateral Declaration of Independence
UDR	Ulster Defence Regiment (of the British Army)
UNESCO	United Nations Educational Scientific and Cultural Organisation
UFF	Ulster Freedom Force (Unionist paramilitary force)
UFF	Ulster Freedom Fighters (another Unionist para-military force)
UUUC	United Ulster Unionist Council
UVF	Ulster Volunteer Force (Unionist paramilitary force)
UPNI	Unionist Party of Northern Ireland
UWC	Ulster Workers' Council

Appendix 4

A Note About Money

Until 1971, when sterling was decimalised, I have given prices in old money, with the approximate value in decimalised coins in brackets. Because of inflation, these figures bear very little relation to the value of money today.

However, before going into that, let me try to sort out the old money. When I started to be aware of money as the principal determining factor behind most of my other activities, we thought in terms of pounds, shillings and pence, known as £sd. There were twenty shillings in a pound, twelve pence in a shilling, and four farthings in a penny. Prices were quoted right down to halfpennies and farthings, and the coins available included farthings, halfpennies, pennies, threepenny bits, tanners (6d), shillings (1s), florins (2s) and half-crowns (2/6) and there were notes for ten shillings (10/- or 10s) and £1. To make matters more complicated, many professionals charged for their services in guineas; a guinea was worth 21 shillings or £1 1s.

Inflation is a modern phenomenon. It started at the outbreak of World War One. Prices remained stable from about 1790 until 1914, according to an excellent article by John Windsor in the *Independent*, in February, 1994, on the value of the pound in your pocket. Then the cost of living rose by 15 per cent in the first four days of the war, and by the end of 1914, food prices had doubled and taxes were also rising rapidly to pay for the war.

According to a graph which appeared with the article, a modern £1 would have been worth approximately £50 in 1900 and about the same until August, 1914. By the mid-Twenties, a £1 note of that period would have bought about £20 worth of goods, rising to about £35 in the mid-Thirties, after the depression, and then dropping fairly consistently since, with a flat around £33 during the war years. Since the war, and particularly since the Seventies, inflation has soared, with the result that today it would cost £33 to buy what you could have bought for £1 at the end of World War Two, and £50 to buy what you could have bought for £1 in 1914.

Then a bottle of whiskey cost roughly 3s 6d (about 16p). Today one (the same article, made and packaged in the same way) costs nearly £10. I take whiskey as an example because, unlike motor cars and package holidays and cigarettes and video tapes, whiskey has remained a constant factor in our lives since Elizabethan times; whether you drink it or not, it gives you a fair idea of the way money has changed in value over the years.

Index

Index

Ireland This Century

Index

Index

Index

☐	The Lost Years	Tony Gray	£9.99
☐	Saint Patrick's People	Tony Gray	£6.99
☐	Walking Through Ireland	Robin Neillands	£6.99
☐	Irish Folk and Fairy Tales	Michael Scott	£6.99
☐	Irish Myths and Legends	Michael Scott	£5.99

Warner Books now offers an exciting range of quality titles by both established and new authors which can be ordered from the following address:

Little, Brown and Company (UK),
P.O. Box 11,
Falmouth,
Cornwall TR10 9EN.

Fax No: 01326 317444
Telephone No: 01326 372400
E-mail: books@barni.avel.co.uk

Payments can be made as follows: cheque, postal order (payable to Little, Brown and Company) or by credit cards, Visa/Access. Do not send cash or currency. UK customers and B.F.P.O. please allow £1.00 for postage and packing for the first book, plus 50p for the second book, plus 30p for each additional book up to a maximum charge of £3.00 (7 books plus).

Overseas customers including Ireland, please allow £2.00 for the first book plus £1.00 for the second book, plus 50p for each additional book.

NAME (Block Letters) ....

....

ADDRESS ....

....

....

☐ I enclose my remittance for ....

☐ I wish to pay by Access/Visa Card

Number ☐☐☐☐☐☐☐☐☐☐☐☐☐☐☐☐

Card Expiry Date ☐☐☐☐